"In this work one finds a mature reflthroughout Scripture that is sensitive to both diachronic and synchronic concerns in locating this paradigm within the wider biblical-theological landscape. Readers of this volume will not only appreciate the insights this study generates in the reading of particular biblical books and individual passages, they will also be rewarded by the guidance this volume provides in navigating through numerous contested issues in contemporary biblical scholarship. As such, both introductory and advanced students will benefit from this study."

David W. Pao, professor of New Testament and chair of the New Testament department, Trinity Evangelical Divinity School

"Estelle deftly guides the reader, from Genesis through Revelation, to a central teaching of the Bible—the exodus of the Israelites and the unrivaled rule of God. Drawing from a well of primary and secondary sources, this well-written volume is carefully researched and hermeneutically sensitive. Most of all, this book gazes at Christ's work in delivering his people from the slavery of sin and leading them through the waters of redemption. Certainly recommended!"

Benjamin L. Gladd, associate professor of New Testament, Reformed Theological Seminary

"Scripture presents salvation in Jesus Christ through the grammar of Israel's exodus out of Egypt. Estelle's book, pulling together the riches of current scholarship on the topic, ably sets forth how the New Testament authors conveyed the wonders of Christ's new exodus after the theological pattern of the old. Along the way, *Echoes of Exodus* demonstrates the unity of both God's purposes and his word."

L. Michael Morales, professor of biblical studies, Greenville Presbyterian Theological Seminary

"Informed by classic Reformed theology and the most modern methods, Bryan Estelle presents what may be the most careful and extensive study of the exodus available. His study is a model of an intertextual and biblical theological study of a theme in Scripture, and not just any theme, but one of crucial importance to understanding the message of salvation in the gospel. I recommend this book to all serious students of the Bible and to pastors who want to preach in a way that honors the coherence of Scripture."

Tremper Longman III, Distinguished Scholar of Biblical Studies, Westmont College

ECHOES
of
EXODUS

Tracing a Biblical Motif

BRYAN D. ESTELLE

An imprint of InterVarsity Press
Downers Grove, Illinois

InterVarsity Press
P.O. Box 1400, Downers Grove, IL 60515-1426
ivpress.com
email@ivpress.com

©2018 by Bryan Estelle

All rights reserved. No part of this book may be reproduced in any form without written permission from InterVarsity Press.

InterVarsity Press® is the book-publishing division of InterVarsity Christian Fellowship/USA®, a movement of students and faculty active on campus at hundreds of universities, colleges, and schools of nursing in the United States of America, and a member movement of the International Fellowship of Evangelical Students. For information about local and regional activities, visit intervarsity.org.

All Scripture quotations, unless otherwise indicated, are taken from The Holy Bible, New International Version®, NIV®. Copyright © 1973, 1978, 1984, 2011 by Biblica, Inc.™ Used by permission of Zondervan. All rights reserved worldwide. www.zondervan.com. The "NIV" and "New International Version" are trademarks registered in the United States Patent and Trademark Office by Biblica, Inc.™

Cover design: David Fassett
Interior design: Daniel van Loon

ISBN 978-0-8308-5168-3 (print)
ISBN 978-0-8308-8226-7 (digital)

Printed in the United States of America ∞

InterVarsity Press is committed to ecological stewardship and to the conservation of natural resources in all our operations. This book was printed using sustainably sourced paper.

Library of Congress Cataloging-in-Publication Data
A catalog record for this book is available from the Library of Congress.

| P | 23 | 22 | 21 | 20 | 19 | 18 | 17 | 16 | 15 | 14 | 13 | 12 | 11 | 10 | 9 | 8 | 7 | 6 | 5 | 4 | 3 | 2 | 1 |
| Y | 37 | 36 | 35 | 34 | 33 | 32 | 31 | 30 | 29 | 28 | 27 | 26 | 25 | 24 | 23 | 22 | 21 | 20 | 19 | 18 |

TO

my mother

CONTENTS

Acknowledgments ix

Abbreviations xiii

Introduction 1

1. Hermeneutical Foundations — 19
2. The Past Is Prologue: Creation and Exodus — 61
3. The Exodus Motif: A Paradigm of Evocation — 92
4. The Psalms and the Exodus Motif — 121
5. Isaiah's Rhapsody — 149
6. Exile and Post-exile: The Second Exodus Revisited — 182
7. Jesus as the New Exodus in Mark and Matthew — 208
8. The Exodus Motif in Luke–Acts — 236
9. The Exodus Motif in Paul — 263
10. The Exodus Motif in 1 Peter — 286
11. The Exodus Motif in Revelation: Redemption, Judgment, and Inheritance — 298

Conclusion 314

Appendix: Intertextuality 327

Bibliography 353

Author Index 377

Subject Index 381

Scripture Index 387

ACKNOWLEDGMENTS

Climbing a major mountain is a joint venture requiring the greatest degree of interdependence and trust. So also is writing a book like this. Climbers know that each peak has unique challenges. Every ascent involves hard work and a willingness to undergo a "suffer fest." An eight-thousand-meter peak requires years of apprenticeship, knowledge of altitude and how it affects the human body, and lots of endurance. A rock and ice face like Cerro Torre or Fitzroy in Patagonia, or a Grade VI multiday ascent on Half Dome or El Capitan in Yosemite, demands a different set of technical skills and lots of experience, perhaps even more so than an eight-thousand-meter-peak in the Himalayas. Solo climbers are a rare breed. They take on greater risks without the psychological support and mental fortitude that comes through sharing climbing adventures with others. After all, courage is contagious. Writing a scholarly book should not be a solo endeavor. The margins for risk and death are too great. No wonder Flannery O'Connor described writing a book as "giving birth to a sideways piano."[1]

Westminster Seminary in California (WSC) provided sources of funding that allowed me to work on this project. First, therefore, I am thankful especially to the board of trustees at WSC. This project was researched and written over a couple of sabbaticals but especially the last one. The board of trustees is very gracious with their sabbatical policy, and I hope that the support of board members is rewarded in some slight way when they take up this book and read. Additionally, I am indebted

---

[1] "Baboons Differ with Giraffes," interview with Flannery O'Connor by Celestine Sibley, *The Atlantic Constitution*, February 13, 1957, 24. Reprinted in *Conversations with Flannery O'Connor*, ed. Rosemary M. Magee (Jackson: University Press of Mississippi, 1987).

to the library staff at WSC, especially James Lund, Katherine VanDrunen, John Bales, and Brian Hecker. I appreciated their goodwill, competence, and forbearance especially with each new interlibrary loan request. They resupplied my research constantly by retrieving numerous books and articles quickly and efficiently.

It causes me mental anguish to try to recall all the people who helped me write this book and imparted the courage to attempt to do so. I owe a great debt of gratitude to so many. Harold Bloom said (roughly) years ago: teaching is a three in one with reading and writing. He's right. Some people may look at the footnotes and think they are weighted too heavily with my colleague's work at WSC as if it is some kind of mutual congratulatory love-fest, but that has not been my aim. I have merely learned so very much from them that I wanted to acknowledge a debt of gratitude. I'm sure they deserve more attribution than I have given in places. Moreover, many other colleagues from other sympathetic institutions (and nonsympathetic ones) will recognize their names in the footnotes as well.

Although I have tried to list everyone to whom I am indebted, I am sure I've left someone out. Don Collet, professor of Old Testament at Trinity School of Ministry, has been one of my best conversation partners on hermeneutical matters during our annual confab at SBL. My greatest appreciation is directed to my faculty colleagues, especially those who read and commented on some part of this book: Steve Baugh, John Fesko, Mike Horton, Dennis Johnson, David VanDrunen, and Josh VanEe. Each of these brothers heard or read drafts of this work in progress, offering helpful criticism and suggestions. I am not first and foremost a New Testament scholar. Therefore, I turned to New Testament colleagues to check some of my work. I must mention my special appreciation for Steve Baugh, Lee Irons, Dennis Johnson, and Guy Waters. Each read sections of my book and offered feedback.

Moreover, one must always pay one's respects to mentors. There are former professors whose influence is tremendous and profoundly affected this book, even years before its composition. I could never have executed this project without them: M. Futato, M. G. Kline, A. Fitzgerald,

S. Fassberg, R. Murphy, M. P. O'Connor, S. Griffith, D. Johnson, E. De Marcellis, and especially Doug Gropp. They exercised a formative influence over me that I am still recognizing with each new dawn.

My pastor, Rev. Zach Keele, deserves special mention. Zach, with whom I have enjoyed so much time on trips to, from, and in the mountains and in discussing all matters textual, but who has also brought me into the Lord's presence on so many occasions through his faithful preaching, was the most enriching conversation partner throughout various stages of this project. He will hear his own voice in much of my writing, for which I have to beg his forgiveness if I haven't given appropriate attribution at any point. There are a few points in this book where I don't honestly know whether the ideas are original to me or to him. One of the greatest jewels in friendship and definitely one of the greatest blessings a professor can have is a well-informed and thoughtful friend with whom he can dialogue about ideas. Zach has been such a conversation partner. It is a rare commodity when conversation becomes such that true and genuine intellectual exchange, growth, and maturity happens. I know how to read my Bible better thanks to Zach. I owe thanks to one of my former pastors as well, Rev. Alfred Poirier, who read the manuscript and as always offered many humorous and encouraging words. I am grateful that Rev. Joel Fick also read a draft and gave some helpful feedback on a very important point.

More students than I can remember deserve mention. Some are mentioned in the footnotes along the way. My research assistant years ago, Gideon Park, retrieved many articles and books that served my curiosity well and allowed me to read from paper, which I prefer. Many other students gave their input to some aspect of this project. Eric Chappell and John Stovall each read chapters and made helpful comments. Since he is a master of the Spanish tongue, Dan Masters assisted me with the translation of Horacio Simian-Yofre's article. Erik Erderma wrote a paper for me on the so-called combat motif in the Bible that spurred much thinking on my part. Matthew Tyler, a student in my elective on the exodus motif, asked a question that spurred me on to think more deeply about what exactly the exodus motif is. He deserves credit, although to my knowledge he does not know it, for helping me think about the exodus motif as a synecdoche for the whole salvation matrix.

Finally, one could not have asked for a better partner with whom to be tied, so to speak, than Dan Reid, IVP Academic editorial director. His advice and support with this book are much appreciated. Grateful is the best word I can come up with to describe his early interest in this project. He kept pressing me to keep my argument singularly focused. He worked patiently on my chubby prose and improving its style. He asked probing questions, guiding my writing in such a manner that it made my argument clearer and stronger. He shepherded this project to its final conclusion. Additionally, I am grateful to all the IVP staff for assisting in this project. Kelli Garvey also cut my wasted words by reading some earlier draft chapters. Katie Terrell also greatly improved my style by helping me state clearly what I wanted to say, all in the midst of raising kids and supporting her pastor, who happens to be her husband.

This book is dedicated to my mother, who first inculcated me with a love of the mountains and encouraged me to use my mind in service of our common Lord. Her patience and love throughout the years toward me has truly been a reflection of God's love for all of us stubborn sinners. My only regret is that my father did not live long enough to see this publication come to light. Even so, his enthusiasm at seeing an outline of a draft was encouragement enough.

ABBREVIATIONS

ABD	*Anchor Bible Dictionary*. Edited by David Noel Freedman. 6 vols. New York: Doubleday, 1992
ANF	*Ante-Nicene Fathers*
BETL	Bibliotheca Ephemeridum Theologicarum Lovaniensium
Bib	*Biblica*
BZAW	Beihefte zur Zeitschrift für die alttestamentliche Wissenschaft
BZNW	Beihefte zur Zeitschrift für die neutestamentliche Wissenshaft
CBQ	*Catholic Biblical Quarterly*
CBQMS	Catholic Biblical Quarterly Monograph Series
CurBR	*Currents in Biblical Research*
ET	English translation
FAT	Forschungen zum Alten Testament
HSM	Harvard Semitic Monographs
Int	*Interpretation*
JBL	*Journal of Biblical Literature*
JETS	*Journal of the Evangelical Theological Society*
JNES	*Journal of Near Eastern Studies*
JSNT	*Journal for the Study of the New Testament*
JSNTSup	Journal for the Study of the New Testament Supplement Series

JSOT	*Journal for the Study of the Old Testament*
JSOTSup	Journal for the Study of the Old Testament Supplement Series
JTI	*Journal of Theological Interpretation*
JTS	*Journal of Theological Studies*
LXX	Septuagint
MT	Masoretic Text
NICNT	New International Commentary on the New Testament
NICOT	New International Commentary on the Old Testament
NIGTC	New International Greek Testament Commentary
NT	New Testament
NTS	*New Testament Studies*
OT	Old Testament
OTL	Old Testament Library
RTR	*Reformed Theological Review*
SBLDS	Society of Biblical Literature Dissertation Series
SBLMS	Society of Biblical Literature Monograph Series
SBLSymS	Society of Biblical Literature Symposium Series
SNTSMS	Society for New Testament Studies Monograph Series
VT	*Vetus Testamentum*
VTSup	Supplements to Vetus Testamentum
WBC	Word Biblical Commentary
WTJ	*WTJ*
WUNT	Wissenschaftliche Untersuchungen zum Neuen Testament

INTRODUCTION

Interpreting what texts mean is a great intellectual challenge whether one is a biblical scholar who seeks to understand the truth in the scriptures or a Supreme Court justice who seeks guidance from the constitution in adjudicating legal disputes.
Raymond W. Gibbs Jr.

Humans love stories. A good yarn can keep someone seated, turning page after page, without becoming restless. The exodus event does that for me. I am fascinated by the way it is reactualized and recontextualized in subsequent biblical books. Throughout the Old Testament, there are reminiscences of the exodus event again and again. The lexical, conceptual, and influential allusions to this founding event of the ancient Hebrew nation resonate throughout the Bible: in the Psalms, Prophets, and the postexilic literature. Yet the ripples do not stop in the Hebrew Bible. The New Testament literature appeals to the exodus event as well. Of the numerous references in the New Testament to the Old Testament, the exodus event comes in a noble third, trailing behind only the prophet Isaiah and the Psalms in number of citations.[1] It serves as the organizing paradigm for several of the Gospels and influences the book of Acts. Paul's two most doctrinal letters, Romans and Galatians, lean heavily on the exodus for their theology. The apostle Peter puts an ecclesiastical spin on the exodus, and Revelation ties all the

---

[1] Otto A. Piper, "Unchanging Promises: Exodus in the New Testament," *Int* 11 (1957): 3-22.

threads together in John's tapestry of consummation. I have set on climbing a big wall of narration. In short, I want to relate the greatest story ever told.

The biblical writers' use of the exodus event is no mere repetition, no base recapitulation. Rather, it is taken up, transformed, "eschatologized," and ultimately repackaged into a tapestry that mesmerizes readers and draws them into the drama of salvation. No biblical reader can walk away from the performance unchanged. To trace the allusions throughout this corpus of biblical literature is not only an exercise in curiosity and aesthetic entertainment. Consider the following questions: Why would Paul refer to the exodus event as "under the cloud"? Why would Peter address his church in language evocative of Israelite identity? Why would the prophets invoke the ancient creation combat motif to express theology if they were committed monotheists? What is the purpose of the "way of the Lord" language in Isaiah 40:1-11, arguably one of the most influential passages at Qumran and elsewhere in the Second Temple period? Why would Jesus himself, at the transfiguration, discourse with Elijah and Moses about his own *exodon*? What, we may ask, is the purpose of these allusions? Are they poetic influence, metaphor, citation, or something altogether different? My goal throughout this book is to help readers grow in their "allusion competence," especially in their ability to recognize scriptural allusions to the exodus motif.

The exodus event is what Walter Brueggemann calls "the Exodus grammar of Yahweh." He comments, "The Exodus recital, either as a simple declarative sentence enacting Israel's primal theological grammar or a fuller narrative, becomes paradigmatic for Israel's testimony about Yahweh. It becomes, moreover, an interpretive lens to guide, inform, and discipline Israel's utterances about many aspects of its life."[2]

This book is about the continuing thread of the exodus motif in the Old Testament and New Testament. Students, pastors, and biblical scholars will come to appreciate how interconnected the Scriptures are

---

[2]Walter Brueggemann, *Theology of the Old Testament: Testament, Dispute, Advocacy* (Minneapolis: Fortress, 1977), 178.

and how a biblical motif works through allusion and transformation of that motif. From the perspective of the Hebrews, a more important topic than the exodus motif could hardly be chosen. Martin Noth considered the Hebrew exodus from Egypt to be a primary confession or article of faith (*Urbekenntnis*).³

What is the exodus motif? The following pages will demonstrate that the exodus motif is a much bigger concept than merely the liberation of the Hebrews from the oppressive iron furnace of the Egyptians. It is about God's crafting a people for himself by bringing them to the very abode of his presence at Mount Sinai. Yet there is more. Just as there was an anticipated goal at the beginning of creation in the Garden of Eden, so also there is an anticipated goal for Israel. The deliverance from Egypt did not stop at Sinai, where God meets with his people. The deliverance was intended to include the Promised Land. In the immediate context of the Hebrew Bible, this means the land of Canaan. However, the final goal of the exodus deliverance and salvation itself includes something greater than the Promised Land. It is nothing less than the grandest gift imaginable: heaven itself, which I will refer to as "the world-to-come" in this book.⁴ Mishnaic Hebrew came to express the world in the future as *ʿôlām hābāʾ* (world-to-come). This Hebrew construction is often used to contrast "world" in an eschatological context with the present world (*ʿôlām hazzeh*). This is where the exodus motif finds it fulfillment, in the world-to-come (cf. Rev 21:3).⁵

---

³Martin Noth, *Überlieferungsgeschichte des Pentateuch* (Darmstadt: Wissenschaftliche Buchgesellschaft, 1960), 52. ET: *A History of Pentateuchal Traditions*, trans. Bernhard W. Anderson (Chico, CA: Scholars Press, 1981), 49.

⁴The word *heaven* has a wide application in the Scriptures. First, it is a real place, since the Nicene Creed says that Christ "came down from heaven." In Scripture it sometimes means the atmospheric heavens or the stellar heavens where astral bodies reside. There are also the "third heavens," where God resides and the glorified body of Christ now reigns. Then there is the sublime use of the word by which Christians are described as being already introduced into a realm by virtue of their regeneration and union with Christ. In the English language, the word is used for the domain of space travelers as well as the domain of God, where he assembles those whom he saves. See the terse summary of Charles Hodge, *Commentary on the Epistle to the Ephesians* (Grand Rapids: Eerdmans, 1950), 113-16. Also see the fine summary in Xavier Léon-Dufour, *Dictionary of Biblical Theology*, updated 2nd ed., trans. P. Joseph Cahill and E. M. Stewart (Boston: St. Paul, 1967), 229-32.

⁵This language will be used throughout the book for the goal of the exodus motif (and new exodus as well).

In introducing the importance of this pervasive theme, I hope that readers will be swept up into this grand story of redemption. As has been suggested,

> No other OT motif is as crucial to understand. No other event is so basic to the fabric of both Testaments. Our concepts of deliverance and atonement, of God dwelling with his people, of God taking a people for himself and so forth have their roots in this complex of events. And precisely because it so permeates the Bible, the interpretation of the exodus and its motif usage are a challenge.[6]

Undoubtedly, the exodus motif is one of the most important themes in the Bible to interpret.[7] Understanding the use of this motif in Scripture is vital to reading our Bible and hearing its message. As Geerhardus Vos declared years ago, "The exodus from Egypt *is* the Old Testament Redemption."[8]

I am not saying the exodus motif is the central theme in Scripture.[9] Nevertheless, it is a significant organizing theme. The hazard of choosing one major organizing theme of biblical theology is that reductionism often follows close behind.[10] Moreover, in our postmodern context, an attitude of suspicion exists toward any grand story or metanarrative (*grand récit*). This is primarily the result of a Lyotard's critique of modern, Western epistemology.[11] Therefore, writing a biblical theology (even one limited to tracing a motif) runs the risk of marginalizing certain voices within the scriptural material.[12] Any attempt at

---

[6]Leland Ryken, James C. Wilhoit, and Tremper Longman III, eds., *Dictionary of Biblical Imagery* (Downers Grove, IL: InterVarsity Press, 1998), 253.

[7]See Stephen Dempster's passionate appeal, "Exodus and Biblical Theology: On Moving into the Neighborhood with a New Name," *Southern Baptist Journal of Theology* (1997): 4-23.

[8]Geerhardus Vos, *Biblical Theology: Old and New Testaments* (Grand Rapids: Eerdmans, 1954), 109.

[9]Claiming central dogmas has caused trouble for biblical theologians in the past; nevertheless, it cannot be denied that the exodus motif is a central narrative since it is the paradigmatic salvation event in the OT and very influential for how the NT authors describe salvation.

[10]Karl Möller, "The Nature and Genre of Biblical Theology: Some Reflections in the Light of Charles H. H. Scobie's 'Prolegomena to a Biblical Theology,'" in *Out of Egypt: Biblical Theology and Biblical Interpretation*, ed. Craig Bartholomew et al., Scripture and Hermeneutics 5 (Grand Rapids: Zondervan, 2004), 41-64.

[11]See Jean-François Lyotard, *The Postmodern Condition: A Report on Knowledge*, Theory and History of Literature 10 (Minneapolis: University of Minnesota Press, 1984).

[12]See Craig G. Bartholomew and Michael W. Goheen, "Story and Biblical Theology," in Bartholomew et al., *Out of Egypt*, 144-71.

biblical theology must avoid flattening out all biblical genres or ignoring other motifs and themes.[13] And while the current cultural climate is not conducive to telling the grand story of the exodus motif in all its dimensions, I am convinced that I must try for at least the following reason.

The exodus motif is one important way that the Bible tells us about Christ—not only about his person, but also about what he has accomplished in his work. The centrality of Scripture is Christ, and this book will take pains to demonstrate this hermeneutical principle as we trace the exodus motif through redemptive history as revealed in the Old Testament and New Testament.[14] The exodus motif offers a way of explaining God's grand narrative—or meganarrative—of redemption for sullied, sinful men, women, and children. In some cultural contexts, it might prove difficult to understand and see this as a grand narrative, since it might be construed as the master story of one's adversary.[15] Nevertheless, the exodus motif is the Bible's grand narrative, and it is one of the best stories because it encompasses all the major aspects of God's work of salvation through Christ: redemption from sin, suffering, and the tyranny of the devil (the exodus from Egypt and Pharaoh); bringing us into the very presence of God (represented at Sinai); wilderness wanderings (pilgrimage toward a special place); and possession of the land of Canaan (ultimately symbolizing entitlement to the world-to-come; cf. Heb 4) in order to be a unified, holy people in a place where they might worship God perpetually. Such is the

---

[13] Möller, "Nature and Genre," 59.
[14] Michael S. Horton, *Covenant and Eschatology: The Divine Drama* (Louisville, KY: Westminster John Knox, 2002), 17-18, and Kevin Vanhoozer, *The Drama of Doctrine* (Louisville, KY: Westminster John Knox, 2005), 296-97.
[15] Consider, e.g., the testimony of Richard B. Hays in his recent book *Reading Backwards: Figural Christology and the Fourfold Gospel Witness* (Waco, TX: Baylor University Press, 2014), xiv-xv. The most frequent question he received from the audience during the presentation of his lectures in Cambridge was whether his argument "might impact conversations between Christians and Jews. Does a theological affirmation of the christological exegesis of Israel's Scriptures de facto invalidate Judaism and generate a hostile supersessionist understanding of the relationship between Israel and the church? The question is both important and complicated." Hays's response is that Christian figural readings do not annihilate the significance of the Hebrew Scriptures; rather, they "affirm its reality."

meganarrative of redemption with all its major theological themes: redemption and forgiveness, presence with God, which entails union and communion with God, sanctification through the pilgrim way, holy community in the kingdom of God, and positive righteousness won by the Savior qualifying one who believes for entitlement to the world-to-come. Nothing is more needed today than studies of Scripture that help us bridge the gulf that has been created in paradigms of salvation. Let me explain.

I was stunned by the paradigm shift that had occurred in the academy when I emerged from the Semitics library at the Catholic University of America as a newly minted PhD in 2000–2001, ready to begin my academic career. Forensic metaphors for salvation were being replaced by metaphors of participation. This could be traced to the more distant influence of Albert Schweitzer and in more recent decades to the influence of E. P. Sanders on Pauline theology.[16] Sanders's emphasis on participation in Christ vis-à-vis juridical concepts of salvation is evident in *Paul and Palestinian Judaism*, where he argues that "the main theme of Paul's theology is found in participationist language rather than on juridical conceptions of atonement."[17] The influence coming in the wake of these works has been felt far and wide.[18]

Sanders, it is true, may be credited with chastening the academy for its caricatures of Judaism and changing the paradigm for New Testament studies.[19] Additionally, he pioneered the "new perspectives" on Paul, giving birth to trends that are far from waning.[20] Sanders has been called

---

[16]See Albert Schweitzer, *The Mysticism of Paul the Apostle* (London: Black, 1931; repr., Baltimore: Johns Hopkins University Press, 1998), and E. P. Sanders, *Paul and Palestinian Judaism: A Comparison of Patterns of Religion* (Minneapolis: Fortress, 1977), 453-72, 502-8, 514, 548-49.

[17]Sanders, *Paul and Palestinian Judaism*, 552.

[18]See, e.g., Richard B. Hays, "What Is 'Real Participation in Christ'?" in *Redefining First-Century Jewish and Christian Identities: Essays in Honor of Ed Parish Sanders*, ed. Fabian E. Udoh (Notre Dame, IN: University of Notre Dame Press, 2008), 336-51.

[19]He particularly helped focus attention away from merely Greco-Roman backgrounds and onto Jewish works as a background for understanding New Testament writings. See, e.g., the introduction of R. Michael Fox in *Reverberations of the Exodus in Scripture* (Eugene, OR: Pickwick, 2014), xi.

[20]See, e.g., Stephen Westerholm, "What's Right About the New Perspective on Paul," in *Studies in the Pauline Epistles: Essays in Honor of Douglas J. Moo*, ed. Matthew S. Harmon and Jay E. Smith (Grand Rapids: Zondervan, 2014), 230-42. I refer to the "new perspectives" for emphasis since this

the "godfather if not the grandfather" of the new perspective on Paul.²¹ The category of participation in Christ has become a central topic in discussions of Paul's theology of grace.²²

My own project attempts to bridge a huge gulf that has been created between participationist and forensic descriptions of salvation.²³ Both elements must be included in any description of the plan of salvation presented in the Bible.²⁴ Union and communion, participation and relationship with God—this is a vitally important category when talking about the salvation of sinners. Even so, one cannot pit this against judicial and legal categories.²⁵ Just as a marriage between a man and a woman is one of the most powerful biblical metaphors for God's relationship to his blood-bought people, so too we cannot eviscerate the forensic element out of this image or it will lose its power. That institution has a legal basis. Indeed, the relationship between God and Israel is also portrayed in terms of a marriage bond, and that relationship comes with demands.²⁶ The Old Testament is largely unique in this regard compared to world religions and even Islam since it focuses on a

---

is not one homogeneous movement, nor do the writers often pigeonholed into this label all agree with one another.

²¹N. T. Wright, *The Paul Debate: Critical Questions for Understanding the Apostle* (Waco, TX: Baylor University Press, 2015), 71.

²²For recent treatments, see Stanley K. Stowers, "What Is Pauline Participation in Christ?," in Udoh, *Jewish and Christian Identities*, 352-71, and John M. G. Barclay, "Grace and the Transformation of Agency in Christ," in Udoh, *Jewish and Christian Identities*, 372-89.

²³For bibliographical references, see Michael J. Gorman, *Inhabiting the Cruciform God: Kenosis, Justification, and Theosis in Paul's Narrative Theology* (Grand Rapids: Eerdmans, 2009), 3n6.

²⁴Consider Gorman, *Inhabiting the Cruciform God*, who goes all in on the participationist side and encourages a greater appreciation for *theosis*. More precisely, he tries to bridge the gap between those who emphasize the juridical model and those who emphasize the participationist model by suggesting instead that Paul has one soteriological model: justification by co-crucifixion (which he labels JCC). Or, for a more mitigated position, but one that still makes unconditional promise the foundation of covenant theology and downplays the forensic foundation of salvation, see Scott W. Hahn, *Kinship by Covenant: A Canonical Approach to the Fulfillment of God's Saving Promises*, Anchor Yale Bible Reference Library (New Haven, CT: Yale University Press, 2009).

²⁵For a helpful, terse outline of the debate, see N. T. Wright, *Paul and the Faithfulness of God*, Christian Origins and the Question of God 4 (Minneapolis: Fortress, 2013), 779. On the importance of the doctrine of union with Christ during the Reformation and its subsequent development, see J. V. Fesko, *Beyond Calvin: Union with Christ and Justification in Early Modern Reformed Theology (1517–1700)*, ed. Herman J. Selderhuis, Reformed Historical Theology 20 (Göttingen: Vandenhoeck & Ruprecht, 2012).

²⁶See Robin Routledge, "The Exodus and Biblical Theology," in Fox, *Reverberations*, 191-97. See Jer 2.

relationship with one transcendent, personal God who loves someone that has not loved him first.[27]

I did not set out in this project to prove this claim. Rather, I was merely developing an elective course at the institution where I teach. Nevertheless, the more I observed the biblical data as it unfolded, the more I began to realize that I had stumbled into a manner of describing salvation that was inclusive of both the union and communion side of salvation ("participation") and the forensic basis of salvation. These ways of describing salvation are not exclusive, forcing us to emphasize one or the other. I am referring to the ditch often created by those who emphasize participationist categories (sometimes referred to as "being in Christ" or "union with Christ") over against juridical categories (i.e., declarative justification of the individual saint) in their presentation of biblical salvation.[28] In short, both are necessary.

Biblical Motifs and Intertextuality

A motif is like a theme, but it accomplishes more. Leland Ryken says it is "a discernible pattern composed of individual units, either in a single work or in literature generally."[29] Concurrent with the influence of a literary approach to the Bible, the analysis of motifs has been applied to biblical literature with ever-increasing frequency.

Recent studies in biblical narrative have demonstrated an ancient reader's difficulty in grasping abstract ideas. In other words, so much of the biblical story and message is not given in bare, abstract propositions. Shemaryahu Talmon says there is a "dearth of systematic presentation of speculative thought [in the Hebrew Bible]."[30] Generally speaking, truth derived from narrative must be an aggregate of particulars peppered throughout the biblical text. Only after sustained reading of a

---

[27] See Iain Provan's analysis in *Seriously Dangerous Religion: What the Old Testament Really Says and Why It Matters* (Waco, TX: Baylor University Press, 2014), 186-90.
[28] Not all New Testament scholars would equate "union with Christ" with "participation." So much depends on how one defines terms.
[29] Leland Ryken, *Words of Delight: A Literary Introduction to the Bible* (Grand Rapids: Baker, 1987), 361.
[30] Shemaryahu Talmon, "Literary Motifs and Speculative Thought in the Hebrew Bible," *Hebrew University Studies in Literature and the Arts* 16 (1988): 150-68.

biblical story does a reader of the narrative arrive at the point of truth being conveyed.³¹

Talmon has proposed the following definition for a literary motif as it applies to biblical studies:

> A literary motif is a representative complex theme that recurs within the framework of the Hebrew Bible in variable forms and connections. It is rooted in an actual situation of anthropological or historical nature. In its secondary literary setting, the motif gives expression to ideas and experiences inherent in the original situation and is employed by the author to reactualize in his audience the reactions of the participants in that original situation. *The motif represents the essential meaning of the situation, not the situation itself.* It is not a mere reiteration of the sensations involved, but rather a heightened and intensified representation of them.³²

This definition has many salutary features. Motifs, according to Talmon, make a story come alive through resonances. A motif is a bridge-building literary tool for spanning centuries of elapsed time: it can make an ancient text come alive for subsequent hearers.

Talmon is an extremely sensitive reader of the Hebrew text. If he means, as John Wright says, that the "ideas and expressions in the original situation give rise to the symbol, and become a motif," which is somewhat disassociated from the original situation itself, then I cannot but agree.³³ Although Talmon focuses on the fact that biblical narrative is selective in its historiography, I would not draw such a sharp bifurcation between "the essential meaning of the situation" and "the situation itself." The way to the world-to-come is through the earth. Concrete symbols give way to symbols that embody transcendent truths.

Literary concerns and historicity should not be pitted against each other. This book will help the reader understand the exodus motif in the

---

³¹Ibid., 151.
³²Shemaryahu Talmon, "The Desert Motif in the Bible and in Qumran Literature," in *Literary Studies in the Hebrew Bible: Form and Content* (Jerusalem: Magnes Press), 225-26 (emphasis mine).
³³See, e.g., John Wright, "Spirit and Wilderness: The Interplay of Two Motifs Within the Hebrew Bible as a Background to Mark 1:2-13," in *Perspectives on Language and Text: Essays and Poems in Honor of Francis I. Andersen's Sixtieth Birthday, July 28, 1985*, ed. Edgar W. Conrad and Edward G. Newing (Winona Lake, IN: Eisenbrauns, 1987), 269-98, esp. 289.

texts of the ancient Hebrews and the texts of early Christians. For example, we will trace the use of the Old Testament in the New Testament, the use of mythical concepts in biblical literature, biblical theology, and biblical history. One of the most important things I wish to achieve is to break new ground in one area: how to understand evocation and allusion in biblical literature. Gilbert Highet recognized years ago, in tracking down Greek and Roman influences on Western literature, that this is no simple task:

> It is a difficult art, the art of evocative quotation. The theory held by the romantics that all good writing was entirely "original" threw it into disrepute. It has been further discredited by the misapplication of scholarship and the decline in classical knowledge . . . for readers do not like to think that, in order to appreciate poetry, they themselves ought to have read as much as the poet himself. Also, they feel, with justice, that hunting down "allusions" and "imitations" destroys the life of poetry, changing it from a living thing into an artificial tissue of copied colours and stolen patches. Still, it remains true that the reader who knows and can recognize these evocations without trouble gains a richer pleasure and a fuller understanding of the subject than the reader who cannot.[34]

This is true as well with the study of the Bible, especially the Bible in its original languages: the reader who can recognize evocation will have a better understanding and appreciation of the material. As Benjamin D. Sommer has recently commented, "Indeed, the constant reworking of biblical material is a hallmark of Jewish literature, a hallmark that is already prominent in the Bible itself."[35] The technical term for evocation is *intertextuality*, which is "how the Bible relates to itself in its own system of cross-reference. . . . It has to do with the way in which parts of the Bible and finally the two Testaments relate to one another."[36] In other words, later biblical authors build on, allude to, cite from, and

---

[34]Gilbert Highet, *The Classical Tradition: Greek and Roman Influences on Western Literature* (New York: Oxford University Press, 1957), 157-58.
[35]Benjamin D. Sommer, "Inner-biblical Interpretation," in *The Jewish Study Bible*, ed. Adele Berlin and Marc Zvi Brettler (Oxford: Oxford University Press, 2004), 1833.
[36]Christopher Seitz, *Prophecy and Hermeneutics* (Grand Rapids: Baker Academic, 2007), 228.

repurpose earlier portions of Scripture.[37] As we will see in chapter one, biblical scholars often use the term *intertextuality* in manifold and sometimes confusing ways. This has become such a problem that some have even argued for abandoning the term altogether. I am not in favor of abandoning the term; rather, I think we need a careful analysis of *how one should carry out intertextual studies*. Early on in this study, we will seek to define our terms closely and carefully. Thus, instead of abandoning the term, I will attempt to revivify what I think is a responsible use of the term vis-à-vis an irresponsible, or at least less rigorous, understanding of intertextuality.

When performing intertextual analysis, some citations and allusions are easy to recognize; however, "recognition of intertextual elements are, in many cases, not conspicuous and are only ascertainable through the performance of an attentive textual analysis," as Magdolna Orosz correctly recognizes.[38] Thankfully, now more than ever before, resources are available to help the biblical interpreter identify quotations and allusions in the biblical text. Excellent and reliable lexicons, commentaries, concordances, and monographs identify and discuss allusions. And many of these resources can be loaded on computers, enabling quick searches.[39]

In this book I will attempt to revivify a responsible use of typology, which has fallen out of favor in the academy. Indeed, typology and intertextuality are not unrelated, nor are they mutually exclusive, despite the fact that mainstream biblical scholars are disinclined to use typological exegesis at present.[40] In exploring the exodus, we will use typology rather broadly. We will speak of both literary typology (retrojective and forward

---

[37]See the important article by Joseph A. Fitzmyer, "The Use of Explicit Old Testament Quotations in Qumran Literature and in the New Testament," in *The Semitic Background of the New Testament* (Grand Rapids: Eerdmans, 1997), 3-58. Fitzmyer builds a taxonomy for the way in which Old Testament literature is quoted in Qumran and the New Testament: (A) The Literal or Historical Class (pp. 17-21), (B) The Class of Modernized Texts (pp. 21-33), (C) The Class of Accommodated Texts (pp. 33-45), (D) The Class of Eschatological Texts (pp. 46-52.).

[38]Magdolna Orosz, "Literary Reading(s) of the Bible: Aspects of a Semiotic Conception of Intertextuality and Intertextual Analysis of Texts," in *Reading the Bible Intertextually*, ed. Richard B. Hays, Stefan Alkier, and Leroy A. Huizenga (Waco, TX: Baylor University Press, 2009), 197.

[39]As a beginning, see the helpful book by G. K. Beale, *Handbook on the New Testament Use of the Old Testament: Exegesis and Interpretation* (Grand Rapids: Baker Academic, 2012).

[40]As is recognized, for example, by Brueggemann, *Theology of the Old Testament*, 178.

looking, as will be explained below) and typology in the more common sense found in the history of interpretation: a divinely designated, shadowy type anticipating and looking forward to a fulfillment in the antitype (i.e., the real thing).

In addition to tracing the exodus motif, I am also interested in and concerned about the discipline of biblical theology. The primary purpose of biblical theology is the study of God's unfolding plan of redemption in Scripture. It has to do with understanding God's revelation as given in different eras. Such study concerns itself with "three characteristics that are common to every action to which God commits Himself *in time*," says Klaas Schilder. He goes on to identify those properties: "(1) Such revelation is always a true one, and (2) Such revelation is never a complete one, and (3) Such revelation is always a growing one."[41] These principles attend every ongoing revelation of God in Scripture. Following this threefold nature of revelation are certain demands on persons who receive it. This becomes important as we explore the contrasts among varying responses to God's revelation.

Many biblical theologies are too ambitious. As James Barr comments, to add another book that essays the "grandiose task of verbalizing the theology of the whole" may, by its very ambitions, "invite mockery."[42] Barr questions whether ambitious Old Testament biblical theologies are the best way to pursue biblical theology. He suggests that the real work of biblical theology lies along more modest lines in the areas of tracing one theme, or investigating one area of Old Testament background or one area of Old Testament tradition.[43]

Outline of the Book

Here is how we will proceed. Chapter one discusses intertextuality and hermeneutics generally. This chapter develops a *text theory* within a

---

[41]Klaas Schilder, *Christ in His Suffering*, trans. Henry Zylstra (Grand Rapids: Eerdmans, 1938), 87-88.
[42]James Barr, *The Concept of Biblical Theology: An Old Testament Perspective* (Minneapolis: Fortress, 1999), 53, 60. See Barr's insightful comments on pp. 52-61 about the ever-increasing number of large volumes trying to write *the* theology of the Old Testament.
[43]Ibid., 53.

philosophy of language that interacts with recent trends. If readers are interested in drilling deeper, they can consult the more detailed account found in the appendix. This is a complex and technical subject, and consequently its technical jargon needs no justification.

Chapter one also looks at allusions. How do they work? How is allusion distinct from related terms? Here the main issue is how the author of the text, the original audience, and the reader are all involved in the process of determining meaning. Is discerning the original author's intention actually possible, and if so, what does this mean? What is the primary and proper horizon from which to commence a study of the meaning of a given text? Is it the horizon of the reader, the audience, the author, or the historical situation of the original audience? In this discussion, we will observe how allusions to the exodus function. Chapter one also deals with typology. Although the term *typology* is not always used univocally, I am not going to avoid the term.[44] The exodus event has been considered a type throughout the history of Old Testament interpretation. I explore how the mode of biblical typology was employed by the early Hebrew and Christian writers as a legitimate interpretation of Old Testament texts.

Once these theoretical issues have been discussed, we will be ready to dive into the biblical text in earnest. Chapter two is about the foundations of the exodus motif as they are found in the biblical creation account. The past is prologue here. Thus, we turn to the beginning of the Scriptures to see that creation itself informs the way the story plays out. In creation, the big themes that will provide the backdrop for so much of the rest of the book are put in place: mountain, wilderness, avian (bird) imagery, alienation, and promise. Creation is important for its connection with covenant. Once we see that creation and covenant are connected, we are prepared to see the connections with the exodus. Covenant becomes a structuring device, especially in Genesis but also in Exodus.[45] In my view, covenant is best defined as a legal transaction in

---

[44]Pace Fitzmyer, *Semitic Background*, 22.
[45]Rolf Rendtorff, "'Covenant' as a Structuring Concept in Genesis and Exodus," *JBL* 108, no. 3 (1989): 385-93.

which there are divinely sanctioned commitments.[46] This definition is broad enough to encompass a host of biblical covenants. Moreover, it does not prejudice the relational over against the legal. Biblical covenants function as "instruments of the divine government."[47]

Having laid the foundations, we come to the heart of the matter in chapter three: a discussion of the exodus motif as a paradigm. We explore the foundational salvific event of the Old Testament and build a platform for future discussion. The deliverance of God's people becomes a crucial motif in Scripture from this point forward.

In chapter four we see how the threads of the exodus motif are woven into the pattern and tapestry of the Psalms. We will also see the function of the exodus motif: Israel is called to a new level of understanding in light of God's faithfulness in the past. We will see not only how biblical themes are interwoven at this point but also how the themes and ideas of the surrounding cultures are strategically employed. God as the divine warrior will now conquer the enemies of his people just as he subdued the ancient and tumultuous waters of chaos.

Chapter five deals with Isaiah's use of the exodus motif. Something "new" is going to take place, according to the prophets. This has been called the "Isaianic new exodus." From different vantage points and in various ways, Isaiah teaches us that the foundational salvific event of the exodus is a paradigm for announcing an altogether new event of salvation. What was a mere shadow is going to break on the horizon of the future with a new brilliance. In Isaiah 40–55 we will observe a fusion of a series of creation/redemptive themes in more than a dozen passages.

Next, chapter six handles the exilic and postexilic periods. Here I turn to the two other major prophets, Ezekiel and Jeremiah. The prophets are important for our understanding of how the exodus motif plays out in the New Testament; however, one more link is necessary before we turn to the New Testament's use of this theme. After the Babylonian exile,

---

[46]Meredith G. Kline, *Kingdom Prologue: Genesis Foundations for a Covenantal Worldview* (Overland Park, KS: Two Age Press, 2000), 1-6.

[47]See Meredith G. Kline, *Genesis: A New Commentary*, ed. Jonathan G. Kline (Peabody, MA: Hendrickson, 2016), 18.

the exodus motif continues to influence the manner in which the biblical authors describe salvation history. Indeed, references to the exodus motif during the postexilic period of redemptive history mark the transition to the New Testament. The "new thing" that the prophets anticipated is realized in the coming of the King, who inaugurates his kingdom. Scholarship has recognized this especially in the use of particular Hebrew phrases and formulas in Ezra–Nehemiah having to do with the exodus and an analysis of the prayers of Nehemiah. Moreover, the exodus pattern becomes the paradigm of the Gospels to describe this new and profound realization.

When we come to the Gospels in chapter seven, we observe the mediatorial role that the ideology of the exodus plays in formulating the message of the arrival of King and kingdom. In this chapter I consider Mark and Matthew. Here the Isaianic new exodus paradigm is evoked to demonstrate that the exodus motif has become "eschatologized." The exodus has become a future event promised on the basis of God's past action in delivering his people. In chapter eight I will consider Luke–Acts. Now a reformulation of the exodus event appears along cosmogonic, earth-shaking lines: the *new* exodus is a creative event declaring who the true Israel is.[48] Moreover, we begin to see that the foundation story of the exodus is mediated through Isaiah especially, but other Old Testament Scriptures as well.

As one would expect, all this evocation flowing from the exodus could not possibly leave the apostle Paul untouched. Indeed, the influence of the exodus motif on the apostle is pervasive, and we will be selective in what we discuss in chapter nine. As N. T. Wright says, "The theme of 'new Exodus' is never far away from the mind of Paul, or indeed of other early Christians."[49] The exodus motif has been identified by scholars as being pervasive and influential for two of Paul's

---

[48]New Testament scholars have not achieved any consensus regarding what exactly "new exodus" means. For a survey, see Daniel Lynwood Smith, "The Uses of 'New Exodus' in New Testament Scholarship: Preparing a Way Through the Wilderness," *CurBR* 14, no. 2 (2016): 207-43.

[49]N. T. Wright, *The Paul Debate: Critical Questions for Understanding the Apostle* (Waco, TX: Baylor University Press, 2015), 38. Indeed, in an earlier work Wright had claimed that this was the narrative that had dominated so much early Christian thought; see *Paul and the Faithfulness of God*, 1105.

most important and doctrinal books: Galatians and Romans. Chapter nine discusses the influence of the exodus motif on these two books as well as some other references in Pauline literature such as Colossians 1:12-14 and 1 Corinthians 10:1-10.

The apostle Peter also makes prominent use of the exodus motif, especially in 1 Peter 1:1–2:10. Chapter ten interacts with the particular contribution of Petrine texts. These letters contribute to the development of the exodus motif from an ecclesial perspective. In 1 Peter 1–2, Christians are now redeemed by the spotless blood of the Lamb and become the new people of God, the fulfillment of the promise of that royal priesthood. We also begin to see the special function of the exodus motif unfold with new clarity in the these epistles. The people of God are caught up and participate in the new exodus so that they might serve God and one another as a new royal priesthood of God.

Chapter eleven brings us to the end of the biblical corpus with an examination of the exodus motif in Revelation. Here, all the strands come together in the consummation of the ages. Revelation shows similarities to 1 Peter, but John advances on Peter's argument. Indeed, Christians are seen as the new kingdom of priests, no longer pilgrims in a strange land. The divine warrior themes so common in the exodus motif become prominent once again. The church's victory is seen as complete; typology throughout Scripture is now fulfilled, and the consummation of the ages has come. The kingdom of Christ and his people has become the kingdom of this world.

Chapter twelve attempts to bring the arguments together under the rubric of biblical theology. Having traced the particulars of Scripture's use of the exodus motif, we view the whole from the parts. I analyze what contribution our study makes to the discipline of biblical theology.

Should you speed-read this book? Probably not. I recommend reading from beginning to end slowly and carefully in order to discern the flow of the argument. I have deliberately organized it with such a view in mind. Skipping ahead to read the treatment on any particular passage or topic may lead to misunderstanding a part in light of the whole, or vice versa.

The exodus motif is one way the masterful and mysterious plan of God is made plain to those readers of Scripture willing to invest the energy. As Paul E. Deterding has said, "If the church's proclamation is to be truly apostolic, we must also declare that God's dealings with Israel in Egypt are not bare, historical facts with no application to ourselves. Rather, we are to proclaim that in the death and resurrection of Jesus Christ, in our own conversion, and in the immanent consummation, God fulfills His mighty acts of old for us."[50] Understood properly, the story of an ancient nation delivered from captivity, led into the desert, and brought to a new land is full of life-changing news for a modern world.

---

[50]Paul E. Deterding, "Exodus Motifs in First Peter," *Concordia Journal* 7, no. 2 (March 1981): 64.

One

HERMENEUTICAL FOUNDATIONS

Mi amar le-mi u-matay ("who said unto whom and when").[1]
CHANA KRONFELD

> *Theory was to be understood (by the Greeks) as itself the highest realization of practice.*
> MARTIN HEIDEGGER

There is wide consensus among literary critics that Milton was a precursor to Wordsworth as Shakespeare was to Keats. These literary giants influenced subsequent poets.[2] Can we observe the same kind of literary dynamic happening among biblical authors? For example, is Isaiah influenced by the creation account and the exodus motif when allusions are made in his writings? If so, how? Do the Gospel writers refer to the Prophets when they make allusions to the exodus? If so, how? More important, what does this tell us about how the Hebrew Bible is informing and influencing the narrative of Jesus as the agent of the new exodus? In the introduction we discussed motifs and their use in Scripture, highlighting their references to past events. In this chapter we will look at intertextuality, allusion, and typology.

---

[1] This "is the standard opening of a Bible quiz in an Israeli school, and the standard 'lead-in' of many Israeli jokes." Chana Kronfeld, *On the Margins of Modernism: Decentering Literary Dynamics* (Berkeley: University of California Press, 1996), 114.

[2] However, Milton criticism has been diverted with finding allusions that the writer himself may not have even been aware of. See, e.g., Dale C. Allison Jr., *The New Moses: A Matthean Typology* (Minneapolis: Fortress, 1993), 22.

Simply stated, intertextuality is the manner in which the various books of the Bible interact. In other words, authors in Scripture often allude to, cite, echo, comment on, and even at times "revise" or "accommodate" other scriptural texts.[3] When studying a passage in the Bible that references another passage, we are given a window into an author's understanding of the other scriptural texts, especially when metaphors are used. But the reader cannot be left out of the equation when it comes to understanding meaning, especially when it comes to identifying motifs and metaphors. Indeed, in the final analysis, "it is the reader who 'completes' the reading and engenders the metaphor's tenor [i.e., meaning]."[4] My primary goal in this chapter is to provide the reader with a brief introduction to intertextuality. A secondary goal is to look at the literary side of hermeneutics.

Hans-Georg Gadamer is well known in the field of philosophical hermeneutics. One chief concern of Gadamer's was to develop what he called "effective history," or *Wirkungsgeschichte*. This is essentially the *historical continuum* shared by an interpreter and the phenomena he or she studies, which is ultimately the basis of understanding.[5] Enter the topics of allusion and typology.

Literary theorists suggest all kinds of reasons for the deliberate use of allusion. For example, Benjamin Sommer, an Isaiah scholar, introduces the notion of delight and pleasure.[6] Playfulness may contribute to the use of allusion since we delight in alluding to other authors and we delight as human beings in recognizing allusions. The primary reason Scripture uses allusions, however, has to do with typology. "Allusions commonly merge with typology," claims Bruce Waltke. He goes on to say, "The Old

---

[3] I am indebted for the latter term to Joseph A. Fitzmyer, SJ, "The Use of Explicit Old Testament Quotations in Qumran Literature and in the New Testament," in *The Semitic Background of the New Testament* (Grand Rapids: Eerdmans, 1997), 3-58.

[4] Øystein Lund, *Way Metaphors and Way Topics in Isaiah 40–55*, FAT 28 (Tübingen: Mohr Siebeck, 2007), 35.

[5] See Kurt Mueller-Vollmer, introduction to *The Hermeneutics Reader: Texts of the German Tradition from the Enlightenment to the Present*, ed. Kurt Mueller-Vollmer (New York: Continuum, 2000), 39-41, 256-92, esp. 256.

[6] See Benjamin D. Sommer, *A Prophet Reads Scripture: Allusion in Isaiah 40–66* (Stanford, CA: Stanford University Press, 1998), 18-19.

Testament is full of types of people and historical events, but none surpasses Moses and Israel's exodus from Egypt."[7] Although typological interpretation has fallen on hard times in recent decades, it is a method of biblical interpretation with a time-honored pedigree in the church. The topic needs to be revisited in a serious manner, and the concept needs to be retrieved. In the discussion that follows, I will often use the terms *figural reading* and *typology* synonymously, although I realize that in much secondary literature distinctions are made between the two.

Finally, I will discuss the controversial concept of the rule of faith, or *regula fidei*. This hermeneutical principle was commonplace in the biblical interpretation of the early church. Recently, it has regained attention. The payoff is theological since, at its most basic level, the rule of faith is concerned to identify Christ with Yahweh as revealed in the Old Testament Scriptures.

A Brief History of Intertextuality

The term *intertextuality* was coined by the French literary theorist Julia Kristeva (b. 1941) in her 1969 book Σημειωτικη *[Sēmeiōtikē]: Recherches pour une sémanalyse*.[8] Turbulent events in France in May 1968 provoked a crisis in literary criticism in order to attempt to transform society.[9] Moved by what she perceived as a crisis in meaning within Western literature, Kristeva sought to mediate the ideas of Russian literary thinker Mikhail Bakhtin (1895–1975) to the Western world.[10] Bakhtin was one

---

[7]Bruce Waltke with Charles Yu, *An Old Testament Theology: An Exegetical, Canonical, and Thematic Approach* (Grand Rapids: Zondervan, 2007), 133, 138.

[8]Originally published in 1969 by Éditions due Seuil and published in English as Julia Kristeva, *Desire in Language: A Semiotic Approach to Literature and Art*, ed. Leon S. Roudiez, trans. Thomas Gora, Alice Jardine, and Leon S. Roudiez (New York: Columbia University Press, 1980). Also see *The Kristeva Reader*, ed. Toril Moi (New York: Columbia University Press, 1986); and Mastrangelo Bove, "The Text as Dialogue in Bakhtin and Kristeva," *Revue de l'Université d'Ottawa* 53 (1983): 117-24.

[9]See Gary A. Phillips, "Poststructural Intertextuality," in *Exploring Intertextuality: Diverse Strategies for New Testament Interpretation of Texts*, ed. B. J. Oropeza and Steve Moyise (Eugene, OR: Cascade, 2016), 106-28, esp. 106-9.

[10]Some may think that engaging authors such as Kristeva entails taking on the ideological baggage associated with poststructuralist theorists. I disagree since interest in their ideas (e.g., intertextuality and "echo" within literature) does not entail accepting their ideological framework. See the comments of Richard B. Hays, *The Conversion of the Imagination: Paul as Interpreter of Israel's Scripture* (Grand Rapids: Eerdmans, 2005), 172-74.

of the leading twentieth-century thinkers about the nature of literature and texts.[11] He had analyzed Dostoyevsky's novels and come to the conclusion that speaking merely of authorial intent in literature was shortsighted. Every character carries a voice that interacts with many other previous and contemporary voices inside and outside the text.

Consequently, to understand meaning in any given literary text, a reader needs to be aware of the myriad influences, cultural and intertextual, that are represented in the text. Kristeva's methods were weighted more toward a synchronic than a diachronic approach. Looking at a topic synchronically means considering something across a slice of time, looking at language as a functional whole. In contrast, a diachronic approach is concerned with the text's history, how it came into its present form through time. Here the aim is to give a historical evaluation of a topic through time. The synchronic approach is usually connected with reader-centered methods, whereas the diachronic approach is customarily joined to an author-centered methodology. This distinction is related to the thinking of the father of modern linguistics, Ferdinand de Saussure (1857–1913). (The curious reader can learn more about him by turning to the appendix.)

Intertextuality and Biblical Studies

In biblical studies, the work of Michael Fishbane represents a seminal perspective on the field of intertextuality with his focus on the reuse of the Hebrew Bible within the Hebrew Bible itself.[12] With methodological

---

[11] See Katerina Clark and Michael Holquist, *Mikhail Bakhtin* (Cambridge, MA: Harvard University Press, 1984). For a recent application of Bakhtin to certain aspects of systematic theology, see Kevin J. Vanhoozer, *First Theology: God, Scriptures and Hermeneutics* (Downers Grove, IL: InterVarsity Press, 2002), and especially his more recent work, *Remythologizing Theology: Divine Action, Passion, and Authorship* (Cambridge: Cambridge University Press, 2010). Vanhoozer's work is creative, deeply informed, and helpful in many respects; however, there are some areas where I demur at his suggestions, e.g., his construals that challenge a classic approach to the impassibility of God.

[12] Michael Fishbane, *Biblical Interpretation in Ancient Israel* (Oxford: Clarendon, 1985). Other works of Fishbane that deal with innerbiblical interpretation are "Torah and Tradition," in *Tradition and Theology in the Old Testament*, ed. Douglas A. Knight (Philadelphia: Fortress, 1977), 275-300; *Text and Texture: Close Readings of Selected Biblical Texts* (New York: Schocken, 1979); "Revelation and Tradition: Aspects of Inner-biblical Exegesis," *JBL* 99 (1980): 343-61; "Inner-biblical Exegesis: Types and Strategies in Interpretation in Ancient Israel," in *The Garments of Torah: Essays in*

precision and clarity, Fishbane notes the many ways in which the scribes of the Hebrew Bible commentated on the received text (the *traditum*) by incorporating their own exegetical insights into a subsequent product (the *traditio*). He argues that at each stage of the development of the Hebrew Bible, the *traditum* was transformed, revised, and even reinterpreted for subsequent generations.

In New Testament studies, the work of Richard B. Hays on Paul has been groundbreaking with respect to intertextuality.[13] This is especially the case with Hays's use of *metalepsis*, or *transumption*, a poetic and rhetorical device in which a later author draws on older work in order to suggest a connection or interplay between the two texts.[14] Specifically, metalepsis is the use of allusion that "evokes resonances of the earlier text *beyond those explicitly cited.* The result is that the interpretation of a metalepsis requires the reader to recover unstated or suppressed correspondences between two texts."[15] Following Fishbane and Hays, a deluge of papers, articles, and books on intertextuality have flooded the biblical studies guild.[16] Some have suggested jettisoning the term *intertextuality* altogether because of the varied uses of the term. Rather, we must be

---

Biblical Hermeneutics (Bloomington: Indiana University Press, 1989), 3-18; *The Exegetical Imagination: On Jewish Thought and Theology* (Cambridge, MA: Harvard University Press, 1998); and "Types of Biblical Intertextuality," in *Congress Volume: Oslo 1998*, ed. A. Lemaire and M. Sæbø, VTSup 80 (Leiden: Brill, 2000), 38-44.

[13]Richard B. Hays, *Echoes of Scripture in the Letters of Paul* (New Haven, CT: Yale University Press, 1989). More recently Hays has been applying his methods to the Gospels: *Reading Backwards: Figural Christology and the Fourfold Gospel Witness* (Waco, TX: Baylor University Press, 2014). His newest work, *Echoes of Scripture in the Gospels* (Waco, TX: Baylor University Press, 2016), should actually be read as the precursor to *Reading Backwards*. Hays's work has inspired young scholars to apply his methods to other sections of Scripture as well. See, e.g., Brandon D. Crowe, *The Obedient Son: Deuteronomy and Christology in the Gospel of Matthew*, BZNW 188 (Boston: De Gruyter, 2012).

[14]Hays, in *Echoes of Scripture in the Letters of Paul*, describes metalepsis as follows: "When a literary echo links the text in which it occurs to an earlier text, the figurative effect of the echo can lie in the unstated or suppressed (transumed) points of resonance between the two texts" (20). More recently, in *Reading Backwards*, he defines it as "the practice of citing a fragment that beckons readers to recover more of the original subtext in order to grasp the full force of the intertextual link" (42). His use of *metalepsis* and the influence here is dependent on Hollander, not Harold Bloom or his students. For a summary and recent criticisms of this notion, see Alec J. Lucas, "Assessing Stanley E. Porter's Objections to Richard B. Hays's Notion of Metalepsis," *CBQ* 76, no. 1 (January 2014): 93-111.

[15]Hays, *Conversion of the Imagination*, 2.

[16]For surveys of the literature, see P. K. Tull, "Intertextuality and the Hebrew Scriptures," *CurBR* 8 (2000): 59-90.

more precise in our use of terms and concepts since failing to recognize intertextual links may result in a loss of meaning and falsely presuming intertextual links may result in a distortion of meaning.[17]

How are we to define *intertextuality*? A minimal definition is how "in one artistic text there coexist, more or less visibly, several other texts."[18] Applied to biblical studies, it is the recognition that "the interpretation of the Bible begins with the Bible itself."[19] Here Leland Ryken's simple definition is helpful: intertextuality is "a situation in which the full meaning of a text depends on its interaction with another text."[20] Even at this point, one must recognize cultural influences on the Scriptures and the reader's role as well. A definition commended by W. J. C. Weren is perhaps inclusive enough to capture all these factors, since by "intertextuality" he means "research into the relationships between texts and the functions of these relationships."[21] I appreciate the functional definition given by James H. Charlesworth also: "Intertextuality is the attempt to appreciate the meaning of a text by focusing on the text (or texts) within it; that is, quoted in it or echoed in it."[22] Such mental recognition by a reader often depends on what I am calling "allusion competence."

A character portrayed in a novel may say to a jealous husband, "I will not have you misinterpret my handkerchief!"[23] Readers may immediately recognize such an allusion if they are current on their Shakespeare. However, this requires some level of literary competence, which undergirds an allusion competence. The character could have said to her jealous

---

[17]Paraphrasing John Sailhamer as quoted by Richard L. Schultz, "The Ties That Bind: Intertextuality, the Identification of Verbal Parallels, and Reading Strategies in the Book of the Twelve," in *Thematic Threads in the Book of the Twelve*, BZAW 325 (Berlin: De Gruyter, 2003), 45.
[18]Hans-Peter Mai, quoted in Christopher B. Hays, "Echoes of the Ancient Near East?," in *The Word Leaps the Gap: Essays on Scripture and Theology in Honor of Richard B. Hays*, ed. J. Ross Wagner, C. Kavin Rowe, and A. Katherine Grieb (Grand Rapids: Eerdmans, 2008), 24.
[19]Benjamin D. Sommer, "Inner-biblical Interpretation," in *The Jewish Study Bible*, ed. Adele Berlin and Marc Zvi Brettler (Oxford: Oxford University Press, 2004), 1829.
[20]Leland Ryken, *Words of Delight: A Literary Introduction to the Bible* (Grand Rapids: Baker, 1987), 361.
[21]Quoted in Kenneth Litwak, *Echoes of Scripture in Luke–Acts: Telling the History of God's People Intertextually*, JSNTSup 282 (New York: T&T Clark, 2005), 27.
[22]See James H. Charlesworth, "Intertextuality: Isaiah 40:3 and the Serek Ha-Yaḥad," in *The Quest for Context and Meaning: Studies in Biblical Intertextuality in Honor of James A. Sanders*, ed. Craig A. Evans and Shemaryahu Talmon (Leiden: Brill, 1997), 218.
[23]I am indebted to Carmela Perri, "On Alluding," *Poetics* 7 (1978): 289-307, for the following illustration.

husband, "I will not have you make me into a Desdemona," or even more explicitly, "I will not have you make us into Desdemona and Othello from Shakespeare's play *Othello*."[24] The latter examples are much more explicit. Even if readers don't know the play, they can understand the allusion with a little bit of research.

In other words, in order for readers to recognize allusions, they must be aware of what is being referred to, which is an act of informed intelligence.[25] In the interpretation of Scripture, the reader must keep in mind the human author as well as the divine author. The Old Testament can be used consciously by a New Testament writer, who can be influenced by it unconsciously as well.[26] So what are we doing as students of the Bible when we use an intertextual approach, and how ought we to use the terminology now in vogue?[27]

Reader Oriented or Author Oriented?

The answer to the above question is that both reader and author are important. For the sake of clarity, we should restrict the term *intertextuality* to the reader-oriented, synchronic approach (although not exclusively).[28] On the other hand, two terms have gained currency for the more author-oriented, diachronic approach: innerbiblical exegesis and innerbiblical allusion. I will adopt the term *innerbiblical exegesis* for the diachronic approach since my understanding of allusion with regard to the exodus will focus on diachronic concerns. The upshot of this is that when I use *intertextuality*, I

---

[24]Ibid., 290.

[25]Figural (i.e., typological) interpretation will take both the divine authorship and intentions and the human authorship and intentions of the Scriptures seriously. Here Calvin may be our guide. Let it be perfectly clear what I am saying: "It is not possible for Calvin to talk *singularly* about the *human* author's intention: for him this is never separate from the divine Author's intention," as Sujin Pak declared recently in "Calvin on the 'Shared Design' of the Old and the New Testament Authors: The Case of the Minor Prophets," *WTJ* 73 (2011): 257.

[26]A point used to good effect by A. Denaux, "Old Testament Models for the Lukan Travel Narrative," in *The Scriptures in the Gospels*, BETL 131 (Leuven: Leuven University Press, 1997), 271-99.

[27]Many examples can be cited with regard to confusion or imprecise use of terminology. See, e.g., Stanley E. Porter, "The Use of the Old Testament in the New Testament: A Brief Comment on Method and Terminology," in *Early Christian Interpretation of the Scriptures of Israel: Investigations and Proposals*, ed. Craig A. Evans and James A. Sanders, JSNTSup 148 (Sheffield: Sheffield Academic Press, 1997), 79-97.

[28]On this, see the extensive discussion in the appendix.

am talking about a literary connection in which one text influences another, and I am less concerned about chronological precedence. When I use the term *innerbiblical exegesis*, I am assuming that one text influenced a subsequent biblical text, even diachronically. In my judgment there can be no ultimate rapprochement between the two approaches (synchronic and diachronic) if they both want to own the term *intertextuality*.[29]

I am suggesting a theory that takes seriously the text and its original horizon, which includes both human and divine authors, and the process by which readers come to understand the literary and theological meaning of a scriptural text and realize that meaning may be "updated" by the new horizons of subsequent readers. As traditional approaches to philology have emphasized for centuries, readers have an ethical obligation and a responsibility to work hard and earnestly listen to what an author or narrator is saying, and to do justice to those words by not twisting them to fit one's own interpretation.[30]

Sometimes determining quotations and allusions depends on an interpreter's commitment to either the reader or the author.[31] My theory of influence and intertextuality does not ignore the historical side of an author or the psychology of the reader, for the two must be wedded for a full understanding of meaning. This approach runs against the grain of much interpretation in literary circles.

---

[29]This is more restrictive than the recent work, from which I have benefited greatly, by Will Kynes, *My Psalm Has Turned into Weeping: Job's Dialogue with the Psalms*, BZAW 437 (Boston: De Gruyter, 2012), 29. Kynes seeks to use the term more broadly by suggesting "intertextualities in dialogue" (by modifying Ben-Porat and Hays) since he notes that writers often fluctuate between diachronic and synchronic approaches in their analysis of allusions.

[30]See Vanhoozer, *First Theology*, 161; Grant R. Osborne, "Hermeneutics and Paul: Psalm 68:18 in Ephesians 4:7-10 as a Test Case," in *Studies in the Pauline Epistles*, ed. Mathew S. Harmon and Jay E. Smith (Grand Rapids: Zondervan, 2014), 159-180, esp. 160. Also see Vanhoozer's excellent discussion in *Is There a Meaning in This Text? The Bible, the Reader, and the Morality of Literary Knowledge* (Grand Rapids: Zondervan, 1998), 367-441.

[31]See, e.g., Stanley E. Porter, "Further Comments on the Use of the Old Testament in the New Testament," in *The Intertextuality of the Epistles: Explorations of Theory and Practice*, ed. Thomas L. Brodie, Dennis R. MacDonald, and Stanley E. Porter (Sheffield: Sheffield Phoenix Press, 2006), 105, who points out the differences between Hays and Christopher Stanley. In this regard, Porter sides with Stanley. See Christopher Stanley, *Paul and the Language of Scripture: Citation Technique in the Pauline Epistles and Contemporary Literature*, SNTSMS 74 (Cambridge: Cambridge University Press, 1992) and Stanley, *Arguing with Scripture: The Rhetoric of Quotations in the Letters of Paul* (New York: T & T Clark, 2004).

In the last half century, this "de-authoring" of texts and concomitant focus on the act of interpretation has "shifted attention to the reader, encouraging the procedures of [synchronic] intertextuality."[32] Has this been a good move? Whereas Julia Kristeva opened the gate for this new approach, Roland Barthes (1915–1980), perhaps the most influential among the new literary critics in France in the 1960s, sauntered through it. Barthes states,

> Classic criticism has never paid any attention to the reader; for it, the writer is the only person in literature. We are now beginning to let ourselves be fooled no longer by the arrogant antiphrastical [antiphrasis is the rhetorical device that uses a word in an opposite sense to its usual meaning] recriminations of good society in favour of the very thing it sets aside, ignores, smothers, or destroys; we know that to give writing its future, it is necessary to overthrow the myth: the birth of the reader must be at the cost of the death of the Author.[33]

Surely, this is a gaffe of immense proportion when it comes to respecting any author, let alone the divine author.[34] In this system of reference, Sommer suggests, "it is the reader who interprets signs in the text by associating them with related signs in the reader's own mind."[35] As far as literary-critical theories are concerned, some would even say that the poststructuralistic reaction to Barthes has led to a radical shift from how the signs of a text work to the "perception of those signs in the mind of the reader."[36] In other words, in this approach *the meaning* is merely generated by the reader.[37]

By contrast, I am suggesting that human intentionality is accessible, though discovering what that exactly is has many challenges.[38] Indeed,

---

[32]Jay Clayton and Eric Rothstein, "Figures in the Corpus: Theories of Influence and Intertextuality," in *Influence and Intertextuality in Literary History*, ed. Jay Clayton and Eric Rothstein (Madison: University of Wisconsin Press, 1991), 16.
[33]Roland Barthes, "The Death of the Author," in *Image, Music, Text*, trans. Stephen Heath (New York: Hill and Wang, 1977), 148.
[34]Michael S. Horton, *People and Place: A Covenant Ecclesiology* (Louisville, KY: Westminster John Knox, 2008), 62.
[35]Sommer, *Prophet Reads Scripture*, 7.
[36]Grant R. Osborne, *The Hermeneutical Spiral: A Comprehensive Introduction to Biblical Interpretation*, 2nd ed. (Downers Grove, IL: IVP Academic, 2006), 475.
[37]For helpful criticism of Barthes, see Vanhoozer, *First Theology*, 211-13, 244-45.
[38]See the famous article on the "intentionalist fallacy" made clear: W. K. Wimsatt Jr. and M. C.

human intentionality is fairly consistent across cultures and artifacts and among individuals in their communication, whether written or otherwise.[39] Barthes's theory, which sought to marginalize or even get rid of the author of a text, suppresses history, biography, and psychology.[40] I will not. Truth is at stake.[41]

Determining Literary Connections: Criteria for Establishing Relationship

Within the context of innerbiblical exegesis and intertextuality, one of the first tasks for the reader of Scripture is to determine whether an actual influence exists between one text and another. Scholars who are concerned to establish and interpret a link have made various proposals for accomplishing this. What criteria should we use to determine the influence of one scriptural text on another?

Sharing language. The foremost criterion for establishing a link between texts is *shared lexical features*.[42] When dealing with New Testament quotations of Old Testament texts, a debate ensues as to whether the New Testament author interpreted the Old Testament citation or quotation in line with the original Old Testament context.[43] An example of

---

Beardsley, "The Intentional Fallacy," *Sewanee Review* 54 (1946): 468-88. This important essay was later published by Wimsatt in *The Verbal Icon: Studies in the Meaning of Poetry* (London: Methuen, 1954). Wimsatt and Beardsley were not against authorial intent; they merely wanted it properly nuanced.

[39] See the excellent book by Raymond W. Gibbs Jr., *Intentions in the Experience of Meaning* (Cambridge: Cambridge University Press, 1999), 332-34. Gibbs, a cognitive psychologist, provides a robust defense of intentionalism across cultures in written and oral communication, but he also recognizes that there may be different ways of recognizing intentions among people in different kinds of interpretive activities.

[40] Ibid., 252-56.

[41] See Ann Jefferson, "Structuralism and Post-structuralism," in *Modern Literary Theory: A Comparative Introduction*, ed. Ann Jefferson and David Robey, 2nd ed. (London: B. T. Batsford, 1986), 92-121. She comments in relation to Barthes, "Truth is similarly found to have no real status in the literary text. Far from ordering and creating literature from without, Barthes shows truth to be a mirage produced by one of his five codes. By posing an enigma and deferring its solution, the hermeneutic code pulls off a sleight of hand which makes delayed information synonymous with truth. Truth is not something fixed and solid beyond and behind the literary text, and to which the text can be reduced: it is simply what comes last in the text" (110).

[42] G. D. Miller, "Intertextuality in Old Testament Research," *CurBR* 9 (2010): 295.

[43] See G. K. Beale, *Handbook on the New Testament Use of the Old Testament: Exegesis and Interpretation* (Grand Rapids: Baker Academic, 2012).

this is found in Psalm 68. At the end of the psalm (Ps 68:33-35), the psalmist appeals to the universal rule of God. The tone becomes eschatological and universal. The apostle Paul quotes this psalm in Ephesians 4:7-16. There is significant development from the context of the original psalm but also coherence. Enter the topic of typology.

When Paul quotes Psalm 68, there is typological development and heightening. But another point is significant for the purposes of biblical typology.[44] In Ephesians 4:8, when the apostle says *dio legei*, "therefore it says," he is citing Scripture in a manner that is not customary for the apostle.[45] Paul is marking by the use of the preposition "therefore" (*dio*, in consequence of this) the inference of what Scripture says in Psalm 68:18. The effect of this is that Paul is essentially claiming, "(Because) to each one of us grace was given ... *therefore*, ... Scripture says, 'When he ascended on high ...'"[46] Stephen M. Baugh explains that the apostle is essentially teasing out the meaning of Psalm 68, seeing in that text a preliminary announcement of the gospel (cf. Gal 3:8). For Paul, claims Baugh, the psalm is part of the organic development of how the apostle understands redemptive revelation. "Organic" is merely communicating continuity. Both author and reader are important here for understanding. In Ephesians there must be a merging of horizons. Yes, there is development and it is forward looking; however, the idea culminating in Christ's distribution of gifts to men (Eph 4:11) was inchoate in Psalm 68, and that is the reason for the psalm being written in a mysterious and preliminary way.

Sharing content. Other ways may be established to link texts. Sometimes there is no direct citation or quotation from another passage in Scripture but merely overlap in content without direct citation. An example of this may be seen in 1 Peter, which is treated later in the book.

Sharing form. In the instance of authors citing each other explicitly, innerbiblical exegesis is clear. But a similar use of form or even structures

---

[44]The following is a summary of Steve Baugh's work on Ephesians. See Stephen M. Baugh, *Ephesians*, Evangelical Exegetical Commentary (Bellingham, WA: Lexham Press, 2016), 321-26.

[45]See ibid. Only in three other places does this occur in Scripture: a composite quote in Eph 5:14, Jas 4:6 (a quote from Proverbs), and Heb 10:5.

[46]Baugh's translation.

can also signal influence. Little research and writing has been developed in this area. Yet in my view similar patterns can provide important clues to influence. Indeed, similar structures between texts may be allusive. Take Isaiah 5 as an example. This chapter's influence on the vineyard parables in the Gospels is notable, but consider how the form of the passage, a softer and more general pattern, may have influenced them as well. For example, the structure of Matthew 23 seems to have been influenced by the form of Isaiah 5 (notice the "woe" oracles in both passages).

Now that we have seen some criteria for determining links between biblical texts, how are these links used by biblical authors in constructing their texts and furthering their theology?

Interpreting the Connection and Exegetical Function

In what follows, I offer my definitions and criteria for determining allusions. The first area is the most general in literary circles: influence.

Evocation and influence. While I am interested in innerbiblical discourse that attempts to make diachronic judgments, to speak of evocation and influence is a better path. Some have gone so far as to say, "Inner-biblical discourse requires that we begin with diachronic observations and judgments."[47] *Influence*, moreover, is a term used in literary-critical circles to broadly describe links between various themes in texts.[48] Strictly speaking, influence should refer to relations between mere texts. However, influence studies often comment on shared intellectual backgrounds.[49] In considering the exodus motif, an expanded definition and sense of influence "allows one to shift one's attention from the transmission of motifs between authors to the transmutation of historically given material."[50] This associative strategy has had a long history, but in modern literary criticism no one has been more influential than Harold

---

[47] W. M. Schneidewind, "'Are We His People or Not?' Biblical Interpretation During Crisis," *Bib* 76 (1995): 550.
[48] See Louis A. Renza, "Influence," in *Critical Terms for Literary Study*, ed. Frank Lentricchia and Thomas McLaughlin (Chicago: University of Chicago Press, 1990), 186.
[49] Clayton and Rothstein, "Figures in the Corpus," 3.
[50] Ibid., 6.

Bloom (b. 1930).⁵¹ Bloom's theory of poetry "remains essentially a theory of literary influence."⁵² Bloom maintains that authors are always engaging their predecessors when they write; indeed, they are under the influence of their predecessors. But Bloom also notes that there is a constant tilt toward originality in literature, an agonizing desire to say something different from those who have gone before us. Because of this, some have suggested that Bloom himself is caught in a "vicious oedipal circle" of his own making,⁵³ though Bloom thinks this is a caricature of his work and an unfair reading.⁵⁴ What, then, is allusion? We now look at precisely how scholars have referred to the various kinds of influence.

Quotation. Until recently, quotation has been the primary category recognized and discussed in scriptural intertextuality and innerbiblical studies. The issue is whether a quotation must contain some kind of citation formula (e.g., "it is written"). Stanley E. Porter has offered a critique of the definitions and methodology of scholarship in this area.⁵⁵ Since some quotations do not have introductions (e.g., "it is written"), Porter calls quotations without an introduction formula "direct quotations." However, I will us "quotation" for those marked with some kind of introductory formula.

Subtle citation. By contrast, a subtle citation is a quotation that does not have an introductory formula (e.g., "it is written"). This category may encompass a fairly literal citation without an introductory formula or a citation with some alteration of the word order of the cited text but not to the same degree as allusions. Porter uses the term *paraphrase* to cover this; however, I am trying to keep terms to a minimum. While there has been some discussion in biblical scholarship on this dynamic, especially in Paul, a consensus has not been achieved.⁵⁶

---

⁵¹Harold Bloom, *The Anxiety of Influence: A Theory of Poetry* (New York: Oxford University Press, 1973).
⁵²James K. Chandler, "Romantic Allusiveness," *Critical Inquiry* 8 (1982): 462.
⁵³See Renza, "Influence," 192 .
⁵⁴Harold Bloom, *Anatomy of Influence: Literature as a Way of Life* (New Haven, CT: Yale University Press, 2011), 9
⁵⁵Porter, "Use of the Old Testament," 92. However, Porter later distinguished between "formulaic quotation" and "direct quotation"; see Porter, "Further Comments," 107-8.
⁵⁶See, e.g., Dietrich-Alex Koch, *Die Schrift als Zeuge des Evangeliums: Untersuchungen zur Verwendung und zum Verständnis der Schrift bei Paulus*, Beiträge zur historischen Theologie 69 (Tübingen: Mohr, 1986). For a summary of Koch's views and Stanley's interactions, see Christopher R. Bruno,

Allusion. An allusion is usually defined as a tacit or indirect reference to another text, although this definition is inadequate. More recently, a semantic and pragmatic approach has been suggested as a better way to understand how allusions function in literature.[57] Allusions are usually more fragmentary or periphrastic than quotations.[58] But defining and describing the semantic meaning of allusions should not be overly formalized.[59] Even so, as Ziva Ben-Porat observed, it is important to distinguish between "allusion in general and literary allusion."[60] Allusion in general merely makes indirect reference to known facts.[61] Literary allusion, by contrast, is restricted to a "device for simultaneous activation of two texts."[62] But this might even be a reduction, for literary allusion is not merely a device but, in Viktor Shklovsky's words, "an essential modality of the language of literature."[63]

Some would express uncertainty about whether an allusion to an Old Testament text by a subsequent Old Testament narrator or a New Testament writer was intended.[64] Most, however, would maintain the intentional aspects of allusion. As James Chandler puts it, "An allusion is an intentional echo of an earlier text: it not only reminds us; it means to remind us."[65] Porter defines allusion as "nonformal invocation by an author of a text (or person, event, etc.) that the author could reasonably have been expected to know (for example, the Old Testament in the case

---

"Readers, Authors, and the Divine Author: An Evangelical Proposal for Identifying Paul's Old Testament Citations," *WTJ* 71 (2009): 311-21, esp. 314-15.

[57] See Carmela Perri, "On Alluding," *Poetics* 7 (1978): 289-307. For bibliography on other recent theoretical treatments on allusion, see Udo J. Hebel, "Towards a Descriptive Poetics of *Allusion*," in *Intertextuality*, ed. Heinrich F. Plett (New York: De Gruyter, 1991), 135-64.

[58] John Hollander, *The Figure of Echo: A Mode of Allusion in Milton and After* (Berkeley: University of California Press, 1981), 64.

[59] Hans-Peter Mai, "Bypassing Intertextuality: Hermeneutics, Textual Practice, Hypertext," in Plett, *Intertextuality*, 30-59. Concerning the demand that the description of allusion not be formalized too strictly, see Hebel, "Descriptive Poetics," 153.

[60] Ziva Ben-Porat, "The Poetics of Literary Allusion," *PTL: A Journal for Descriptive Poetics and Theory of Literature* 1 (1976): 106; Ben-Porat, "The Poetics of Allusion" (PhD diss., University of California, Berkeley, 1967).

[61] Ben-Porat, "Poetics of Literary Allusion," 105.

[62] Ibid., 107,

[63] Quoted in Robert S. Kawashima, "Comparative Literature and Biblical Studies: The Case of Allusion," *Proof* 27 (2007): 334.

[64] See Fitzmyer, *Semitic Background*, 8.

[65] Chandler, "Romantic Allusiveness," 463.

of Paul)."[66] In a subsequent article, however, Porter maintains that allusion (unlike his category "paraphrase") may or may not be intentional and is distinguished from paraphrase by the amount of similar language and precision that is used.[67] Even so, others have maintained that further nuance is necessary in defining allusion in the Bible. Will Kynes, for example, says that quotations are explicit references to earlier expressions and are intended by the author, whereas echoes are unintentional references to earlier expressions. Allusions, for Kynes, fall in a gray area since they are intentional implicit references to earlier expressions.[68] It seems prudent to maintain that allusions fall under the rubric of authorial intent, especially since readers need to recognize markers in order to actualize an allusion in their own minds.[69] Authors usually intend that readers recognize the allusions they are attempting to make.

What seems evident in recent studies of allusion is a change in direction from the criteria of explicit and implicit to allusion as an intertextually relational device.[70] A biblical example from the apostle Paul illustrates this. Paul in Galatians 4 alludes to Abraham as having two sons, his son by the slave woman and his son by the free woman (Gal 4:23-31). Most readers of the Bible will know who he is speaking about.

Allusions must be overt enough for subsequent audiences to recognize.[71] Nevertheless, the question again presents itself: Where does meaning happen—with the reading audience or with the author? Certain methodologies have focused on the pragmatic, intertextual patterning that occurs in the reader's perception of the text.[72]

---

[66]Porter, "Use of the Old Testament," 95.
[67]Porter, "Further Comments," 109.
[68]Kynes, *My Psalm*, 31-32.
[69]A former student, Tim Wilson, expressed eloquently, "Intention by the author is especially important because it changes how a reader must process and understand an allusion. If a text is merely an echo of another text and the allusion is not intentional, then the primary purpose of allusion is no longer valid. While the echo may be interesting, the reader is not required to ponder an unstated point."
[70]See Mai, "Bypassing Intertextuality," 136-38.
[71]See Christopher A. Beetham, *Echoes of Scripture in the Letter of Paul to the Colossians*, Biblical Interpretation 96 (Leiden: Brill, 2008), 12. Beetham follows Porter's emphasis on an author-oriented approach to allusions.
[72]See Elaine Rusinko, "Intertextuality: The Soviet Approach to Subtext," *Dispositio* 4, nos. 11/12 (1979): 213-35.

Echoes and reminiscence. Echo is another crucial concept, if also the most abstract, for this study on the exodus motif.[73] Some maintain that echoes are less explicit than allusions, just as allusions are less explicit than quotations, whether subtle or direct.[74] This is a good starting point. However, as mentioned above, the discussion of these categories has moved beyond explicit versus implicit toward intertextual relations. Often in recent biblical studies, echo and allusion are used interchangeably. Perhaps they should be further distinguished. For example, Christopher Beetham sees a substantial difference between allusion and echo, primarily based on whether an "essential interpretive link" may be located—that is, whether there is a marker for the reader. If it is present, the reference is to be identified as an allusion. If not, then it is an echo.[75] We will use *echo* in this book when there is a less sustained, less distinguishable reference.[76] This becomes important, for example, in recognizing echoes in Paul, who in some instances may not have intended to refer to the exodus but nevertheless does. In other words, Paul's mind was so filled with Scripture that he naturally weaves it into his discourse. His DNA was biblical to the very core.[77] Whether it is in Scripture itself or in English literature echoing classical literature and themes, there are always secondary or derivative reflections for the sensitive ear and observant eye to catch. "Texts are haunted by echoes," John Hollander maintains.[78]

In biblical studies, no one has raised the issue of echoes more than Richard B. Hays in *Echoes of Scripture in the Letters of Paul*.[79] Hays's study

---

[73]Porter, "Further Comments," 109.
[74]See Beetham, *Echoes of Scripture*, 20.
[75]Ibid., 192.
[76]A similar categorical distinction is used by John Frederick Evans, "An Inner-biblical Interpretation and Intertextual Reading of Ezekiel's Recognition Formulae with the Book of Exodus" (ThD diss., University of Stellenbosch, 2006), 70.
[77]See, e.g., Sylvia C. Keesmaat, *Paul and His Story: (Re)Interpreting the Exodus Tradition*, JSNTSup 181 (Sheffield: Sheffield Academic Press, 1999), 49.
[78]Ibid., 23.
[79]In Hollander's beautiful book on the nature of allusion, *The Figure of Echo*, he begins by noting the analogy of allusion with nature. Just as there are surfaces throughout the natural world (mountains, rocks, caves, forests, etc.) that can produce serial echoes, so literature (especially poems) raises questions of the rebounding nature of language itself in subsequent reflecting literary surfaces (cf. 21-22).

is itself haunted by Hollander's thesis. "The volume of intertextual echoes varies in accordance with the semantic distance between the source and the reflecting surface," Hays suggests.[80] In other words, it may be difficult for a modern reader to appreciate an echo because of the distance between an ancient text and its modern interpreter. How is the ancient material being *used* and *changed* in subsequent echoic texts? In a subsequent echo, is the author changing or perhaps advancing the earlier text in some manner?

Hays is interested in and sensitive to the role that the horizon of the subsequent reader plays in the intricate web of meaning. This leads to a significant hermeneutical question: "If echo is a metaphorical way of talking about a hermeneutical event, an intertextual fusion that generates new meaning, in whose mind does that event occur, and how are claims about intertextual meaning effects to be tested?"[81] It is at this crucial point that a tension in hermeneutics is brought forth: the relationship between text, author, and reader(s), or even text(s), author(s), and reader(s). Once again the hermeneutical question surfaces: Where does meaning occur?

Hays offers five possible answers to this crucial question: (1) "The hermeneutical event occurs in Paul's mind.... (2) The hermeneutical event occurs in the original readers of the letter.... (3) The intertextual fusion occurs in the text itself.... (4) The hermeneutical event occurs in my act of reading.... (5) The hermeneutical event occurs in a community of interpretation."[82] Hays is not a piecemeal thinker. He is able to synthesize data and make significant systematic claims. He states, "I am neither prepared to embrace the doctrine of any of the hermeneutical schools represented by these five options (let the reader understand) nor inclined to jettison any of the elements of interpretation to which they draw attention." He continues, "The working method of this book should be understood as an attempt to hold them all together in creative tension. This is a daunting task, of course, particularly when we are seeking to interpret ancient texts that interpret in turn still more ancient texts."[83]

---

[80]Hays, *Echoes of Scripture in the Letters of Paul*, 23.
[81]Ibid., 26.
[82]Ibid.
[83]Ibid., 27.

For Hays, this all leads to the concept of future or later figurations (i.e., extensions of the original plain sense). Building on the notion that one can indeed discern echoes in Scripture, echoes that even the apostle Paul and his contemporaries experienced, Hays suggests, "The reader will share with the author [whose intentions may be discerned] the requisite 'portable library' to recognize the source of allusion."[84] For Hays, however, this ability to plumb an author's (in this case Paul's) intentions should not cause us to limit our interpretation to that. Such a limitation of merely recognizing Paul's intended scriptural echoes would be to "impose a severe and arbitrary hermeneutical restriction." The fact of the matter is that "later readers will rightly grasp meanings of the figures that may have been veiled from Paul himself. Scripture generates through Paul new figurations."[85] New potential meaning lies in the act of figuration.[86]

These views of Hays's, some of which focus on the reader, not the author, have been criticized because they allegedly leave no appeal to any evidence apart from the experience of reading.[87] The term *echo*, according to Hays's critics, may still be useful, but it must be defined for "thematically related language of some more general notion or concept," whereas allusion will refer to "a specific person, place, or literary work."[88]

In my own thinking, I am not eclipsing authorial intent. Keeping focused on the intentions of the divine author will help us steer clear of unsubstantiated claims in our understanding of the text. The divine authorial intent may mean that human authors say more than they recognize at the time. This means that it might be reductionistic to limit

---

[84] Ibid., 29.
[85] Ibid., 33. Even Beetham, who sides with Porter on the side of authorial intent, recognizes the possibility of new figurations when he asks, "What new figuration has Paul created in alluding to or echoing the past text?" (*Echoes of Scripture*, 36).
[86] Hays states, "Anyone who has ever acted in a play knows the experience of discovering that lines from the play come unexpectanly to mind in real-life situations different from the original dramatic context. The aptness of the quoted line does not depend on exact literal correspondence between the original meaning and the new application. Indeed, the wit and pleasure of such quotations lie partly in turning the words to a new sense. In such cases, the act of quotation becomes an act of figuration, establishing metaphorical resonance between drama and life" (*Echoes of Scripture in the Letters of Paul*, 33).
[87] Porter, "Allusions and Echoes," 38.
[88] Ibid., 39.

the meaning of a text merely to the human author of Scripture.[89] Biblical writers knew what they were doing when they wrote, but they may not have known all they were doing. They may have known only partially.[90] The view, for example, that the meaning an ancient prophet held in his mind when writing is the only meaning possible may not allow for a very thick understanding of the multiple meanings and significations a text may generate.[91] As Michael Horton states, "The original human author may never have intended his or her words to be put to use in later, often quite distanciated, contexts, but the divine speaker is doing just that."[92] As biblical interpreters, we have to maintain a divine author–centered approach to discovering and understanding the function of innerbiblical references, whether they are of the Old Testament referencing itself or the New Testament referencing the Old Testament.[93] This entails coherence between the original text and the quoted text, a hermeneutic already discussed.

Consequently, with regard to the inspiration of Scripture, we can never be singularly focused on the human author's intention but must also consider the divine author's intention.[94] Human authors may make unintentional allusions, but the divine author of Scripture never does.[95] Focusing on the divine author does not mean neglecting the human side. As Augustine once said, how the divine author composes the various books is "like an ineffably gifted artist combining movements into a sung

---

[89] See Douglas J. Moo, "The Problem of the Sensus Plenior," in *Hermeneutics, Authority, and Canon*, ed. D. A. Carson and John D. Woodbridge (Grand Rapids: Zondervan, 1986), 199.

[90] See J. G. Machen, *The Christian Faith in the Modern World* (Grand Rapids: Eerdmans, 1947), 48.

[91] See, e.g., the seminal and classic essay by David C. Steinmetz, "The Superiority of Pre-critical Exegesis," *Theology Today* 37 (April 1980): 27-38, esp. 28; reprinted in *Ex Auditu* 1 (1985): 74-82, and in *A Guide to Contemporary Hermeneutics: Major Trends in Biblical Interpretation*, ed. Donald K. McKim (Grand Rapids: Eerdmans, 1986), 65-87.

[92] Michael S. Horton, *Covenant and Eschatology: The Divine Drama* (Louisville, KY: Westminster John Knox, 2002), 182. See also Machen, *Christian Faith*, 48.

[93] See, e.g., Bruno, "Readers," and Pak, "Calvin."

[94] See, e.g., Richard B. Gaffin Jr., "The Redemptive-Historical View," in *Biblical Hermeneutics: Five Views*, ed. Stanley E. Porter and Beth M. Stovell (Downers Grove, IL: IVP Academic, 2012), 89-110. Gaffin says, "A redemptive-historical orientation requires giving careful attention to this instrumental role of the human authors of the biblical documents, but that is not due to captivation with the 'humanity' of Scripture or at the expense of downplaying its primary divine authorship" (96).

[95] Bruno, "Readers," 320.

poem."[96] Since we are examining Scripture, which has a divine author and human authors, we need to discuss both. At one and the same time, every word of Scripture is the word of God and the word of man. God's word and man's words in the Bible are identical. The divine and the human are united in perfect harmony. The divine influence is primary, and the human is secondary. In this interrelationship between the divine and human intentionality, the latter becomes the fit vehicle for the former.[97] Moreover, this act of figuration through allusion and echo is not open-ended. That is to say, it is closed and restricted by the canon of Scripture, revealed in the sixty-six books of the Bible. This dynamic, furthermore, falls under the ongoing illumination of the Holy Spirit in those interpreters who are regenerated Christians.

Returning to Hays's proposal, we find that Porter rejects Hays's audience-oriented definition and description of echo. While Porter wants to retain the concept of echo, he qualifies it vis-à-vis Hays as a more general thematic reference in contrast to an allusion, which Porter sees as an attempt to bring an "external person, place, or literary work into a contemporary text."[98] Nevertheless, I see Hays's view as true *with some qualification* (further discussed below). I would emphasize the organic unity of Scripture and its internal coherence of meaning and intentions, both human and divine—something sorely lacking in recent debates. I would also accent that the Old Testament Scriptures really do broker christological truth in and of themselves and therefore exert christological and theological pressure on the New Testament writers.

One aim of this book is to advance our understanding of this issue as we observe the exodus motif unfold through redemptive history. With

---

[96]Michael Cameron, *Christ Meets Me Everywhere: Augustine's Early Figurative Exegesis*, Oxford Studies in Historical Theology (Oxford: Oxford University Press, 2012), 31.

[97]This is not to suggest that the divine author's intention is completely separate from or hidden from the human author; rather, the divine author provides a larger context within the framework of a developing canon. This is more commendable than a *sensus plenior*, "fuller sense" approach practiced by Roman Catholicism, especially when it is defined as the meaning intended by God but not by the human author. See William Sanford LaSor, "The *Sensus Plenior* and Biblical Interpretation," in McKim, *Guide to Contemporary Hermeneutics*, 47-64. Also see Moo, "Problem of the Sensus Plenior," 179-211.

[98]Porter, "Allusion and Echo," 40.

the exodus motif as our guiding theme, we will see how quotation, subtle citation, allusion, and echo become tools by which the authors of Scripture "work" the motif. Notice that this arrangement allows for all three categories of agency to stay active: the author, the text, and the audience or subsequent readers. Consider figure 1.1: this grouping gives us four broad categories for identifying how any biblical author is using the exodus motif.[99] Obviously these are literary categories.

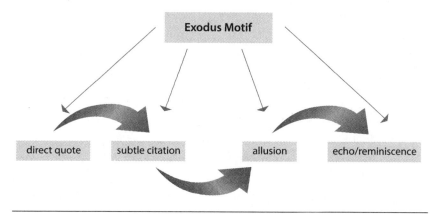

Figure 1.1. Biblical authors' use of the exodus motif

We turn now to the second goal in this chapter: the development of a proper use of typology as a key to understanding the exodus motif in Scripture.

Typology and symbols. Friedbert Ninow provides one of the most helpful historical surveys of the use and study of typology as a way of understanding the Scriptures.[100] Although typological exegesis was frequently practiced in the early church, it was often practiced without careful constraints, and its practice frequently slipped into allegory.[101]

---

[99]Although the illustration has been adapted, for the arrangement of the boxes in linear fashion, I am indebted to Christoph Uehlinger, "Subtle Citations? Identifying and Evaluating Interplays Between Images and Texts" (paper presented at the Annual Meeting of the Society of Biblical Literature, Baltimore, November 2013).
[100]Friedbert Ninow, *Indicators of Typology Within the Old Testament: The Exodus Motif* (Frankfurt: Peter Lang, 2001), 15-97.
[101]See the excellent introductory discussion in Vanhoozer, *Is There a Meaning*, 113-20.

From the outset, it is important to recognize that typology is integrally related to symbol in Scripture.

Symbols in Scripture are gateways into appropriate typological method and practice.[102] However, often in the practice of biblical interpretation, symbols have been inappropriately wrested from their material moorings. Historical essences and legitimate external references of words to phenomena outside the text were left behind as figural readings of the biblical text were generated. The result was a "free-range allegory" that attempted to secure some kind of deeper meaning.[103] The wings of human imagination lifted a variety of often ungrounded, abstract meanings from the biblical text. John Wright sums up a better understanding of the function of symbols, one that realizes that the way to the transcendent is through the material, not bypassing it: "A symbol points beyond itself to the thing being symbolized and must be able to disclose what transcends it. The symbol needs to be socially acceptable, *being born out of man's experience*. It has its own innate power. A symbol never has a one-to-one correspondence, but is always multiple, suggests other symbols, and may be perceived differently by different people."[104] Hijacked by a free-range allegory, the suggested meanings and senses of Scripture's symbols seemed fanciful and exaggerated to post-Enlightenment sensibilities. They lacked textual grounding and historical control.

Characteristic of much of the history of typological interpretation is the fact that many have defined the term *typology* and its hermeneutical method according to their own fancy.[105] Consequently, eighteenth- and nineteenth-century rationalism, especially that of Johann S. Semler and Johann D. Michaelis, took a skeptical view of the unity of the Old and New Testaments. This introduced trouble for the typological method of interpretation, which had previously assumed a unity of the Old and New

---

[102]See the excellent introductory discussion in Edmund P. Clowney, *Preaching and Biblical Theology* (Phillipsburg, NJ: P&R, 1961), 100-112.

[103]I am indebted to my friend Don Collett for the term "free-range allegory."

[104]John Wright, "Spirit and Wilderness: The Interplay of Two Motifs Within the Hebrew Bible as a Background to Mark 1:2-13," in *Perspective on Language and Text: Essays and Poems in Honor of Francis I. Andersen's Sixtieth Birthday, July 28, 1985*, ed. Edgar W. Conrad and Edward G. Newing (Winona Lake, IN: Eisenbrauns, 1987), 269 (emphasis mine).

[105]Ninow, *Indicators of Typology*, 17.

Testaments. Indeed, for many prior to this point, the Old Testament was somehow incomplete without the New and was therefore open-ended. Prior to the rise of serious biblical criticism in the Enlightenment, the Scriptures by and large were assumed to be one organic whole. With the advent of Enlightenment biblical criticism, however, the focus shifted to the distinct and individual contributions of various books of the Bible, and the assumed homogeneity of the inspired Scriptures was questioned. Source criticism, trying to identify the various editorial strands and traditions within the biblical corpus, consumed the energies of talented and well-trained biblical scholars.

This higher-critical scholarship, which until recently was the method most prominent in biblical studies, seeks to identify different sources, traditions, and strands that make up the received text of the Old Testament. This dissecting of the text has been devastating to the story and plot structure of the Scriptures. "To dissect biblical narrative . . . is to misunderstand its inner nerve and the special character of its means of communicating revelatory truth," says Christopher Seitz, summarizing Hans Frei's important work.[106]

Presently, however, there are major upheavals within the inherited nineteenth-century source-critical consensus theory just as there are major upheavals over the method called "tradition history" in Old Testament studies. Anyone familiar with biblical studies at the highest levels of scholarship knows that the discipline can be characterized by "methodological disarray, lack of consensus on key questions, the triviality of a great deal of historical scholarship, and a problematic relation to the Bible's religious readership."[107] In the midst of these methodological debates, scholars fall at various points on a spectrum between the historical certainty of the exodus and skepticism with regard to how much

---

[106]Christopher R. Seitz, *Figured Out: Typology and Providence in Christian Scripture* (Louisville, KY: Westminster John Knox, 2001), 55, with reference to Hans Frei, *The Eclipse of Biblical Narrative: A Study in Eighteenth and Nineteenth Century Hermeneutics* (New Haven, CT: Yale University Press, 1974).

[107]Michael C. Legaspi, *The Death of Scripture and the Rise of Biblical Studies*, Oxford Studies in Historical Theology (Oxford: Oxford University Press, 2010), 167. See especially chap. 1 of Legaspi's book for further details.

history is represented in the book of Exodus.[108] Some scholars commendably attempt to bridge the different approaches of synchronic and diachronic studies to the book of Exodus.[109]

I do not think that typology is an outdated, overworn, or fanciful method. What is needed is a typological method with hermeneutical controls. If we neglect typology, we risk missing some truth that the divinely inspired author intended. Anticipatory symbols are introduced into the biblical narratives with divine intention in order to set up the pedagogical relationship of type and antitype, promise and fulfillment. Typology is not mere pedagogy, however. These truths are communicated with power to effect change in the addressee.

Ninow well summarizes how typology can function in our understanding of the exodus motif: "One of the major characteristics of these passages that connect the past with the future is the prophetic indication. In each case, where the text reveals a *Vorbild* [type]–*Nachbild* [antitype] relation, it is the prophet who uses the historical context of the *Vorbild* to 'create' a future vision of events molded after the *Vorbild* using similar language and imagery."[110] Typology teaches that Old Testament events, individuals, laws, cult, and the nation itself looked beyond themselves for their ultimate fulfillment and interpretation. In a very real and profound sense, when we study the history of Israel, we see that she was not behind the times but was actually ahead of her time.

Shadows Looking Forward and Shadows Descending

The first level in a responsible use of typology is promise; the second is fulfillment. Typology entails continuity and unity but also discontinuity.

---

[108] See the survey of James K. Hoffmeier, "'These Things Happened': Why a Historical Exodus Is Essential for Theology," in *Do Historical Matters Matter to Faith? A Critical Appraisal of Modern and Postmodern Approaches to Scripture*, ed. James Hoffmeier and Dennis Magary (Wheaton, IL: Crossway, 2012), 99-134.

[109] See the stimulating study by Mark S. Smith, *The Pilgrimage Pattern in Exodus*, JSOTSup 239 (Sheffield: Sheffield Academic Press, 1997). Although Smith is devoted to source-critical analysis, he demonstrates great willingness to listen to and learn from others approaching the text from a different vantage point, namely, a synchronic literary approach. Although it is primarily a work based on tradition-history analysis, the same is true of Thomas B. Dozeman's *God on the Mountain: A Study of Redaction, Theology and Canon in Exodus 19–24*, SBLMS 37 (Atlanta: Scholars Press, 1989).

[110] Ninow, *Indicators of Typology*, 244.

Throughout, however, there is one biblical meganarrative with multiple manifestations and adumbrations: one kingdom, one king, ultimately one people. The exodus informs all of these levels. But the exodus from Egypt is a prototype that inaugurates the promise. Fulfillment was yet to come. Typology, or an appropriate figural reading of Scripture, goes beyond a mere literalistic meaning. Typological readings trump any reading of the exodus as a mere political liberation, but typological readings are not divorced from liberation either, since the historical occasion of the exodus is the foundation on which the extended meaning is built.

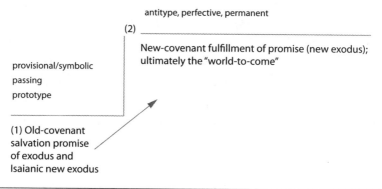

Figure 1.2. Forward-looking typology

To illustrate this forward-looking typology, we may set it out as shown in figure 1.2. Consider the following example. In the typological situation, the Isaianic new exodus is the fruit of the earlier exodus from Egypt. Likewise, the new exodus of the new covenant, which finds its nexus in the coming of Christ, is the further fruit of the former Isaianic new exodus, along with other Old Testament Scriptures. In other words, the New Testament uses exodus imagery mediated through and transformed by the Psalter and Isaiah. In addition, Jeremiah, Ezekiel, Hosea, and many other Old Testament Scriptures exert theological pressure relating to a new exodus on the Gospel writers, Paul, and Peter. This is not merely analogy. It is typology. In this relationship between type and antitype, there is escalation between promise and fulfillment.[111] These are

---

[111]Ninow, *Indicators of Typology*.

not mere empty shadows. The shadows are grounded in reality and are just as real as the fulfillment.

Geerhardus Vos's construal of typology in the book of Hebrews is helpful to consider.[112] The book of Hebrews makes a significant claim as to how biblical typology works, and Vos's explanation of what that writer is doing applies also to other New Testament writers, even if they are not as explicit as Hebrews. Vos wishes to explain how the writer of Hebrews conceives of typology in Hebrews 10:1, where, as Vos puts it, "we read: 'the law having a shadow (*skia*) of the good things to come, not the very image (*aute eikoon*) of the things. . . .' Thus we see that the law lacked something that we of the new covenant possess, namely *the very image*."[113] Vos homes in on the contrast between *image* and *shadow*. He says we might be inclined to think the shadow was not the very body or substance, but the image is; however, he is especially concerned to note the nuance that the author of Hebrews is suggesting by asking how shadow and image can be used as correlative terms. Next, he suggests two possibilities for understanding this passage: one from the perspective of an artist and the other from the perspective of philosophy. The perspective of philosophy is the more difficult but more plausible way to explain the typology. Vos then produces a diagram (represented in fig. 1.3 with slight modification).[114]

Vos explains that when Hebrews speaks of this shadowing as coming down, it means from heaven to earth.[115] This is somewhat different from a typology that is merely "shadowing forward." In other words, the Old Testament type is a shadow of the heavenly reality, not merely shadowing forward to the New Testament. Moreover, Vos says that the word *eikoon* [sic] in Greek can have the meaning of "archetype," a meaning "which precisely suits our purpose here."[116] This means, for Vos, that the New Testament is speaking of a reality that came down in substance, not just as a representation.

---

[112]See Geerhardus Vos, *The Teaching of the Epistle to the Hebrews*, ed. and rewritten by Johannes G. Vos (Phillipsburg, NJ: P&R, 1956), 55-64.
[113]Ibid., 55.
[114]The "B" of the triangle in fig. 1.3 was left out in the original book. Since Vos explains it, it seems to have been an oversight.
[115]Ibid., 58.
[116]Ibid.

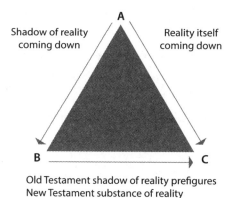

Old Testament shadow of reality prefigures
New Testament substance of reality

A represents the heavenly reality.
B represents the Old Testament, which is a *shadow* of the heavenly reality.
C represents the New Testament, which is the *substance* of the heavenly reality.
B prefigures C because B is the shadow of A and C equals A.

Source: Geerhardus Vos, *The Teaching of the Epistle to the Hebrews*, ed. and rewritten by Johannes G. Vos (Phillipsburg, NJ: P&R, 1956), 57.

Figure 1.3. Vos's typology

Among Vos's examples is Hebrews 9:24. The passage speaks of the earthly tabernacle as the *antitype* of the true one (*antitypa tōn alēthinōn*). Here the Old Testament is the actual antitype! But how can this be if the New Testament antitype is usually understood as fulfillment? For Vos, "to find the original *type*, of which the Old Testament is the antitype, then, we must go back of the Old Testament to heaven. This heavenly type was shown to Moses on Mount Sinai."[117] Vos maintains that this kind of typology is peculiar to Hebrews, in contrast with Paul and Peter.[118] In fact, this seems not to be the case. Although it is not as explicit in Paul, there are instances where the same kind of dynamic exists. We saw one example earlier, where Paul quotes Psalm 68 in Ephesians 4:8. There the apostle says *dio legei*, "therefore it says." The substance, or in Vos's language, the heavenly reality, was present in the Old Testament. A similar use of the preposition occurs in Hebrews 10:4-5 (cf. Heb 10:10), where

---
[117]Ibid.
[118]Ibid., 59.

a psalm (Ps 40:6-8) is also quoted. The writer of Hebrews "understands the cited passage as a word addressed by the Son to the Father on the occasion of the incarnation, which the psalmist, as it were, overheard."[119] Once again, the organic development of Scripture helps one grasp the New Testament use of the Old Testament.

Vos understated his claims about this triangle of heaven, Old Testament, and New Testament. This kind of typology is not only found in Hebrews but also plausibly lies behind some of Paul's conceptual constructions. Thus, while "shadowing *down*" (from heaven to earth) typology is conspicuous in Hebrews, it seems that Paul and perhaps even other New Testament writers understood this as well.[120] The heavenly substance was already residing in Old Testament typology, and such a construal may have been working in Paul's mind as well.[121]

Literary typology. We can add another arrow to the triangle (see fig. 1.4). This two-way arrow represents the necessity of reading both ways and the fact that such a reading may strengthen one's interpretation. This is what we may call "literary typology." For example, one might read

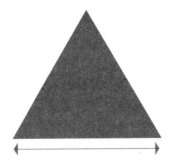

Figure 1.4. Ezekiel's use of the "recognition formula," i.e., "I am the Lord your God," which is much more "negative" or connoting judgment vis-a-vis the use of the formula in the book of Exodus

---

[119]William Lane, *Hebrews 9–13*, WBC 47B (Dallas: Word, 1991), 263, quoted in Baugh, *Ephesians*, 331.
[120]Galatians 3:8 is one of the clearest examples. The Scripture foresaw the justification of the Gentiles, although it awaited the arrival of Christ and the "faith" that would be put in him (Gal 3:23). The seed is Christ (Gal 3:16), to whom the promise was made, and it was still awaiting fulfillment until Christ should arrive in the flesh (Gal 3:19).
[121]Private conversation with Professor Baugh.

backward in the intertextuality of text reception, from Ezekiel to Exodus, to see a certain "potential" that is "latent in the recognition formula [i.e., 'I am the Lord your God,' of Exodus]." In other words, the formula is changed in its communicative intent to sound a note of judgment in the book of Ezekiel, whereas it was primarily positive in the book of Exodus.[122] Such a two-way reading will become evident when we later engage Psalm 77.

This is one way to protect against only reading texts in a unidirectional manner. As Robert Wall has contended, "Progressive revelation tends to define intertextual practices unidirectionally."[123] This can be hazardous, or at least not contribute to as full an interpretation as possible. In other words, as we attempt to understand the echoic nature of language and literature, in this case biblical literature, it is vital to look backward as well as forward in the canon in order to understand allusions.

I take the position that literary typology is often retrojective. But it may also be forward-looking. In the words of Fishbane, this is "where one historical event serves as the prototype for the descriptive shaping of another."[124] Since the Christian church is committed to the New Testament as an integral part of her canon, literary typology should be considered from a retrospective viewpoint after Christ's death and resurrection and the coming of the Holy Spirit.[125]

Returning to our discussion of intertextuality and a dialogical process, we can integrate these notions of typology into a Bakhtinian frame of reference (although with some qualification). Bakhtin says,

> Even *past* meanings, that is, those born in the dialogue of past centuries, can never be stable (finalized, ended once and for all)—they will always change (be renewed) in the process of subsequent, future development of the dialogue. At any moment in the development of the dialogue, there are immense, boundless masses of forgotten contextual meanings, but . . .

---

[122]Evans, "Inner-biblical Interpretation," 267.
[123]See Robert W. Wall, "The Canonical View," in Porter and Stovell, *Biblical Hermeneutics*, 197.
[124]Fishbane, *Biblical Interpretation*, 358. Fishbane actually categorizes typologies into four categories in this section of his book: (1) cosmological-historical, (2) historical correlations, (3) spatial correlations, and (4) biographical (see 352-79).
[125]See Beale, *Handbook*, 22-27.

[in] subsequent development along the way, they are recalled and reinvigorated in renewed form (in a new context). Nothing is absolutely dead: every meaning will have its homecoming festival.[126]

Let us consider a biblical example. As Joshua is about to lead the Israelites into the Promised Land, the Lord speaks: "The LORD said to Joshua, 'Today I will begin to exalt you in the eyes of all Israel, so they may know that I am with you as I was with Moses. Tell the priests who carry the ark of the covenant: "When you reach the edge of the Jordan's waters, go and stand in the river"'" (Josh 3:7-8). As Fishbane states, "The reader is made to anticipate a correlation between the past exodus and the present conquest from the outset."[127] Notice these two texts in counterpoint to one another in table 1.1.

Table 1.1. Textual links between Exodus and Joshua

By the blast of your nostrils the waters piled up. The surging waters stood up like a wall [nēd]; the deep waters congealed in the heart of the sea. (Ex 15:8 NIV)	And as soon as the priests who carry the ark of the LORD . . . set foot in the Jordan, its waters flowing downstream will be cut off and stand up in a heap [nēd]. (Josh 3:13 NIV)

What is the result of the Lord's marvelous intervention on the people's behalf? The people come to fear Joshua *just as* they had Moses.[128] There are further links. For example, the Israelites "are depicted as celebrating their entrance into the land of Canaan, in the first month, with the cake ritual and paschal offering of the Passover."[129] Another dictional link between the foundational exodus event and the conquest is formed when Joshua, just before the invasion of Jericho, is commanded by the theophanic angel messenger, "Take off your sandals, for the place where

---

[126]Bakhtin, "Methodology," quoted in Magdolna Orosz, "Literary Reading(s) of the Bible: Aspects of a Semiotic Conception of Intertextuality and Intertextual Analysis of Texts," in *Reading the Bible Intertextually*, ed. Richard B. Hays, Stefan Alkier, and Leroy A. Huizenga (Waco, TX: Baylor University Press, 2009), 204.
[127]Fishbane, *Biblical Interpretation*, 358.
[128]Ibid. See also the detailed discussion in Charles David Isbell, *The Function of Exodus Motifs: Theological Didactic Drama*, Studies in the Bible and Early Christianity 52 (Lewiston, NY: Edwin Mellen, 2002), 97-110.
[129]Fishbane, *Text and Texture*, 124.

you are standing is holy" (Josh 5:15; cf. Ex 3:5). As Fishbane points out, "On the brink of battle, about to complete the preexodus promises of God to the patriarchs, Joshua is again addressed as a new Moses."[130]

So we might wonder, what is the purpose of these retrojective typologies? We will turn to this topic shortly, but first notice another dynamic in this complex web of allusive and typological discourse. Sometimes there is a liturgical reflex among the Israelites, where we observe a conflation of various allusions and typologies. We will see this pattern repeatedly, and we will consider it again when we look at Psalm 114. It is worth quoting Fishbane at length on this point:

> Recollection of the ancient exodus from Egypt serves the speaker as a hedge against despair and a catalyst towards renewed hope. . . . The simultaneous capacity of the exodus paradigm to elicit memory and expectation, recollection and anticipation, discloses once again its deep embeddedness as a fundamental structure of the biblical historical imagination. But it further discloses just what is so variously and diffusely indicated elsewhere in the Bible; namely, that the events of history are prismatic openings to the transhistorical. Indeed, the very capacity of a historical event to generate future expectation is dependent on the transfiguration of that event by the theological intuition that in it and through it the once and future power of the Lord of history is revealed. Without such a symbolic transformation, the exodus would never have given birth to hope.[131]

It is not merely retroactive typology that is displayed in the Scriptures. Sometimes typologies, according to Fishbane, "can also provide the linguistic and ideologic prism for projective forecasts of future redemption."[132] This can even take place through allusive sound play in the Hebrew Bible, as demonstrated by Jonathan Kline's work.[133] The exodus motif, therefore, also has a shaping influence for the future in the canonical context, as we shall see in chapter five when we turn to the Prophets.

---

[130]Ibid.
[131]Ibid., 140.
[132]Fishbane, *Biblical Interpretation*, 360-61.
[133]Jonathan G. Kline, *Allusive Soundplay in the Hebrew Bible*, Ancient Israel and Its Literature 28 (Atlanta: SBL Press, 2016). See the discussion on Is 41:16-20 in chap. 5 below.

The same is true with regard to Isaiah 40–55.[134] Not only will the same God who acted wondrously, salvifically, and powerfully in the first exodus act again; he will act in a new and determinative way to rescue the exilic community from their oppressors (i.e., Babylon), deliver them through the desert (instead of the sea), and bring them into Zion through a restoration.[135] The forward-looking mentality shapes Isaiah's message, but it does not lack backward references either. Now the picture looks backward beyond the original exodus and through allusion treads the typological path all the way back to creation.

I agree with Fishbane when he says that the exodus event can generate future expectation. Ultimately, however, we will see the threads come together and find their fulfillment in the Messiah, Jesus himself. Indeed, Anthony Ceresko has linked the sufferings of the servant in Isaiah and the exiles in Isaiah 40–55 with the preexodus sufferings of Israel in Egypt.[136]

Now I want to turn our attention to the distinction between allegory and typology and then to a preeminent exegete of the Scriptures, John Calvin. Calvin developed a system of hermeneutics for preaching and teaching biblical texts that is a fusion of all the various horizons I have been suggesting.

Allegory and Typology: Clearing Up Definitional Discrepancies

During the Middle Ages, the allegorical method and interpretation derived from Alexandrian theology and philosophy was dominant in biblical exegesis. Part and parcel of the interpretative method during this period was the notion that one could interpret literature according to the fourfold sense, or exegetical *quadriga*. This consisted of the literal or

---

[134]Some of the following ideas were originally addressed in my "The Exodus Motif in Isaiah," *New Horizons* 29, no. 1 (January 2008): 5-7.

[135]See Bernhard W. Anderson, "Exodus Typology in Second Isaiah," in *Israel's Prophetic Heritage: Essays in Honor of James Muilenburg*, ed. Bernhard W. Anderson and Walter Harrelson (New York: Harper, 1962), 177-95.

[136]Anthony R. Ceresko, "The Rhetorical Strategy of the Fourth Servant Song (Isaiah 52:13–53:12): Poetry and the Exodus—New Exodus," *CBQ* (1994): 42-55.

historical sense together with the threefold spiritual sense: the moral or tropological, the allegorical, and the anagogical.[137] The term *quadriga* is from Latin, meaning a four-horse chariot. Simply stated, the *quadriga* is a method of reading the Scriptures that maintains that a passage has four possible meanings, not one.

Currently, there is a debate about the usefulness of the terms *allegory* and *typology*. The traditional and customary way of presenting matters is that allegory was the method used by Origen and others in the early church, which gave flight to all kinds of imaginative and fanciful interpretations. The allegorical method supposedly extracts "symbolic meaning from the text. It assumes that a deeper, more sophisticated interpretation is to be found beneath the obvious meaning of the passage."[138] Allegory, as Hans Frei noted, "is the literary personification of abstract qualities, usually personal attributes—virtue, reason, faith, courage."[139] The history of the development of allegorical hermeneutics is a long and fascinating story, but a detailed treatment is beyond the purview of this chapter.[140] Even so, some general comments are in order.

Modern advocates of the allegorical method include Peter Leithart.[141] Leithart enjoins a reading of all texts typologically, which for

---

[137]For the most detailed treatment of this, see Henri de Lubac, *Medieval Exegesis*, trans. Mark Sebanc and E. M. Macierowski, 3 vols. (Grand Rapids: Eerdmans, 1998–2009), esp. vols. 1 and 2 since they deal with the four senses of Scripture. Also see Charles Kannengiesser, *Handbook of Patristic Exegesis: The Bible in Ancient Christianity* (Leiden: Brill, 2004), 1:536-74, including an excellent bibliography.

[138]Craig A. Evans, "The Old Testament in the New," in *The Face of New Testament Studies: A Survey of Recent Research*, ed. Scot McKnight and Grant R. Osborne (Grand Rapids: Baker Academic, 2004), 133.

[139]Hans Frei, "Karl Barth: Theologian," in *Theology and Narrative: Selected Essays*, ed. George Hunsinger and William C. Placher (New York: Oxford University Press, 1993), esp. 168-69.

[140]See Tzvetan Todorov, *Theories of the Symbol*, trans. Catherine Porter (Ithica, NY: Cornell University Press, 1982).

[141]See, e.g., Peter Leithart, *Deep Exegesis: The Mystery of Reading Scripture* (Waco, TX: Baylor University Press, 2009). I have criticized Leithart's positions elsewhere, especially his sacramental hermeneutics; see "Passover and the Lord's Supper: Continuity or Discontinuity," in *Children and the Lord's Supper*, ed. Guy Waters and Ligon Duncan (Fearn, UK: Mentor, 2011), 31-58. I hesitate to give a completely negative assessment of the book since there is much to be commended; nevertheless, such an assessment *is* necessary in a chapter on typology, especially since Leithart claims he is trying to revive something like the *quadriga*. For a more popular and accessible example of what Leithart is trying to accomplish, see Leithart, "The

him is different from what I am proposing as typology.[142] Leithart, in my judgment, blurs the distinction between allegory and typology. Greg Beale, on the other hand, offers a more helpful definition and method of biblical typology, which includes the elements of typological heightening and prophetic foreshadowing. Beale defines typology as *"the study of analogical correspondences among revealed truths about persons, events, institutions, and other things within the historical framework of God's special revelation, which, from a retrospective view, are of a prophetic nature and are escalated in their meaning."*[143] This definition retains an accent on the historical as do most modern treatments of typology.[144] I think Mark Gignilliat goes too far in asserting, "Typology *is* allegorical or figural reading."[145] What is needed are precise distinctions between allegory, typology, and analogy.

It is true that medieval exegetical methods cannot be reduced to merely allegorism, since a variety of interpretive patterns can be observed.[146] Even so, according to leading literary theorists, allegory should be distinguished from typology. Typology, which is grounded in the text, is the more responsible methodology according to some biblical scholars.[147] In typological exegesis, history is important and reflective of divine design. This provides, in contrast to the allegorical method, restraints on ungrounded interpretive proclivities and fanciful flights of imagination. Moreover, such a historical focus in interpretive methodology extends at least as far back as

---

Quadriga or Something Like It: A Biblical and Pastoral Defense," in *Ancient Faith for the Church's Future*, ed. Mark Husbands and Jeffrey P. Greenman (Downers Grove, IL: IVP Academic, 2008), 110-25.

[142]Leithart, *Deep Exegesis*, 74.

[143]Beale, *Handbook*, 14.

[144]Perhaps most influential in modern hermeneutics of typology has been the classic of Leonhard Goppelt, *Typos: The Typological Interpretation of the Old Testament in the New*, trans. Donald H. Madvig (Eugene, OR: Wipf and Stock, 2002), esp. 52-53.

[145]Mark Gignilliat, "Paul, Allegory, and the Plain Sense of Scripture: Galatians 4:21-31," *JTI* 2, no. 1 (2008): 135-46.

[146]See esp. Richard A. Muller and John L. Thompson, "The Significance of Precritical Exegesis: Retrospect and Prospect," in *Biblical Interpretation in the Era of the Reformation: Essays Presented to David C. Steinmetz in Honor of His Sixtieth Birthday*, ed. Richard A. Muller and John L. Thompson (Grand Rapids: Eerdmans, 1996), 335-45, esp. 343-44.

[147]E.g., Ninow, "Indicators of Typology Within the Old Testament," and Beale, *Handbook*, 13-27.

Augustine.¹⁴⁸ Even so, some scholars, such as Frances M. Young, have seen typology, with its emphasis on historical consciousness, as a modern construct.¹⁴⁹ However, we must be careful not to caricature the past by suggesting that figures such as Origen always practiced a free-range allegory. Young and Peter W. Martens provide a good review of the issues and debates between Origenist allegorical methods and the Antiochenes, including the question of whether Origen has been fairly represented among modern interpreters.¹⁵⁰

It seems, indeed, that Origen has often been unfairly caricatured. For example, there may be some good reasons that Origen was less interested in historical matters than we moderns are. For instance, he did not have the same access to sources we have today, which would have equipped him to read in a more critical manner.¹⁵¹ Nevertheless, even surveying the literature and coming to a more sympathetic reading of Origen, I myself remain unconvinced that Reformers such as Calvin were merely attempting to revalorize or repristinate the medieval *quadriga*.

As Frei has noted, "Calvin's rejection of allegorical and anagogical readings of biblical texts was, if anything, even more pronounced than Luther's."¹⁵² The fact of the matter is that Calvin more often than not did not speak well of what he thought Origen's methods were.¹⁵³ In fact, it may be said that Origen, at least for Calvin, leads the list of those who do bad exegesis.¹⁵⁴ Although John Thompson contends

---

¹⁴⁸See, e.g., Cameron, *Christ Meets Me Everywhere*, 297-98; David Dawson, *Christian Figural Reading and the Fashioning of Identity* (Berkeley: University of California Press, 2002); Erich Auerbach, "Figura," from *Scenes from the Drama of European Literature: Six Essays by Erich Auerbach* (New York: Meridian, 1959), 42-43.
¹⁴⁹Frances M. Young, *Biblical Exegesis and the Formation of Christian Culture* (Cambridge: Cambridge University Press, 1997), 152-53.
¹⁵⁰See ibid., 209-13, and Peter W. Martens, "Revisiting the Allegory/Typology Distinction: The Case of Origen," *Journal of Early Christian Studies* 16, no. 3 (Fall 2008): 283-317.
¹⁵¹See Gerald Bray, "The Church Fathers and Biblical Theology," in *Out of Egypt: Biblical Theology and Biblical Interpretation*, ed. Craig Bartholomew et al., Scripture and Hermeneutics 5 (Grand Rapids: Zondervan, 2004), 30.
¹⁵²Frei, *Eclipse of Biblical Narrative*, 25.
¹⁵³See John L. Thompson, "Reformer of Exegesis? Calvin's Unpaid Debt to Origen," in *Calvin: Saint or Sinner*, ed. Herman Selderhuis (Tübingen: Mohr Siebeck, 2010), 113-41.
¹⁵⁴Ibid., 120.

that it would be hazardous to suggest that Calvin never read Origen directly, whether Calvin picked up this posture toward Origen from primary sources (i.e., reading Origen himself) or from secondary sources (namely, Melanchthon, Bullinger, Bucer, and Erasmus) is open to debate and consideration.[155] Brevard Childs may be right when he says, "Calvin rejected any dichotomy between the literal and spiritual senses.... Calvin spoke of the *versus scripturae sensus* which is both literal and spiritual, the single true sense of the text."[156] However, that evaluation by Childs hardly validates what some would say of Calvin, situating him merely in the stream of medieval exegesis. John Thompson offers a measured judgment based on the extant sources: "In reforming exegesis ... Calvin did not really abandon allegory. Instead, *he moderated it*, he renamed it, and he expanded the letter to absorb much of what was formerly conveyed by 'spiritual' exegesis."[157] I see the Reformation as mitigating the excesses it received from the medieval hermeneutical tradition.

The Rule of Faith: Reading Forward

Finally, we turn to the so-called rule of faith. This principle has an honored pedigree stretching back at least as far as Irenaeus.[158] Regrettably, many modern interpretations of Irenaeus's use of the rule of faith as a metanarrative of God's work stretching from creation to consummation are flawed.[159] His approach was more subtle. More unfortunately still, sometimes the way the rule of faith is set forth today makes it sound as if it is liable to subjectivism, of de facto

---

[155]Ibid.
[156]Brevard S. Childs, "The Sensus Literalis: An Ancient and Modern Problem," *Beiträge zur alttestamentlichen Theologie; Festschrift für Walther Zimmerli zum 70. Geburtstag* (Göttingen: Vandenhoeck & Ruprecht, 1976), 87.
[157]Thompson, "Reformer of Exegesis?," 141.
[158]See Robert W. Wall's essay, "Canonical View," 111-30. For fuller treatments of Irenaeus, see David Jeffrey Klein, "Jeremiah, Exegesis, and the Rule of Faith: Theological Interpretation in Practice" (ThM thesis, Regent College, 2013), 84-86.
[159]See Nathan MacDonald, "Israel and the Old Testament Story in Irenaeus's Presentation of the Rule of Faith," *JTI* 3, no. 2 (2009): 281-98.

creating a canon above the canon of Scripture.[160] Therefore, a positive and nuanced construal of the rule of faith is necessary. Christopher Seitz carefully defines the rule of faith in the following manner: "The rule of faith is the scripturally grounded articulation, based upon a proper perception of the hypothesis of Scripture, that Jesus Christ is one with the god who sent him and who is active in the Scriptures inherited, the Holy Spirit being the means of testifying to his active, if hidden, life in the 'Old Testament' and our apprehension of that."[161] This is a helpful way of expressing the rule of faith since it focuses on the rule as embodying "an ontological judgment about God's being, which in turn affects the way the Scriptures of Israel must be read."[162] This is not merely ontology in the Greek, metaphysical sense. Rather, ontology is used here in the sense of what Scripture claims to be reality. God has already revealed himself in the Scriptures of Israel; therefore Jesus, who is one with God, must be a witness to Christ.[163] Although strictly speaking, God and his actions should not be separated; nevertheless, this move expresses the important truth that God exists independently and apart from the way he expresses himself, for example, in history or typology. Jesus is revealed to be the unified pattern of aggregate parts of Scripture, not some reconstructed hypothesis taken from decontextualized bits and pieces of Scripture that make sense as a narrative but are foreign to the canon of truth and the Scripture's own christological narrative.[164]

---

[160]This is a liability in Wall's presentation, and Gaffin in his essay, correctly, criticizes it, citing the distinction of the canon of Scripture being the "norming norm," which Muller has foregrounded from Reformed orthodoxy, *norma normans—norma normata*. The former—the *norma normans* is Scripture—and the latter are the creeds and confessions that express the theological sense of the Scriptures. See, e.g., Richard Muller, *Post-Reformation Reformed Dogmatics*, vol. 2, *Holy Scripture: The Cognitive Foundation of Theology*, 2nd ed. (Grand Rapids: Baker Academic, 2003), 106. See also Gaffin, "The Redemptive-Historical Response," in Porter and Stovell, *Biblical Hermeneutics*, 183.

[161]Christopher R. Seitz, *The Character of Christian Scripture: The Significance of a Two-Testament Bible*, Studies in Theological Interpretation (Grand Rapids: Baker Academic, 2011), 198.

[162]Klein, "Jeremiah," 82.

[163]Ibid., 83.

[164]On this, see ibid., 81–87, and Young, *Biblical Exegesis*, 19–20.

Often the rule of faith has been misunderstood to be something like figure 1.5, as demonstrated by David Jeffrey Klein.[165]

Figure 1.5. The rule of faith misunderstood

Klein, writing on the rule of faith and the book of Jeremiah in particular, proposes instead the description of the rule of faith in figure 1.6, building on Seitz.[166]

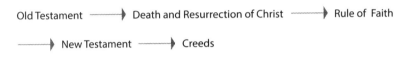

Figure 1.6. The rule of faith as proposed by Klein

Therefore, the proper "location of the rule is between the two testaments. The rule of faith looks back to Israel's scriptures and also anticipates and helps shape the emerging New Testament witness."[167] In my judgment this not only escapes the charge of a canon above the canon; it actually guards the canon because a proper interpretation of the Old Testament influences the New Testament. Such a view also forces the exegete to engage seriously with the Old Testament Scriptures on their own terms before moving to the New Testament. We are undertaking a "ruled reading" in this book.

The importance of this construal of the rule of faith is that it preserves the christological sense of the Old Testament Scriptures themselves, which were exerting christological and theological pressure in their own right on the apostolic witness. In other words, by expounding interpretation in this manner, the literal sense of the Old Testament Scriptures is not merely the function of the retrospective readings performed by

---

[165]I am indebted to Klein for his simplified manner of expressing this; see Klein, "Jeremiah," 87-88. Klein is representing Seitz, *Character of Christian Scripture*, 192.
[166]Seitz, *Character of Christian Scripture*, 198-99.
[167]Klein, "Jeremiah," 199-200.

New Testament authors.[168] Nor is the meaning of Scripture construed merely along christotelic lines.[169] This approach, as Lane Tipton says,

> asserts that the Old Testament, on its own terms and in light of a grammatical-historical "first reading," cannot sustain a typological reading that is Christ-centered. That is, the Old Testament is not intrinsically centered on the kingdom, person, and work of Christ. . . . Typology, a reading of the Old Testament that construes it as both revealing and anticipating Christ in provisional forms, is only recognized in terms of a retrospective "second reading" of the Old Testament in light of its surprise fulfillment in Christ.[170]

The Old Testament promises, prophecies, and sacrifices; circumcision; the Passover lamb; and many other types and ordinances serve figural or typological purposes that were sufficient for the time and were more fully realized as redemptive history progressed. These typological signifiers really did broker the truth of Christ, even though those Old

---

[168] An example of this are the frequent construals of Richard Hays. Here I am indebted to Professor Don Collett for his incisive analysis. See the construal of 1 Corinthians 10 in Hays, *Echoes of Scripture in the Letters of Paul*, 91; cf. Hays, *First Corinthians*, Interpretation Commentary (Louisville, KY: Westminster John Knox, 1997), 160. Hays suggests that Paul is drawing a rather "fanciful" analogy between Israel and the church in this passage. Furthermore, Paul's reading of Israel's wilderness sojourn is an "imaginative act of reading Exodus as metaphor for human experience. Hence Paul's metaphors should not be pressed" (*Echoes of Scripture in the Letters of Paul*, 91), lest we fall into the error of "supposing that the Old Testament itself interprets these events as sacramental symbols or that Jewish tradition before Paul had conceived of these events as figurative foreshadowings of future realities" (160). The same kind of claim is made in Hays's recent book *Echoes of Scripture in the Gospels*. Here Hays deals with the notion of a "redefinition" of messianic expectations: from militaristic messiahship to one who would not "fight with weapons of war but who would trust God to vindicate him and give the victory." He goes on to say that "this interpretation of the riddle makes sense *only in the retrospective light of the cross and resurrection*" (55, emphasis mine). In my view of typology, these are foreshadowings of future realities. See, e.g., the discussions under "Isaiah 41:16-20" in chap. 5 below and in chap. 9 on my treatment of Paul.

[169] See, e.g., Peter Enns, "Fuller Meaning, Single Goal: A Christotelic Approach to the New Testament Use of the Old in Its First-Century Interpretive Environment," in *Three Views on the New Testament Use of the Old Testament*, ed. Kenneth Berding and Jonathan Lunde (Grand Rapids: Zondervan, 2008), 167-217, esp. 213-15. Also see his earlier book, *Inspiration and Incarnation: Evangelicals and the Problem of the Old Testament* (Grand Rapids: Baker Academic, 2005), 113-66. For a critique of the christotelic approach, see Lane G. Tipton, "The Gospel and Redemptive-Historical Hermeneutics," in *Confident of Better Things: Essays Commemorating Seventy-Five Years of the Orthodox Presbyterian Church*, ed. John R. Muether and Danny E. Olinger (Willow Grove, PA: The Committee for the Historian of the OPC, 2011), 185-213.

[170] Lane G. Tipton, "Jesus in the Old Testament," in *No Uncertain Sound: Reformed Doctrine and Life* (Philadelphia: Reformed Forum, 2017), 12.

Testament saints lived in a historical economy of *Logos asarkos*, when the Word had not yet been made flesh.[171]

Conclusion: Calvin and Vitringa as Model Exegetes

Spiritual versus literal readings of Scripture are not the real issue in hermeneutics today. In this chapter we have discussed a text theory engaging intertextuality, typology, allegory, and the rule of faith. What the discussion has demonstrated is that the real issue today is how the referentiality of biblical texts functions, not merely the cold war of spiritual versus literal hermeneutics that has been so commonplace in the past.

After looking at recent trends, we focused on intertextuality. This important area of study can assist the biblical exegete in making more precise distinctions between biblical citations, allusions, and echoes. We also considered a responsible use of typology with allegory and briefly discussed the rule of faith. In my judgment, Calvin and Vitringa embodied many of these methods to one degree or another.

David Steinmetz's interest in the superiority of precritical exegesis is well known. Premodern exegetes employed many methods before the rise of the critical method, and these interpreters demonstrated significant insight and acumen over and over again and are undeserving of the chronological snobbery so often voiced by modern exegetes.[172] Richard A. Muller's discussion of Calvin's exegetical and hermeneutical methods in light of late-medieval exegetical methods highlights the genius of Calvin's methods.[173] Muller shows that Calvin took great pains to emphasize a more textual, grammatical, and historically oriented hermeneutic of biblical texts. Calvin related

---

[171] See the incisive critique of christotelic readings and the sensus plenior in Don Collett, "Reading Forward: The Old Testament and Retrospective Stance," *Pro Ecclesia* 24, no. 2 (2015): 178-96. He is not using *Logos asarkos* in the typical tangle of post-Barthian worries about the "hidden" God who exists behind the God revealed in Scripture.

[172] Muller and Thompson, "Significance of Precritical Exegesis," 336.

[173] Richard A. Muller, "The Hermeneutic of Promise and Fulfillment in Calvin's Exegesis of the Old Testament Prophecies of the Kingdom," in *The Bible in the Sixteenth Century*, ed. David C. Steinmetz, Duke Monographs in Medieval and Renaissance Studies 11 (Durham, NC: Duke University Press, 1990), 68-82. G. Sujin Pak makes similar claims in her study; see Pak, *The Judaizing Calvin: Sixteenth-Century Debates over the Messianic Psalms*, Oxford Studies in Historical Theology (New York: Oxford University Press, 2010).

the Old Testament to the New along the lines of promise and fulfillment. Furthermore, he coupled the idea of an extended meaning in the text that can relate a single sense to several referents, which in turn can encompass the entire kingdom of God.[174] Calvin's method was derived, no doubt, from classical rhetoric,[175] for he was steeped in work of the ancient Roman rhetorician Quintilian.[176] Calvin used a technical term from rhetoric, *complexus*, "indicating a connection in discourse as important to the meaning of a text as the grammatical *sensus*."[177] In short, as Muller has demonstrated, Calvin shows great antipathy to the allegorical method. He would not move in his exegesis from the grammatical and historical sense to allegory; however, says Muller, he did "develop the *complexus* of ideas presented in a text to cover an extended meaning virtually identical in content to that covered by allegory or trope but more closely governed by the grammatical and historical *sensus* of the text."[178] Thus, Calvin took great pains not to separate the *sensus historicus* from the *sensus literalis*. This is something narrative theology customarily does do, however, for a variety of reasons.[179]

What is needed today in biblical studies is the *via media* of the eighteenth-century biblical scholar Campegius Vitringa (1659–1722).[180] Vitringa was famous in his own time for his monumental work on the prophet Isaiah. He was unflinching in his commitment to the historical

---

[174] Other scholars will subsume this under "referent expansion." See Darrell L. Bock, "Single Meaning, Multiple Contexts and Referents," in Berding and Lunde, *Three Views*, 114.
[175] Muller, "Hermeneutic," 73.
[176] See Naphtali Lewis and Meyer Reinhold, *Roman Civilization, Sourcebook II: The Empire* (New York: Harper, 1966), 287-91.
[177] Muller, "Hermeneutic," 73.
[178] Ibid.
[179] Horton, *Covenant and Eschatology*, 176.
[180] See the excellent discussion in the dissertation of Charles Kelly Telfer, "The Exegetical Methodology of Campegius Vitringa (1659–1722), Author of the *Commentarius in Librum Prophetiarum Jesaiae*" (PhD diss., Trinity Seminary, 2015). The dissertation (reworked and modified) has been published as Charles K. Telfer, *Wrestling with Isaiah: The Exegetical Methodology of Campegius Vitringa (1659–1722)*, Reformed Historical Theology 38 (Göttingen: Vandenhoeck & Ruprecht, 2016). For a general overview of Vitringa's life, work, and influence, see Telfer, "Campegius Vitringa Sr. (1659–1722): A Biblical Theologian at the Turn of the Eighteenth Century," in *Biblical Theology: Past, Present, and Future*, ed. Carey Walsh and Mark W. Elliott (Eugene, OR: Cascade, 2016), 18-32.

sense and using historical research to understand the text. But he was critical of his contemporary Hugo Grotius for being preoccupied with how Isaiah speaks to events of his own day without understanding how Isaiah spoke to the future, namely, how he spoke of Christ and the future people of God. For Vitringa, someone like Grotius was too historicist. Vitringa maintained that the great gospel of the Old Testament, Isaiah, was focused on Christ. But he was also critical of another contemporary, Johannes Cocceius, whom he perceived as too much invested in the allegorical method. So Vitringa proposed a *via media* between the historicism of Grotius and the allegorism of Cocceius.

In the chapters that follow, my aim is to apply with rigor the kind of interpretive approach that Calvin and Vitringa embodied. Analyzing echoes of the exodus motif provides an excellent opportunity for applying and illustrating this approach.

Two

THE PAST IS PROLOGUE

Creation and Exodus

The striking similarity between the flood and Sinai, between Noah and Moses, is of great theological significance for the interpretation of each story. For each story is a critical moment. First for the future of the world, then the future of Israel is in the balance. The world, while still in its infancy, has sinned and brought upon itself Yahweh's wrath and judgment. Israel has only just been constituted a people, God's chosen people, yet directly it has sinned and incurred Yahweh's wrath and judgment. Each time the same question is raised. How, before God, can a sinful world (in general) or a sinful people, even God's chosen people (in particular), exist without being destroyed? Each time the answer is given that if the sin is answered solely by the judgment it deserves, then there is no hope. But in addition to the judgment there is also mercy, a mercy which depends entirely on the character of God and is given to an unchangingly sinful people.

R. W. L. MOBERLY

Cosmology in the ancient world was not merely about the structure and origin of the universe; it was also about its very governing principles. This is why creation was such a fundamental concern for the ancients, for "to know the origin of something is somehow to know its essence."[1] Where does the problem of human plight begin, and where is the solution to that failed human project? Or, to frame

---

[1] Richard J. Clifford, *Creation Accounts in the Ancient Near East and in the Bible*, CBQMS 26 (Washington, DC: Catholic Biblical Association, 1994), vii.

it according to the subject of this book, how might creation be related to the exodus motif?

The problem of how creation is related to the doctrine of redemption, or the doctrine of election, stands at the very center of almost all significant endeavors in the field of Old Testament theology.[2] In the previous chapter I suggested how typological interpretation needs to be part of the reader's toolbox when examining the exodus motif. In this chapter I aim to set forth how integral a right understanding of the covenantal structures of the early chapters of Genesis is for tracing the exodus motif throughout Holy Scripture.

Francis Watson, building on Aristotle's *Poetics*, maintains that "properly integrated narratives have a beginning, a middle and an end. 'A beginning is that which does not necessarily come after something else, although something else exists or comes about after it.'"[3] If we are going to understand the role of the exodus motif in Scripture, then we must start at the beginning with creation since Genesis 1 casts its shadow on the entire Bible.

Suggesting that Israel's creation theology arose early goes against the academic consensus. Rolf Rendtorff summarizes this state of affairs, suggesting that creation theology was born in Israel during the monarchy.[4] Or, as H. H. Schmid states about the current academic milieu, "OT scholarship is nearly unanimous in regarding creation faith in ancient Israel as chronologically late and theologically secondary."[5] The systemic ramifications of such a position for our understanding of Old Testament theology cannot be understated. This position will necessarily affect our understanding of the covenants. It will also influence our understanding of the role of law and wisdom in ethics during various epochs of the life of ancient Israel. And finally, as we trace the exodus motif throughout Scriptures, it

---

[2] Rolf Rendtorff, *Canon and Theology: Overtures to an Old Testament Theology*, trans. and ed. Margaret Kohl (Minneapolis: Fortress, 1993), 95.
[3] Francis Watson, *Text and Truth: Redefining Biblical Theology* (Grand Rapids: Eerdmans, 1997), 225, quoting Aristotle's *Poetics* 7.
[4] Rendtorff, *Canon and Theology*, 93-94.
[5] H. H. Schmid, "Creation, Righteousness, and Salvation: 'Creation Theology' as the Broad Horizon of Biblical Theology," in *Creation in the Old Testament*, ed. Bernhard W. Anderson, Issues in Religion and Theology 6 (Philadelphia: Fortress, 1984), 103.

will influence whether we think there is some kind of innerbiblical exegesis (i.e., diachronic influence) happening, for example, with the creation themes so prominently mixed with exodus themes in Isaiah (see chap. 5).

Perhaps no one is more responsible for the notion of creation traditions arising late in the development of Israelite religion than Gerhard von Rad. When von Rad published *Das formgeschichtliche Problem des Hexateuchs* in 1938,[6] he posited that various traditions were behind the final form of the Pentateuch, each having its own independent existence and development before reaching final form. For example, many scholars think that the exodus tradition originated at Bethel. And for von Rad, not only was the exodus tradition independent of the creation tradition, but salvation faith had priority, temporally and otherwise, over any tradition of creation faith. I take the opposite view that creation is the foundation of covenant and therefore of salvation as well. With that in mind, we will begin with the large structures found in Genesis 1–15, which form the backdrop for the exodus motif. It is crucial to develop this relationship between creation and covenant, which is also the relationship between Genesis and Exodus.

Genesis 1:1–2:3: The Creation of the World and Its Priest-King

Genesis 1 is the magisterial account of the creation of humankind.[7] The intended original design here is the one city of God. From the very beginning record of redemptive history, God is portrayed as the One who owns creation and rules over it. Unlike other stories of creation in the ancient Near East, God is not portrayed merely as builder or warrior. He speaks and the creation comes into existence. The creation account is no mere mythological revisionism, as if it were formed as a reflex to surrounding pagan cosmologies that may or may not have influenced the

---

[6]Gerhard von Rad, *Das formgeschichtliche Problem des Hexateuch*, Beiträge zur Wissenschaft vom Alten (und Neuen) Testament 78 (Stuttgart: Kohlhammer, 1938) (= his *Gesammelte Studien zum Alten Testament*, 9-86); ET: *The Problem of the Hexateuch and Other Essays*, trans. E. W. Trueman Dicken (New York: McGraw-Hill, 1966), 1-78.

[7]*Magisterial* in the sense of the passage that represents the work of a "master workman," who speaks ex-nihilo (out of nothing) creation into existence with authority.

author of Genesis. As Eugene Merrill puts it, the notion of God's sovereignty over the watery abyss is not meant to support the notion entertained by some that the "creation account of Gen 1 is a primitive legendary tradition (*Chaoskampf*) scrubbed clean of offensive pagan polytheism."[8] Rather, this first book of Scripture offers us the true divine deposit, a narrative portrayal of absolute beginnings and the organizing of the visible and invisible heavens and earth. From the beginning, the Eden narrative is presented in the imagery of ancient Near Eastern cosmic-mountain ideology. The waters of creation are chaotic waters that must be subdued so that humans may ascend the mountain of God to worship him.[9] This ideology serves as the conceptual backdrop for "Israel's cultus so that approaching YHWH in worship at the temple was comprehended, beyond the inevitable metonymy given the temple's locale atop the hill of Zion, via a narrative liturgy: a mythopoeic journey to the cosmic mountain of God."[10] In other words, Genesis 1 is relating creation to the temple cult. The cosmos is a large temple, and the act of creation is probably to be considered against the backdrop of ancient Near Eastern understanding of the cosmos as a large temple-palace.[11] This pattern will be recapitulated in the tabernacle.[12] Indeed, there are even deliberate echoes and parallels between the Genesis 1 description of creation, the construction of the ark as a virtual temple, and the construction of the tabernacle.[13]

Because this is so from the beginning, the Scriptures represent God as the Lord of creation and history.[14] The very structure of Genesis as a

---

[8] See Eugene H. Merrill, "The Meaning and Significance of the Exodus Event," in *Reverberations of the Exodus*, ed. R. Michael Fox (Eugene, OR: Pickwick, 2014), 7.

[9] L. Michael Morales, *The Tabernacle Pre-figured: Cosmic Mountain Ideology in Genesis and Exodus*, Biblical Tools and Studies 15 (Leuven: Peeters, 2012), 5-6. This pattern becomes crucial for the flood and exodus narratives as well. Many passages in Scripture demonstrate God's sovereignty over the waters, which can be used for judgment (cf. Job 9:8; 26:10; 38:8-11; Ps 24:2; 29:3, 10; 33:6-7; 74:12-17; 89:8-10; 104:5-7; Prov 8:29; 30:4; Is 40:12; 50:2; 51:9; 54:9; Jer 5:22; Amos 5:8; 9:6; Nahum 1:4; Hab 3:15; Mt 8:26-27; Rev 21:1).

[10] Ibid., 33.

[11] Ibid., 78.

[12] Ibid., 87.

[13] Ibid., 146-47.

[14] See, e.g., Charles H. H. Scobie, *The Ways of Our God: An Approach to Biblical Theology* (Grand Rapids: Eerdmans, 2003), 106-8.

whole teaches a kind of philosophy of history. God operates and manifests his redemptive plan through families and through the covenant community, which he institutionalizes and administrates.

Not only is God the king, but according to Genesis 1:26, humanity is created according to the *imago Dei* with a royal function. As Randall Garr puts it, "Created 'in our image' and 'in the image of God,' represents both levels of divine authority that governs the cosmos. Humankind represents God's community of co-rulers, responsible for performing the justice and enacting the sovereign will of God."[15] This is apparent in Genesis 1 and becomes even more explicit in Genesis 2–3, when Adam names the animals and takes care of the garden. It becomes clear especially in Psalm 8, which is an inspired commentary on the early chapters of Genesis.

Another point here that informs our discussion of the exodus motif is that the creation of the world at the beginning of time is a constructive process, a reflection, a mirror, of the temple of God and its predecessor, the tabernacle.[16] Indeed, the creation of the world and the construction of the temple and the tabernacle stand in a complementary parallel relation to one another.[17] The temple in Israel will later become the "architectural embodiment of the cosmic mountain."[18] Within ancient Near Eastern studies, this concept is familiar and commonplace knowledge.[19] This relationship between cosmos and temple is represented not only at the conceptual level but at the linguistic level as well.

Why is this important? Because it indicates that the creation at the beginning of time is a sacred space, just as the tabernacle and the temple were later recognized to be spaces of sacred presence. God was

---

[15] W. Randall Garr, *In His Own Image and Likeness: Humanity, Divinity, and Monotheism*, Culture and History of the Ancient Near East 15 (Leiden: Brill, 2003), 219.

[16] This point is eloquently discussed by Jon D. Levenson, *Sinai and Zion: An Entry into the Jewish Bible* (San Francisco: Harper & Row, 1985), 137-45.

[17] Ibid., 141-44.

[18] John M. Lundquist, "The Common Temple Ideology of the Ancient Near East," in *Cult and Cosmos: Tilting Toward a Temple-Centered Theology*, ed. L. Michael Morales (Leuven: Peeters, 2014), 52. This article is a reprint from *The Temple in Antiquity: Ancient Records and Modern Perspectives*, ed. Truman G. Madsen (Provo, UT: Religious Studies Center, Brigham Young University, 1984), 53-76.

[19] Lundquist, "Common Temple Ideology," 54.

a divine protectorate to the first human pair in the garden. Hovering over the face of the waters, the Spirit's presence maintained Eden as a sanctuary, a place of protection, security, and preservation.[20] The combination of the verb *rāḥap* (to hover) with the noun *tōhû* (without form) in Genesis 1:2 occurs again only in Deuteronomy 32:10-11, where *tōhû* is now applied to the situation where God enters into another act of creation: in the exodus event in which his particular people are created in the wilderness.[21]

Indeed, in my view the land of Israel was a sacred space as well, for it was intended to be a picture of heaven or, better, the world-to-come. All the activities conducted by the first couple in their Edenic space were royal and holy because the place was holy: it was a prototypical sanctuary. The original couple not only had a royal mandate; they also had a priestly function to perform. At the end of Genesis 1:31, there is an important phrase, "And God saw all that he had made, and it was very good." The reader should note that the approbative formula ("and it was good") used so regularly in the cadence of the first six days is conspicuously absent from the seventh day. Perhaps the writer intended to communicate that the story of human history is not over yet, as Garr notes suggestively, and therefore approval is withheld.[22] The goal of eschatological rest had not been achieved yet.

The entire creation account is oriented to this climactic Sabbath rest. God declared that all his work was very good, but then he rested on the seventh day (Gen 2:2-3; Ex 31:16-17). God does not grow weary like humans (Is 40:28). So what is the nature of this resting? It is a royal resting following in the wake of his royal work, which was the building of his cosmic house. In short, it symbolizes his enthronement over creation. This is echoed in God's enthronement above the ark of the covenant, which as a virtual temple symbolized God's presence to the people of Israel. This divine Sabbath rest becomes the exemplar and

---

[20]See Meredith G. Kline, *Genesis: A New Commentary*, ed. Jonathan G. Kline (Peabody, MA: Hendrickson, 2016), 10. The participle in Gen 1:2 and the verb in Deut 32:11 listed above are in the *piel* in the text.
[21]Meredith G. Kline, *Images of the Spirit* (Grand Rapids: Baker, 1980), 14-18.
[22]Garr, *In His Own Image*, 239-40.

pattern for Israel's goal of the land of Canaan as Sabbatical goal of rest (see Heb. 3:1-11).

In Exodus, the Israelites needed rest from their hard labors (Ex 5:5). When God guided the people in their wilderness wanderings, he promised that he would go before them and give them rest (Ex 33:14). The goal of their liberation was not merely political. Nor was it merely rest. The ultimate goal was worship (Ex 5:1; 7:16; 8:1, 20; 9:1, 13; 10:3). As we shall observe, the ultimate rest God provides for his own is only found in the eternal world-to-come (Heb 3:1-11), where God is enthroned over his city, which is his gathered people, who worship him in the city of the lamb (Rev 21:1-8; 22:1-3).[23]

Genesis 2:4-3:24: The Sanctuary of God and Covenant Crises
The Garden of Eden was a prototypical sanctuary. Adam was not only assigned the role of a vassal ruler there; he was also the prototypical priest who was to guard Eden, the sanctuary of God.[24] This cultic interpretation of the garden scene was the standard rabbinical interpretation.[25]

Ezekiel 28 also represents Eden as a cosmic mountain. In the ancient Near East, sacred mountains were the "meeting place of heaven and earth, where celestial and mundane reality came together."[26] The later Temple Mount, from a theological perspective, "was at the intersection point of heaven and earth."[27] Adam constituted the prototypical priest, and the Garden of Eden was a prototypical sanctuary/

---

[23]Meredith G. Kline, *Kingdom Prologue: Genesis Foundations for a Covenantal Worldview* (Overland Park, KS: Two Age Press, 2000), 33-41.

[24]For extensive argumentation and bibliography on this issue, see my "The Covenant of Works in Moses and Paul," in *Covenant, Justification, and Pastoral Ministry: Essays by the Faculty of Westminster Seminary California*, ed. Scott Clark (Phillipsburg, NJ: P&R, 2007), 89-136. Also see Gordon J. Wenham, "Sanctuary Symbolism in the Garden of Eden Story," in *I Studied Inscriptions from Before the Flood*, ed. Richard S. Hess and David Toshio Tsumura (Winona Lake, IN: Eisenbrauns, 1994), 399-404; G. K. Beale, *The Temple and the Church's Mission: A Biblical Theology of the Dwelling Place of God*, New Studies in Biblical Theology 17 (Downers Grove, IL: InterVarsity Press, 2004), 81-99.

[25]Morales, *Tabernacle Pre-figured*, 100.

[26]William J. Dumbrell, "A Foreshadowing of the New Creation," in *Biblical Theology: Retrospect and Prospect*, ed. Scott Hafemann (Downers Grove, IL: InterVarsity Press, 2002), 57.

[27]Karel van der Toorn, "Theology, Priests, and Worship in Canaan and Ancient Israel," in *Civilizations of the Ancient Near East*, ed. Jack M. Sasson et al. (New York: Charles Scribner's Sons, 1995), 3:2052.

temple. Interestingly, many scholars have come to view the high priest of Israel as a second Adam.[28] The ground on which Adam and Eve walked was truly holy. God was present. He sanctified this first holy place. There God reigned, and Adam reigned under God. The garden was constituted a temple by God's holy reign, and it was his holy realm: this was a theocracy.[29]

Theocracy entails the coalescence of God's rule, reign, and realm. Here the cultic (religious worship along the vertical plane) intersects with culture (humankind's horizontal cultural pursuits, including the political) to form a unique institution that arises at sundry times and in various epochs of redemptive history. It starts in the Garden of Eden.[30] The thoughtful reader will begin to see the profound ramifications of this for Adam's duty and function in the garden. The end point (or telos) of creation is a summons to worship.[31]

In Genesis 2:15 we read that Adam was placed within the garden to tend it and guard it.[32] Two trees were prominent: the testing tree and the tree of life. One warned of curse and potential death. The other adumbrated promise and reward.[33] Interestingly, temples elsewhere in the ancient Near East were associated with a tree of life.[34] Adam's primary responsibility was as a priestly vassal king to protect the garden, the sanctuary of God, from unholy intruders. As the story reveals, Adam failed to discharge this duty. The consequences were dire for him and Eve and the entire human race. Adam could no longer ascend the Edenic mountain to be in God's presence, for no one can approach God

---

[28]Morales, *Tabernacle Pre-figured*, 258-63.
[29]See Michael Fishbane, *Biblical Text and Texture: A Literary Reading of Selected Texts* (New York: Schocken, 1979), 17.
[30]Kline, *Kingdom Prologue*, 51.
[31]Morales, *Tabernacle Pre-figured*, 91.
[32]The translation of these two verbs, especially the latter, is most often lost in English versions. The places in the Pentateuch where these two verbs occur together are in contexts where the Levite's duties include guarding and protecting the sanctuary.
[33]See the study of Tryggve N. D. Mettinger, *The Eden Narrative: A Literary and Religio-historical Study of Genesis 2–3* (Winona Lake, IN: Eisenbrauns, 2007), esp. 47-58. Mettinger claims the tree of life was unknown to Adam and Eve and would be revealed to them once they obeyed, a position from which I demur, although I do agree with him that it would only become accessible to them after they obeyed.
[34]Lundquist, "Common Temple Ideology," 63.

unprepared or without the requisite holiness. He must descend.[35] Indeed, from a canonical perspective, the gate liturgy that becomes so significant later in redemptive history ("Who shall ascend?"; see Ps 15, 24, 118) is initiated at this point.

Even so, God declared his mercy in the so-called protevangelium (first gospel) as recorded in Genesis 3:15-21. There was judgment and there was a common curse following Adam's sin, common in that it fell on all of Adam's descendants. However, there was also the corollary blessing: mercy and grace—in a word, redemption.[36]

The Connection Between Creation and Exodus

Creation is therefore the foundation for salvation and election, the creation of a royal priesthood people of God. For the biblical writers, what takes place in the exodus, together with the covenantal enactment at Sinai in the formation of the nation of Israel, is intimately connected with what happened in the creation covenant. In developing this view I have taken my cue from Geerhardus Vos. Starting with the creation story in the primeval history and positing its antecedent and foundational quality for what follows is vital for a healthy biblical theology.[37]

Building on Vos's approach, we will be looking at how all the foundational elements of a biblical worldview are in compliance with God's world and its interim structures. God designs each epoch of world history in such a manner that it is conducive to the accomplishment of his redemptive plans at any given period in history. That is to say that all the subsequent covenantal eras or epochs, including the role of the exodus within those patterns of interim structures, serve the unfolding

---

[35] Morales, *Tabernacle Pre-figured*, 114.
[36] I agree with the traditional Reformed view that, following in the wake of this announcement of the gospel, there is one organic covenant of grace throughout history, although with distinct administrations. See the Westminster Confession of Faith, chaps. 7 and 11.
[37] Geerhardus Vos, *Biblical Theology: Old and New Testaments* (Grand Rapids: Eerdmans, 1948), 16: "The main problem will be how to do justice to the individual peculiarities of the agents in revelation. These individual traits subserve the historical plan. Some propose that we discuss each book separately. But this leads to unnecessary repetition, because there is so much that all have in common. A better plan is to apply the collective treatment in the earlier stages of revelation, where the truth is not as yet much differentiated, and then to individualize in the later periods where greater diversity is reached."

development and plan of God's salvation of a people for himself. These foundational elements are provided in the opening chapters of the Bible, specifically Genesis 1–15 and following. This revelation applies to the theocratic-specific applications found especially in the Mosaic covenant. But more importantly, it applies to the distinctions brought about by the instituting of common grace after the fall (Gen 3), which is God's way of providing the soil, or a stable platform, on which God will carry out his plan in redemptive history.

Genesis 4–5: The Foundation of the City of Man

Genesis 4 is crucial to our understanding of the exodus motif. Our interpretation of this passage will systemically affect our reading of the exodus motif, whether we view it from merely a political perspective or from one that is primarily spiritual and redemptive. The exodus has been a focal point for liberation theologians and deliverance politics, and it continues to exercise some of the best minds in biblical scholarship and biblical theology.[38] But it is often overlooked that Genesis 4 (and especially Genesis 9) discusses God's instituting the city of man, putting in place a legal system for restraint against unbridled vengeance.

Before we begin our discussion of Genesis 4 and the beginnings of the city of man, we should set out our understanding of common grace,[39] which provides the backdrop for the unfolding of redemptive special grace. Common grace has been an important teaching of the church for centuries. It explains God's mercy toward the world in providing structures that allow Christians and non-Christians to live together in relative peace. God restrains the wickedness of humans through civil society and law. God benevolently provides rain for the righteous and the

---

[38]Consider, e.g., the spirited interchange between Jon D. Levenson, George Pixley, and John J. Collins in *Jews, Christians, and the Theology of the Hebrew Scriptures*, ed. Alice Ogden Bellis and Joel S. Kaminsky, SBLSymS 8 (Atlanta: Society of Biblical Literature, 2000), 213-75. For excellent work on how the narrative of the exodus has influenced and shaped politics and political rhetoric for centuries in a profound and systemic manner, see Michael Walzer, *Exodus and Revolution* (New York: Basic Books, 1985), and more recently John Coffey, *Exodus and Liberation: Deliverance Politics from John Calvin to Martin Luther King Jr.* (New York: Oxford University Press, 2014).

[39]See John Murray, "The Free Offer of the Gospel," in *Collected Writings* (Carlisle, PA: Banner of Truth Trust, 1982), 4:113-32.

unrighteous. God works through rulers that do not believe in him in order to bring about stability and civic good.

Common grace accounts for the fact that, after the fall, God demonstrates grace and mercy in allowing humankind to have a city even though they have broken covenant with God. After Abel offers an acceptable sacrifice to God, his brother Cain kills him because God had not accepted his own sacrifice (Heb 11:4). Cain fears retribution and revenge from Abel's kin, for God declares that he will now be a "vagrant and wanderer on the earth" (Gen 4:12, author's translation). Cain's plaintive cry to God is instructive: "My punishment is more than I can bear. Today you are driving me from the land, and I will be hidden from your presence; I will be a restless wanderer on the earth, and whoever finds me will kill me" (Gen 4:13-14).

What is the essence of Cain's lament, especially his concern to be hidden from the face of God? To be denied access to the face of God is "to be abandoned to the mortal perils of a lawless world.... He will be denied God's judicial oversight."[40] This is confirmed in the Psalter's understanding of what banishment from the face of God means. Often the psalmist appeals for judicial oversight in the midst of persecution from enemies. Cain's great fear is that he will be "exposed to lawless men bent on vengeance. He will be *ex lex* on a God-forsaken earth."[41] What is God's response to this concern of Cain's? Verse 15 tells us: "'Not so; anyone who kills Cain will suffer vengeance seven times over.' Then the LORD put a mark on Cain so that no one who found him would kill him" (Gen 4:15).

The pronouncement by God begins with a formal, solemn affirmation with the Hebrew word *lākēn*, "therefore." Nahum Sarna sums up well the importance of this word: "[It] frequently introduces a solemn declaration, while the formulation of the reassurance derives from the realm of law. The unusually emphatic language is directed first to Cain, in order

---

[40]Meredith G. Kline, "Oracular Origin of the State," in *Biblical and Near Eastern Studies: Essays in Honor of William Sanford LaSor*, ed. Gary A. Tuttle (Grand Rapids: Eerdmans, 1978), 132-33. In much of what follows on the explication of Gen 4, I am indebted to this article.
[41]Ibid., 134.

to allay his mortal fear, and then to the world at large, as a kind of royal proclamation that has the force of law. It states that despite his crime, Cain still remains under God's care."[42] God is setting up a legal system for restraint against unbridled vengeance. As Iain Provan puts it, "Retribution is not to be excessive; it is to be just. God had promised Cain a special level of deterrence in his case as a vulnerable outsider to organized society. A heavy price would be exacted from any community that killed him."[43] Scripture nowhere gives any direct evidence for prescriptions on government.[44] Nevertheless, it seems that God is setting up a legal system here that will be more fully developed in Genesis 9, where we see that the Noachian covenantal arrangement provides the foundation for *jurisgenerative* authority structures.[45] God says that he shall be avenged "sevenfold" (*šibʿātayîm*) if Cain is killed. This demonstrates that the stipulated retribution will be perfect, divine in origin and authority.[46] This is not to excuse Cain but to set a precedent for the future. Genesis 4, therefore, "expresses through narrative principles that are of fundamental importance in biblical law."[47]

Other evidence further corroborates the divine origin of these principles. Many English versions translate verse 15 in such a way that it sounds as if it is Cain who will be avenged. After all, the verb "shall be taken" (*yuqqām*) is in the passive, so it leaves it up to the interpreter to determine who the subject (or, more precisely, the ultimate agent) of the

---

[42]Nahum M. Sarna, *Genesis*, JPS Torah Commentary (Philadelphia: Jewish Publication Society, 1989), 35.
[43]Iain Provan, *Seriously Dangerous Religion: What the Old Testament Really Says and Why It Matters* (Waco, TX: Baylor University Press, 2014), 202.
[44]See David VanDrunen, "Legal Polycentrism: A Christian Theological and Jurisprudential Evaluation," *Journal of Law and Religion* (forthcoming). Polycentrism holds that there are multiple sources of law, whereas the classical positivist notion is a monocentric view of law: law comes from a single source, i.e., the properly constituted political authorities. VanDrunen argues that polycentrism may be more plausible and coherent with the biblical data.
[45]I am indebted to VanDrunen for this term, which he applies in his own analysis to Gen 9 and the Noachian covenant.
[46]Kline, "Oracular Origin," 135. Kenneth Matthews says that seven is here a "figure of speech meaning completeness or fullness [and] expresses the certainty and severity of God's vengeance against a vigilante." *Genesis 1–11:26*, New American Commentary 1A (Nashville: Broadman & Holman, 2001), 278.
[47]Gordon Wenham, *Genesis 1–15*, WBC 1 (Waco, TX: Word, 1987), 117.

action is.⁴⁸ In other words, it is often misinterpreted and rendered as "(Cain) will be avenged." This is most likely the wrong analysis.

It was George Mendenhall who noted the important political and legal overtones of the verbal root *nqm* when he wrote, "Instead of representing merely a primitive custom incompatible with any stable peaceful society, the root *NQM* has to do with the very foundations of political legitimacy and authority long before the time of Moses."⁴⁹ Mendenhall recognized that the use of *nqm* probably signaled the intervention and authority of Yahweh, and this strongly implies that God himself is the subject of the action of this verb. I agree with this analysis, but I would take it even farther.

When passive or passive-like verbs are used in Semitic languages, the reader must interpret who the agent or originator of the action is. These passives can serve different purposes. One very important purpose—and I think Genesis 4:15 is an example—is the passive's use as a substitute for royal or divine agency. At times, this has the net effect of increasing the authority of the initiator or originator of the action.⁵⁰

New Testament scholars analyze certain Greek passives in a similar manner. It is often said that these passive constructions, where the implied unspecified agent is God, are used to avoid irreverence toward God. These are called "divine passives."⁵¹ When a Gospel writer declares that the veil of the sanctuary *was rent* in two, it is clear on a little reflection that God is the ultimate agent of the action.

God sets a "sign" (*'ōt*) for Cain. Many commentators have missed the significance of this because they assume that it must refer to a physical sign or mark. However, a sign can also be verbal in nature.⁵² In this view,

---

⁴⁸Most parse the verb as a *hophal*, the passive of the *hiphil*. The root *nqm*, however, has no known *hiphil* and is more likely to be the rare *qal* passive. See Paul Joüon, *A Grammar of Biblical Hebrew*, trans. and rev. T. Muraoka (Rome: Pontifical Biblical Institute, 1991), §58. Some lexicons also parse this as a *pual*; however, I think it is parsed correctly as a *hophal*, but note at the end of the note that Joüon actually argues for a *qal* passive.

⁴⁹Quoted in Kline, "Oracular Origin," 136.

⁵⁰See Bryan Estelle, "The Use of Deferential Language in the Arsames Correspondence and Biblical Aramaic Compared," *Maarav* 13, no. 1 (2006): 43-74.

⁵¹ See, e.g., Raymond E. Brown, *The Death of the Messiah: From Gethsemane to the Grave*, Anchor Bible Reference Library (New York: Doubleday, 1994), 2:1100-1106.

⁵²Cf. Francis Brown, S. R. Driver, and Charles A. Briggs, *A Hebrew and English Lexicon of the Old Testament* (Oxford: Clarendon, 1907), 16-17.

the sign corresponds to the divine response in Genesis 4:15a,[53] and therefore the verse in question with the following infinitive has the effect of filling out the substance of God's response to Cain, which might be freely translated, "Thus Yahweh gave Cain an *'ōt* to the effect that everyone who came upon him would not be out to kill him."[54] Cain, and the world at large, would not be subjected to lawless chaos; rather, the world would be judicially structured. God's common grace would exercise restraint against evil.

What did humankind do with this common grace that God established for the benefit of a stable order? Through a tremendously compressed recording of history in Genesis 4:17-26, we see cultural growth and subsequent prosperity: inventions, artistic enterprises, the emergence of occupations, and technologies. However, in Genesis 4:18 and following, we read of Lamech, who ran roughshod over the establishment of God's previously established legal restraint, and we see how far the state of the world has drifted from God's oracular origin of that restraint. God implemented the city of man to maintain a kind of civic righteousness on the part of humankind generally—not just for the community of faith, but also for those who do not profess Yahweh as their God. In other words, in the wake of Genesis 3, humankind does not need to acquiesce to some kind of fatalistic notion that injustice must run rampant and unchecked.[55] From the perspective of the Scriptures, this arrangement allows for peaceful and stable order in which the purposes of God for redemptive history may march forward. Now the world would be marked by two cities, not just one city, as was the design before the fall of humans.

In Genesis 4 we see Lamech rise to power. Through an act of severe self-aggrandizement, and with evil avarice and hubris, Lamech tramples on the institution of marriage by taking to himself two wives (Gen 4:19). Then he despises the good gifts of civil restraint by boasting of taking a life for a bruise (Gen 4:23)! In short, he practices injustice. His

---

[53]Kline, "Oracular Origin," 138.
[54]Ibid.
[55]See the insightful comments of Provan, *Seriously Dangerous Religion*, 134-46.

insolence knows no bounds. Lamech boasts in his infamous sword song: if God was to be avenged "sevenfold," then he will be avenged "seventy-sevenfold" (Gen 4:24).

More significant is the rising of the community of faith in the midst of that generation whose evil waxed. God raises a seed that comes not from the line of Cain but from Adam and Eve's third son, Seth, who "calls on the name of the Lord." Here, before the flood, we have an introduction to the godly line of the covenant community in ancient days, by which we mean the covenant community of God who bears God's name in the midst of the city of man. God is already busy crafting a people, a royal priesthood (this too will provide a vital theme for the unfolding plot line of the exodus motif). This is a crucial passage, well placed just before Genesis 5, since it records a genealogical account leading up to Noah. The distinctive feature of these people in Genesis 5 is that they are God's people, for here the Sethites (cf. Gen 4:25-26) are "beginning to call on the name of the Lord." This common biblical idiom has to do with making the faith of the heart known in an external expression of worship, often making known the name of the Lord among hostile peoples.

The picture is analogous to the covenant people of God in the present age of the church. The very structure of the genealogy in Genesis 5 advertises the family structure of this cultic community, an altar-oriented people who call on the name of the Lord. It is a covenant community living and pilgrimaging in the midst of the common-grace city of man. They are simultaneously citizens of the covenant community and citizens of a world marked by common grace.

What should the stance of the covenant community be during this time? The parallels between the Sethite community of Genesis 4–5 and our own age is striking. All people are citizens of the world in which they find themselves. Therefore, they are subject to a particular nation's laws and order. Meredith Kline sums up the proper role of the Sethites: "Though they must not neglect their part in building the common city, they were also to fulfill with eager hope their distinctive covenantal mission. Though full citizens in the city of man, they were faithfully to maintain within it their altar to the name of Yahweh and remember that they were also citizens of his yet unseen heavenly city."[56] This altar-oriented people is to be in the world but not of the world.

This is not a theocracy. What is recorded has instructive importance for later generations of God's people. It is not a theocratic political commonwealth; it is a manifesto for pursuing dual citizenship, one heavenly and the other earthly. The altar-oriented people of God, whether they find themselves as pilgrims in the prediluvian era, in the time of the patriarchs, at the height of Roman civilization, or in the twenty-first century, must always recognize the general lordship of God over every area of their lives. At certain points in history, God can and does allow holy kingdom institutions to coexist with non-holy institutions.

The chief concern of Genesis 5 is the genealogical account leading up to the cycle of narratives concerning Noah and his family. Here we see that God has a plan. This period of history, in its huge global sweep before the crisis of the flood, "is not so much the history of the Sethites *per se* as it is the history of the covenant institution."[57] The literary structure of the genealogy in chapter 5 is concerned with the Sethites, which is not to say that all the believers were in the line of Seth; even so, those who were believers were more closely aligned with the line of Seth. We will see a similar pattern in Genesis 11. There the covenantal family will be closely aligned with Shem. The main point, however, is that a covenantal family is living in the midst of the common-grace city of man.

Genesis 6-8

The discussion we began in Genesis 4 concerning the city of man would not be complete without seeing its connection in Genesis 6:1-4. This completes in many respects the picture presented in Genesis 4. It reads,

> Now it came about, when men began to multiply on the face of the land, and daughters were born to them, that the sons of God saw that the daughters of men were beautiful; and they took wives for themselves,

---
[56]Kline, *Kingdom Prologue*, 199-200.
[57]Ibid., 195.

whomever they chose. Then the Lord said, "My spirit shall not strive with man forever, because he also is flesh; nevertheless his days shall be one hundred and twenty years." The Nephilim were on the earth in those days, and also afterward, when the sons of God came in to the daughters of men, and they bore children to them. Those were the mighty men of old, men of renown. (Gen 6:14, author's translation)

This strange passage has occasioned numerous comments from commentators over the years.[58] What is at issue is the interpretation of the phrase "the sons of God." The various interpretations may be grouped under three categories: (1) "sons of God" are nonhuman beings, such as angels, demons, or spirits; (2) "sons of God" are superior men of some kind, such as kings or other rulers; (3) "sons of God" are the godly descendants of Seth in contrast with the godless descendants of Cain. Each of these three views has a plausible defense.[59]

The Sethite interpretation has few adherents today[60] despite its honored place among Christian exegetes in the past.[61] One may understand its attractiveness, since it avoids the difficult, if not offensive, notion of the first view: that supernatural beings copulated with human beings, the daughters of men. This bowdlerizing interpretation—however popular even among such luminaries as Augustine, Calvin, and Luther—is specious on philological grounds.[62]

The angelic/demonic position has a time-honored pedigree in Jewish literature, in the literature of the early Christian fathers, and in very early apocalyptic literature. Nevertheless, this understanding is strained even within its immediate context and may run against Jesus' own statement about the nature of angelic marriage and reproduction (cf. Mt 22:30; Mk 12:25).[63] But one supporting fact is that in Ugaritic literature

---

[58]For a good overview to the issues, see Wenham, *Genesis 1–15*, 136-47.
[59]Bruce K. Waltke with Cathi J. Fredericks, *Genesis: A Commentary* (Grand Rapids: Zondervan, 2001), 116-17.
[60]Rita F. Cefalu, "Royal Priestly Heirs to the Restoration Promise of Gen 3:15: A Biblical Theological Perspective on the Sons of God in Genesis 6," *WTJ* 76 (2014): 351-70.
[61]Wenham, *Genesis 1–15*, 40.
[62]Ibid., 116.
[63]It is true, nevertheless, that Christian interpreters have appealed to other scriptural passages to support their view of the fallen angels here (cf. 1 Pet 3:19-20; 2 Pet 2:4; Jude 6).

(contemporary in time and close in proximity to the Israelites) "sons of God" often refers to gods of the Pantheon.

The second option holds the most promise because it fits well the biblical and cultural context. Defenders of this view often point out that the Bible does refer to human rulers as divine judges (cf. Ps 82:1-7). The point is that the Bible reflects the practice of contiguous cultures round about the Israelites: kings and rulers are called the "sons of God" because they bear a divine, vassal status in that they rule in the God's stead. Thus, this passage echoes the same kind of self-aggrandizing spirit among royalty and tyrants that was evident in Lamech in Genesis 4: these kings run roughshod over the legal restraints that God has put in place by practicing polygamy, arrogating to themselves the name "the sons of God" (literally in Gen 6:4, "the men of the name"), and perverting justice as "divine" kings.[64] They lust for a name of power. These arrogant royal figures have transgressed God's boundaries in the spheres of family and spheres of family and civil restraint. The correspondence between Genesis 4 and 6 is too close to ignore.

Sin now waxes strong, so strong that it threatens to squash the people of God. An important contrastive parallel to the closing of the magisterial creation story of Genesis 1 now moves the plot line along: "God saw all that he had made, and it was very good" (Gen 1:31), and "God saw the earth, and it was very corrupt" (Gen 6:12, author's translation). The parallel here is obviously intentional.[65] However, Noah and his family become the exception to God's universal evaluation. Indeed, Noah is considered "righteous" (*ṣaddîq*) by God in Genesis 7:1 and "unblemished" or "blameless" (*tāmîm*) in Genesis 6:9. Michael Morales brings out the didactic purpose: "Only the righteous will be delivered through the waters to the holy mount."[66] As always in redemptive history, holiness is necessary to experience union and communion with God. Ultimately, Noah points the way forward to the true deliverer,

---

[64]Meredith G. Kline, "Divine Kingship and Sons of God in Genesis 6:1-4," *WTJ* 24 (1962): 187-204.
[65]Rolf Rendtorff, "'Covenant' as a Structuring Concept in Genesis and Exodus," *JBL* 108, no. 3 (1989): 385-93.
[66]Morales, *Tabernacle Pre-figured*, 166.

whose righteousness and blamelessness is perfect.[67] But more immediately, Noah brings to the fore the principle that "only the blameless may dwell in God's holy mount."[68] Noah is portrayed as a priest.[69] However, it is not merely by virtue of his office that the typology of Noah is triggered.[70] Rather, Noah is a type of Christ both by virtue of his office and by virtue of his righteousness and blamelessness. He had these characteristics by Spirit-wrought grace. As Protestants who love to showcase the grace of God *alone*, we must not be timid about recognizing such God-designed typology in certain Old Testament saints, even if it involves the approbation of the "righteous."[71]

The narrative records that God makes a covenant with Noah and his family. He will deliver them through the judicial waters, a virtual "trial by ordeal."[72] The waters of judgment on humanity actually become the waters of deliverance for God's people (cf. 1 Pet 3:20).[73] The purpose of the deluge was to purify the earth.[74] "It is curious how little importance is attached to God's covenant with Noah in surveys of Old Testament theology," laments Rendtorff.[75] The Noachian covenant has indeed received too little attention vis-à-vis the Mosaic and royal covenants. Patrick D. Miller is correct when he states, "It may be that the theological enterprise needs to discern the relationship between Mosaic and

---

[67]See my short article "Noah: A Righteous Man?," *Modern Reformation* 19, no. 5 (September/October 2010): 27. When comparing the imperfect righteousness of a mere creature (even one as great as Noah) to the antitype, namely Christ, it is imperative to note the disparity between the type and the antitype, who was without sin.

[68]Morales, *Tabernacle Pre-figured*, 166.

[69]Ibid., 169.

[70]Pace Jeffrey J. Niehaus, *Biblical Theology: The Common Grace Covenants* (Wooster, OH: Weaver Books, 2014), 1:178-79.

[71]Besides, we have memorialized in Holy Scripture the fact that Noah seemed to enjoy "pulling the cork" too much, a sin that led to other sins in his family (cf. Gen 9:20-29).

[72]The only direct account in Scripture of the "trial by ordeal" judicial procedure is in Num 5; however, for a quick introduction to this phenomenon in the ancient Near East and its influence on the Bible, see my *Salvation Through Judgment and Mercy: The Gospel According to Jonah* (Phillipsburg, NJ: P&R, 2005). Also see P. Kyle McCarter, "The River Ordeal in Israelite Literature," *Harvard Theological Review* 66, no. 4 (1973): 403-12. For a full discussion of this phenomenon, see the unpublished dissertation of T. S. Frymer-Kensky, "The Judicial Ordeal in the Ancient Near East" (PhD diss., Yale University, 1977).

[73]Morales, *Tabernacle Pre-figured*, 202.

[74]Ibid., 129.

[75]Rendtorff, *Canon and Covenant*, 109.

Noahic covenants." He continues by suggesting, "Rather than legitimating a particular political order or dynamic, or a particular theological establishment, by rooting it in creation, the Noahic covenant legitimates *God's* structures of creation for humankind, precisely those that belong to the natural world's capacity and not just humankind."[76]

I would say that God legitimates the structures of creation, and it is for humankind. A stable "platform" is provided on which God enacts redemption. But more precision is needed with regard to what Noachian covenant is being talked about. Are we talking about the covenant made with Noah and his family in the ark (Gen 6:18), or are we talking about the covenant recorded in Genesis 9, after Noah and his family have disembarked?

The Covenant of Genesis 6:18 and Its Relation to the Noachian Covenant (Gen 8:20-9:17)

We turn now to an often overlooked question. Did the earliest reference to *bərît*, "covenant," in Genesis 6:18 refer to Noah and his family only, or did it also refer to humankind outside the ark? Putting the question another way, was it a common-grace covenant made with all humankind, or was it a salvific covenant for Noah and his family alone?

One place to look for the answer is in the literary structure of Genesis 6:13-21. The passage may be divided into two sections, 6:13-16 and 6:17-21, with each section beginning with a statement of God's intentions: "I am going to put an end to all people" (Gen 6:13), and "I am going to bring floodwaters on the earth to destroy all life under the heavens" (Gen 6:17). The first section has to do with the ark's construction; the second section has to do with the ark's occupants. This can be demonstrated pictorially (see fig. 2.1).

---

[76]Patrick D. Miller, "Creation and Covenant," in *Biblical Theology: Problems and Perspectives; In Honor of J. Christiaan Beker*, ed. Steven J. Kraftchick, Charles D. Myers Jr., and Ben C. Ollenburger (Nashville: Abingdon, 1995), 165. To be perfectly fair in representing Miller, he sees "the nations . . . susceptible to the same divine *blessing, mercy,* and *redemption* as is Israel," and cites Gen 17, Jonah, and passages that include other nations in this redemptive activity (e.g., Amos 9:7; Is 19:20), but in doing so he confuses the categories by saying that "the covenant with Noah, therefore, has incorporated the whole creation." At least some of these passages are the outworking of the blessing promised to Abraham and have little to do with the inclusivity of the Noachian covenant.

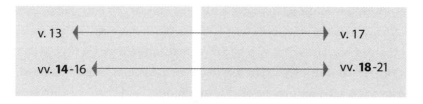

Figure 2.1. Relationship of Genesis 6:13-16 and 6:17-21

Notice the key relationship between verses 14 and 18. Genesis 6:14 says, "So make yourself an ark of cypress wood; make rooms in it and coat it with pitch inside and out." Genesis 6:18 says, "But I will establish my covenant with you, and you will enter the ark—you and your sons and your wife and your sons' wives with you." Verse 18 is a counterpart of verse 14. Note also the contrast between verses 17 and 18, "All will be destroyed, but I will establish my covenant with you; and you shall enter the ark" (author's translation).

So the covenant here is the covenant of salvation, which is narrated in the flood episode. The language in Genesis 6:18 is that of *establishing* a covenant with Noah and his family. The covenantal addressees are Noah and his family, not the whole world.[77] So the covenant described in 6:18 is a redemptive covenant with Noah and his family: by this covenant "God commits himself to save the community that was calling on his name and to bestow on them his holy kingdom, in the ark."[78] The covenant described in Genesis 8:22–9:17 is a nonredemptive covenant, one that is made in order to provide a stable world order in which God can carry out his redemptive plan. It is a common-grace covenant.[79]

However, in Genesis 8:1 we read that "God *remembered* [*zākar*] Noah and all the wild animals,"[80] which clearly shows the fulfillment of God's intentions stated earlier in the Noachian cycle. In other words, at this

---

[77] It used to be thought that this form of the verb, the *hiphil* of *qûm*, was not used for initiating a covenant but rather was employed for the performing of previously assumed covenantal obligations. This view is no longer tenable.
[78] Kline, *Genesis*, 36.
[79] Ibid.
[80] The root *zkr* is used throughout the Bible in terms of fulfillment of a covenant; cf. Ex 6 and Lev 26:41-42.

point God's intentions have been fulfilled, at least in part, *for Noah and his family*, not the whole wide world. As Kline puts it, "What was presented in Genesis 6 as divine purpose is recounted in Genesis 8 as execution of that purpose."[81] The world has been created anew.[82] Indeed, "if the creation account may be read as an exodus from chaos to cosmos, the deluge narrative reads as an exodus from the old creation to the new."[83] This deliverance out of the chaotic waters of the flood foreshadows the future narratives of Zion as the hope of the nations, the city to which peoples will eventually come.[84]

Consequently, this covenant is not the same postdiluvian covenant made with all creation recorded in Genesis 8:22–9:17; rather, it is a covenant that is salvific in nature, made with the community of the covenant, Noah and his family. It is a partial fulfillment of the covenant of grace already described in Genesis 3:14-21.[85] The Noachian remnant in the ark was not the ultimate fulfillment of that initiated covenant of grace but only a type of its eventual and ultimate fulfillment.

It is important not to confuse the covenants of Genesis 6 and 9. The one made with Noah and his family in 6:18 is a sub-administration of the covenant of saving and redemptive grace, and a covenant of common grace is made later with Noah and all the earth (cf. Gen. 9:13, 17). The latter covenant (Gen 9) involved those inside the community of faith and those outside. Not so the covenant of 6:18, which is made strictly with Noah and his family. The benefits of the latter covenant (Gen 9) were strictly secular, not holy, not offering salvation, and not having to

---

[81] Kline, *Kingdom Prologue*, 231.
[82] Morales, *Tabernacle Pre-figured*, 143. I do not have the space to discuss the details of the correspondences between the creation narrative, the flood, and the exodus. For a good discussion of the details, consult ibid., 137-43.
[83] Ibid., 143.
[84] See ibid., 155.
[85] For myself, all historical administrations of the gospel after the fall come under the rubric of this covenant of grace, in which the operative principle is indeed grace. This remains programmatic throughout redemptive history. The fundamental condition to obtain eschatological blessing (i.e., heaven) is faith and remains the same in both the Old Testament and the New Testament; however, there are less general conditions that apply to the temporal-blessing distinctions between the two covenants (the old and the new). See, e.g., the excellent nuanced discussion by Zacharias Ursinus, *The Commentary of Dr. Zacharias Ursinus on the Heidelberg Catechism*, trans. G. W. Willard (1852; repr., Phillipsburg, NJ: P&R, n.d.), 98-100.

do with the holy city of God.[86] A conflation of the covenants of Genesis 6 and 9 creates a confused understanding of the relationship between God's people and the wider culture. Why? The covenant of grace is made with God's kingdom, with a special people who are called to be holy.[87]

Genesis 9 and Common Grace

As we have seen, the Genesis 9 covenant is a covenant of common grace.[88] It is not a redemptive covenant since it is made with all creation. This covenant is a resumption of the covenant of common grace already established in Genesis 4. Since God had destroyed the world, there is a need to reestablish and reassert the interim structures of the world previously founded, especially with respect to restraint against sin. For some authors, this is the vital beginning of law for all humankind, what later writers, using nonbiblical language, will call the "state of nature" from which humanity moves toward becoming civilized or political, especially with the Noachian laws containing respect for animal life and especially human life.[89] This category is vital for a correct understanding of the exodus motif in Scripture. It allows us to answer precisely whether the

---

[86] For an excellent treatment of the Noachian covenant, see David VanDrunen, *Divine Covenants and Moral Order: A Biblical Theology of Natural Law*, Emory University Studies in Law and Religion (Grand Rapids: Eerdmans, 2014), 95-132.

[87] Now, this does not mean that all who are in the ark, or the covenant community, are saved (i.e., elect). Only at the end of time will the circle of the elect and the circle of the covenant community coincide. The sin of Ham (Gen 9:22, 25) would seem to indicate that not all of Noah's household were indeed saved. No, at this time the consummating of the kingdom ark was still only at the level of typological sign.

[88] Some Reformed theologians, though not all, have interpreted this Noachian covenant as a covenant of common grace. This is in distinction from the covenant of grace revealed elsewhere in which God promised salvation to his distinctive, chosen people through the atoning work of Jesus Christ. Some examples of significant Reformed theologians who interpret the Noachian covenant as a covenant of common grace include Herman Witsius, *The Economy of the Covenants Between God and Man: Comprehending a Complete Body of Divinity*, trans. William Crookshank (1822; repr., Phillipsburg, NJ: P&R, 1990), 2:239 (originally published in 1677); Wilhelmus à Brakel, *The Christian's Reasonable Service*, trans. Bartel Elshout (Ligonier, PA: Soli Deo Gloria, 1992–1995), 4:384 (originally published in 1700); Abraham Kuyper, *De Gemeene Gratie* (Kampen: J. H. Kok, 1945), 11-100 (originally published in 1902–1904); Herman Bavinck, *Reformed Dogmatics*, vol. 3, *Sin and Salvation in Christ*, ed. John Bolt, trans. John Vriend (Grand Rapids: Baker Academic, 2006), 218-19 (originally published in 1895–1901); and Kline, *Kingdom Prologue*, 164, 244-46.

[89] See Leon R. Kass, *The Beginning of Wisdom: Reading Genesis* (Chicago: University of Chicago Press, 2003), 173-87.

exodus is foremost a spiritual liberation or a political liberation.[90] Notice that there is no blood transaction in this covenant, unlike the redemptive covenant God made with Abraham.

What is the structure of this passage, and what can it teach us about God's covenantal dealings with humankind? Notice the chiastic structure here: stability in nature (Gen 8:20-22) followed by further specification of the interim stable world (Gen 9:1-7) followed by stability in nature again (Gen 9:8-17). As Kline notes, "Genesis 8:20-22 does double duty; it is the closing section of the deluge narrative and the opening A-section of an A.B.A'-structured record of the postdiluvian covenant of common grace (8:20–9:17)."[91] Moreover, "the *stabilizing of nature* is the subject of the opening (8:20-22) and concluding (9:8-17) sections. The central B-section (9:1-7) presents regulations for the cultural sphere."[92]

This is a covenant not of redemptive but of common grace. It did not bestow a holy kingdom on the people. Rather, this covenant is marked by the regularity of the common world after the judgment of the flood. It is made by the unbloody sign of the rainbow, and, according to Genesis 9:1, it is made with all the earth. This covenant consecrates no one. The central section in this structure (Gen 9:1-7) opens and closes with the family function of procreation, and the central section deals with humans' dominion.[93]

In Genesis 8:22–9:17, God promises a stable, temporal realm of common grace.[94] Notice the importance, once again, of maintaining the distinction between the common-grace order in Genesis 9 from the

---

[90] Such an analysis demonstrates that this is important for public policy from a Reformed perspective. See David VanDrunen, "The Importance of the Penultimate: Reformed Social Thought and the Contemporary Critiques of the Liberal Society," *Journal of Markets and Morality* 9, no. 2 (Fall 2006): 219-49.

[91] Kline, *Genesis*, 41.

[92] Ibid. (emphasis mine).

[93] Ibid.

[94] Kline sums up, "The covenant of Genesis 8:20ff. does not promise the restoration-consummation of the paradise order envisaged as the goal of redemption. It does not produce the everlasting perfection of the blessings of nature but merely provides for a partial and temporary limitation on the infliction of the curses of nature. . . . It does not culminate in the new heaven and earth; on the contrary it is terminated by the final cosmic cataclysm, which it only for a while postpones" (*Kingdom Prologue*, 248-49).

special redemptive-grace covenant announced in Genesis 6:18. If you do not separate these two, there will be confusion in your covenantal analysis between a truly redemptive covenant (Abrahamic) and a nonredemptive covenant (Noachian) and consequently in your systematic theology.

The far-reaching and perpetual language of "everlasting covenant" demonstrates the permanence of these matters. As we are about to discuss the cultural program set forth in these covenants, we have to see their perpetuity until the coming of the final eschaton. We find the same kinds of stipulations and regulations governing the institutions that were put in place back at Genesis 4:15, which was a correlative response of common grace to the common curse discussed at 3:16-19. The importance of the family now emerges in verses 1 and 7 of Genesis 9, again demonstrating the primacy of the family. The new world order that emerges at this point focuses on foundational laws and the rudiments of civil society.[95] Again, we see that it is supplementary. In verses 2-4 the rule for humans to rule over the subhuman creation is reinstated. In verses 5-6 foundational law and the primary responisiblities of a civil society are reinstituted. The charter of the city is given here again; therefore, it is an important passage describing one of the primary responsibilities of the state.

The Covenant of Grace in Redemptive History

The Abrahamic covenant, a manifestation of the covenant of grace, marks a point in which "repeated declarations of these promises and God's oaths of covenant ratification and confirmation dominate this division [11:27–25:11]."[96] The narrative in Genesis 12 offers the solution to the plight of Genesis 3–11.[97] Even so, the covenant of grace is constantly pregnant with all the promises for God's future covenantal kingdom. It was originally pronounced in Genesis 3:15-21, but it comes to the fore again in Genesis 12 and the Abrahamic narratives. Within

---

[95]Kass, *Beginning of Wisdom*, 173-77.
[96]Kline, *Genesis*, 53.
[97]N. T. Wright, *The Paul Debate: Critical Questions for Understanding the Apostle* (Waco, TX: Baylor University Press, 2015), 84.

my own ecclesiastical tradition, the Westminster Assembly (1643–1648) sums it up this way:

> Man, by his fall, having made himself uncapable of life by that covenant, the Lord was pleased to make a second, commonly called the covenant of grace; wherein he freely offereth unto sinners life and salvation by Jesus Christ; requiring of them faith in him, that they may be saved, and promising to give unto all those that are ordained unto eternal life his Holy Spirit, to make them willing, able to believe.... This covenant was differently administered in the time of the law, and in the time of the gospel. ... Under the gospel, when Christ, the substance, was exhibited, the ordinances in which this covenant are dispensed are the preaching of the Word, and the administration of the sacraments of baptism and the Lord's Supper.... There are not therefore two covenants of grace, differing in substance, but one and same, under various dispensations.[98]

Genesis 12 stands over against everything that happened in Genesis 11 (Tower of Babel). In Genesis 12 we read that "all the peoples on earth will be blessed through you," and the ratification of the promise occurs in Genesis 15. The animal is cleft in two, and God passes between the parts to ensure the fulfillment of the covenant (cf. Gal 3; Rom 4). God condescends—not only saying he will do this, but swearing by himself, of which none can swear higher. This covenant is unilateral. God fulfills it, and its sole condition is faith on the part of participants.[99] That does not mean, however, that it is unconditional in its administration. God expects ethical conformity of his elect people, a royal priesthood for whom he secures salvation: "Through an arrangement of divine grace,

---

[98]Westminster Confession of Faith, chap. 7. The text is taken from Chad Van Dixhoorn, *Confessing the Faith: A Reader's Guide to the Westminster Confession of Faith* (Carlisle, PA: Banner of Truth, 2014), 95-102. Van Dixhoorn's book has the most reliable text historically to date. Reformed theologians have understood this covenant of grace to be continuous throughout history after the fall, administered through a series of distinct covenants. These covenants are nonetheless organically related. For example, the covenant initiated at Sinai—in its substance—is part of the administration of the covenant of grace. However, the Mosaic covenant and the Mosaic "economy" need to be distinguished. The same Westminster Confession of Faith, for example, uses the term *law* to refer to the Sinai covenant-administration by way of synecdoche (in which a part is taken for the whole). See Westminster Confession of Faith 25.2, 7.5-6, and Westminster Shorter Catechism 27.

[99]See Westminster Confession of Faith 7.6 (and supporting proof texts, esp. Rom 4:16-17, 23-24) with its accent on the essential condition of faith in the covenant of grace.

not human works, the Abrahamic Covenant entailed human obligations."[100] The Abrahamic covenant has forensic foundations, but ethical conformity to God's holy standards are also important.[101] Building on Herman Bavinck, Michael Horton notes, "The works that believers are called to 'walk in' are the way *of* life, not the way *to* life."[102]

How then do the programmatic chapters of Genesis 1–15 relate to the exodus motif? Even as early as Genesis 15, we have a hint of the exodus to come. For in Genesis 15:13-14 God declares that Abram's people will be afflicted for four hundred years; however, God will redeem them from this slavery through a supernatural act of grace and holy war judgment, all of which is "a prefiguration of the eternal messianic salvation."[103] (See Genesis 9:25-26, where God adumbrates, through a pun, that God will subdue Canaan.)[104] Nevertheless, the covenant must not be separated from creation.

Connecting Creation and Covenant

How should biblical theology connect creation and covenant? The notion that creation is covenantal has been called a "dubious doctrine."[105] But a line of evidence demonstrates that creation is in fact covenantal. Meredith Kline has argued that "man's creation as image of God means . . . that the creating of the world was a covenant-making process."[106] David VanDrunen summarizes the argument:

> For Kline, the very act of creation in God's image entails the establishment of the covenant, with its requirement of obedience and its prospect of eschatological reward or punishment. By separating these two acts, older theologians seemed to be caught on the horns of a dilemma, namely being

---

[100] Kline, *Genesis*, 55.
[101] See Kline, *Kingdom Prologue*, 320.
[102] Michael Horton, *The Christian Faith: A Systematic Theology for Pilgrims on the Way* (Grand Rapids: Zondervan, 2011), 617.
[103] Kline, *Genesis*, 64.
[104] Ibid.
[105] Guy Prentiss Waters, *The Federal Vision and Covenant Theology: A Comparative Analysis* (Phillipsburg, NJ: P&R, 2006), 25-26.
[106] See Kline, *Kingdom Prologue*, 92. The reader interested in pursuing the full argument may find it in Kline, *Images of the Spirit*.

compelled to speak of a natural knowledge of the works principle while feeling constrained to defend the meaningfulness of a covenant relationship that is not simply superfluous. By identifying these two acts, Kline has no such dilemma. God's creating Adam in his image and the establishment of the covenant are aspects of the same act, and thus Adam's image-derived natural human knowledge that obedience brings eschatological life was at the very same time covenantal knowledge of the special relationship that he enjoyed with God.[107]

Creation as a covenantal act is important for several reasons, not least being its eschatological dimension. As Horton argues, "The image is to be understood in this account as an office or embassy, *a covenantal commission with an eschatological orientation.*"[108] Covenant comes to the foreground as well in the creation of the particular people of God during the exodus. "At the heart of the Book of Exodus is the establishment of a special covenant relationship between God and the Israelites,"[109] writes T. Desmond Alexander. God is crafting a special people, a royal priesthood, for himself. (This will become clear when we look at 1 Peter and Revelation.)

Moreover, creation as a covenantal act is important from the standpoint of imagery that recurs throughout the Bible, in both the Old and New Testaments. For example, mountain imagery present in the beginning reoccurs later in the Bible.[110] Eden imagery is evoked in the second-exodus motif of Isaiah and in postexilic texts. There the people God is crafting for himself return to an Edenic place through a way prepared by God—not through the sea, but a highway cleft through the desert.[111] Wilderness imagery, issuing from the creation

---

[107]David VanDrunen, "Natural Law and the Works Principle Under Adam and Moses," in *The Law Is Not of Faith: Essays on Grace and Works in the Mosaic Covenant*, ed. Bryan Estelle, J. V. Fesko, and David VanDrunen (Phillipsburg: NJ: P&R, 2008), 291.
[108]Michael S. Horton, *Lord and Servant: A Covenant Christology* (Louisville, KY: Westminster John Knox, 2005), 104.
[109]T. Desmond Alexander, *From Paradise to the Promised Land: An Introduction to the Main Themes of the Pentateuch* (Grand Rapids: Baker, 1995), 82.
[110]See Bryan D. Estelle, "The Covenant of Works in Moses and Paul," in *Covenant, Justification, and Pastoral Ministry: Essays by the Faculty of Westminster Seminary California*, ed. Scott Clark (Phillipsburg, NJ: P&R, 2006).
[111]T. Stodalen, *Echoes of Eden: Genesis 2–3 Symbolism of the Eden Garden in Biblical Hebrew Literature*, Contributions to Biblical Exegesis and Theology 25 (Leuven: Peeters, 2000).

narrative and the expulsion from the garden, and the pilgrimage theme are both part of the exodus motif as it is woven throughout redemptive history.[112]

But the greatest significance of creation as covenant lies in the interim world structures laid down in these early chapters of Genesis. Although it is true that God sovereignly rules over the entire world, one of the key questions developed early in Genesis is *how* God rules the kingdoms he has established. The structuring of the early chapters is programmatic for the doctrine of two kingdoms: the *regnum gratiae* (kingdom of grace) and the *regnum potentiae* (kingdom of power). The *regnum gratiae* is where God rules over the *ecclesia militans* (the church militant) as its redeemer. The *regnum potentiae*, or the civil kingdom, is governed by God's universal, general, or natural rule over the world and its affairs through the civil magistrate. This is Paul's understanding of civil authority in Romans 13:1-7. All legitimate authority is derived from God, even civil authority.

These distinctions have a long pedigree in Christianity.[113] Bernard Lewis, the doyen of Middle Eastern studies and professor at Princeton, states in a way commanding attention:

> Throughout Christian history, and in almost all Christian lands, church and state continued to exist side by side as different institutions, each with its own laws and jurisdictions, its own hierarchy and chain of authority. The two may be joined, or, in modern times, separated. Their relationship may be one of cooperation, of confrontation, or of conflict. Sometimes they may be coequal, more often one or the other may prevail in a struggle

---

[112]Shemaryahu Talmon, "The Desert Motif in the Bible and in Qumran Literature," in *Literary Studies in the Hebrew Bible: Form and Content* (Jerusalem: Magnes Press, 1993); Richard B. Gaffin Jr., "The Usefulness of the Cross," *WTJ* 41 (1979): 228-46.

[113]See esp. VanDrunen, *Natural Law*. At a more popular level, see VanDrunen, *Living in God's Two Kingdoms: A Biblical Vision for Christianity and Culture* (Wheaton, IL: Crossway). Also see VanDrunen, "Natural Law, Custom, and Common Law in the Theology of Aquinas and Calvin," *University of British Columbia Law Review* 33, no. 3 (2000): 699-717; VanDrunen, "The Context of Natural Law: John Calvin's Doctrine of the Two Kingdoms," *Journal of Church and State* 46 (Summer 2004): 503-25; VanDrunen, "The Two Kingdoms: A Reassessment of the Transformationalist Calvin," *Calvin Theological Journal* 40 (2005): 248-66. See also Paul Helm, *John Calvin's Ideas* (Oxford: Oxford University Press, 2004), 347-88; William J. Bouwsma, *John Calvin: A Sixteenth Century Portrait* (New York: Oxford University Press, 1988), 73-76.

for the domination of the polity. In the course of the centuries, Christian jurists and theologians devised or adapted pairs of terms to denote this dichotomy of jurisdiction: sacred and profane, spiritual and temporal, religious and secular, ecclesiastical and lay.[114]

Thomas Peck (b. 1822), who labored alongside Southern Presbyterian theologian R. L. Dabney for years at Union Theological Seminary and then replaced him as chair of systematic theology, states the key issues laconically:

> Christians are all agreed that Jesus, their Saviour, is King of kings and Lord of lords, not only in the sense that He is the greatest of kings, but in the sense that all earthly kings and lords are subject to His authority. But the question is, whether civil rulers derive their authority from Him, as Mediator, or whether they derive their authority from God, as moral governor of mankind. Christ says that, "His kingdom is not of this world." This is His solemn testimony before a civil magistrate whose authority He recognises. (See John 19:10,11; Rom. 13:1, etc.)[115]

The heart of the issue is the twofold authority or jurisdictional distinctions by which God rules his world.[116]

Understanding God's organization of the post-fall world, so that there are different ends for the church and common culture, for the kingdom of God and the civil kingdom, will help us understand the exodus motif, guiding our interpretation of the exodus along spiritual lines rather than merely political ones.

Conclusion

We have been striving for a "thicker" understanding of the biblical imagery of exodus, in which creation is not separated from the whole. As Schmid states, creation is "not a peripheral theme of biblical theology but it is plainly the fundamental theme."[117] Francis Watson suggests:

---

[114] See Bernard Lewis, *What Went Wrong? Western Impact and Middle Eastern Response* (New York: Oxford University Press, 2002), 98.
[115] Thomas E. Peck, "Church and State," *Southern Presbyterian Review* 16, no. 2 (October 1863): 135.
[116] VanDrunen, *Natural Law*, 67.
[117] H. H. Schmid, "Creation, Righteousness, and Salvation," 111.

Biblical scholars who isolate texts relating to creation from their canonical context are in fact reflecting and reinforcing assumptions and prejudices characteristic of their own particular time and place. . . . They are displaying a tendency, deeply ingrained in modern biblical studies, to emphasize and to exaggerate the boundaries that demarcate one text from another. Within a canonical context, one can afford to be fairly relaxed about textual boundaries, since the significant boundary is that which divides canonical from non-canonical writings.[118]

In the next chapter, we will begin to see how the exodus serves as a significant motif in the Scriptures, starting with the founding event itself, the departure from the iron furnace of the Egyptians.

---

[118]Watson, *Text and Truth*, 267. For a cautionary approach to the theological interpretation of Scripture movement (in which Francis Watson is a key player), see the recent article by Nathaniel Gray Sutanto, "On the Theological Interpretation of Scripture: The Indirect Identity Thesis, Reformed Orthodoxy, and Trinitarian Considerations," *WTJ* 77 (2015): 337-53.

Three

THE EXODUS MOTIF

A Paradigm of Evocation

Come ye faithful, raise the strain
of triumphant gladness!
God hath brought forth Israel
into joy from sadness;
loosed from Pharaoh's bitter yoke
Jacob's sons and daughters;
led them with unmoistened foot
through the Red Sea waters.

'Tis the spring of souls today;
Christ hath burst his prison,
and from three days' sleep in death
as a sun hath risen;
all the winter of our sins,
long and dark is flying
from his light to whom we give
laud and praise undying.

JOHN OF DAMASCUS, TRANS. JOHN MASON NEALE

The exodus is a great story. It draws us in and entices us to sit, listen, and relish a grand narrative. The book of Exodus tells of a leader raised up for the liberation of a downtrodden, captive people through miraculous means and a tyrant getting his comeuppance in the end. It is also about the true King, who takes back his rightful throne in dominion over his blood-bought subjects. This victory is construed along legal lines,¹ but it is also construed along relational lines. Salvation does not come in simple binary terms, either as forensic or as participatory. Both the legal and the relational are crucial.

The conflict in the story is dynamic and constantly unfolding. It is not merely an earthly battle. As we saw in chapter two, the exodus must first and foremost be understood in its cosmological dimensions: "Israel's deliverance is a work of new creation."² Indeed, it recapitulates many of the same themes of creation. However, the story advances with new complexity.³ As we will see in the final resolution of the canonical story in Revelation 21, the outcome is construed according to familial and marriage imagery, an intimate, participatory category with a legal foundation.

In the exodus, one royal king engages in combat with another. The possession of a people is at stake. And the stakes are high: tyranny, oppression, servitude, liberation, the freedom of individuals, and a community are on the line. The honor of kings is in jeopardy. Seated around a campfire with the warm glow of flames and shadows dancing on the trees, we might listen to this story as told by a gray-bearded sage—and we would find it satisfying enough. But there is a sequel to this initial installment. As the story unfolds, we realize it is a story of epic proportions.⁴

The exodus motif is much bigger than merely the liberation of the Hebrews from the iron furnace of the Egyptians. It is about a great king forming a people by bringing them to the very abode of his presence at Mount Sinai, where the "preeminent theophanic revelation of God" occurs.⁵ We see the worldview of the ancients represented here: one must pass through the waters as a trial by ordeal in order to approach the cosmic

---

¹David Daube, *The Exodus Pattern in the Bible* (London: Faber and Faber, 1963).
²L. Michael Morales, *The Tabernacle Pre-figured: Cosmic Mountain Ideology in Genesis and Exodus*, Biblical Tools and Studies 15 (Leuven: Peeters, 2012), 195.
³Warren Austin Gage, *The Gospel of Genesis: Studies in Protology and Eschatology* (Winona Lake, IN: Carpenter Books, 1984), 20-21.
⁴For a transdisciplinary perspective on Israel's exodus from Egypt, see the website Exodus: Out of Egypt, http://exodus.calit2.net/. The international conference on which the website is based was held May 31 to June 3, 2013, in Calit2's Qualcomm Institute at UC San Diego and brought together experts from around the world. I am grateful to my son, Sean, who formerly worked at Calit2's Qualcomm Institute, for bringing the conference to my attention.
⁵Morales, *Tabernacle Pre-figured*, 205.

mountain and worship God.[6] The divine presence lost in Eden becomes the central catastrophe in the biblical drama. The building of the tabernacle according to a model (*tabnît*) as God's presence or dwelling (*miškān*) in the midst of his people at least partially resolves that problem.[7] This constitutes the major theme of Exodus as a book, if not biblical theology as a whole.[8] Also introduced at Sinai is the notion of contingency. The Abrahamic covenant was made on the basis of unconditional promises delivered by God. The Sinaitic covenant, albeit part of the administration of the covenant of grace, by contrast, is radically contingent (see, e.g., Ex 19:5).[9]

Nevertheless, the exodus motif is about more than divine presence. Just as there was an anticipated goal at the beginning of creation in the Garden of Eden, so also there is an anticipated goal for Israel: a gathered people of God, turfed in the presence of almighty God. The goal of the exodus deliverance is not fulfilled at Sinai, where the great King meets with his people.[10] The goal of the exodus is ultimately a deliverance of a people, a "called out assembly," to the Promised Land. To this end the exodus has an ecclesiological purpose, broadly defined.[11] The connection between land, wilderness wanderings, and God's presence must not be severed.

In the Hebrew Bible, of course, the land is Canaan.[12] Within the meganarrative of the Old Testament, that land became forfeit. God

---

[6]Ibid., 1-50, 209.
[7]Ibid., 249.
[8]Ibid., 275.
[9]See the deft comparison by Michael Walzer, *Exodus and Revolution* (New York: Basic Books, 1985), 77-79. As discussed in chap. 2, historically, the Sinai covenant has been defined as part of the administration of the covenant of grace (Westminster Confession of Faith 7.5-6). At times, however, the confessional standards also use the term *law* to refer to the Sinai covenant-administration by way of synecdoche (Westminster Confession of Faith 25.2; 7.5-6; Westminster Shorter Catechism 27).
[10]Morales, *Tabernacle Pre-figured*, 206-9.
[11]Ibid., 196.
[12]Walter Vogels, quoted in R. Michael Fox, *Reverberations of the Exodus in Scripture* (Eugene, OR: Pickwick, 2014), 19, maintains that this very point may be reinforced by a literary chiasm within the early books of the Bible that demonstrates that the giving of the Torah is the climax between Egypt and the conquest of Canaan:
  A Israel in Egypt (Ex 1–10)
    B Passover and the Crossing (Ex 11:1–15:21)
      C Journey in the Wilderness (Ex 15:22–18:27)
        X Sinai (Ex 19:1–Num 10:10)
      C' Journey in the Wilderness (Num 10:11–Deut)
    B' Crossing and Passover (Josh 1–5)
  A' Israel in Canaan (Josh 6–24)

told Israel it would become so (cf. Deut 31:14-22). Nevertheless, God will restore them from their exile (cf. Deut 32), even their continued sense of exile that lasted into the New Testament period. However, even Canaan is not the ultimate goal. The final goal of the exodus deliverance and salvation encompasses something greater than Canaan, the grandest gift imaginable. It is entitlement to the ultimate mountain, the final resting point for the people of God, the world-to-come itself.[13] There the issue of divine presence in the midst of God's people is ultimately resolved.[14]

Frank M. Cross and David Noel Freedman considered the Song of the Sea (Ex 15:1-18), the very center of the book of Exodus, to be a "sort of 'national anthem' of Israel, celebrating the crucial and central event of her history."[15] The Song of the Sea provides a kind of fulcrum between the first and second parts of the book. The Song of the Sea must be viewed against the broader context of the book of Exodus, for the Song tells us what the book is all about.[16] First, it is about God as the true King who is an absolute sovereign. Additionally, it defines for us what constitutes the exodus motif. We will observe reverberations of the ideas presented here throughout the rest of Scripture.

I am primarily interested in seeing the grand story (the meganarrative) of the exodus motif as opposed the various alleged traditions that some

---

[13] Even when God showed Abram the land (cf. Gen 13:14-17) before the Israelites had taken possession of it, God promised that this would be their land "forever" (v. 15). Even as early as this, there was an "intimation of the antitypical level of meaning in the covenant promises; for earthly Canaan is not eternal, but the consummate inheritance of the saints in the new heavens and earth is forever." See Meredith G. Kline, *Genesis: A New Commentary*, ed. Jonathan G. Kline (Peabody, MA: Hendrickson, 2016), 58-59.

[14] See the treatment of Rev 21 at the end of the book.

[15] Frank Moore Cross Jr. and David Noel Freedman, "The Song of Miriam," *JNES* 14 (1955): 237. There are actually two songs in Ex 15, the Song of the Sea (Ex 15:1-18) and the Song of Miriam (Ex 15:19-21), both of which are genuinely archaic poetry, although this notion is challenged recently by Mark Smith (see below). See Cross and Freedman, *Studies in Ancient Yahwistic Poetry* (1975; repr., Grand Rapids: Eerdmans, 1995), 1-45; Thomas B. Dozeman, *Exodus*, Eerdmans Critical Commentary (Grand Rapids: Eerdmans, 2009), 333-44. The relationship between these two songs has received much discussion.

[16] When I refer to the Song of the Sea in this chapter, I am referring to Ex 15:1-21, which therefore includes the Song of Miriam (vv. 19-21).

scholars suggest were collected and sewn together at a later date.[17] In short, the book of Exodus should be read as "theological didactic drama."[18]

Although we will be approaching the book of Exodus from a synchronic canonical perspective, in the interest of establishing the chronological priority of the exodus event for subsequent echoes, it is important to address the composition date for the Song of the Sea. In the first chapter, I introduced the tension that exits between a diachronic and synchronic point of view in hermeneutics and intertextuality. In the next section, I am making an argument on historical and linguistic grounds, that the exodus story is diachronically prior to the many echoes later in scripture that cite, allude to, or echo its significance.

The Importance of the Wilderness Theme

Martin Noth concluded that the exodus was not only the center of the book of Exodus but also the "point of crystallization" of the entire Pentateuch.[19] Nevertheless, after tracing the development of five themes (promise to the patriarchs, guidance out of Egypt, guidance in the wilderness, guidance into the arable land, and revelation at Sinai), Noth posited that the oldest theme, the exodus tradition, was only later joined to the theme of the land, which, according to him, needed a "bridging" theme. Thus the theme of the wilderness wanderings entered the exodus tradition at a final formative stage.[20] From Noth's perspective, the theme of wilderness wandering was not present at the beginning of the composition and was marginalized even in the final form of the Pentateuch. Noth's hypothesis continues to exercise tremendous influence on the interpretation of the book of Exodus.[21]

---

[17] See, e.g., Gary A. Rendsburg, "The Literary Unity of the Exodus Narrative," in *"Did I Not Bring Israel Out of Egypt?" Biblical, Archaeological, and Egyptological Perspectives on the Exodus Narratives*, ed. James K. Hoffmeier, Alan R. Millard, and Gary A. Rendsburg (Winona Lake, IN: Eisenbrauns, 2016), 113-32. Rendsburg deals primarily with Ex 1–14.

[18] Charles David Isbell, *The Function of Exodus Motifs in Biblical Narratives: Theological Didactic Drama*, Studies in the Bible and Early Christianity 52 (Lewiston, NY: Edwin Mellen, 2002).

[19] Martin Noth, *Überlieferungsgeschichte des Pentateuch* (Darmstadt: Wissenschaftliche Buchgesellschaft, 1960), 52. ET: *A History of Pentateuchal Traditions*, trans. Bernhard W. Anderson (Chico, CA: Scholars Press, 1981), 51.

[20] Noth, *History of Pentateuchal Traditions*, 46-62.

[21] Dozeman, *Exodus*, 15.

Others have argued that the wilderness theme plays a more central role in the story. But even here the themes of land and exodus are viewed as disjointed. Thomas B. Dozeman, for example, has argued that the wilderness/pilgrimage theme was not an original component in the plot structure of the exodus but was later inserted by Deuteronomistic editors. Its particular contribution was to separate the element of divine power in the exodus from the outcome of the land inheritance of the Israelites.[22] For Dozeman, the first half of Exodus (1:1–15:21) is about the power of God, whereas the latter half is about God's presence with Israel in the world.[23] The loss of God's presence among his people, the central catastrophe since the fall into sin, has been somewhat resolved in the establishment of the tabernacle. Indeed, there are many literary parallels between God's building of the world as a cosmic temple in Genesis 1 and the microcosmic world of the tabernacle.[24] However, from Dozeman's perspective, the wilderness tradition transforms the story into salvation history.

My own view, in contrast to Noth's and Dozeman's, is that we need to read the exodus event as an orderly and unified story celebrating liberation from the iron furnace of the Egyptians, and this includes, from the start, the wilderness wanderings culminating in the conquest of the land. Within this larger narrative, the poem in Exodus 15 "occupies the fulcrum-point of the book linking the preceding and following sections."[25]

In Walter Brueggemann's terms, the Israelites were going to be "turfed" in the land, and the Jordan represented the boundary of "confidence of at-homeness . . . the moment of empowerment or enlandment, the decisive event of being turfed and at home for the first time."[26] The wilderness theme triggers a transformation to salvation history in which the land is promised to the wandering-in-the-wilderness Israelites. The salvation from the bondage of Egypt has already been accomplished, and

---

[22] Thomas B. Dozeman, *God at War: Power in the Exodus Tradition* (Oxford: Oxford University Press, 1996).
[23] Dozeman, *Exodus*, 44.
[24] See Morales, *Tabernacle Pre-figured*, 250.
[25] Mark S. Smith, *The Pilgrimage Pattern in Exodus*, JSOTSup 239 (Sheffield: Sheffield Academic Press, 1997), 47.
[26] Walter Brueggemann, *The Land: Place as Gift, Promise, and Challenge in Biblical Faith*, Overtures to Biblical Theology, 2nd ed. (Minneapolis: Fortress, 2002), 43.

it is the promise of land that is in view as early as the Song of the Sea. Even at this early stage, the grand story of salvation, with all its constituent parts, is evident, although only in shadowy form.

The goal of the land for the people, the holy abode mentioned in the Song of Moses (Ex 15:13, 17), was probably first comprehended at Sinai but for different reasons than others have suggested.[27] As Brian D. Russell states, "Exodus 15 designates Sinai as YHWH's inheritance and divinely made sanctuary."[28] Although the earliest audience likely understood this to refer to Sinai, in subsequent times and later audiences this national anthem was used for the legitimizing of later, competing Yahwistic shrines.[29] For example, it could be adapted in Joshua 3–5 for Gilgal, and the author of Psalm 78 could extend its use to refer to Shiloh and even Jerusalem, or Zion.[30]

From Sinai to Zion

We see, then, that the reference to Sinai in the Song of the Sea is not static. It can refer to Mount Zion as well. As Jon Levenson puts it, "Sinai was a kind of archetype, a mold into which new experiences could be fit. . . . That mold served as a source of continuity which enables new norms to be promulgated with the authority of the old and enabled social change to take place without rupturing the sense of tradition and the continuity of historic identity."[31] Ultimately, the significance of this movement is that the reader is encouraged to embrace not merely Sinai, but Zion as well, as both a past and future ideal.[32]

In chapter one we saw how Psalm 68 uses an allusion that was moored in the exodus tradition and presents God as a warrior who scatters his

---

[27]See Noth, *History of Pentateuchal Traditions*, 9. He suggested that the P narrative was not oriented toward the land but rather Sinai was the center of this priestly source, and therefore when those editors inserted Ex 19:1 to Num 10:10, this effectively fronted Sinai and made it overshadow later identifications of the mountain references with Zion.

[28]Brian D. Russell, *The Song of the Sea: The Date of Composition and Influence of Exodus 15:1-21*, Studies in Biblical Literature 101 (New York: Peter Lang, 2007), 95.

[29]Ibid., 86-96.

[30]This fits with the hermeneutic discussed in chap. 1 under the topic of *complexus* (see the section "Conclusion: Calvin and Vitringa as Model Exegetes").

[31]Jon D. Levenson, *Sinai and Zion: An Entry into the Jewish Bible* (San Francisco: Harper & Row, 1985), 18.

[32]Thomas B. Dozeman, *God on the Mountain: A Study of Redaction; Theology and Canon in Exodus 19–24*, SBLMS 37 (Atlanta: Scholars Press, 1989), 153.

enemies. Levenson notes an interesting aspect of this shift from Sinai to Zion. In most passages in the Hebrew Bible, when this motif (i.e., God emerging as a divine warrior from a mountain) appears, it is not from Sinai that he comes but from Zion. As Levenson puts it, "The transfer of the motif from Sinai to Zion was complete and irreversible, so that YHWH came to be designated no longer as 'the One of Sinai,' but as 'he who dwells on Mount Zion' (Is 8:18)."[33] For Christians, in light of the quotation of Psalm 68 in Ephesians 4, this movement extends even further: the divine warrior is none other than the Messiah who has come, Jesus Christ.

The Hebrews, unlike their ancient Near Eastern neighbors, were not inclined to represent images visually. Rather, they represented ideas by "painting in words."[34] Thus the Song of the Sea's references to Yahweh's abodes in a mountain/land (Ex 15:13, 17) are highly evocative imagery.

Shemaryahu Talmon demonstrates how this works.[35] In the Hebrew Bible, *har* (mountain) and *midbār* (desert) become antithetical terms, the latter having temporal connotations and referring to the forty years of wandering, a period characterized by disobedience as well as God's guidance and revelation.[36] The former term, *har*, is connected with the Hebrew conception of space.[37] Ancient mythological thought (especially cosmogonies) assigned special significance to unusual places, which were considered unalterably holy. But biblical authors rejected this notion.[38] For them, "there is no place, not even a mountain, which is sacred by itself."[39] What makes unusual places like mountains holy is God's presence. "Mountains represent—not only in Israelite thought— the *axis mundi*, the connecting link between heaven and earth."[40] The

---

[33] Levenson, *Sinai and Zion*, 91.
[34] See Shemaryahu Talmon, "הר and מדבר: An Antithetical Pair of Biblical Motifs," in *Literary Motifs and Patterns in the Hebrew Bible: Collected Studies* (Winona Lake, IN: Eisenbrauns, 2013), 55-76, esp. 56.
[35] Ibid.
[36] Ibid., 60-64.
[37] Ibid., 65.
[38] Ibid.
[39] Ibid.
[40] Ibid., 66. For further development of this symbolism of the cosmic mountain among the Hebrews and other cultures, see Mircea Eliade, *The Sacred and the Profane: The Nature of Religion*, trans.

Hebrew Bible repeatedly represents mountains as the abode of deity (e.g., Hab 3:3; Ps 78:26).[41] Yahweh is even referred to as a "mountain god" in 1 Kings 20:23-28.[42] Subsequently and consequently, "sanctuary" and "mountain" became historically identical.[43] "After all previously chosen places were rejected (Pss 68:15-17; 78:67), God's presence came to rest upon Mt. Zion (Pss 68:17; 78:68; 132:13-18), 'his holy mountain' (Is 11:9; 27:13; 66:20; Jer 31:23; Joel 2:1; 4:17; Zech 8:3; Ps 3:5; 43:3; 48:2; Dan 9:16, 20); 'his own mountain,' which he had created for himself (Exod 15:17; cf. Ps 78:54)."[44] In turn, this becomes eschatologized. An ideal vision developed and coalesced into mountain imagery of a future age.[45] The desert will be replaced by the city of Jerusalem. "Mount Zion takes the place of Mount Sinai as the locale of the new giving of the law (Isa 2:3 = Mic 4:2), and the Davidic king, not Moses, is center stage (Is 11:1-10; Jer 17:14-26; 22:1-4; Hos 3:5; Amos 9:11-15; Mic 5:1-2 etc.)."[46] Furthermore, this theme of presence on the mountain gives way to God's presence in the temple. In later times, when one went up to the temple, it was "*as though* you were 'in heaven.'"[47] Others have argued that the biblical "way" motif points toward the goal of Zion/Jerusalem.[48]

The Unfolding Meaning of the Exodus

With each turn in our exploration of the exodus motif, more meaning unfolds. It is much larger than mere liberation from Egypt. The narrative of escape and liberation from Egypt turns on the fulcrum of the Song of the Sea (Ex 15:1-21) and prepares us for Israel's wilderness journey

---

Willard R. Trask (New York: Harcourt, Brace & World, 1959), 36-59, and Gerhard van der Leeuw, *Religion in Essence and Manifestation* (New York: Harper & Row, 1963), 1:52-55.

[41]Ibid.
[42]Ibid., 67.
[43]Ibid.
[44]Ibid., 67-68.
[45]Ibid.
[46]Ibid., 69.
[47]See N. T. Wright, *Paul and the Faithfulness of God*, Christian Origins and the Question of God 4 (Minneapolis: Fortress, 2013), 96-101, quotation on 97.
[48]See Markus P. Zehnder, *Wegmetaphorik im Alten Testament*, BZAW (Berlin: De Gruyter, 1999), 463ff. However, this point has been criticized recently for not recognizing that Zion/Jerusalem is the addressee in relevant passages, not the endpoint of the "way" (*derek*) metaphor in Isaiah.

culminating at the foot of Mount Sinai (Ex 15:22–18:27).[49] Israel's Sinai sojourn in Exodus 19–40 is a meticulously organized masterpiece that climaxes in the descent of the Spirit on the tabernacle.[50] This in turn adumbrates the descent of God's glory on the Solomonic temple. Against the canonical backdrop of Torah, Moses becomes a new Adam figure. Whereas Adam descended the mountain of God in Eden, with his way back to God's presence barred by the cherubim, Moses is a new Adam entering the "new paradisiacal Presence of God."[51] Adam was barred from God's presence at the glory-filled mountain summit in Eden. Moses alone makes the ascent up Sinai, where the glory of the Lord filled the summit. Moses alone at this particular point is the ascender.[52] This provokes the question, why would the writer to the Hebrews contrast that mountain with something much better, arrival at another mountain? "You have not come to a mountain that can be touched and is burning with fire; to darkness, gloom and storm.... But you have come to Mount Zion, the city of the living God, to the heavenly Jerusalem" (Heb 12:18, 22). After Israel's stumbling fall, who alone will be able ascend the mount of God to provide *the way* into God's presence again so that his people may worship him?[53] Although Moses is the ascender now, ultimately he prefigures Christ, who becomes *the* ascender in the course of redemptive history.

Russell argues that the very structure of the Song of the Sea in Exodus 15:1-21 reflects just such a central organizing function.[54] Verses 1-12 and 19-21 look backward to the events surrounding Israel's liberation

---

[49]For a treatment of "covenant relationship as journey" in the so-called Deuteronomistic History, using a cognitive metaphor model popularized by Lakoff and Johnson, see Michael J. Seufert, "A Walk They Remembered: Covenant Relationship as Journey in the Deuteronomistic History," *BibInt* 25 (2017): 149-71. Seufert develops a network of lexemes used as metaphors to demonstrate covenant relationship as journey.
[50]Morales, *Tabernacle Pre-figured*, 246.
[51]Ibid., 214.
[52]Ibid., 224.
[53]Ibid., 224-31. See also Jonathan Burnside, *God, Justice, and Society: Aspects of Law and Legality in the Bible* (Oxford: Oxford University Press, 2011), 49-50. Burnside develops a nuanced discussion of spatial levels at just this point to demonstrate that the Sinai story is focusing on the one who may ascend.
[54]Russell, *Song of the Sea*, 45-55.

from the oppression of the Egyptians. Verses 13-18 of the Song, however, anticipate the pilgrimage through the wilderness. Therefore, since the Song of the Sea seems to have an internal structure that serves as a microcosm of the whole book of Exodus, it only makes sense to take our cue from the Scriptures themselves as to what constitutes the exodus motif—namely, *both the deliverance from the enemies of Israel in Egypt and the wilderness wanderings as described in the Sinai pilgrimage, which culminate in the arrival at the foot of the mountain of God.*[55] The wilderness wanderings do not play a minor role in the whole exodus complex. They are crucial for understanding the story and theology of the book of Exodus.

Talmon analyzed the occurrences of *midbār* into three geographical areas: grazable land in southern Palestine, borderland between the desert and cultivated land, and the desert proper.[56] John Wright adds a fourth category not covered by Talmon: Judean wilderness with its deep wadis and yet its proximity to major population centers.[57] The wilderness is symbolic for a rite of passage between the exodus and the Promised Land. As Talmon has demonstrated, in the theology of the Hebrew Bible, this wilderness motif denotes a place of punishment and "a necessary transitory state in the restoration of Israel to its ideal mode of life."[58] It is this "betweenness" that is crucial. Other studies have recently confirmed that the Sinai pericope extends all the way to the end of the book of Exodus.[59] Complexity enters the picture when we realize that the wilderness motif gives rise to numerous later symbolic ideas, sometimes seemingly conflicting ones.[60] But the main point here is that the wilderness is a strong trigger for symbolic use later in Scripture.

---

[55] See ibid., 47.
[56] Shemaryahu Talmon, "The Desert Motif in the Bible and Qumran Literature" in *Literary Studies in the Hebrew Bible: Form and Content* (Jerusalem: Magnes Press, 1993), 216-54.
[57] John Wright, "Spirit and Wilderness: The Interplay of Two Motifs Within the Hebrew Bible as a Background to Mark 1:2-13," in *Perspectives on Language and Text: Essays and Poems in Honor of Francis I. Andersen's Sixtieth Birthday, July 28, 1985*, ed. Edgar W. Conrad and Edward G. Newing (Winona Lake, IN: Eisenbrauns, 1987), 269-98.
[58] Ibid., 217.
[59] E.g., see Morales, *Tabernacle Pre-figured*, 208, who is building on the work of Niccacci.
[60] Wright, "Spirit and Wilderness," 273.

The Jewish people have recognized for a long time the importance of this transitional period in the wilderness, for it was memorialized in *Sukkot*, or the Festival of Booths.[61] The desert becomes iconic, "the place where they entered the dangerous sphere of freedom, where 'everything is possible.' The desert represents the time separating what was already given (liberation from Egypt) from what was not yet a reality (the Promised Land)."[62] This will become important for the biblical theological analysis of subsequent books in Scripture that reflect back on the exodus motif.[63]

It is not merely to Sinai that God guided the people whom he was crafting as his own. Sinai represented God's presence to these liberated Hebrew slaves.[64] Being in his presence was one outcome of this remarkable deliverance. Mount Sinai was considered a cosmic mountain, the meeting place between heaven and earth.[65] Sinai was indeed a potent symbol.[66] But God delivered his people from Egypt in order to give them the land that he had promised to Abraham. This is evident from the programmatic statement recorded in Exodus 6:6-8:

> Therefore, say to the Israelites: "I am the LORD, and I will bring you out from under the yoke of the Egyptians. I will free you [*rhyomai*] from being slaves to them, and I will redeem you [*lytroō*] with an outstretched arm and with mighty acts of judgment. I will take you as my own people, and I will be your God. Then you will know that I am the LORD your God, who brought you out from under the yoke of the Egyptians. And I will bring you to the land I swore with uplifted hand to give to Abraham, to Isaac and to Jacob. I will give it to you as a possession [*klēros*]. I am the LORD."

---

[61]See, e.g., James K. Hoffmeier, "'These Things Happened': Why a Historical Exodus Is Essential for Theology," in *Do Historical Matters Matter to Faith? A Critical Appraisal of Modern and Postmodern Approaches to Scripture*, ed. James Hoffmeier and Dennis Magary (Wheaton, IL: Crossway, 2012), 117-18.

[62]Jacques Ellul, *Reason for Being: A Meditation on Ecclesiastes*, trans. Joyce Main Hanks (Grand Rapids: Eerdmans, 1990), 44.

[63]See, e.g., Ulrich Mauser, *Christ in the Wilderness: The Wilderness Theme in the Second Gospel and Its Basis in the Biblical Tradition* (London: SCM Press, 1963).

[64]See Dozeman, *God on the Mountain*, 12-17, for a discussion of the mountain as theological symbol of divine presence.

[65]See the excellent book by Richard J. Clifford, *The Cosmic Mountain in Canaan and the Old Testament*, HSM 4 (Cambridge, MA: Harvard University Press, 1972).

[66]For a discussion of symbol, see O. Ducrot and T. Todorov, *Encyclopedic Dictionary of Sciences of Language* (Baltimore: Johns Hopkins University Press, 1979), 99-105.

It is clear from this passage that "God's deliverance of the Israelites out of Egypt was a *means* to an *end*."[67] I have cited the Greek words of the Septuagint at strategic points in this paradigmatic passage because these will become crucial for later echoes, especially in Isaiah and Paul. The use of ironic allusion to this passage will also become evident in Ezekiel. The Septuagint writers often use *rhyomai* and *lytroō* ("deliver/liberate" and "redeem," respectively) as central terms for expressing God's deliverance from Egypt.[68] Moreover, the land is often called "the inheritance," *klēros*.[69]

Nevertheless, God's goal for the royal priesthood of people that he was erecting as his own was that they would ascend to a much greater end than merely Canaan. God intended to grant them—all those Israelites who believed in a messiah to come and all future believers that believed a messiah had come—entitlement to the world-to-come itself. Second Peter declares, "But in keeping with his promise we are looking forward to a new heaven and a new earth, where righteousness dwells" (2 Pet 3:13). This was the ultimate bliss envisioned by the story: union and communion with God as a "turfed" people. Enlandment was the ultimate goal, and nothing less than world-to-come was meant by that land promise.

This is what the exegetical data suggests and the canonical Scriptures corroborate with regard to the exodus motif. The exodus motif is the course of salvation in miniature. It is a synecdoche.[70] It includes in story format, and with broad brush strokes, the whole matrix of Christian salvation.[71] Of course, Canaan becomes a kind of synecdoche for Zion. "As important as Sinai is in the march, it lies midway between Egypt and Canaan (Zion)," says Michael Horton.[72] Zion, especially

---

[67]Christopher A. Beetham, *Echoes of Scripture in the Letter of Paul to the Colossians*, Biblical Interpretation 96 (Leiden: Brill, 2008), 84.
[68]See ibid., 84-85, for the many references.
[69]See ibid., 84, for the many references. Sometimes *klēronomia* is also used for "inheritance."
[70]Synecdoche is a figure of speech by which a more inclusive term or the material of a thing is used for a less inclusive term or vice versa.
[71]See my "The Art of Synecdoche: Exodus and Conquest in Scripture," in *Modern Reformation* 22, no. 6 (November–December 2013): 28-33.
[72]See Michael S. Horton, *People and Place: A Covenant Ecclesiology* (Louisville, KY: Westminster

Jerusalem, is the goal. More precisely, the new Jerusalem is the goal (Rev 21). The contribution of this book is to suggest that a close-grained reading of the exodus motif throughout Scripture substantiates this very principle: eschatological rest is the final goal, not Sinai alone. If we foreshorten that vision, we confuse the Abrahamic and Sinaitic covenants or miss the essence of human dominion.[73] This view of the exodus motif is a reflection of the foreshadowing in the creation pattern as described in Genesis 1. Just as God worked and achieved an eschatological goal, so humans, created in God's image, are destined toward that goal. As David VanDrunen has written, "If human dominion was meant to resemble divine dominion, then it seems that human dominion must also include working in this world, passing a judicial test, and entering into an eschatological rest."[74]

Viewed structurally and canonically, the central thrust of the Song of the Sea transcends mere political liberation. For the Song climaxes with the proclamation that the Lord is king: "The LORD reigns forever and ever" (Ex 15:18). This is an extremely significant point.[75] The question of who is ultimately the king is a fundamental concern in the Song of the Sea and the exodus motif more generally. The Hebrew root *mlk* (reign, rule) occurs fifteen times in Exodus 1–15, but fourteen of those occurrences are references to the pharaoh as king. As Dozeman states, "Holy war is central for exploring Yahweh's salvific power in the exodus. . . . Throughout the narrative divine strength is measured as a confrontation of wills between Yahweh and Pharaoh."[76] Legal language abounds

---

John Knox, 2008), 290-93, quotation on 292; and David VanDrunen, *Divine Covenants and Moral Order: A Biblical Theology of Natural Law*, Emory University Studies in Law and Religion (Grand Rapids: Eerdmans, 2014), 69-74, who makes a similar point. The point made above is not intended to communicate that the Mosaic covenant is not part of the administration of the covenant of grace, a standard position of Reformed theology to which I cordially adhere.

[73]Horton, *People and Place*, 293.

[74]See VanDrunen, *Divine Covenants*, 72.

[75]Its significance will also be seen in the last chapter of this book, where the point is made that Rev 11:15 quotes this verbatim.

[76]Dozeman, *God at War*, 26. More recently, Dozeman makes the same point: "Exodus 7:8–15:21 narrates the direct conflict between Yahweh and Pharaoh over the fate of the Israelites as a war between kings. The participation of Yahweh in war suggest that the story of the exodus is in the tradition of holy war" (*Exodus*, 176).

in this face-off. As David Daube pointed out years ago, "*Shillaḥ*, 'to dismiss,' 'to let go,' occurs some forty times in the exodus; from 'after that he will let you go,' through 'let my son go' and 'let my people go,' to the second thoughts of the Egyptians after the escape, 'why have we done this that we have let Israel go from serving us?' *This is legal language*."[77] In other words, there is a forensic foundation to this salvation event. The only verbal use of the root *mlk* as applied to Yahweh is the one just cited in the Song of the Sea, and the point seems to be that although there has been a significant threat to Yahweh's sovereign rule, Yahweh alone reigns in reality.[78] This is integrally connected with what I said in chapter two about the Sabbatical patterning of history. Just as the goal of creation was Sabbatical rest under the royal rule of God the king, so the goal of liberation from bondage to this tyrant is rest, which is expressed in worship (Ex 5:1; 7:16; 8:1, 20; 9:1, 13; 10:3). This is important to keep in mind as we trace the use and function of the exodus motif in Scripture. Not only does the kingship of God play a crucial role in this ancient poem, it permeates the Psalter as well.[79] Ultimately the people of God find their rest in the enthronement of God Almighty and the Lamb of God ruling in the midst of his bride (Rev 21:9-10; 22:1-3), which is the eternal community of the redeemed (Rev. 21:2).

Exodus 14-15: Salvation and Song of the Sea

Exodus 14 relates in prose what chapter 15 represents in poetry. The Song of the Sea (Ex 15:1-21) is not merely a disconnected repetition of the narrative story of Exodus 14 but a victory hymn celebrating God's deliverance and salvation. In fact, Exodus 14 constitutes Yahweh's control over the chaotic waters in such a way that it symbolizes Israel's death and rebirth. Morales writes, "Entering the waters, the sons of Israel die; emerging out of the waters, they are reborn."[80] It is death for

---

[77] Daube, *Exodus Pattern in the Bible*, 29.
[78] Russell, *Song of the Sea*, 51.
[79] O. Palmer Robertson, *The Flow of the Psalms: Discovering Their Structure and Theology* (Phillipsburg, NJ: P&R, 2015), 200.
[80] Morales, *Tabernacle Pre-figured*, 203.

the Egyptians but life for the Hebrews.[81] Creation language and themes pervade the book of Exodus.[82]

After the lengthy prose narrative in Exodus 14, the Song of the Sea describes Israel's deliverance within the framework of the archetypal journey: through the waters → to the mountain → for worship.[83] The Song reads as follows:[84]

> I will sing of Yahweh.
> He is highly exalted.
> He threw horse and chariotry into the sea.
> Yah is my strength and my defense.
> He has become salvation for me.
> This is my god, whom I admire.
> My father's god, whom I extol.
> Yahweh is a warrior.
> Yahweh is his name.
> Pharaoh's chariots and his soldiery
> He throws into the sea.
> His chosen troops are drowned in the Reed Sea.
> The abyss covers them.
> They go through the deeps like a stone.
> Yahweh, your right hand prevails in power.
> Yahweh, your right smashes the enemy.
> In your great majesty, you smash your foes.
> You send forth your anger.
> It consumes them like stubble.
> At the blast of your nostrils, streams of water pile up.
> Streams of water gather like a dyke.
> Deeps foam up from the sea's heart.
> The enemy says:
> I will pursue and overtake.
> I will divide the spoil.

---

[81] See the excellent discussion and evidence for this in ibid., 198-205.
[82] Ibid.
[83] Ibid., 46.
[84] The following translation and lineation is that of M. O'Connor, *Hebrew Verse Structure* (Winona Lake, IN: Eisenbrauns, 1997), 179-85.

> My gullet will be full of them.
> I will draw out my sword.
> My hand will dispossess them.
> You blow with your wind.
> The sea covers them.
> They sink like lead through the dreadful waters.
> Yahweh, who is like you among the holy gods?
> Glorious One, who is like you among the holy gods
> Revered with praises, performer of wonders?
> You stretch out your right hand.
> Earth swallows them up.
> You lead in your love the people
> Which you redeemed.
> You guide them in your strength to your holy enclosure.
> The peoples hear. They tremble.
> Terror seizes the Philistine rulers.
> The Edomite chiefs are dismayed.
> Panic grips the Moabite lords.
> All the Canaanite rulers collapse.
> Terror and fear fall upon them.
> They are as silent as a stone in the greatness of your arm,
> While your people crosses over, Yahweh,
> While the people crosses over
> Which you purchased.
> You bring them in and set them up on your hereditary height.
> Yahweh, you made a sanctuary site for your reign.
> Lord, your hands made a sanctuary site.
> Yahweh rules forever.
> Sing to Yahweh.

Why repeat the story in poetry? For Julius Wellhausen, repetition meant contradiction and thus became the impetus for identification of various sources. For others, it has become a unifying characteristic that can also build emphasis in biblical literature.[85] For still others, it becomes a kind

---

[85] J. Muilenburg, "Hebrew Rhetoric: Repetition and Style," in *Congress Volume: Copenhagen 1953*, ed. G. W. Anderson et al., VTSup 1 (Leiden: Brill, 1953): 97-111; Robert Alter, *The Art of Biblical Narrative* (New York: Basic Books, 1981).

of mimesis, a form of repetition grounded in similarity and ultimately in an archetype model, "so that difference is viewed in light of a preestablished identity—a third thing, if you will, which precedes the repetition."[86] The importance of this last suggestion is that repetition—the mimesis—always leads one back to the archetypal model.

Although chapter 14 is written in prose and chapter 15 in poetry, this is not merely a retelling of the prose account in poetic diction.[87] Some scholars have compared the two in terms of alleged differences between a J (Yahwist) source (chap. 14) and P (Priestly) source (chap. 15), but what is a more penetrating approach? The sea crossing may be seen as a new creation or rebirth.[88] It merited, therefore, being memorialized in poetry.

There seems to be considerable telescoping and condensation in the Song of the Sea.[89] We do have an analogue in Judges 4 and 5, the battle against Jabin of Hazor in the days of Deborah and Barak. This pattern corresponds with an Egyptian literary genre from the New Kingdom era, which will become significant for our discussion as we progress.[90] The poem seems to be a response of faith, for the narrative of Exodus 14 ends in verse 31 with the people fearing the Lord (*wayyîrəʾû hāʿām ʾet-yhwh*) and believing in the Lord and Moses, his servant (*wayyaʾămînû bayhwh ûbəmôšeh ʿabdô*). This faithful response on the part of the people is immortalized in song and poetry in chapter 15. The poem is an interpretation of the event itself. In the poetic rendition, there is an emphasis on God as the sole agent of salvation; Moses' agency as recorded at the end of chapter 14 recedes into the background. Although there are differences, there are also similarities between Exodus 14 and 15. Examining the similarities can provide insight into the analysis of the poem. For example, the poetic version describes the double action of the waters. In Exodus 15:8, God heaps up the waters with his breath; his wind is

---

[86]Dozeman, *God on the Mountain*, 149.
[87]Nahum Sarna, *Exploring Exodus: The Heritage of Biblical Israel* (New York: Schocken, 1987), 75.
[88]Morales, *Tabernacle Pre-figured*, 73.
[89]Sarna, *Exploring Exodus*, 75
[90]Ibid. The narratives recounting the epic battle of Pharaoh Ramesses II (1290–1224 BCE) against the Hittites and the battle of Pharaoh Merenptah (1224–1211 BCE) against the Libyans.

powerful and showcases his power and control.[91] In verse 10, God covers the enemies with his breath; the effect of the wind is to congeal the waters. Consequently, reading the texts together, with one complementing the other, is a better reading strategy. One account immortalizes the other in song.

Dating the Song

On linguistic evidence alone, one can plausibly set a date as early as the twelfth century BCE. This is the argument of Russell, although it has been challenged recently by Mark Smith. The language of Exodus 15:1b-18 is not just archaizing but genuinely archaic, according to at least eight criteria.[92] Russell argues that the accumulation of archaic elements is without question. Thus, one can posit a twelfth-century date on linguistic evidence alone. Russell concludes that it is the early Iron Age (Iron I) and therefore reflects a twelfth-century-BCE composition date.

Russell then asks about historical allusions in the Song of the Sea and their possible implications for dating. He claims that not only the linguistic data but also the historical allusions in the Song allow for a premonarchic dating of mid-twelfth century. Four lines of evidence suggest an early date: "archaic grammar and syntax, lack of prosaic particles, the use of staircase parallelism, and phrases and word pairs in common with Ugaritic prosody."[93]

---

[91]Wright comments, "Yahweh is seen as using the wind as an instrument in his plan. However, in the poetic Exod 15:8 it is said of God: 'and with the *rûaḥ* of thy nostrils, the waters piled up.' This anthropomorphism is a basic characteristic of the poem which talks about Yahweh as a warrior, refers to his right hand, wrath, nostrils, breath, and to him as a guide. The return of the waters in Exod 14:28 is simply stated as Moses stretching out his hand and the waters returning and covering the Egyptians. But in Exod 15:10 we read: 'Thou didst blow with the breath (*rûaḥ*), the sea covered them'" ("Spirit and Wilderness," 281).
[92]In this section I draw on David A. Robertson, *Linguistic Evidence in Dating Early Hebrew Poetry*, SBLDS 3 (Missoula, MT: Scholars Press, 1972), whose method uses Hebrew poetry of unknown origin with Ugaritic texts and Canaanite glosses from the Amarna letters on the one hand and standard Hebrew poetry on the other (texts from eighth century or later); especially relevant are pp. 28-38 and 147-56. This is supplemented with material from Russell's *Song of the Sea*. For other bibliography on this important issue, see the noteworthy book recently published by Mark Smith, *Poetic Heroes: Literary Commemorations of Warrior Culture in the Early Biblical World* (Grand Rapids: Eerdmans, 2014), 496-514.
[93]See Russell, *Song of the Sea*, 59-73, quotation on 59.

In Exodus 15:14-16, Philistia, Moab, Edom, and Canaan are the nations that have been affected by God's action. Cross and Freedman have argued that this list of nations allows one to post the twelfth century as terminus a quo and the eleventh century as terminus ad quem.[94] We know that Pharaoh Ramesses III foiled the Philistines' attempted invasion of Egypt in about 1190 BCE. Freedman argues that the twelfth century BCE is the most likely date for the Song of the Sea because it makes the most sense of the data. What about Edom, Moab, and Ammon? While evidence for the entire period is sketchy at best, Cross argues that the reference "chiefs of Edom, leaders of Moab" is warranted for premonarchic periods of these nations.[95] There are some who read Exodus 15:14-16 differently, suggesting that it represents Deuteronomistic thought and is much later (fifth century BCE).[96] The conclusion, although not conclusive, nevertheless "does demonstrate true historical memory of the time, and thus leaves open the possibility of a date near the beginning of the Iron Age."[97] On the other hand, such a claim should perhaps be mitigated by Smith's recent treatment, which will undoubtedly encourage more debate on the issue.[98] In conclusion, on the basis of both the linguistic evidence and the historical references within the Song itself, the data seem to support as very plausible an original twelfth-century date of composition.

So what is going on in the contrast between the Song of the Sea in Exodus 15 and the narrative in Exodus 14? I will follow the suggestion that the Song of the Sea is a *triumph hymn* and is therefore meant to celebrate the actual event of the exodus, especially the overthrow of the Egyptians. This is a Hebrew counterpart of a long line of Egyptian

---

[94]Cross and Freedman, "Song of Miriam," 239-40; Peter Craigie, "The Earliest Israelite Religion: A Study of the Song of the Sea (Exodus 15:1-18)" (PhD diss., McMaster University, 1970), 55.
[95]Frank Moore Cross, *Canaanite Myth and Hebrew Epic: Essays in the History of the Religion of Israel* (Cambridge, MA: Harvard University Press, 1973), 124-25.
[96]See Martin L. Brenner, *The Song of the Sea: Ex. 15:1-21*, BZAW 198 (New York: De Gruyter, 1991), 158-67 and 174-75.
[97]Russell, *Song of the Sea*, 79.
[98]Smith, *Poetic Heroes*, 219-20, concludes, "I am hesitant about dating Exodus 15 to the Iron I or even to the tenth century. This means that old-looking features could continue to be used in Iron II A (tenth-ninth centuries)."

triumph hymns (Thutmose III, Amenophis III, Ramesses II, and Merenptah). Even an Assyrian king (Tukulti-Ninurta I) had a similar triumph hymn. Such triumph hymns are seen later in the Bible as well (e.g., in Judg 4–5 and 1 Sam 18:7, "Saul has slain his thousands, and David his tens of thousands").

The Song of the Sea is a precursor, therefore, to the psalmody and poetry that would become commonplace from 1000 BCE onward.[99] In fact, by the time of David, the Israelites were the cultural heirs to some two thousand years of hymns and psalms in the ancient Near East.[100] There are poems such as Exodus 15 and Judges 5 that spanned the interval between 1200 (or approximately 1500 if one takes an early date for the exodus) and 1000 BCE and following.[101] Think of the literary allusions that reverberate from classical literature into French, English, German, or Italian writers. In fact, the affinities between Ugaritic, Hebrew, and Canaanite Phoenician are even closer.[102]

Identifying Exodus 15 as a triumph hymn clarifies the relationship between the prose account in chapter 14 and the poetic account in chapter 15. This triumph hymn functions as a "Hebrew reply (so to speak) to the proud triumph hymns of the New Kingdom pharaohs that ostensibly adorned the walls of Egyptian temples or were blazoned on stelae in the temple courts and beyond," says Egyptologist Kenneth Kitchen.[103] But we may also ask what further purposes this hymn serves in Holy Scripture.

The Purpose of the Song of the Sea

There are only two places where God is called a warrior in the Hebrew Bible. Exodus 15:3 states: *yhwh 'îš milḥāmāh yhwh šəmô*, "The LORD is a warrior, the LORD is his name." The other occurrence is in the new song of Isaiah 42:13. Thus, Exodus 15:3 introduces us to another important theme in the Song of the Sea and a crucial feature of the exodus motif: the theme

---

[99] See K. A. Kitchen, *The Bible in Its World* (Downers Grove, IL: InterVarsity Press, 1977), 95–100, for a brief outline.
[100] Ibid, 95.
[101] Ibid, 98.
[102] A point ably made by Kitchen in ibid., 98.
[103] K. A. Kitchen, *On the Reliability of the Old Testament* (Grand Rapids: Eerdmans, 2003), 252.

of the divine warrior.[104] This theme is intimately connected with the metaphor of God as king. "The Exodus event itself became an important archetype in the biblical tradition, a means of telling and retelling God's acts of deliverance," say Tremper Longman and Daniel Reid.[105]

The purpose of the Song of the Sea is to exalt Yahweh as the only King.

> You will bring them and plant them in your own mountain,
> [lit., *bəhar naḥălātəkā*, "the mountain of your possession"]
> The place you made to dwell in, O Lord,
> The sanctuary, O Lord, which your hands established.
> The Lord will reign forever and ever! (Ex 15:17-18, author's translation)

This is perhaps the earliest biblical use of this metaphor (i.e., God as King).[106] In light of the essential function in the book of Exodus of the root *mlk*, "to rule/reign," the Song of the Sea is a polemic against Pharaoh's self-proclaimed royal divinity.[107]

The Egyptian concept of *ma'at* ("truth," "justice," or "right") is thrown into disarray by Yahweh.[108] John Currid says, "This was a direct challenge

---

[104]See Kevin J. Cathcart, "The Divine Warrior and the War of Yahweh in Nahum," in *Biblical Studies and Contemporary Thought*, ed. M. Ward et al. (Somerville, MA: Greeno, 1975), 68-76; Edgar W. Conrad, *Fear Not Warrior: A Study of 'al tîrā' Pericopes in the Hebrew Scriptures*, Brown Judaic Studies 75 (Chico, CA: Scholars Press, 1985); Peter C. Craigie, *The Problem of War in the Old Testament* (Grand Rapids: Eerdmans, 1978); Frank M. Cross Jr., "The Divine Warrior in Israel's Early Cult," in *Biblical Motifs*, ed. Alexander Altman (Cambridge, MA: Harvard University Press, 1966), 11-30; T. Raymond Hobbs, *A Time for War: A Study of Warfare in the Old Testament*, Old Testament Studies 3 (Wilmington, DE: Michael Glazier, 1989); Sa-Moon Kang, *Divine War in the Old Testament and in the Ancient Near East*, BZAW 177 (Berlin: De Gruyter, 1989); Martin Klingbeil, *Yahweh Fighting from Heaven: God as Warrior and as God of Heaven in the Hebrew Psalter and Ancient Near Eastern Iconography*, Orbis Biblicus et Orientalis 169 (Fribourg: University Press, 1999); Millard C. Lind, *Yahweh Is a Warrior: The Theology of Warfare in Ancient Israel*, Christian Peace Shelf (Scottdale, PA: Herald, 1980); Tremper Longman III, "Psalm 98: A Divine Warrior Victory Song," *JETS* 27, no. 3 (1984): 256-74; Longman, "The Divine Warrior: The New Testament Use of an Old Testament Motif," *WTJ* 44 (1982): 290-307; Gerhard von Rad, *Holy War in Ancient Israel*, trans. and ed. Marva J. Dawn (Grand Rapids: Eerdmans, 1991); Moshe Weinfeld, "Divine Intervention in War in Ancient Israel and in the Ancient Near East," in *History, Historiography and Interpretation: Studies in Biblical and Cuneiform Literatures*, ed. H. Tadmor and M. Weinfeld (Jerusalem: Magnes Press, 1984), 121-47; and Smith, *Poetic Heroes*.

[105]Tremper Longman III and Daniel G. Reid, *God Is a Warrior*, Studies in Old Testament Biblical Theology (Grand Rapids: Zondervan, 1995), 32.

[106]Cf. Marc Zvi Brettler, *God Is King: Understanding an Israelite Metaphor*, JSOTSup 76 (Sheffield: JSOT Press, 1989).

[107]Cf. Sarna, *Exploring Exodus*, 82.

[108]This point is brought out by John D. Currid, *Ancient Egypt and the Old Testament* (Grand Rapids: Baker, 1997), 118-20.

to the power and sovereignty of Pharaoh: could he maintain *ma'at* or not?"[109] In this understanding, the despoiling event of the exodus provides a literary Janus (hinge or fulcrum) from creation looking into the future. The motif becomes theologically charged, freighted with all kinds of potentialities. This would fit with the evidence that Exodus 1–15 owes much of its literary content and form to the creation account.[110]

Cross, in *Canaanite Myth and Hebrew Epic*, claims that creation theology was not a product of the late history of the Israelites, as Gerhard von Rad and other German theologians thought, but rather arose quite early. From his careful analysis of the Song's language, Cross argues that the Hebrews mythologized historical events on the basis of creation themes in ancient Near Eastern cosmogonies. Above all, he argues, the Hebrews did this in the victory at the Red Sea and immortalized the event in the Song of the Sea.

The combat motif is a subtheme of the larger divine warrior theme introduced in the Song of the Sea. This conflict myth has also been called the "combat myth," or *Chaoskampf* (lit., "chaos battle"). The conflict myth is pervasive throughout the Bible, especially in the Psalms and the Prophets and into the postexilic literature (to be discussed later). Richard Clifford introduces the notion:

> One of the most long-lived genres in ancient literature was the so-called combat myth. It lasted as a live genre into the period of full-blown apocalyptic works and had an enormous influence on them. In fact, the genre provided ancient poets with a conceptual framework for reflecting on divine power and human kingship, on the rise and fall of nations. . . . In early biblical poetry it is found in Yahweh's victory over the Pharaoh at the sea (Exodus 15) or over the sea itself (several psalms). No ideal form of the combat myth exists, of course, but a consistent plot line can be abstracted: a force (often depicted as a monster) threatens cosmic and political order, instilling fear and confusion in the assembly of the gods; the assembly or its president, unable to find a commander among the older gods, turns to a young god to battle the hostile force; he successfully

---

[109]Ibid., 119.
[110]See Meredith G. Kline, *Images of the Spirit* (Grand Rapids: Baker, 1980), 13–42.

defeats the monster, creating the world (including human beings) or simply restoring the pre-threat order, builds a palace, and receives acclamation of kingship from the other gods.[111]

Not only is this combat myth reflected in Exodus 15, but it is also evident in the Psalms, Isaiah 40–66, Zechariah 9–14, Daniel 7, and Revelation 12.[112] It was a standard theme in Israel's surrounding cultures. "Important examples of the combat myth in ancient Mesopotamia are the Sumerian *Lugal-e* of the late third millennium, the Akkadian *Anzu*, extant in both an Old Babylonian and an early first millennium version, and the Akkadian *Enuma Elish*, most often dated to the twelfth century BCE," comments Adela Yarbro Collins.[113] "In these myths a monster, usually described as a composite animal, rebels against the king of the gods. These monsters represent political enemies; the chaos they bring is overcome and the new political order is defined over against chaos."[114] In this combat myth, many patterns and characters are noteworthy. According to Robert Oden,

> this pattern consists of four rounds: (1) a Divine Warrior goes forth to battle the chaotic monsters, variously called Sea, Death, Leviathan, Tannin; (2) the world of nature responds to the wrath of the Divine Warrior and the forces of chaos are defeated; (3) the Divine Warrior assumes his throne on a mountain, surrounded by a retinue of other deities; and (4) the Divine Warrior utters his powerful speech, which leads nature to produce the created order.[115]

While no one biblical account seems to convey all the aspects of this battle, once the pattern and characters are clear, we can see that this pervasive myth and stock language stands behind much biblical imagery that has a cosmogonic tone. The characters are common: "For example, the titles Leviathan, Sea, River, Sea Monster (*tannin* or the like), and

---

[111] Richard J. Clifford, SJ, "The Roots of Apocalypticism in Near Eastern Myth," in *The Encyclopedia of Apocalypticism*, ed. John J. Collins (New York: Continuum, 1999), 1:7.
[112] Ibid., 1:30.
[113] Adela Yarbro Collins, "Apocalyptic Themes in Biblical Literature," *Int* 53, no. 2 (April 1999): 123-24.
[114] Ibid.
[115] Robert A. Oden, "Cosmogony, Cosmology," *ABD* 1:1164.

Dragon (*rahab*) all are used of opponents of Yahweh the God of Israel in settings describing the earlier days of the cosmos."[116] The Bible and the ancient Near Eastern material both speak of "the deep" (*təhôm*). C. L. Seow comments:

> In Babylonian mythology, the deep is personified in the figure of monstrous Tiamat, a goddess whose name is related to the Hebrew word *tĕhôm*. It was upon the defeat of Tiamat that Babylon's patron god, Marduk, was able to create the cosmos and establish order. Tiamat's body was split in two like a shellfish. One half of the body became the firmament, the other became the bedrock of the earth.... The deep is regularly associated with other watery monsters against whom Yahweh fought in both the creation of the world and of God's people: Rahab, Leviathan, River, Sea, Tannin, Mighty Waters.[117]

This manner of speech, so common among the ancients, becomes the garb in which certain biblical narratives cloak their ideas. In Scripture the most prominent use of this mythology of the sea water occurs in the exodus.[118] Instead of straining to find natural-world corollaries with the strange vocabulary we find in Scripture, we would do better reading these ancient texts historically and sympathetically, recognizing the mythopoetic language for what it is. The biblical writers attempted to universalize certain truths by embedding in the narrative mythopoetic language mixed with historical realities. The effect was to give these historical events universal and lasting power. This was the biblical authors' world. This was the language with which they garbed their speech. Nevertheless, even while adopting this language, the Bible demythologizes the ancient cosmologies, root and branch, by substituting Yahweh as the one who destroys the chaotic waters.[119]

The debate over which surrounding culture's literature and ideas were most influential on the biblical material—whether east, such as Sumer

---

[116]Ibid.
[117]C. L. Seow, "The Deep," *ABD* 2:125.
[118]See Dozeman, *Exodus*, 299.
[119]See Meredith G. Kline, *Kingdom Prologue: Genesis Foundations for a Covenantal Worldview* (Overland Park, KS: Two Age Press, 2000), 28-29.

and Akkad, or west, such as the Northwest Semitic sources of Ugarit—continues among scholars. Regardless, these ideas were in the air throughout the region. My own view is that the influence of these ideas probably came via the northwest, from Ugarit.

The Bible's Use of "Myth"

How, then, does the Bible use this combat myth? Bernhard F. Batto's *Slaying the Dragon: Mythmaking in the Biblical Tradition* shows how myth is an influential feature in the ancient world with respect to producing literature. He states, "I use the term *mythopoeic* to refer to that process by which new myths are created or old myths are extended to include new dimensions." Batto defines myth in the following way: "Myth is here defined very broadly as a narrative (story) concerning fundamental symbols that are constitutive of or paradigmatic for human existence."[120] Batto is a good example of a scholar who deemphasizes the historical aspect in the Hebrew Bible. For example, in speaking of the exodus motif, he states, "The exodus narrative, for example, is less a historical account than a mythic reinterpretation of this 'event' as a second act of creation.... The Egyptian host is not so much an earthly enemy as an incarnation of the chaos dragon."[121] Notice that for Batto this event stands outside time. He says, "Sagas and legends take place in past time, in secular time, whereas myths take place outside of secular time. Myth stands outside of time as we know it and serves as the *principle* or source of secular time and order. Myth is paradigmatic for the society in which that myth is operative. Such is the purpose of the Exodus."[122] For Batto, therefore, "at every stage of its transmission the exodus was interpreted and embellished by mythopoeisms, often very deliberately."[123]

The fact that the Bible uses mythological forms and language often causes anxiety for Christians. One reason is that when modern people

---

[120]Bernard F. Batto, *Slaying the Dragon: Mythmaking in the Biblical Tradition* (Louisville, KY: Westminster John Knox, 1992), 11.
[121]Ibid., 3.
[122]Ibid., 123.
[123]Ibid., 126.

hear the word *myth*, they usually equate it with *unhistorical* or simply assume that myth is a projection onto history. What should we make of this phenomenon in Scripture? The challenge, in contrast to Batto, is to see how the Bible interacts with these ancient mythic motifs *while still relating history*. For example, the Bible often interacts in a polemical way with the myths of neighboring cultures. Within the conceptual world of the ancient Near East, mythic features are not divorced from the historical. We can maintain the historical element while still recognizing "mythic" elements in the biblical text.[124] I propose the category of *mytho-historic*. My contention is that Batto's position downplays, often even eliminates, the historical element from the biblical exodus motif. This will become evident when we later turn to Psalm 77.

Mytho-historic is properly descriptive of the biblical material. As I suggested earlier, the historic element is fundamental to the biblical story. Mytho-historic recognizes the presence of certain "mythic" features in a text; however, it does not limit or marginalize the significance of the real historical elements. True history can be communicated in an elevated mytho-historic language. Of course, we do not mean historical in a modern, scientific sense. Consider just one luminary from the past century, who says that Scripture "uses the language of everyday experience, which is and remains always true . . . the language of observation, which will always continue to exist alongside that of science and the academy."[125]

History as common grace is the field of operation for special revelation, or redemptive history, as we saw in our analysis of the Noachian covenant (Gen 8:20–9:17). Sometimes there are real cosmogonic elements worked into the narrative. These must be recognized and described with care. It is true that Israel's history took place in the context of the ancient Near East, and it is important to understand the complex interaction of Israel with her contiguous neighbors and their ideas. Israel

---

[124]See, e.g., C. Stephen Evans, *The Historical Christ and the Jesus of Faith: The Incarnational Narrative as History* (Oxford: Oxford University Press, 1996), 48-66.

[125]See Herman Bavinck, *Reformed Dogmatics*, vol. 1, *Prolegomena*, ed. John Bolt, trans. John Vriend (Grand Rapids: Baker Academic, 2003), 446. The paragraph at the bottom of 445 through 447, the last full paragraph, is worth reading for this point.

engaged in vigorous debates and discussions with its neighbors. As Luis Alonso Schökel puts it:

> If we take as models the undoubtedly mythological texts of the ancient Near-East . . . it is clear that the OT has not admitted myths. . . . The Hebrews do not welcome myths as narratives, but they have no difficulty in incorporating mythical motifs into their lyric texts. . . . The most frequent motif is the struggle of God with chaos as he creates or imposes order on the world.[126]

Often these influences from ancient Near Eastern myth reflect the magisterial account of creation. The creation account is reflected in various ways throughout the entire Exodus narrative.[127] For example, the first five verses of Exodus show familiarity with seventy persons descended from Jacob in Genesis 46:26-27. Genesis 1:28 is reflected in Exodus 1:7. The Tower of Babel in Genesis 11 seems to be reflected in Exodus 1:10-11. The ordeal Moses underwent as a baby in Exodus 2:3, being placed into a pitch-covered basket (*tēbāh*), is similar to the episode of Noah covering the ark (*tēbāh*) with tar and pitch. The exodus is seen as second act of creation (esp. chaps. 13–15), and the "Genesis creation account served as the paradigm for Israel's deliverance at the sea."[128] In Exodus 13:21, divine presence brings light into darkness, which equals day one of creation. The waters are divided in Exodus 14:21 (= day two). The dry land emerges in Exodus 14:29 (= day three). Other examples from the creation narrative include references to Deuteronomy 32:10-11 and Genesis 1:2, which describe the Spirit's creative and protective power as evidenced both in the creation of the world and the creation of God's chosen, particular people.[129] The plagues have been described as a kind of de-creation, reducing order to chaos.[130]

---

[126]Luis Alonso Schökel, *A Manual of Hebrew Poetics*, Subsidia Biblica (Rome: Pontifical Biblical Institute, 1988), 17. See also Elmer B. Smick, "The Mythological Elements in the Book of Job," *WTJ* 40 (1977–1978): 213-28; Smick, "Mythopoeic Language in the Psalms," *WTJ* 44 (1982): 88-98.
[127]Currid, *Ancient Egypt*, 113-20.
[128]Ibid., 114.
[129]Here, of course, Currid (ibid., 114-15) is relying on Kline's *Images of the Spirit* and acknowledges that this is the case.
[130]Ziony Zevit, "The Priestly Redaction and Interpretation of the Plague Narrative in Exodus," *Jewish Quarterly Review* 66 (1976): 193-211.

In the Song of the Sea, there is a past, present, and future orientation as well. The kingly thrust of the Song discloses a major concern of its author, to assert that the Lord alone is ruler, not Pharaoh. Moreover, the author of this poem is confident that God's deliverance will usher them into a temple.[131] This is picked up by 1 Kings 6:1, where the author dates the building of the temple according to the exodus (the only such chronological reckoning in the Bible).[132]

Conclusion

As we have examined the Song of the Sea, I have argued that it serves as a fulcrum between the two halves of the book of Exodus. I have also suggested that the prose account in Exodus 14 should be read together with the poetic account in Exodus 15. They are complementary. We have also seen that the Song of the Sea portends movement from one mountain, Sinai, to others, ultimately Zion. The narrative pattern has been set forth, waiting for further detail to fill in: Egypt–waters–wilderness–sanctuary.[133] This movement is important for the theology of subsequent biblical books.[134] Finally, we considered the mythic elements embedded in the Song and saw that the Hebrews regularly used mythological categories without conceding the historical reality of the events recorded. The Song immortalizes an event that marks, through decisive action, a discriminatory judgment by a sovereign King on behalf of his people.[135] Thus, something transcendent has occurred in history. Something so fantastic has taken place, eclipsing the "normal" workings of history, that only poetry could begin to capture and express the earth- and sea-shattering events that had occurred.

As we turn to the Psalter in the next chapter, we will see that the Hebrews expressed their convictions about their own history in some of their very best poetry. These truths, according to the various writers of the psalms, have great consolatory power for both the present and the future.

---

[131] Sarna, *Exodus*, 81.
[132] Ibid., 82.
[133] Morales, *Tabernacle Pre-figured*, 209.
[134] Ibid., 205.
[135] Kline, *Kingdom Prologue*, 220.

Four

THE PSALMS AND THE EXODUS MOTIF

What the Aeneid was to ancient Rome, Exodus is to ancient Israel.
THOMAS W. MANN

> *They are not monuments, but footprints. A monument only says, "At least I got this far," while a footprint says, "This is where I was when I moved again."*
> WILLIAM FAULKNER

If the Psalms contain some of the richest and deepest theology in the Hebrew Bible and express the whole range of human emotions, then what is their specific contribution to the unfolding nature of the exodus motif? C. S. Lewis, in his *Reflections on the Psalms*, said,

> If the Scriptures proceed not by conversion of God's word into a literature but by taking up of a literature to be the vehicle of God's word, this is not anomalous....
>
> If the Old Testament is a literature thus "taken up," made the vehicle of what is more than human, we can of course set no limit to the weight or multiplicity of meanings which may have been laid upon it. If any writer may say more than he knows and mean more than he meant, then these writers will be especially likely to do so. And not by accident.[1]

That insight by Lewis, outlined in his customary prose, precisely describes what we observe in the Psalter's treatment of the exodus motif.

---

[1] C. S. Lewis, *Reflections on the Psalms* (New York: Harcourt, Brace, 1958), 116-17.

We have seen how the exodus serves as a paradigm for later citation and allusion in the Scriptures. We also noted how the Song of the Sea is a microcosm of the whole book of Exodus and observed how scholars have recently argued that the very structure of Exodus seems to include both the liberation from Egypt and the wilderness wanderings. I demonstrated how important these matters are for the exodus motif. If these things are true, then it makes sense to take our cue from the Scriptures themselves as to what constitutes the exodus motif. The exodus motif includes both the deliverance from the enemies of Israel in Egypt and the broader wilderness wanderings as described in the Sinai pilgrimages, which culminate in the arrival at the foot of the mountain of God. This mountain setting is not mere background.[2] The significance of the mountain setting at Sinai is symbolic. We saw in the last chapter that, more than merely an itinerary stop, the mountain was meant to symbolize a cosmic mountain in the ancient Near East, a place where the divine presence was disclosed and an essential relationship was established between God and his people. However, that reference to the mountain of God, originally understood as Sinai but later applied to Zion, shows movement from one mountain to another. Not Sinai but Zion in Canaan is intended to be the Mount Everest of the exodus motif, at least for the Old Testament. In the New Testament there is further movement, for Zion finds its location in a heavenly realm (cf. Heb 12).

I suggested that the exodus story is a synecdoche for the meganarrative of the entire biblical picture of salvation. Consequently, I proposed a way of reading Scripture that seriously engages the original horizon of the text and the process by which readers understand the meaning of the text in many subsequent horizons. In Kevin Vanhoozer's words, I am emphasizing the process of *intersubjectivity* that occurs when the church reads Scripture.[3] As we observe the unfolding tapestry of the exodus motif, we are engaging in a reading strategy where we observe "both the

---

[2]See Thomas B. Dozeman, *God on the Mountain: A Study of Redaction, Theology and Canon in Exodus 19–24*, SBLMS 37 (Atlanta: Scholars Press 1989), 13.

[3]Kevin Vanhoozer, "Imprisoned or Free? Text, Status, and Theological Interpretation in the Master/Slave Discourse of Philemon," in *Reading Scripture with the Church: Toward a Hermeneutic for Theological Interpretation*, ed. A. K. M. Adam et al. (Grand Rapids: Baker Academic, 2006), 51-93.

interpersonal interaction of the Spirit of God with the human authors of the Bible (inspiration) and the interpersonal interaction of the Spirit of God with the human readers of the Bible (illumination)."[4]

Since the last chapter established that the exodus is the paradigm for later echoes, this chapter will demonstrate how the exodus motif ripples throughout the Scriptures, especially the Psalter. Specifically, we will try to discern how the Psalms evoke the language and memory of the exodus. The influence of the exodus motif on the Psalms is a large topic, so this chapter will be selective. It will serve to demonstrate the kind of analysis of the Psalms that one can perform in light of the exodus motif.

Psalm 114: God Conquers the Sea

Psalm 114 begins, "When Israel went forth from Egypt" (author's translation), leaving no doubt about its roots in the exodus tradition. The verb the author uses, "went forth" (from *yāṣāʾ*), is commonly associated with exodus traditions. Allusions to the exodus can be detected in this psalm as well.[5] In verse 1, Jacob and Israel are listed as subjects. However, in verse 2, Judah and Israel are the subjects, though not as specific people but as geographic areas. (The verb is feminine and is used with a proper name, referring only to cities or countries and not individuals.)[6] Whereas Calvin understood this reference to Judah to be the Messiah, the immediate point seems to focus on conquering the land of Canaan and God establishing his sanctuary. As we have seen, the scope of the exodus motif extends to the Promised Land. Clearly, the first stanza of this psalm has in mind the events of the exodus and conquest.[7] The psalm unfolds as follows:

> When Israel came out of Egypt,
>   Jacob from a people of foreign tongue,

---

[4]Ibid., 76.
[5]Daniel J. Estes, "The Psalms, the Exodus, and Israel's Worship," in *Reverberations of the Exodus in Scripture*, ed. R. Michael Fox (Eugene, OR: Pickwick, 2014), 41.
[6]Stephen A. Geller, "The Language of Imagery in Psalm 114," in *Lingering over Words: Studies in Ancient Near Eastern Literature in Honor of William L. Moran*, ed. Tzvi Abusch, John Huehnergard, and Piotr Steinkeller (Winona Lake, IN: Eisenbrauns, 1990), 179-94, esp. 182.
[7]Tremper Longman III and Daniel G. Reid, *God Is a Warrior*, Studies in Old Testament Biblical Theology (Grand Rapids: Zondervan, 1995), 81.

> Judah became God's sanctuary,
>> Israel his dominion.
> The sea looked and fled,
>> the Jordan turned back;
> the mountains leaped like rams,
>> the hills like lambs.
> Why was it, sea, that you fled?
>> Why, Jordan, did you turn back?
> Why, mountains, did you leap like rams,
>> you hills, like lambs?
> Tremble, earth, at the presence of the Lord,
>> at the presence of the God of Jacob,
> who turned the rock into a pool,
>> the hard rock into springs of water. (Ps 14)

In this psalm God is portrayed as a god who stills the chaotic and tumultuous waters. Language from the conceptual world of ancient Near Eastern mythology is woven into many of these psalms.[8] Since in Western culture the concept of myth in ordinary language usually implies "historically untrue" (as we noted in the last chapter), we need to be careful in dealing with this issue. And the danger sometimes is not saying enough.

As Baal, a god of the Ugaritic pantheon, conquers Yam, the divinized sea, and proceeds to build a palace, so God is portrayed in the Psalms as an omnipotent architect after subduing foes. As Babylonian Marduk, the divine king, conquers Tiamat, the sea monster, and cleaves her in two to build a temple, the Psalms portray God conquering enemies and establishing his chosen, created people in the land.[9] This similarity does not reduce the biblical text to mere myth. Rather, it shows that this was the cultural language of divine action in that day, and the Hebrews were apparently comfortable using such language without accepting all the baggage that accompanied it. Recognizing this helps us appreciate why

---

[8]See, e.g., Bernhard W. Anderson, "Exodus and Covenant in Second Isaiah and Prophetic Tradition," in *Magnalia Dei: The Mighty Acts of God; Essays on the Bible and Archaeology in Memory of G. Ernest Wright*, ed. Frank Moore Cross, Werner E. Lemke, and Patrick D. Miller Jr. (Garden City, NY: Doubleday, 1976), 346.
[9]Geller, "Psalm 114," 183.

the psalmists expressed themselves in the manner they did, and it assists us in understanding how an ancient audience would have heard these psalms when they were recited and sung.

In Psalm 114:3 and following, the poet invokes the literary device of personification. The sea and the Jordan are both portrayed as piling up (personified as obstacles) and as fleeing like enemy forces in battle. The imagery would resonate with the audience as allusions to the historical event of the exodus. This personification works by grouping discrete particulars into a collective notion. The mythopoetic parallels, besides resonating with the ancient audience, drive home the point that the divine sovereign conquers evil and threatening forces on behalf of his people. The Israelites found the sea "terrifying and uncontrollable."[10] They were landlubbers, and the unknown would have added to their fear. Even so, God levels the obstacles before his people, brings forth order from chaos, and establishes his own sanctuary in Canaan, a place where his people may dwell safely.[11] Figuratively, this Promised Land signifies the world-to-come. Here as elsewhere, the mighty divine warrior "reflects a cosmological conflict that is reflected in historical warfare but ultimately reaches its origins in the spiritual realm."[12]

A stark contrast is made in this psalm between the sea fleeing and the land rejoicing because God has subdued evil. The hills now dance in jubilation because God establishes his sanctuary in Judah and Israel.[13] The exodus motif has been pushed forward toward its intended goal: "Israel is a new creation, its formation is a culminating divine act equivalent to the establishment of the cosmos."[14] Earlier we noticed the unmistakable connection between the exodus-redemption of Israel and the obvious allusion to the magisterial creation.[15] The psalm extends this poetically. This supports the notion that the exodus motif is not merely liberation. God is

---

[10] A. A. Macintosh, "Christian Exodus: An Analysis of Psalm 114," *Theology* 72, no. 589 (1969): 318.
[11] Geller, "Psalm 114," 186.
[12] Longman and Reid, *God Is a Warrior*, 78.
[13] Geller, "Psalm 114," 186.
[14] Ibid., 187.
[15] See, e.g., Meredith G. Kline, *God, Heaven, and Har Magedon: A Covenantal Tale of Cosmos and Telos* (Eugene, OR: Wipf and Stock, 2006), 34-35.

making Israel into a new creation. Just as God rescued his people in the past when he came with cosmic disturbances and intervened, so too he comes in the present and future with another intervention. This pattern characterizes how God customarily treats his own people: he has acted on their behalf in the past and stands ready to act on their behalf in the future.[16]

This psalm was the first in a series of psalms known as the Hallel (or Egyptian Hallel) that were used regularly in the celebration of the Passover and were almost certainly sung by Jesus himself at the Last Supper.[17] "When Israel went out of Egypt" is what Jesus experienced as a child, and as we will see when we turn to the Gospels, this exodus is fulfilled by Jesus in the most profound sense.[18] But as we turn to the last psalm of the Egyptian Hallel, Psalm 118, we will be seeing the nexus in this series of psalms between their retrojective look at the Passover and their projective look toward Christ. As Dale C. Allison puts it, "The God of the exodus is also the God of the Promised Land. The point is continuity in salvation-history."[19]

Psalm 118: Gate Liturgy for the Return of the King

In Psalm 118 the references to the exodus are straightforward. On the psalm's original horizon of the ancient Near East, it bears striking similarities with other gate liturgies, especially Babylonian ones. A gate liturgy is a protocol that a king or general follows in order to enter a walled city. Other gate liturgies include Psalm 15 and Psalm 24. An example from the ancient Near East is quoted by Hans-Joachim Kraus: "To perform prostration and prayer, I who had (already) gone down into the grave, entered Esalgila [the temple of Marduk in Babylon] and returned to Babylon."[20] Yet despite some striking similarities between biblical and

---

[16]Claus Westermann, *Praise and Lament in the Psalms*, trans. Keith R. Crim and Richard N. Soulen (Atlanta: John Knox Press, 1981), 97.
[17]Macintosh, "Christian Exodus," 318.
[18]Klaas Schilder, *Christ in His Suffering*, trans. Henry Zylstra (Grand Rapids: Eerdmans, 1938), 282.
[19]Dale C. Allison, *The New Moses: A Matthean Typology* (Minneapolis: Fortress, 1993), 24.
[20]Hans-Joachim Kraus, *Psalms 60–150: A Commentary*, trans. Hilton C. Oswald, Continental Commentary (Minneapolis: Augsburg, 1989), 399. The Babylonian gate liturgy continues:
    At the "Gate of Plenty" superfluity [an excessive amount of something] was given to me.
    At the "Gate of the . . . Protective Deity" my protective deity approached me.

Babylonian gate liturgies, there are also differences. Kraus notes that in the ancient Near Eastern account, "a person who is rescued from death enters the gate to thank his god Marduk. A high official is involved. The rites of the Babylonian cultus [i.e., religion] accompany the act, which begins with a cleansing at the gate."[21] The degree of difference between these two ancient songs will become more evident as we continue.

Determining the original horizon of the psalm is difficult, and many suggestions have been made.[22] However, certain internal features of the psalm are evident. Psalm 118:19-27, for example, makes it clear that the participants here are entering the temple and proceeding to the altar. In verse 27 we read, "Bring the sacrifice, bound, to the horns of the altar" (author's translation). The psalm would have been sung as part of a festival procession on its way to the gates of the righteous (v. 20), or "portal of Yahweh."

The psalm is a kind of victory psalm that was sung following a major military conquest. There may also be significant parallels with other coronation rites found in the ancient Near East, particularly in Egypt.[23] When the participants reached the gate, they had to give a declaration of loyalty and only the "righteous" would pass through the "portals of Yahweh" into the temple (see, e.g., Is 26:2, "Open the gates that the righteous nation may enter"). So the singer of this psalm wants to walk through the "portals of righteousness" (v. 20) to offer thanks for some victory that God had provided.

At the "Gate of Salvation" I beheld salvation.
At the "Gate of Life" I met life.
At the "Gate of the Sun's Rising" I was (again) counted among the living.
At the "Gate of Beaming Wondrous Beauty" my good omens beamed forth.
At the "Gate of Redemption from Sin" my debt was freed.
At the "Gate of Praise" my mouth asked.
At the "Gate of Redemption from Misery" I was released from misery.
At the "Gate of Water Cleansing" I was sprinkled with the water of cleansing.
At the "Gate of Salvation" I met Marduk.
At the "Gate Decorated with Luxuriance" I fell down at the feet of parsimony [frugality]....
    They who had (already) celebrated his burial, now they sat at the meal of joy.
  When the Babylonians saw that (Marduk) had brought him to life, all mouths glorified his greatness.

[21]Ibid.
[22]For details see Andrew C. Brunson, *Psalm 118 in the Gospel of John: An Intertextual Study on the New Exodus Pattern in the Theology of John*, WUNT 158 (Tübingen: Mohr Siebeck, 2003), 23-45.
[23]Othmar Keel, *The Symbolism of the Biblical World: Ancient Near Eastern Iconography and the Book of Psalms*, trans. Timothy J. Hallett (Winona Lake, IN: Eisenbrauns, 1997), 256-68.

Individual and corporate voices intermingle as the main speaker in this psalm. It may well be that the singular "I" (Ps 118:5-21) stands for a larger group. Perhaps the main speaker acts in some representative capacity.[24] Or perhaps more likely, the main speaker was, at least at one time, a royal figure, a king, and he is singing of a literal military victory.[25]

Germane to our purpose is the reference to the Song of the Sea. Just as the Hebrews celebrated God's victory over the Egyptians by singing a song, so this psalm is sung to solemnize God's victory in battle. In fact, Exodus 15:2, "The LORD is my strength and my defense; he has become my salvation," is directly quoted in Psalm 118:14 and alluded to in verse 21 and verse 28 at the psalm's conclusion. Indeed, the statement that "the LORD is a man of war" in Exodus 15:3 is a leitmotif of Psalm 118.

Notable as well is how Psalm 118:16 picks up the wording of Exodus 15:6 with slight adaptation (see table 4.1). These repetitions show us that Psalm 118 is to be read and understood in light of the exodus event.

Table 4.1

Exodus 15:6	Psalm 118:16
Your right hand, LORD, was majestic in power.	The right hand of the LORD is exalted!
Your right hand, LORD, shattered the enemy.	The right hand of the LORD is triumphant!

As noted earlier, Psalm 118 concludes the six Hallel Psalms, which were associated with the Passover meal. On the canonical level, Psalm 118 is quoted more times in the New Testament than any other. As many as thirty-five citations or allusions to Psalm 118 appear in the New Testament, being absent only in James and Jude. Especially significant is the quotation of the psalm in John 12:12-19, a monument to Jesus' triumphal entry into Jerusalem. This influence alone tells us that Psalm 118 deserves our careful attention.[26]

---

[24]Leslie Allen, *Psalms 101–150*, WBC 21 (Waco, TX: Word, 1983), 123.
[25]Brunson comes to the conclusion that this psalm was a "king's psalm, associated especially with the Feast of Tabernacles, which during the monarchy was the royal festival *par excellence*, celebrating Yahweh's kingship and the king's role as Yahweh's representative" (*Psalm 118*, 44).
[26]See Brunson, *Psalm 118*, for details.

Psalm 23: Shepherding to a New Land and a New Covenant

Psalm 23 is a favorite psalm of Christians even though it is not directly cited in the New Testament.[27] It too builds on the exodus motif, albeit much more indirectly than Psalm 118.

Here again we see that the exodus motif is a miniature picture of salvation, a synecdoche for the entire salvation event. Psalm 23 focuses on the relationship between God and his people as it is transacted in the temple. Here we see the immanent presence of the Divine Shepherd setting a banquet and ushering his flock into the Promised Land.

As we saw in chapter one, there is a constant tilt toward originality in literature. The same was true of Hebrew poetry, where we see both a desire to adhere to tradition and an inclination toward originality.[28] Although Psalm 23 (unlike Psalm 118 or Psalm 78) lacks a direct reference to the exodus motif, David Noel Freedman has demonstrated that a new-exodus theme is recognizable in this psalm. He maintains that once we recognize this theme, the tension between two apparently conflicting images—Yahweh as shepherd and Yahweh as divine host—is relieved. Significantly, Freedman points out that the psalm's concluding statement, "And may I dwell in Yahweh's house forevermore," refers to settlement in the Land of Promise.[29] Michael L. Barré and John S. Kselman have extended Freedman's insight with a new-covenant motif. This is based on the common seventh- to sixth-century themes of the "new exodus, the new trek through the wilderness, and the restoration and resettlement in the land."[30] Additionally,

---

[27]The reader may wonder why I do not interpret this psalm as a psalm composed by David. The titles and authorship of the Psalms are a vexed and complex issue. My view is that the preposition *lamed* ("to" or "for") attached to David's name does not necessarily imply authorship. See Peter C. Craigie, *Psalms 1–50*, WBC 19 (Waco, TX: Word Books, 1983), 33-35. For an alternative view, see Bruce K. Waltke and James M. Houston with Erika Moore, *The Psalms as Christian Worship: A Historical Commentary* (Grand Rapids: Eerdmans, 2010), 89-92.

[28]Susan E. Gillingham, *The Poems and Psalms of the Hebrew Bible* (Oxford: Oxford University Press, 1994), 190.

[29]David Noel Freedman, "The Twenty-Third Psalm," in *Michigan Oriental Studies in Honor of George G. Cameron*, ed. L.L. Orlin et al. (Ann Arbor: Department of Near Eastern Studies, The University of Michigan, 1976), 139-66.

[30]Michael L. Barré and John S. Kselman, SS, "New Exodus, Covenant, and Restoration in Psalm

Freedman notes the parallels between Psalm 23 and Psalm 143 (we will return to Psalm 143 when we deal with Paul). The following translation of Psalm 23 by Barré and Kselman sets out the pattern, which demonstrates a new exodus, a new march through the wilderness, and a new covenant restoration:

> Yahweh himself is my shepherd;
>   I lack nothing.
> In grassy meadows he makes me lie down.
> Beside tranquil waters
>   he guides me;
>   he restores my life;
>   he leads me
> in straight paths, for his name's sake—
> even when I walk through the valley of deep darkness[31]—
>   I fear no evil, for you are with me.
> Your rod and your staff—
>   they alone vindicate me.
> You spread a table before me
>   in the sight of my foes;
> You anoint my head with oil,
>   my cup runs over.
> (Henceforth) may only (your) covenant blessings pursue me
>   all the days of my life;
> And may I dwell in Yahweh's house
>   forevermore.

Freedman notes the significance of the verb *rādap*, "to pursue," in Psalm 23:6 and other places in the Hebrew Bible. He concludes that the psalm is meant to communicate divine accompaniment.[32] Barré and Kselman view it as a song of "new exodus and restoration to the

---

23," in *The Word of the Lord Shall Go Forth: Essays in Honor of David Noel Freedman in Celebration of His Sixtieth Birthday*, ed. Carol L. Meyers and M. O'Connor (Winona Lake, IN: Eisenbrauns, 1983), 98.

[31] Even the language of "very deep shadow" is not only "a part of the metaphor of the shepherd," says Craigie, "but again has associations with the Exodus and the wandering through the 'deep shadow' of the wilderness (Jer 2:6)" (*Psalms 1–50*, 207).

[32] Freedman, "Twenty-Third Psalm," 297–98.

Promised Land"³³ and understand the reference to *ṭôb wāḥesed* (goodness and mercy) in Psalm 23:6 as covenantal language, and more specifically new-covenant language.³⁴ The same authors also point out the use of these motifs in light of a reverse of the covenant curses in Deuteronomy 28.³⁵ From this and other ancient Near Eastern evidence, they argue that the psalm has to do with a new exodus, a new march through the wilderness, and a new covenant.³⁶

These conclusions fit aptly with our argument that the exodus serves as the foundation for subsequent biblical allusions. Although Barré and Kselman speak of an "idealization of the old Sinai covenant," I would speak in terms of the fulfillment of the Abrahamic promises and the unconditional promises of the Davidic covenant coming into their own. And I would add that this faithful covenant love is accomplished by a new and better covenant than Sinai: *a covenant with unconditional promises founded on God's grace.* What humans could not do, God will do by his own initiative. The Mosaic covenant is beginning to become obsolete.³⁷

The psalm's goal is settlement in the Land of Promise, but that resting point ultimately is not Canaan but the world-to-come. Its eschatological hope is not only for renewed settlement in a place but also for renewed relationship. As Walter Brueggemann puts it, Psalm 23 "knows that evil is present in the world, but it is not feared. Confidence in God is the source of new orientation."³⁸ This future hope elicits present peace.

---

³³See also Mark S. Smith, "Setting and Rhetoric in Psalm 23," *JSOT* 14 (1988): 61-66. Smith's argument supports the necessity of an exodus typology of the exile and restoration in addition to the exodus-wilderness pattern proposed by Freedman, especially for suggesting a historical datum that accounts for the movement toward the feast and the reference to the temple in v. 6.
³⁴Barré and Kselman, "New Exodus," 104.
³⁵Ibid., 107.
³⁶Ibid., 113-14.
³⁷Barré and Kselman are much closer to the mark in quoting W. L. Holliday: "The old contract is a dead letter; it is in the wastebasket, so God is going to draw up a new one which is different from the old one in crucial respects.... God will draw up a new sort of contract for a new sort of relationship altogether, so that all the old difficulties will be gone and forgotten" (ibid., 115).
³⁸Walter Brueggemann, *Message of the Psalms: A Theological Commentary* (Minneapolis: Augsburg, 1984), 156.

Psalms 78: A Hymnic Recital of the Exodus Sojourn

The date of the composition of Psalm 78 has been variously interpreted.[39] I believe it is thus far unsolved, but there is plausible evidence to date the psalm in the late eighth century BCE.[40]

The literary structure of the psalm is fairly self-evident. Anthony F. Campbell notes that it can be divided into two major recitals with the following structure:

I. Introduction (vv. 1-8)
II. Recital of History (vv. 9-72)
    A. Recital of Rejection (vv. 9-58)
        1. First Recitation: emphasis on Israel's rebellion (vv. 12-39)
        2. Second Recitation: emphasis on Yahweh's deliverance (vv. 40-58)
    B. Rejection of Israel by Yahweh (vv. 59-64)
    C. Recital of Election (vv. 65-72)[41]

Deformation in strict linear order of historical events for theological purposes is evidenced in this psalm as it is elsewhere in the Hebrew Bible.[42]

It is obvious that the first two verses introduce the psalm within the context of wisdom. In verses 1-4, "the thought of the introduction progresses from the identification of the speaker who announces himself as authoritatively retelling the old traditions of Yahweh's glorious deeds to

---

[39] Unless stated otherwise, translations of this psalm following is Michael Patrick O'Connor's, *Hebrew Verse Structure* (Winona Lake, IN: Eisenbrauns, 1997), 263-78.

[40] Brian D. Russell, *The Song of the Sea: The Date of Composition and Influence of Exodus 15:1-21*, Studies in Biblical Literature 101 (New York: Peter Lang, 2007), 127. David A. Robertson, *Linguistic Evidence in Dating Early Hebrew Poetry*, SBLDS 3 (Missoula: Scholars Press, 1972), 150-51, states, "The dating of individual psalms is a most precarious undertaking. Usually all that can be said is that nothing absolutely prohibits a dating in such and such a time; positive evidence favouring such a date is seldom forthcoming." However, he continues, "Positive clues suggesting a date between 930 and 721 can be detected, in at least one Psalm. This is Ps 78. The forms of standard poetic Hebrew are overwhelmingly predominant in it.... The reason for dating Ps 78 between 930 and 721 is the polemic against the northern kingdom which is evident at three places in the psalm." For another detailed analysis on date, composition, structure, and meaning, see Markus Witte, "History and Historiography in Psalm 78," in *Deuterocanonical and Cognate Literature: Yearbook 2006*, ed. Núria Calduch-Benages and Jan Liesen (New York: De Gruyter, 2006), 21-42.

[41] Anthony F. Campbell, "Psalm 78: A Contribution to the Theology of Tenth Century Israel," *CBQ* 41 (1979): 60-61. The outline above is simplified from the more elaborate and detailed analysis in the article.

[42] Witte, "History and Historiography," 27.

the present generation."⁴³ Then, in verses 5-7, the subject changes to the fidelity of the present generation vis-à-vis the infidelity of their forefathers, in this case the Ephraimites described in verses 8-11. This may be a commentary on 2 Kings 17:7-18, a passage permeated with reasons for the failure of God's people. The attitude here up through verse 67 is consonant with the Bible's expressed attitude of the southern kingdom toward the northern kingdom, and some have surmised that this is genuinely reflected here.⁴⁴

The psalm is meant to untangle a riddle, a "parable," which is why it begins in categories that clearly belong to the wisdom tradition. This mystery is untangled when one notes well the wonder, terror, and awe of God working graciously in the midst of the outworking mystery of iniquity among the Israelites. The real mystery of history, according to this psalmist, is God's mercy persisting in the midst of recurring apostasy.⁴⁵

Susan Gillingham has noted that Psalm 78 "offers the most explicit combination of the Exodus and David/Zion tradition in the Psalter."⁴⁶ In the first historical table (Ps 78:12-39), the "miracle of the sea appears as God's primary miracle."⁴⁷ One interesting thing in Psalm 78 is the apparent references to both Exodus 14 and Exodus 15, the Song of the Sea. The psalm seems to cut comfortably across both narrative and hymn. This supports the point made in chapter three that Exodus 15 is a triumph hymn similar to those of the Pharaohs and probably not the product of some later redactor, and that it is integral to the story of Exodus 14 but placed in hymnic form. Therefore, for this psalmist of the eighth century, the narrative and hymn of Exodus 14–15 were already of one piece. Notice that Psalm 78:13 echoes what we find in the Song of the Sea (Ex 15:8):

He split the sea. He brought them across.
He made the waters stand like a dyke [*nēd*]. (Ps 78:13)

---

⁴³Richard J. Clifford, "Zion and David: A New Beginning: An Interpretation of Psalm 78," in *Traditions in Transformation*, ed. Frank M. Cross (Winona Lake, IN: Eisenbrauns, 1981), 131.
⁴⁴Susan E. Gillingham, "Exodus Tradition and Israelite Psalter," *Scottish Journal of Theology* 52, no. 1 (1999): 30.
⁴⁵Ibid., 33.
⁴⁶Ibid., 28.
⁴⁷Witte, "History and Historiography," 31.

> At the blast of your nostrils, streams of water pile up.
> Streams of water gather like a dyke [*nēd*]. (Ex 15:8)[48]

The verb "to split" (*bāqaʿ*), for the parting of the sea, as Campbell says, is otherwise found in Exodus 14:21, and the reference to the waters standing up as a wall provides a "stronger echo."[49] The next verse in the psalm echoes Exodus 14:19-20:

> He led them by day by a cloud. He led them all night by firelight. (Ps 78:14)

> The angel of the Lord, who had gone before the camp of Israel, moved and went behind them; and the pillar of cloud moved from before them and stood behind then and went between the camp of the Egyptians and the camp of Israel. And there was the cloud and the darkness and it gave light at night, and neither one was able to draw near the other. (Ex 14:19-20, author's translation)

These juxtaposed texts nicely demonstrate that the psalmist is cutting across both traditions.[50] The psalm also explicitly recalls the exodus wonders by its references to Zoan (Ps 78:12, 43). This is the name of the city in the delta of the Nile that the Israelites probably worked on (cf. Num 13:22; Is 19:11, 13; 30:4; Ezek 30:14), often called Tanis (cf. LXX, Jerome, and Targums) but also apparently called Rameses (Ex 1:11) or even Avaris.[51] Other references to the exodus appear in these verses as well.[52]

The upshot of these allusions and indeed the whole discussion is the sad irony expressed by the psalm.[53] God has been gracious to them. He has protected them. Sometimes blessing has even been cloaked in curse, but nevertheless God has constantly blessed—yet they still sin against him. The theme of continuously failing to serve God is emphasized in

---

[48]Translations are from O'Connor, *Hebrew Verse Structure*, at 266 and 181.
[49]Campbell, "Psalm 78," 64.
[50]Although Campbell argues for independence of pentateuchal traditions.
[51]See John Goldingay, *Psalms*, Baker Commentary on the Old Testament Wisdom and Psalms (Grand Rapids: Baker Academic, 2007), 2:490.
[52]See Campbell, "Psalm 78."
[53]See Marvin E. Tate, *Psalms 51–100*, WBC 20 (Dallas: Word, 1990), 281-82.

several parts of the psalm.[54] "In [spite] of all this they still sinned and did not believe in his wonders" (Ps 78:32, author's translation). Here the mystery of iniquity is displayed. However, the mystery of God's grace comes right on its heels.[55] Although verse 35 affirms, "He finished their days in a vapor of dismay,"[56] the *vav* conjunction in verse 38 is contrastive, thus speaking of God's compassionate concern for his people despite their recalcitrance:

> But he is compassionate . . .
> He covers [gnomic usage, meaning customary] over iniquity,
> He does not destroy!
> He frequently [Heb. *wǝhirbāh*] turned back his anger
> He stirs up none of his wrath. (author's translation)

What should one conclude from this movement in the psalm? What is the essential difference with what has gone before? Exodus 15 was Israel's faith response, and Psalm 78 picks up the exodus motif and moves it forward, specifically in the sense of covenantal obligations. The movement is expressed through ethical demands based on a certain sapiential understanding. The communicative intent of the psalm seems to be exhortative. They are to remember! As Markus Witte aptly summarizes, "The way leading from Egypt to Zion (cf. Exod 15:13; 1 Kings 8:16; 2 Chr 6:5-6) and from the Torah to the temple is actualized and becomes alive in the process of remembering."[57] Even so, this is remembering that entails making a decision.[58]

Psalm 77: The Past Is for Present Encouragement

Gillingham writes, "At first sight, Ps 77 does not appear to use the Exodus tradition in any obvious way."[59] However, some have suggested it is a communal lament, which suggests a similar crisis to Psalm 78:67

---

[54]Witte, "History and Historiography," 31.
[55]Witte states, "The Psalmist . . . says that insofar as the human being basically tends to sin, God's willingness to forgive and his grace alone enable the human being to survive" (ibid., 33).
[56]Tate states, "The meaning of Ps. 78:33 is probably that of the swift and unexpected end of life, which can happen as quickly as breath. But the idea of futility may also be present" (Psalms, 282).
[57]Witte, "History and Historiography," 36-37.
[58]Ibid., 28.
[59]Gillingham, "Exodus Tradition," 31.

and following, and therefore may have been edited alongside Psalm 78. Others have suggested the first half of Psalm 77 is an individual lament and the second half of the psalm is a hymn.[60] Gregory M. Stevenson notes, "Interpreters do not debate the obvious presence of the exodus tradition in the hymnic section of Psalm 77, yet they typically ignore its presence in the lament portion due to the lack of explicit imagery."[61] The many details binding together the first half of the psalm with the second half suggest that "Psalm 77 is the literary creation of a single poet, drawing on the national traditions of the Book of Exodus."[62] There is also a notable chiasm that cuts across the two parts of the psalm and thus binds it together with a marvelous change in tone at the pivot point:

A (vv. 9-10): The psalmist's questioning of the creedal confession in Exodus 34:6

   B (v. 11): End of the lament: the psalmist's statement that Elyon's right hand has changed

      C (vv. 12-14): Beginning of the hymn: the incomparability of God, whose acts and Wonders in the past serve as the basis for the psalmist's hope in the present

   B' (vv. 15-16): The answer to B (v. 11): God still redeems his people with his mighty arm

A' (vv. 17-21): The answer to A (vv. 9-10): the hymnic theophany shows God to be still the God who redeemed Israel, whom he guided at the sea with his *ḥesed* and who revealed himself to Moses as *rab ḥesed*.[63]

Here the exodus tradition merges with Canaanite mythological traditions found in verses 17-21 (ET = 16-20). "Pharoah and the Egyptians have been completely replaced here as the enemy. Only the sea remains as the object of God's wrath. . . . It was through the lens of the myth

---

[60]John S. Kselman, "Psalm 77 and the Book of Exodus," *Journal of the Ancient Near Eastern Society of Columbia University* 15 (1983): 51-58.
[61]Gregory M. Stevenson, "Communal Imagery and the Individual Lament: Exodus Typology in Psalm 77," *Restoration Quarterly* 39, no. 4 (1997): 227.
[62]Kselman, "Psalm 77," 57.
[63]The chiastic structure is reproduced from ibid., 58.

that the universal meaning of the exodus was revealed to Israelite believers, thereby enabling the exodus to become the primary paradigm of salvation in the Hebrew Scriptures."[64] As noted earlier, the Israelites were landlubbers for the most part and had very little contact with the sea. For the Israelites, the sea, "like the desert, was a non-world, hostile to the populated and the cultivated land."[65] Usually viewed as a hostile threat, the sea only once appears "as an instrument for salvation rather than destruction."[66] Psalm 77 relates its consoling message through such imagery:

> For the director of music. For Jeduthun. Of Asaph. A psalm.
>
> I cried out to God for help;
>   I cried out to God to hear me.
> When I was in distress, I sought the Lord;
>   at night I stretched out untiring hands,
>   and I would not be comforted.
>
> I remembered you, God, and I groaned;
>   I meditated, and my spirit grew faint.
> You kept my eyes from closing;
>   I was too troubled to speak.
> I thought about the former days,
>   the years of long ago;
> I remembered my songs in the night.
>   My heart meditated and my spirit asked:
>
> "Will the Lord reject forever?
>   Will he never show his favor again?
> Has his unfailing love vanished forever?
>   Has his promise failed for all time?
> Has God forgotten to be merciful?
>   Has he in anger withheld his compassion?"

---

[64]Bernard F. Batto, *Slaying the Dragon: Mythmaking in the Biblical Tradition* (Louisville, KY: Westminster John Knox, 1992), 149. This previous point, however, should be understood with regard to my previous critical comments ("The Bible's Use of 'Myth'") in chap. 3.
[65]Ibid., 11.
[66]Ibid., 12.

> Then I thought, "To this I will appeal:
> > the years when the Most High stretched out his right hand.
> I will remember the deeds of the Lord;
> > yes, I will remember your miracles of long ago.
> I will consider all your works
> > and meditate on all your mighty deeds."
>
> Your ways, God, are holy.
> > What god is as great as our God?
> You are the God who performs miracles;
> > you display your power among the peoples.
> With your mighty arm [*zərôaʿ*, cf. Is 51:9] you redeemed [*gāʾal*, cf. Is 51:10] your people,
> > the descendants of Jacob and Joseph.
>
> The waters saw you, God,
> > the waters saw you and writhed;
> > the very depths [*təhôm*, cf. Is 51:10] were convulsed.
> The clouds poured down water,
> > the heavens resounded with thunder;
> > your arrows flashed back and forth.
> Your thunder was heard in the whirlwind,
> > your lightning lit up the world;
> > the earth trembled and quaked.
> Your path [*derek*, cf. Is 51:10] led through the sea [*yām*, cf. Is 51:10],
> > your way through the mighty waters [*māyim rabbîm*, cf. Is 51:10],
> > though your footprints were not seen.
>
> You led your people like a flock
> > by the hand of Moses and Aaron.

God's enemy in this psalm has been personified by the water whereas previously it was the Pharaoh and his minions. Why is this so? What motivates this kind of literary reflex on the part of the psalmist? To answer these questions, we must look at a related matter that occurs time and again in both the Psalms and the Prophets.

As we have noted, the combat motif can be seen as a subplot of the divine warrior motif that was discussed briefly in the previous chapter.[67] The basic outline of the ancient Near Eastern combat myth is this: a battle between "God (Marduk, Baal) and the sea (Tiamat, Yamm, Lothan) establishes cosmic order, the kingship of God, and his right to a palace (temple)."[68] It is evident that the psalmists use mythopoetic language to articulate their ideas, but in such a way that Israel's articulation of these ideas is often one step removed from the worldview of her neighbors: there is adaptation but not wholesale adoption.

Earlier we saw that neither the historical dimension nor the Bible's use of mythopoetic language should be marginalized. For the biblical writer, both elements probably stood in tension. As Frank Moore Cross has noted, "In Israel, myth and history always stood in strong tension, myth serving primarily to give a cosmic dimension and transcendent meaning to the historical, rarely functioning to dissolve history."[69] The distinctiveness of the biblical material seems to take pains to protect the Creator/creature distinction. Scripture is disinclined to cozy up with any view that would make Yahweh part of his creation or in some sense on a par with it, or perhaps even subject to it.[70]

---

[67] I would like to express my appreciation for many of the ideas in this section that a former student, Erik A. Erderma, brought to my attention in his Westminster Seminary California award-winning unpublished student paper, "The Biblical Usage of the Combat Myth in the Psalms."

[68] Jon D. Levenson, *Sinai and Zion: An Entry into the Jewish Bible* (San Francisco: Harper & Row, 1985), 152-53.

[69] Frank Moore Cross, *Canaanite Myth and Hebrew Epic: Essays in the History of the Religion of Israel* (Cambridge, MA: Harvard University Press, 1973), 90.

[70] See Lynn Clapham, "Mythopoetic Antecedents of the Biblical World-View and Their Transformation in Early Israelite Thought," in Cross, Lemke, and Miller, *Magnalia Dei*, 116: "We must recognize and deal with an element in biblical thought which sets it apart from its mythopoetic environment. Although depicted as the Divine Warrior and King, Yahweh is never a manifestation of or encompassed within any part of nature. The notion that the divine transcends every aspect of the universe is always assumed in Israel's treatment of Yahweh's relations with both history and nature. This feature alone radically distinguishes the Divine Warrior in biblical tradition from the same motif in adjacent cultures and produces important consequences. Although Yahweh is free to use the storm wind and associated meteorological phenomena in holy warfare, he stands over and separate from them (cf. Exodus 15), unlike the divine warriors Baal, Marduk, or Zeus.... This means that Yahweh's political hegemony cannot seriously be challenged by one or another power of nature whatever form it may take.... Yahweh's kingship stands above the fluctuations of seasons or cycles in nature. This also means that relations between Yahweh and Israel may take political

Just as some strands in Psalm 78 seem to cut across both Exodus 14 and Exodus 15, so also in Psalm 77 something like this happens again, but differently. Stevenson has argued, "The dilemma of being caught between one's expectations of God and one's perceptions of reality stands at the center of Psalm 77."[71] He appeals to Michael Fishbane's use of retrojective typology (see chap. 1) to justify this claim. "God's role in past events provides a basis for interpreting God's role in present events."[72] Surprisingly, however, this recollection brings not comfort but pain. For Stevenson this psalm of lament helps the individual identify as a "type" of the Israelite slave who is undergoing distress. The psalmist hearkens back to the wonders of the exodus, but bewilderment follows because of God's apparent inactivity in the present distress. In verses 7-10, the heart of the lament, the psalmist muses on whether God has forgotten to show mercy. The tone changes, however, in verses 11-20.

Now we find a perception of reality from the viewpoint of the Song of the Sea (Ex 15).[73] Whereas verses 1-10 had been from the reference point of the slaves in servitude in Egypt, verses 11-20 shift in tone toward hope and faith as represented in the hymn of Exodus 15. Many verbal and conceptual parallels between Exodus 15 and Psalm 77:13-20 support this point. The psalmist reasons that just as God has worked on his people's behalf in the past, so he will deliver them in the present and the future.[74] This reassurance is largely accomplished through recontextualizing personal memory "within the sphere of community memory."[75] This is a common theme in many of the psalms, especially ones that allude to the exodus motif. For example, Psalm 135:8-14 uses the same dynamic, which is to console and encourage on the ground of what God has done in the past, especially through the exodus. Essentially, the same

---

and historical forms of long duration, permitting the structure of covenantal relationships . . . which govern that relationship. It also means that even in those periods of Israel's history in which the imagery associated with the Divine Warrior permitted the strong resurgence of mythopoetic themes (principally the ideology of the monarchy and apocalyptic), the actions of God in the historical continuum provide the important clues for Israel's self-understanding."
[71]Stevenson, "Communal Imagery," 217.
[72]Ibid., 218.
[73]Ibid., 223.
[74]Ibid., 225.
[75]Ibid.

truth comes to the fore: what the Lord has done in former times becomes the hope of God's people, who glory in what he will do in the future.

Although there are strong links between the exodus motif and Psalm 77, Stevenson notes some significant distinctions and differences as well. For example, God's presence recedes into the background in the way that the psalmist refers to God's actions in the past. This is done through the dry-shod motif. Regarding Psalm 77:19, "Your path led through the sea . . . though your footprints were not seen," Stevenson says, "That God delivers his people without visible footprints is of great significance for the psalmist, whose suffering arises from the perceived absence of God."[76] The exodus motif is employed in a nuanced style. Individual lament has been tied to the progression of typology, or figuration. Retrojective typology looks back to the wonders of God as he has performed mighty deeds on behalf of his people. But this has a projective outlook as well, as one turns to the hymnic section of the psalm. The psalmist places himself in the midst of the journey, one grounded in the great exodus event, whose process ultimately leads the faithful out of distress to deliverance and a posture of steadfastness. The past informs the present and the future and instills hope. Faith and confidence in God is engendered even when God is not seen. "God's presence need not always be detectable for his deliverance to be certain."[77]

When times of bewilderment overshadow God's people, they can meditate on his mighty works of the past. And so they redouble their courage for present and future challenges. We now turn to two historical psalms, both closely related to one another.

Psalm 105: Historical Path to the Promised Land

Psalm 105 is clearly to be paired with Psalm 106. Yet despite the similarities between these two psalms, they are quite different in their redemptive-historical perspectives.[78] The psalms balance each other, with Psalm 105 telling the history of redemption, featuring the covenant and

---

[76]Ibid., 226.
[77]Ibid.
[78]See O. Palmer Robertson, *The Flow of the Psalms: Discovering Their Structure and Theology* (Phillipsburg, NJ: P&R, 2015), 174–77.

settlement in the land, while Psalm 106 brings us back to earth with a story of constant rebellion.[79] Psalm 105 is hymnic in style.[80] Claus Westermann calls it an "expanded hymn of the imperatival type."[81] Bernhard Anderson calls it a "storytelling Psalm" (in the mood of hymnic praise).[82] Its cultic context is possibly reflected in 1 Chronicles 16. The psalm is probably exilic, possibly postexilic, and may reflect a provenance of the Babylonian exile.

The order of the plagues in the psalm is strikingly different from the exodus tradition.[83] Noteworthy is the fact that the plagues are represented up to verse 37, and then the psalm switches back to the exodus event itself. Kraus notes the "sovereign rule of God" is a major theme in the psalm.[84] Psalm 105 stands in stark contrast to most postexilic stories about Israel's history from the Second Temple period. There is a smooth progression of Israelite history from Abraham to Moses and then inheriting the land and keeping the law.[85] Other stories showcase constant rebellion and failure on the part of Israel.

Kraus discerns the following structure of the psalm:

vv. 1-6 = introduction

vv. 7-11 = beginning of main section (the leading thought is announced: Yahweh's faithfulness to his covenant and promise)

vv. 12-15 = journeys of the patriarchs

vv. 16-23 = Joseph's destiny

---

[79]N. T. Wright, *Paul and the Faithfulness of God*, Christian Origins and the Question of God 4 (Minneapolis: Fortress, 2013), 118. Or, as Wright says in his more recent book, *The Paul Debate: Critical Questions for Understanding the Apostle* (Waco, TX: Baylor University Press, 2015), "the former [Ps 105] telling the story of the Exodus as a splendid triumph, the latter [Ps 106] going back over the same narrative from (as it were) the seamy side, with Israel constantly getting it wrong" (82).

[80]See Kraus, *Psalms 60–150*, 309.

[81]Quoted in Allen, *Psalms 101–150*, 40.

[82]Bernhard W. Anderson, *Out of the Depths: The Psalms Speak for Us Today*, 3rd ed. (Louisville, KY: Westminster John Knox, 2000), 222.

[83]See for recent treatments, Samuel E. Loewenstamm, "The Number of Plagues in Psalm 105," *Bib* 52 (1971): 34-38; Baruch Margulis, "The Plagues Tradition in Psalm 105," *Bib* 50 (1969): 491-96.

[84]Kraus, *Psalms 60–150*, 311.

[85]Wright, *Paul and the Faithfulness of God*, 137.

vv. 24-38 = the exodus from Egypt

vv. 39-41 = miracles of sojourn in the desert

vv. 42-45 = conclusion (reference to the main theme and admonition)[86]

The exodus motif is prominent in Psalm 105. Consider the following passage:

> Then Israel came to Egypt;
>   Jacob sojourned in the land of Ham.
> He made his people very fruitful,
>   more numerous than their foes.
> He changed their heart to hate his people,
>   to plot against his servants.
> He sent his servant Moses,
>   and Aaron, whom he had chosen.
> They performed his signs among them,
>   his wonders, against the land of Ham.
> He sent darkness; it was very dark;
>   did they not defy his word?[87]
> He turned their waters into blood
>   and killed their fish.
> Their land teemed with frogs,
>   even the rooms [royal chambers] of their kings.
> Swarms of insects [flies] came at his command,
>   lice, throughout their country.
> He gave them hail for rain,
>   and flaming fire in their land.
> He struck their vines and fig trees,
>   broke down the trees of their country.
> Locusts came at his command,
>   grasshoppers without number [lit., "counting, there is not"].
> They devoured every green thing in their land;
>   they consumed the produce of their soil.
> He struck down every firstborn in their land,

---

[86] Kraus, *Psalms 60–150*, 308.
[87] Krauss (ibid.) says not to read this as a question, against H. Schmidt. MT = "They did not resist his words." The Greek text and Syriac clear this up by removing the negative.

> the first fruit of their vigor [power].
> He led them [i.e., Israel] out with silver and gold;
> > none among their tribes faltered [or stumbled].
> Egypt rejoiced when they left,
> > for dread of Israel had fallen upon them. (Ps 105:23-38, author's translation)

It seems that the exodus motif is being used in a new, positive way.[88] Yahweh's covenant faithfulness is expressed in order to awaken a new obedience.[89]

The exodus motif in this psalm does not stop with the Israelites leaving Egypt. The wilderness wanderings and the goal of the Promised Land is incorporated as well:

> He spread a cloud for a cover [i.e., screen],
> > and fire to light up the night.
> They asked[90] and he brought them quail,
> > and satisfied them with food from heaven.
> He opened a rock so that water gushed forth;
> > it flowed as a stream [or even "river"] in the parched land.
> Mindful of [lit., "He remembered"] his sacred promise
> > to his servant Abraham,
> He led his people out in gladness,
> > His chosen ones with joyous song.
> He gave them the lands of the nations;
> > they inherited the wealth [lit., "fruit of"] of peoples,
> In order that they might keep his laws
> > and observe his teachings.
> > Hallelujah. (Ps 105:39-45, author's translation)

There is an emerging connection between Yahweh's royal rule and his dominion stretching beyond the borders of ethnic Israel.[91]

---

[88]Gillingham, "Exodus Tradition," 41.
[89]Kraus, *Psalms 60–150*, 312.
[90]Literally, "he asked," but as the editors note in the critical edition of the Masoretic Text, many manuscripts have the plural and the *vav* could have fallen out by the common scribal mistake of haplography.
[91]Ibid., 312.

Again we see that the biblical writers think of the parameters of the exodus motif as extending from liberation in Egypt to the wilderness wanderings in Sinai that culminate at that mountain before God's presence, and on to the final goal of rest in the Promised Land according to the Abrahamic promises. We now proceed to the companion of Psalm 105.

Psalm 106: Mercy in Spite of Constant Rebellion

Psalm 106 has the longest treatment of the exodus tradition in the Psalter (Ps 106:7-12).[92] The date can cautiously be asserted since Psalm 106:47-48 is quoted in 1 Chronicles 16:35-36, probably during the latter part of the exile, "when a new administration of the empire was taking over and a new generation of 'Judahites' were beginning to become 'the Jews' (*yehudim* in the religious sense rather than in the political meaning of the word)."[93] Scholars have noted the close links between Psalm 106:45 and Joel 2:13 as well.

The psalm presents a checkered grouping of elements; nevertheless, it follows the form of a complaint or lament, as Leslie Allen concludes: "Formally then the psalm can be defined as a communal complaint strongly marked by hymnic features."[94]

Verses 7-46 make up a large historical section and can be outlined as follows:[95]

vv. 7-12 = the exodus tradition

vv. 13-15 = the craving at the feeding of the quails

vv. 16-18 = Dathan and Abiram

vv. 19-23 = the golden calf

vv. 24-27 = the complaining in the desert

vv. 28-31 = Baal Peor

---

[92] Allen, *Psalms 101–150*, 49.
[93] Samuel Terrien, *The Psalms: Strophic Structure and Theological Commentary*, Eerdmans Critical Commentary (Grand Rapids: Eerdmans, 2003), 733.
[94] Allen, *Psalms 101–150*, 50.
[95] The following outline is from Kraus, *Psalms 60–150*, 316, unless otherwise noted.

vv. 32-33 = waters at Meribah

vv. 34-35 = sins at the occupation of the land

The historical section is set within the following framework:

vv. 1-2 = a summons to thanksgiving and praise (hymnic introit)

vv. 3 = felicitation to the righteous

vv. 4-5 = petition (element of prayer song)

vv. 6 = beginning of the penitential song, after which the main historical section begins

v. 47 = petition (like vv. 4-5)

v. 48 = probably to be disassociated with the psalm itself and is tied to the conclusion of the fourth book of the Psalter

As Kraus concludes, in this psalm "the entire history of Israel is viewed as a single vast judgment of the wrath of YHWH which again and again was interrupted by the helpful intervention of God, by an answer to the cry of distress, and by a merciful remembrance of his covenant."[96]

This psalm picks up where Psalm 105 left off.[97] Whereas Psalm 105 was much more positive, Psalm 106 has a negative tone of admonishment. Verses 6-13 work with the confession of guilt, which stands in relationship to Psalm 105. Allen comments, "Both Psalms review Israel's history, but this one presents a reverse side of the coin. Israel, bound to a faithful God and yet herself unfaithful, is called to a deepened self-understanding, to praise and to trembling hope."[98] W. I. Wolverton points out that the psalm is meant "to *induce* lament as opposed *to* lament."[99] It is like an honest sermon, preached not to please but to be faithful to the text. A demand for ethical righteousness is coming to the fore in these latter psalms.

The use of the Egyptian experience to provide a negative archetype together with its echoes in the wilderness period finds partial parallels

---

[96]Ibid., 321.
[97]Gillingham, "Exodus Tradition," 41.
[98]Allen, *Psalms 101–150*, 53.
[99]Quoted in ibid., 51 (emphasis mine).

elsewhere in the OT, notably in Ps 81 and Ps 95, and thence in the NT, in 1 Cor 10:10-11; Heb 3:7–4:11. Paul uses the saga of human failure and divine wrath and abandonment found in the psalm as a pattern for sin worldwide (Rom 1:18-28). The Exodus complex of events had not only a once-and-for-all significance for salvation and election but also a shadow side.[100]

Nevertheless, despite that it was a fait accompli that Israel as a nation would fail in her obedience (cf. Deut 31:16-17; 32:20-21), the psalmist's recounting of Israel's story "frees history from every form of using fatalism as an excuse and of hope that is presumptuously *naïve*."[101]

However, like a crack in a door through which beams of light shine through into a dark room, the psalm's view of the theological meaning of the history opens up avenues of hope. Psalm 106:28-31 presents Phineas as a model of piety.[102]

Conclusion

We began with Psalm 114 and Psalm 118, both from the Egyptian Hallel, which were sung customarily at Passover in the history of Israel. We noted how mythopoetic language and images were used in Psalm 114 along with the powerful literary device of personification. In poetic strokes, the psalmist drove home that God is sovereign and has subdued his enemies. The beginning of the psalm clearly creates the setting of the exodus but extends it into the Promised Land.

In Psalm 118, the most frequently quoted psalm in the New Testament, we observed that a "gate liturgy" (probably penned on the occasion of a might military victory) could be transformed in its canonical context to instruct God's people that Jesus Christ is the true Messiah-King who has defeated the enemies of his people. Like a snowball set in motion, the exodus event generates new layers of meaning. The new

---

[100] Ibid., 55-56.

[101] Angelo Passaro, "Theological Hermeneutics and Historical Hermeneutics in Pss 105–106," in Calduch-Benages and Liesen, *Deuterocanonical and Cognate Literature*, 50.

[102] See the insightful comments by Passaro in ibid., 52-53. Also see Michael Fishbane, *Biblical Interpretation in Ancient Israel* (Oxford: Clarendon, 1985), 397-99. He recounts, "The intervention of Phineas and Moses were exemplars of hope—no matter that for Phineas and Moses the old *traditum* was aggadically transformed. For, as elsewhere, the fate of a *traditum* lies in its *traditio*—the new *traditum*" (399).

exodus is fulfilled in the person and work of Jesus Christ, and that event far outstrips the miraculous wonders of even the first exodus.

Turning then to the beloved Psalm 23, we noted that Yahweh is painted in images of the divine shepherd and divine banquet host. Two apparently conflicting images actually give way to the image of a new exodus and settlement in the Land of Promise. The themes of new exodus, restoration, and new covenant are prominent, with the old covenant fading as the people's obedience wanes. Thus, the new covenant is beginning to emerge as the solution to the people's sin and breach of their covenantal relations.

In Psalm 78 we noted significant influence of the exodus motif, but the Scriptures have moved the use of the motif forward. Not only is there significant historical recollection, but the motif has also now become eschatologically charged. Israel is enjoined not to behave like her forefathers who forgot the wondrous acts of God and God's gracious disposition despite their former recalcitrance. Psalm 77 contributes a distinctive as a companion to Psalm 78. An individual lamenting is identified with the corporate past sufferings of Israel. God delivers them safely through the sea, his footsteps dry-shod and unnoticeable. Pharaoh and his army are now personified in the Sea, running in defeat before the powerful sovereignty of the Lord. In this we see a strong reflection of the mythological combat motif. This mythopoetic language universalizes the themes, especially that of the Sea as the enemy. Even so, here as elsewhere, Yahweh is portrayed as the divine Sovereign, and the psalmist demonstrates that all enemies flee from him and the creation dances and rejoices at the victory. Psalms 105 and 106 are complementary, two sides of a coin, both commenting on the history of Israel. Whereas Psalm 105 expresses a tone that might be characterized as more positive, Psalm 106 expresses that darkness of Israel's constant rebellion: despite God's constant graciousness, she returns to her waywardness time and time again.

In sum, the exodus motif is reworked and transformed into something new and significant. And the Psalms adumbrate that which is even more manifest in the Prophets as the motif is advanced further into the history of redemption.

Five

ISAIAH'S RHAPSODY

There is vaulting hope in these chapters [of Isaiah]. From first (40:1-11) to last (65:17-25; 66:10-14) there runs through them an overtone of joy like the strains of triumphant music. The pages are suffused with light— light rising from the sun (60:1-3). It is as if the hell and horror had been left behind, and one is moving up a high, sun-drenched summit to the very doors of the Kingdom of God. There is good news to tell (40:9-11; 52:1-12): the night of humiliation has ended, a glorious future lies ahead.

JOHN BRIGHT

Isaiah 40–55 is the linchpin in the relationship between the exodus motif and its development into the new exodus that blooms like spring in the New Testament. We observed hints of the relationship between the exodus and the new exodus in the last chapter, especially with Psalm 118. These chapters of Isaiah have been called the "poetic zenith" of the Old Testament.[1] There is no prophetic text more profoundly evocative of Israel's traditions yet with almost no reference to the Mosaic covenant at Sinai! Claus Westermann went so far as to say, "The place which Deutero-Isaiah gives to the Exodus is so conspicuous that all the other events in Israel's history recede into the background."[2] No prophet gives more prominence to the theme of a second exodus.[3] We shall call this the "Isaianic new exodus."

---

[1] John I. Durham, "Isaiah 40–55: A New Creation, a New Exodus, a New Messiah," in *The Yahweh/Baal Confrontation and Other Studies in Biblical Literature: Essays in Honour of Emmett Willard Hamrick*, ed. Julia M. O'Brien and Fred L. Horton Jr., Studies in the Bible and Early Christianity 35 (Lewiston, NY: Edwin Mellen, 1995), 47.
[2] Claus Westermann, *Isaiah 40–66*, OTL (Philadelphia: Westminster, 1969), 22.
[3] Tremper Longman III, *How to Read Exodus* (Downers Grove, IL: IVP Academic, 2009), 148.

In this chapter, I will show not only how the exodus motif is invoked frequently in Isaiah, as in the Psalms, but also how it is transformed. We can speak of the exodus motif being "eschatologized,"[4] or reworked to describe something in the future: a new creative event. That is, the ingathering of foreign peoples that redefine the people of God, and thus the actual transforming the redemptive story so that God now accomplishes his goals in a hitherto unexpected way.[5]

Isaiah 40–55 is sometimes called the Book of Consolation since its main concern is God's taking pains to reassure his people that he has not forgotten them (cf. Is 40:27–31) nor their way (*derek*). Indeed, God responds to the plight of his people, who find themselves in a "way-less wilderness."[6]

This chapter will not address the thorny issue of whether various sections of Isaiah represent different editors' work. I will refer to the text simply as Isaiah or Isaiah 40–55 and not as Deutero-Isaiah.[7] I am not convinced of a notion of a "third Isaiah" that covers the span of Isaiah 56–66 and that grew out of redaction work on a nucleus of chapters 60–62. Indeed, Shalom Paul has amassed formidable evidence to refute the notion that two different prophets or editors are responsible for Isaiah 40–55 and 56–66.[8]

There is voluminous literature on the "way" motif as it relates to the second exodus.[9] The lexical field for the "way" metaphors varies from

---

[4]See David W. Pao, *Acts and the Isaianic New Exodus* (Grand Rapids: Baker Academic, 2002), 55-59; also Rikki E. Watts's book based on his dissertation, *Isaiah's New Exodus in Mark* (Grand Rapids: Baker Academic, 1997).
[5]For a list of the ways in which creation themes, the flood, and other themes from Israel's epic traditions—including the exodus—deeply influence and serve as a model for the exodus from Babylon, see Shalom M. Paul, *Isaiah 40–66: Translation and Commentary*, Eerdmans Critical Commentary (Grand Rapids: Eerdmans, 2012), 44-46.
[6]Øystein Lund, *Way Metaphors and Way Topics in Isaiah 40–55*, FAT 28 (Tübingen: Mohr Siebeck, 2007), 144.
[7]Some references may be made to other sections of Isaiah in this chapter but only in an ancillary fashion.
[8]Shalom M. Paul, "Is There a Trito-Isaiah?" (paper presented at the Annual Meeting of the Society of Biblical Literature, November 2014). See also Paul, *Isaiah 40–66*, 5-12.
[9]For one of the best surveys of recent literature on this subject in English, the reader may consult Lund, *Way Metaphors*, 3-27. Lund is concerned with both the historicity of the concept and the metaphoricity of the concept in his monograph, with particular attention dedicated to the imagery used in Isaiah 40–55 and the pragmatics of the text. I could have chosen to deal more comprehensively with this topic, e.g., by including such works as Markus P. Zehnder, *Wegmetaphorik im Alten Testament*, BZAW (Berlin: De Gruyter, 1999), who has done the most extensive and systematic

scholar to scholar somewhat, though there is much agreement and overlap among these accounts. The most common word is *derek* (occurring 710 times in the Hebrew Bible), which can be used in both a literal and figurative sense.[10] Other Hebrew words such as *'ōraḥ* (second most frequent with 57 occurrences) and *məsillāh/maslûl* (third most frequent), as well as other less frequently used words, make up the lexical field.[11] We will consider only the most frequently occurring words, which are the only ones in Isaiah 40–55.[12] Indeed, in the translations below, the significant "way" lexemes will be highlighted in Hebrew transliterations when it is helpful for the discussion.

We will see that far from being a mere repetition of the exodus motif, the original exodus has become the means for exhorting and encouraging the exilic Jews in Babylon. While in the past these sixteen chapters of Isaiah have been underappreciated for their metaphorical quality,[13] in recent years their poetry has been scrutinized as a treasure trove of metaphorical riches. Fundamental to this is the "way" metaphor,[14] which would have been easily recognized by ancient Hebrew audiences.[15] And while this consensus has not gone unchallenged,[16] recent studies have

---

work on the lexical field associated with "the way" as it is found in the Bible. However, I have been selective in choosing my conversation partners. A summary of Zehnder's work and of others with regard to the lexemes for "way" can be found in Lund, *Way Metaphors*, 55-60, esp. 60.

[10]There is also a pervasive use of *derek* in the sectarian documents of the Dead Sea Scrolls. It becomes a technical term there. They thought of themselves as "the perfect ones of the Way," and this becomes crucial for our understanding of how the term is picked up in the Gospels, which will be discussed in chap. 7. See James H. Charlesworth, "Intertextuality: Isaiah 40:3 and the Serek Ha-Yaḥad," in *The Quest for Context and Meaning: Studies in Biblical Intertextuality in Honor of James A. Sanders*, ed. Craig A. Evans and Shemaryahu Talmon (Leiden: Brill, 1997), 197-224.

[11]See Lund, *Way Metaphors*, 56-61, for details.

[12]These include *šəbîl, nətîbāh, nātîb, ma'gāl, maslûl, ḥûṣ,* and *'ōraḥ*. These are mentioned by all scholars working in depth on this topic. To this list, Lund adds (given certain nuances) the following: *hālîk, hălîkāh,* and *mahălāh*. See ibid., 56-57.

[13]Hans M. Barstad, *A Way in the Wilderness: The "Second Exodus" in the Message of Second Isaiah,* Journal of Semitic Studies Monograph 12 (Manchester: University of Manchester Press, 1989), 6.

[14]Again, I have been somewhat selective in my conversation partners. See also Yair Hoffman, *The Doctrine of the Exodus in the Bible* (Tel Aviv: Tel Aviv University, 1983); J. Vermeylen "Le motif de la création dans le Deutéro-Isaïe," in *La creation dans l'Orient ancien,* Lectio divina 127 (Paris: Cerf, 1987), 183-240.

[15]Lund, *Way Metaphors*, 38.

[16]See, e.g., Horacio Simian-Yofre, who has questioned criteria for dealing with the second-exodus motif in the Prophets: "Exodo in Deuteroisaías" [Exodus in Deutero-Isaiah], *Bib* 61 (1980): 530-53. Simian-Yofre's criticisms are based on careful analysis of the use of "way" and other lexemes in

answered the major concerns raised against identifying second exodus terms in Isaiah.[17] As Øystein Lund claims, "From the perspective of *language and worldview* the unconscious conventional metaphors become particularly interesting because they reflect an immediately intelligible way of thinking. In our case, it is most likely that the way-metaphor has been so obvious that one has, *without any further thought*, viewed life and history as a way."[18] From a cognitive metaphorical perspective, the image field associated with this kind of metaphor is *life as a landscape* and *life as a journey*.[19]

The Isaianic New Exodus

The themes of exodus and the Isaianic new exodus play a central role in the development of Isaiah 40–55. Carroll Stuhlmueller comments, "The theme of the Exodus, as N. H. Snaith reminds us 'is not merely one of the themes.... It is the prophet's dominant theme.... Basically [it is his] ONE theme, and all else is subservient to it.'"[20] The same God who acted wondrously and powerfully in the first exodus performs a new and

---

Isaiah in comparison with usage elsewhere in the Hebrew Bible. His criticisms primarily have to do with the relationship between the literal/physical use of "way" and its syntagms vis-à-vis metaphorical use. This is similar to so many of Barstad's criticisms of those who usually take the passages we are covering as indicative of a second exodus. Perhaps the greatest contribution Simian-Yofre's article makes to the exegesis of Isaiah is the further precision he brings to the notion of desert and how the Hebrews would have viewed such allusions: ideally or evoking notions of chaos and unsettledness. Here, it seems to me, he has made real gains, basing his research on Talmon's work already discussed in chaps. 1-3 of this book. Even so, his criticisms about literal meaning vis-à-vis figurative or metaphoric meaning have been answered by and large, indirectly if not directly, in the numerous monographs published in recent decades.

[17]Lund, *Way Metaphors*, 39-40. Moving beyond the work of Lakoff and Johnson and invoking the work of D. Peil ("Üb erlegungen zur Bildfeldtheorie," *Beiträge zur Geschichte der deutschen Sprache und Literatur* 112 [1990]: 209-41), Lund explains, "The same phenomenon is, from a more linguistic perspective, described by H. Weinrich and developed by D. Peil. Weinrich and Peil use the designation *Bildfeld* to describe the fact that the connection between source domain and target domain (common terminology in metaphor mapping) is a conventional one and that this combination produces a series of contiguous metaphors. Peil's definition of *Bildfeld* reads (in translation), "An image field is the sum of all possible metaphorical expressions in the context of a relevant key metaphor or basic metaphorical ideal."

[18]Lund, *Way Metaphors*, 38.

[19]Ibid., 145.

[20]Carroll Stuhlmueller, *Creative Redemption in Deutero-Isaiah*, Analecta Biblica 43 (Rome: Biblical Institute, 1970), 59, quoting N. H. Snaith, "Isaiah 40–66," in *Studies in the Second Part of the Book of Isaiah*, VTSup 14 (Leiden: Brill, 1967), 147. However, for Snaith, it is precisely the return from exile, which is a second exodus, to which everything else is made subservient.

determinative "way" in rescuing the exilic community from their oppressors (i.e., Babylon) and delivers through the desert instead of the sea. He will restore them to their home in Zion. Bernhard Anderson identified ten passages with explicit reference to Isaiah's new-exodus theme (Is 40:3-5; 41:17-20; 42:14-16; 43:1-3; 43:14-21; 48:20-21; 49:8-12; 51:9-10; 52:11-12; 55:12-13).[21] Building on Hermann Gunkel's insights (*Schopfung und Chaos und Endzeit*), Anderson demonstrates how prophetic eschatology, especially in Isaiah, is based on the notion that the last days correspond to primeval time (*Endzeit gleich Urzeit*). In other words, the typology of Isaiah picks up on the previous history of Israel's founding event—namely, the exodus—reaching even behind that event to the primeval combat motif. For Anderson, Isaiah draws continuity between events of the past and their greater fulfillment in the present and the future. The former things have been eclipsed by new things, and Israel must now take these things to heart. Mesmerized by the past story, Israel's meganarrative, the people are transformed by that story and what it reveals about their future. This new way inspires hope and a new way of living. Some have linked the sufferings of the servant in Isaiah 40–55 and the exiles with the preexodus sufferings of Israel and Egypt. These sufferings are preparatory, leading again to Israel's deliverance.[22]

Isaiah 40:1-11

The prologue of Isaiah 40 plays a paradigmatic role in Isaiah and in subsequent Scripture. In fact, the first two verses may plausibly be seen as setting a tone for Isaiah 40–55, where their theme is spun into a poetic garb.[23] Indeed, it is a summation of the entire message of the Book of

---

[21]See Bernhard W. Anderson, "Exodus Typology in Second Isaiah," in *Israel's Prophetic Heritage: Essays in Honor of James Muilenburg*, ed. Bernhard W. Anderson and Walter Harrelson (New York: Harper and Brothers, 1962), 177-95; Anderson, "Exodus and Covenant in Second Isaiah and Prophetic Tradition," in *Magnalia Dei: The Mighty Acts of God; Essays on the Bible and Archaeology in Memory of G. Ernest Wright*, ed. Frank Moore Cross, Werner E. Lemke, and Patrick D. Miller Jr. (Garden City, NY: Doubleday, 1976), 339-60.
[22]Anthony R. Ceresko, "The Rhetorical Strategy of the Fourth Servant Song (Isaiah 52:13–53:12): Poetry and the Exodus-New Exodus," *CBQ* (1994): 42-55.
[23]Barstad, *Way in the Wilderness*, 10.

Consolation.[24] While it is true that exodus typology is of some importance in chapters 1–39, it comes to full bloom in Isaiah 40–55. As Rikk E. Watts puts it,

> Exodus typology, of some significance in chapters 1–39, is central to this salvation theme. Although other canonical writings appeal to the exodus tradition, here it is elevated to its most prominent status as a hermeneutic, and according to some commentators, shapes the heart of 40–55 even replacing the first Exodus as *the* saving event. . . . If Israel's founding moment was predicated on Yahweh's redemptive action in the Exodus from Egyptian bondage, then surely a second deliverance from exilic bondage, this time from Babylon, could scarcely be conceived of in other terms than those of the first Exodus?[25]

Books in the ancient world had no table of contents, so the opening lines of a book played a much more important role than they do even in our contemporary literature. Imagine unrolling an entire scroll to read the beginning and the end in order to grasp the text's logic. This would not be a practical approach. Reading Isaiah 40:1-11 would have functioned like an opening introduction for the ancient audience. It was the antechamber into the Book of Consolation.

The structure of the prologue is fairly straightforward with four basic sections:[26]

(a) First section
   Verse 1. The opening declaration sets the tone.
   Verse 2. Comfort is articulated in the parallel statements. Commentators differ in their understanding as to whom this is addressed.

(b) Second section
   Verses 3-5. Imagery is evoked in which a call goes out to prepare the way for a triumphant return. Worthy of note here is that the immediate

---

[24]Bo H. Lim, *The "Way of the Lord" in the Book of Isaiah*, Library of Hebrew Bible/OT Studies 522 (New York: T&T Clark, 2010), 52.
[25]Watts, *Isaiah's New Exodus*, 79-80.
[26]Paul, *Isaiah 40–66*, 127-28. This is basically the same division offered by David Noel Freedman, "The Structure of Isaiah 40:1-11," in *Perspectives on Language and Text: Essays and Poems in Honor of Francis I. Andersen's Sixtieth Birthday, July 28, 1985*, ed. Edgar W. Conrad and Edward G. Newing (Winona Lake, IN: Eisenbrauns, 1987), 167-93; however, Freedman argues that Is 40:5 is "independent of its immediate context, and is in fact the centerpiece and culmination of the poem as a whole" (169, cf. 191-92).

referent is the Syrian Desert, which stretches from Babylon to Israel.[27] The primary concern is for God's presence, evoking the book of Exodus.[28] This will be accomplished through the revelation of God's glory, a reference, as it is in Akkadian, to "a supernatural awe-inspiring sheen that envelops the deity at the moment of revelation."[29] The concluding phrase, "for the mouth of the Lord has spoken it," introduces the third section, which is connected "poetically, structurally, and thematically" to the second.[30]

(c) Third section

Verses 6-8. The supremacy of Yahweh and the permanency of his word over against the transiency of human beings are established, in addition to the evanescence of all things.

(d) Fourth section

Verses 9-11. Jerusalem is to announce to the cities of Judah the news of Yahweh's return. This is the command of a mighty warrior, since "this reflects the common practice of sending messengers from the battlefield to report the results of combat."[31] Yahweh is paradoxically a mighty warrior (v. 10) and also the gentle shepherd (v. 11). As Shalom Paul states, "As in the bygone days of Egypt, God will lead His returning flock through the desert to Israel; cf. Isa 49:9-10; Ezek 34:12; Ps 78:52."[32] This includes Yahweh's *deliverance* of the exiled people.

This opening passage is first and foremost directed to the members of the divine council.[33] A translation of the prologue is offered below.

---

[27]Paul, *Isaiah 40–66*, 130. Some scholars see a reference to the homecoming of the exiles from Babylon as too minimal or even "completely wrong." See, e.g., Barstad, *Way in the Wilderness*, 18-20.
[28]Cf. Ex 33:3, 12-14.
[29]Paul, *Isaiah 40–66*, 131.
[30]Ibid., 132.
[31]Ibid., 134. Barstad, *Way in the Wilderness*, 13, recognizes holy war imagery here.
[32]Paul, *Isaiah 40–66*, 137.
[33]Ibid., 127, relying on Frank Moore Cross, "The Council of Yahweh in Second Isaiah," *JNES* 12 (1953): 274-77. Cross argued that the opening plurals in these imperative verbs were accounted for by the *Gattung* of "divine directives to angelic heralds" (276). Also see Anderson, "Exodus and Covenant," 354. Interestingly, Freedman, "Structure of Isaiah 40:1-11," argues that the speaker at the beginning of v. 6 "is an angel of the throne-room, one who has direct access to the deity and hence is of the first rank" (182). For a different resolution to the problems of the plural imperatives here that ties this passage back to Is 36–39 and therefore sees that the primary background of Is 40:1-11 and the good news proclaimed to be an angelic announcement of victory over the Assyrians, see Matthew Seufert, "Isaiah's Herald," *WTJ* 77 (2015): 219-35, esp. 228-29.

Comfort, comfort [*nāḥam*] my people,
    says your God.
Speak tenderly to Jerusalem,
    and proclaim to her
that her hard service has been completed,
    that her sin has been paid for,
that she has received from the LORD's hand
    double for all her sins.

A voice of one calling:
"In the wilderness [*midbār*] prepare
    the way [*derek*] for the LORD;
make straight in the desert
    a highway [*məsillāh*] for our God.
Every valley shall be raised up,
    every mountain and hill made low;
the rough ground shall become level,
    the rugged places a plain.
And the glory of the LORD will be revealed,
    and all people will see it together.
For the mouth of the LORD has spoken."

A voice says, "Cry out."
    And I said, "What shall I cry?"

"All people are like grass,
    and all their faithfulness is like the flowers of the field.
The grass withers and the flowers fall,
    because the breath of the LORD blows on them.
    Surely the people are grass.
The grass withers and the flowers fall,
    but the word of our God endures forever."

You who bring good news to Zion,
    go up on a high mountain.
You who bring good news to Jerusalem,
    lift up your voice with a shout,
lift it up, do not be afraid;

> say to the towns of Judah,
> "Here is your God!"
> See, the Sovereign LORD comes with power,
> and he rules with a mighty arm.
> See, his reward is with him,
> and his recompense accompanies him.
> He tends his flock like a shepherd:
> He gathers the lambs in his arms
> and carries them close to his heart;
> he gently leads [*nāhal*] those that have young. (Is 40:1-11)

The chapter continues to emphasize the incomparability of God, the futility of idols, and the overall transitory nature of nations.

Where will God appear? A "way" is prepared, not through the desert, but *in* the desert.[34] The imagery is that of a royal road prepared for the sake of easing travel for the king's journey, a liege on a journey to reveal himself in the "hopelessness of desert, exile and catastrophe."[35] Verse 3 has been significant for interpreters ancient and modern. Walther Zimmerli argued that Isaiah 40:3 is a literal highway, while J. Gordon McConville has argued the opposite, that it is metaphor.

The importance of this passage is evident in the Qumran documents, especially the Rule of the Community (1QS). This scroll, along with many others hidden in a cave, was preserved by Jews at Qumran as the Roman army rolled in from the north.[36] Except for the phrase "a voice of one calling," the quotation of Isaiah 40:3 in this Qumran text is verbatim. Additionally, four dots were used to signify the Tetragrammaton (YHWH, the most holy use of the divine name), which occurs after "the way" (*derek*). This is probably due to the consciousness of the Qumran Jews of the ineffableness of God's name.[37] Research of echoes in other Qumran documents lead James Charlesworth to conclude, "This verse is the most important of all the prophetic words of Scripture

---

[34] Erich Zenger, "The God of Exodus in the Message of the Prophets as Seen in Isaiah," in *Exodus, a Lasting Paradigm*, ed. Bas van Iersel and Anton Weiler (Edinburgh: T&T Clark, 1987), 23.
[35] Ibid.
[36] See Charlesworth, "Intertextuality," 197-224.
[37] Ibid., 213.

for the development of the Qumranites' conceptual universe and their self-understanding."[38]

This rich, imaginative poetry is a healing salve for the plaintive cry about the people's plight in verse 27:

> Why do you complain, Jacob?
>   Why do you say, Israel,
> "My way is hidden from the LORD;
>   my cause is disregarded by my God"? (Is 40:27; cf. Ps 74:11; 79:10; 80:13)

God's consolatory word is driven home in the following verses by appealing to his eternal existence, his almighty, tenacious power, and his ineffable understanding.

Isaiah 41:17-20

The beginning of this chapter (Is 41:1-7) is commonly described as a trial scene in which God invites the nations to court in order to establish facts.[39] This leads to three sections in which "comfort and assurance are presented" (Is 41:8-13, 14-16, 17-20).[40] This text also is commonly identified as a second exodus text.[41] A prominent aspect of this pericope is the transformation of the wilderness or the desert. However, the immediately preceding verses are also crucial, for God announces that Israel will be a military force (cf. Is 41:15-16) and that Judah will wipe out all her enemies. Immediately following this, these military responsibilities are reassigned to Cyrus:

> The very task Israel assumed to be uniquely its own, Yahweh has transferred to another agent. The exile confirms the fact that Israel has forfeited its privileged status in Yahweh's plan. In his "new things," Yahweh is free to choose new agents for his service. Given that mention of the "former things" and "new things" end with ch. 48, it is clear that Cyrus is inextricably linked to the "new things." For this reason Cyrus is not a

---

[38]Ibid., 223.
[39]Friedbert Ninow, *Indicators of Typology Within the Old Testament: The Exodus Motif* (Frankfurt: Peter Lang, 2001), 172 (what German exegetes call *Gerichtsrede*).
[40]Ibid. (what German exegetes call *Heilsorakel* or *Erhörungsorakel*).
[41]Ibid. However, Barstad, *Way in the Wilderness*, 26-36, vehemently disagrees with this notion.

parenthesis in the economy of salvation. The election of Cyrus is an eschatological event. In a real, yet incomplete sense, Cyrus's deliverance is the NE [new exodus], the transformation of the wilderness.[42]

As we will observe below, yet another shift occurs: what the nation was to be and Cyrus incompletely fulfilled, a new prophet will bring to completion—a messianic prophecy.[43] Even Calvin's conservative figural exegesis recognized that in Cyrus, a type of Christ, things were foreshadowed that would ultimately find their fulfillment in Jesus' reign.[44]

As we have seen, the wilderness wanderings do not play a minor role in the whole exodus complex, for the wilderness (*midbār*) is symbolic of a rite of passage between the exodus and the Promised Land.[45] And in the wilderness a major question is raised: "Is YHWH with us, or not?"[46] This is significant since with God's presence removed the nation is in jeopardy.[47] Thus the theme becomes an integral part of this narrative. Now, however, they will march through a transformed wilderness, a virtual paradise.[48]

Salvation is cloaked in exodus garb. "In Isaiah 40–55, the emphasis is on salvation," says R. E. Nixon. "As God had led His people from Egypt through the desert by the hand of His servant Moses, so now He would lead them again through the desert through a New Servant, 'an eschatological and Messianic figure'; the God who performs this is the Redeemer, *'ani hu'*—'I am he,' the God of the Exodus."[49] The passage promises with confidence:

---

[42]Lim, *Way of the Lord*, 83. Other writers have also assumed that Cyrus is merely a transitional figure. See, e.g., Durham, "Isaiah 40–55," 54.
[43]Pace Antti Laato, "The Composition of Isaiah 40–55," *JBL* 109, no. 2 (1990): 207-28. Laato, after developing an elaborate chiastic analysis of Isaiah 40–55, claims that the composer's goal was to communicate a new future for the people through Cyrus.
[44]David L. Puckett, *John Calvin's Exegesis of the Old Testament*, Columbia Series in Reformed Theology (Louisville, KY: Westminster John Knox, 1995), 117.
[45]See Shemaryahu Talmon, "The Desert Motif in the Bible and Qumran Literature" in *Literary Studies in the Hebrew Bible: Form and Content* (Jerusalem: Magnes Press, 1993), 216-54.
[46]Ninow, *Indicators of Typology*, 173. Cf. Ex 17:7.
[47]Ibid., 174. Cf. Ex 33:15-16.
[48]Ibid., 174-75.
[49]R. E. Nixon, *The Exodus in the New Testament* (London: Tyndale, 1963), 10.

> The poor and needy search for water,[50]
>> but there is none;
>> their tongues are parched with thirst.
> But I the LORD will answer them;
>> I, the God of Israel, will not forsake them.
> I will make rivers flow on barren heights,
>> and springs within the valleys [*biqʿah*].
> I will turn the desert [*midbār*] into pools of water,
>> and the parched ground into springs.
> I will put in the desert [*midbār*]
>> the cedar and the acacia, the myrtle and the olive.
> I will set junipers in the wasteland,
>> the fir and the cypress together,
> so that people may see and know,
>> may consider and understand,
> that the hand of the LORD has done this,
>> that the Holy One of Israel has created [*bārāʾ*] it. (Is 41:17-20)

The poet has enriched his message about God acting to do something *new* by means of an allusive sound play in the following way.[51] Genesis 7:11 and Psalm 74:15 are the only two places in the Bible that share the vocabulary of the noun "spring" (*maʿyān*) and the verb for "burst apart" (*bāqaʿ*). These two passages also share imagery of abundant water; however, they use that imagery in different ways. Genesis 7:11 uses the imagery of abundant water as an act of de-creation: God reverses the earlier creation event of ordering the dark deep (*təhôm*) by the flood, which is a kind of de-creation. In Psalm 74:15 the image of abundant waters is used to represent God's enemy. There is some debate about whether the allusion is to the creation or the exodus at this point; however, this seems like a false dichotomy. What is significant for our purposes here is that in Isaiah 41:18 the poet has read Genesis 7:11 and

---

[50]The vocabulary invoked here to describe their plight overlaps with language used to describe the Israelites condition of oppression and servitude under Pharaoh (cf. Ex 3:7 and Deut 26:6-7). See Zenger, "God of Exodus," 24. Ninow, *Indicators of Typology*, 173, cites Gen 41:52; Ex 3:17; 4:31; and Deut 16:3 also.
[51]For these insights I am indebted to Jonathan Kline, *Allusive Soundplay in the Hebrew Bible*, Ancient Israel and Its Literature 28 (Atlanta: SBL Press, 2016), 107-10.

Psalm 74:15 in such a manner as to refashion the imagery through paronomasia (i.e., sound play). The verb in the previous two passages (*bāqaʿ*) has been transformed into "valleys" (*bəqāʿôt*). Furthermore, the poet has negated the water imagery of the previous two texts (destruction and splitting apart) to "forge a new message of recreation for the exiles" and communicate "YHWH's outpouring of water in the wilderness in order to provide a path for the exiles to return to the land of exile (water is now a means of vivification)."[52]

Creation language and theology are evident here.[53] Isaiah 41:20, by using the verb "create," signals that this new exodus is in fact a new creation.[54] Charged with exodus theology, it manifests God's glory, emphasizing God's presence and the end of Israel's distress. The exodus theme is "eschatologized." During this forthcoming messianic age, a transformation of the wilderness will occur.[55]

Isaiah 42:14-17

Now Yahweh leads the people in a way they know not. Isaiah 42 opens with God's assurances that they are chosen and there is a brighter future ahead. Again, there is a similar motif of transformation. Leading up to our passage, however, is the revelation of God as warrior (cf. Is 42:13). This bellicose outcry by God is in complete contrast to the calm and restraint that has been expressed before now.[56] This is continued in verse 14, where we pick up our text. It is not unusual in Akkadian texts for a woman's cry in labor to be compared to a warrior's outcry.[57] The exodus tradition is alluded to in Isaiah 42:15 and continues on into verse 16.[58] The original victory song attested in the Song of the Sea, sung by Moses

---

[52]Ibid., 109-10.
[53]Barstad, *Way in the Wilderness*, 28-36.
[54]Ninow, *Indicators of Typology*, 175. This blossoms into full flower possibly in Is 65:17 (a text outside our consideration in this chapter) since it seems that new exodus gives way to new creation here. But this is an important text that ultimately shows influence on Rev 21:1-5, a text I will treat in detail later in the book.
[55]Augustine Stock, *The Way in the Wilderness: Exodus, Wilderness, and Moses Themes in Old Testament and New* (Collegeville, MN: Liturgical Press, 1969), 130.
[56]See Paul, *Isaiah 40–66*, 195
[57]Ibid.
[58]Ibid., 197.

and the Israelites, is now answered in antiphonal cry of a *new* victory song, whose choir constitutes all the people from the ends of the earth (cf. Is 42:6-7).[59] This new song (Isaiah 42:10, "Sing to the LORD a new song") belongs together with the new things (Is 43:14-21, discussed below) that the Lord will do. The new things in the latter part of Isaiah "mean the great unparalleled events about to introduce the future state of Israel."[60] Significantly, this is echoed in the Psalter no less than five times.[61] The new thing ultimately "culminates in the promise of the new heavens and a new earth."[62]

Yet in Isaiah 42:14-17 God's actions seem to contradict his transformation of the wilderness. Even so, the apparent contradiction is resolved in God's acts of judgment "against oppressors and for the oppressed."[63]

> For a long time I have kept silent,
>   I have been quiet and held myself back.
> But now, like a woman in childbirth,
>   I cry out, I gasp and pant.
> I will lay waste the mountains and hills
>   and dry up all their vegetation.
> I will lead the blind [the exiles][64] by ways [*derek*] they have not known,
>   along unfamiliar paths [*nətîbāh*] [they do not know][65] I will guide them;
> I will turn the darkness into light before them
>   and make the rough places smooth.[66]
> These are the things I will do;
>   I will not forsake them.

---

[59] I am indebted to Ninow, *Indicators of Typology*, 176, for this insightful contrast.
[60] Geerhardus Vos, *The Pauline Eschatology* (Phillipsburg, NJ: P&R, 1986), 336.
[61] Ps 33:3; 96:1; 98:1; 144:9; 149:1.
[62] Ibid.
[63] Lim, *Way of the Lord*, 72.
[64] See Lund, *Way Metaphors*, 128. However, the "blindness" may be an indirect criticism of the people despite the overall pericope pertaining to a message of salvation. See ibid., 136.
[65] The NIV unjustifiably drops this repeated phrase, supposedly following the editors' notes in the MT, who consider it *additum*, i.e., "added." Such a move is unnecessary. The clause actually forms a chiastic parallelism with the previous clause; see Paul, *Isaiah 40–66*, 197. The clause is not otiose; rather, it is of immense value in communicating with emphasis the new ethical path on which God will guide them.
[66] Could it be that there is a reversal of the curses listed in Deut 28? I am indebted to Lund, *Way Metaphors*, 133-34, for the possible allusion.

> But those who trust in idols,
>> who say to images, "You are our gods,"
>> will be turned back in utter shame. (Is 42:14-17)

While Horacio Simian-Yofre and Hans Barstad have leveled criticisms against the notion of a new exodus in this text,[67] and they perhaps guard us from overblown exegesis, the weight of evidence is on the side of seeing genuine allusions to the exodus and forward-looking anticipation of a new exodus. Clarifying distinctions between literal and figurative language may go some distance in resolving this debate.[68]

Isaiah 42 has been plagued with discussions about whether the language used here is literal or figurative, especially verse 16 ("I will lead the blind by ways they have not known, along unfamiliar paths . . . , and make the rough places smooth"). In actuality, the issue is how the metaphors function in their literary, social, and cognitive environment here (and for all subsequent readers as well). The literal and the figural should not be sharply bifurcated. Figurative language and metaphor are staples of everyday speech, not just literary adornment. And trends in metaphor theory in recent decades sidestep the issue of literal versus figurative interpretations. The point in its poetic context is that God is going to lead his people along a new way, a way of obedience leading to blessing; however, those who worship idols will not be so blessed. The notion of God leading his people on a road is conventional.[69] The literal, however, generates a figurative sense that people easily understand. Israel's path before the exile was one of repeated failure and disobedience. Even so, God will act decisively to craft a people, and he will help them to walk along the obedient path (*derek*). This path will be a new way of obedience, paths they have not known: "YHWH's own way."[70] A close study of the words in verse 16b in the immediate and canonical context seem to support an ethical sense "that everything that is misguided in the

---

[67] See Simian-Yofre, "Exodus in Deutero-Isaiah," 539-40; Barstad, *Way in the Wilderness*, 37-53.
[68] See, e.g., Lund, *Way Metaphors*, who claims, "It is . . . difficult most of the time to replace a metaphor with literal speech without a loss to meaning and function" (30-31).
[69] Ibid., 137.
[70] Ibid., 138.

people's life will be restored."⁷¹ This "new thing" is explained yet more dramatically in Isaiah 43.

Isaiah 43:1-7

Israel has been blind and deaf (Is 42:18-25); however, like a bereaved father over a prodigal son (cf. Hos 11), God will not give up, for he is kind and compassionate. Isaiah 43 contains a literary frame as evidenced by the repeating vocabulary in verse 1 and verse 7 (see text below).⁷² The passage is permeated by words borrowed from the creation account of Genesis 1–2. Israel is a new work of creation.⁷³ The rare combination *yhwh 'ĕlōhîm*, "the Lord your God" (Is 43:3), may pick up associations with the exodus⁷⁴ and is reminiscent of the Decalogue.⁷⁵ It is plausible that the heaping up of titles is related to the preamble of suzerainty treaties of the Hittites, "terms calculated to inspire awe and fear."⁷⁶ In this passage, God delivers through the waters and the fire, which seems to be a metaphorical merism, expressing totality. God will provide absolute protection.⁷⁷ I have provided the Hebrew in significant places in the following translation in order to highlight the evocations of exodus language.

> But now, this is what the Lord says—
> he who created you [*bōra'ăkā*], Jacob,
> he who formed you [*wəyōṣerkā*], Israel:
> "Do not fear, for I have redeemed you;
> I have summoned you by name [*qārā'tî bəšimkā*]; you are mine.
> When you pass [*ta'ăbir*] through the waters,
> I will be with you;
> and when you pass through the rivers,

---

⁷¹Ibid., 140-41.
⁷²Again, German exegetes refer to this as a *Heilsorakel*, the most common form in which the prophet offers consolation. See Ninow, *Indicators of Typology*, 177.
⁷³Meredith G. Kline, *The Structure of Biblical Authority* (Grand Rapids: Eerdmans, 1972), 88-89.
⁷⁴Ninow, *Indicators of Typology*, 178-79.
⁷⁵Paul, *Isaiah 40–46*, 206.
⁷⁶Kline, *Structure of Biblical Authority*, 114.
⁷⁷Ibid. Merism can be explained as a literary device to express totality through opposite. For example, if I say that my pregnant wife was sick day and night, I am saying that she was sick with our child in her womb all the time during the pregnancy.

> they will not sweep over you.
> When you walk [*hēlēk*] though the fire,
>> you will not be burned;
>> the flames will not set you ablaze.
> For I am the Lord your God [*yhwh ʾĕlōhîm*],
>> the Holy One of Israel, your Savior;
> I give Egypt for your ransom,
>> Cush and Seba in your stead.
> Since you are precious and honored in my sight,
>> and because I love you,
> I will give people in exchange for you,
>> nations in exchange for your life.
> Do not be afraid, for I am with you;
>> I will bring your children from the east
>> and gather you from the west.
> I will say to the north, 'Give them up!'
>> and to the south, 'Do not hold them back.'
> Bring my sons from afar
>> and my daughters from the ends of the earth—
> everyone who is called by my name [*hanniqrāʾ bišmî*],
>> whom I created [*bərāʾtîw*] for my glory,
>> whom I formed [*yəṣartîw*] and made." (Is 43:1-7)

Although there are many allusions to the original exodus from Egypt here, there is also a typological increase.[78] Peoples from all directions of the compass will now be gathered.[79]

Isaiah 43:14-21

Now the Lord provides a way in the wilderness. The new exodus in Isaiah becomes a way to a new creation. It is a way back through the sea and the desert to the restored land expressed in paradisiacal terms. This portion of Scripture very clearly has the exodus in view.[80] Scholars often mark this pericope as beginning with verses 16-18, events that are

---

[78]What German exegetes refer to as *Steitgerung*.
[79]Ninow, *Indicators of Typology*, 179.
[80]Lim, *Way of the Lord*, 55.

concerned with the first thing (*qadmônî*) (v. 18), the past (*ri'šôn*) (v. 18), and then progress to verses 19-21, since the second part is concerned with the new thing or the future (*hădāšah*). To have such a contrast between the former and future things is not uncommon to Isaiah.[81] Here the past becomes solid encouragement for future hope.

> This is what the LORD says—
>   your Redeemer, the Holy One of Israel:
> "For your sake I will send to Babylon
>   and bring down as fugitives all the Babylonians,
>   in the ships in which they took pride.
> I am the LORD, your Holy One,
>   Israel's Creator, your King.
>
> This is what the Lord says—
>   he who made a way [*derek*] through the sea,
>   a path [*nětîbâ*] through the mighty waters,
> who drew out the chariots and horses,
>   the army and reinforcements together,
> and they lay there, never to rise again,
>   extinguished, snuffed out like a wick:
> "Forget the former things [*ri'šōnôt*];
>   do not dwell on the past [*qadmōniyyôt*].
> See, I am doing a new thing [*hădāšāh*]!
>   Now it springs up; do you not perceive it?
> I am making a way [*derek*] in the wilderness
>   and streams in the wasteland
>
> . . . .
>
> to give drink to my people, my chosen,
>   the people I formed for myself
>   that they may proclaim my praise." (Is 43:16-21)

One clear purpose here (and in the Psalms) is to demonstrate the ease with which Yahweh tames unruly forces.[82] The passage exalts the majesty

---

[81]E.g., Is 40:21; 41:4, 22-29; 42:8-9; 43:8-13, 18-19.
[82]Richard J. Clifford, *Fair Spoken and Persuading: An Interpretation of Second Isaiah* (New York: Paulist Press, 1984), 60.

and august rule of Yahweh. In fact, in Isaiah 43:1-21 (we looked merely at 43:14-21 above) there appears to be a fusion or blending of creation and the language of the epics from the surrounding cultures. However, the enemy conquered now is not the sea but the desert. In each case, whether it be sea or desert, a path is laid through it for the people of God to be rescued and set at peace in their own city/land.

Not only would the same God who acted wondrously, salvifically, and powerfully in the first exodus act again, but he would act in a new and determinative way to rescue the exilic community from their oppressors (i.e., Babylon) and deliver them through the desert and bring them into Zion through restoration. Now the return from Babylon to Zion is at hand, as is evidenced in our next text, Isaiah 48:15-21.

Isaiah 48:15-21

I, even I, have spoken;
    yes, I have called him.
I will bring him,
    and he will succeed in his mission [*derek*].[83]

"Come near me and listen to this:

"From the first announcement I have not spoken in secret;
    at the time it happens, I am there."

And now the Sovereign LORD has sent me,
    endowed with his Spirit.

This is what the LORD says—
    your Redeemer, the Holy One of Israel:
"I am the LORD your God,
    who teaches you what is best for you,
    who directs you [root: *drk*] in the way [*derek*] you should go.
If only you had paid attention to my commands,
    your peace would have been like a river,
    your well-being like the waves of the sea.

---

[83] Scholars often pick up at v. 20 here; however, following Lim, *Way of the Lord*, 78-79, I am starting at v. 15. This whole section in Lim's book, on the requirement of "Torah obedience" in light of the parousia of the Lord, is highly suggestive.

> Your descendants would have been like the sand,
> > your children like its numberless grains;
> their name would never be blotted out
> > nor destroyed from before me."
>
> Leave [root: *yṣʾ*] Babylon,
> > flee from the Babylonians!
> Announce this with shouts of joy
> > and proclaim it.
> Send it out [root: *yṣʾ*] to the ends of the earth;
> > say, "The LORD has redeemed his servant Jacob."
> They did not thirst when he led [root: *hlk*] them through the deserts;
> > he made water flow for them from the rock;
> he split the rock
> > and water gushed out. (Is 48:15-21)

This urgent exhortation to flee from Babylon is patterned after the exodus event.[84] Many features signal this allusion. The use of *yāṣāʾ* (to go out) is a significant marker from the book of Exodus (cf. Ex 11:8; 12:41; 13:3-4; 16:1). There it was used as a legal term.[85] The Lord almighty is a suzerain who releases and frees his captive people. As a liberator, he frees his ransomed people. Future reverberations of this legal term, as evidenced here and in other passages in Isaiah, use the same work from the same root. Another allusion is the thirst in the desert and failure to trust (cf. Ex 17:1-7; Num 20:1-13; Ps 78:15-20).[86] However, it is not only a forward-looking mentality that shapes Isaiah's transformation of the exodus motif; he looks backward as well. The author looks back not merely to the exodus but even to the creation, as we see in the next set of verses below.

Rhetorically, Isaiah 48 serves as a literary foil to the revelation of the servant in Isaiah 49. Yahweh is free to appoint whomever he will to carry out his plan of redemption. This is made clear with the refrain "I am Yahweh, I am he" throughout the servant passages. Cyrus becomes a

---

[84]Ibid., 80-82.
[85]David Daube, *The Exodus Pattern in the Bible* (London: Faber and Faber, 1963), 31.
[86]Lim, *Way of the Lord*, 80.

transitional link, a sort of Janus figure.⁸⁷ What the nation of Israel was to fulfill and Cyrus did in a mere military fashion, the new, anonymous servant identified in chapter 49 and following will now complete. Bo Lim states:

> The individual prophet who speaks in 48:16 and 49:1–52:12 now functions as the faithful embodiment of the nation of Israel (49:3) that failed to fulfill its role (cf. 48:1-2). *Yahweh's intention to bring forth justice to the nations will now be realized through an individual.* . . . Whereas Cyrus accomplishes this feat through military conquest, the prophet does so through preaching and suffering.⁸⁸

When we arrive at the Gospels (chaps. 7 and 8 of this book), we will see that this very principle is confirmed: the privileges and responsibilities of Israel are shifted to the Messiah.⁸⁹ Significant in this coalescence between the new exodus and the servant is the shift in rhetorical perspective that takes place at this point in Isaiah.⁹⁰ This new prophet accomplishes his mission through speech, in contrast to the coercive sword of the state represented by Cyrus.⁹¹ The new servant announced in Isaiah 49, like Cyrus, is going to bring Israel back; however, there will be significant changes in the manner, mode, and ultimate object (i.e., ultimate location of the new exodus) with regard to this servant's role.

Isaiah 49:6-13

This chapter marks a major turn in perspective and rhetorical function.⁹² Isaiah 48 concentrated on Israel's recalcitrance. There Jacob is wholly passive. Now chapter 49 opens up with a description of the call and commission of a faithful servant, who is much more active.⁹³ An anonymous

---

⁸⁷The literary term derived from the ancient Roman god of the gates, with two faces looking in opposite directions.
⁸⁸Ibid., 86 (emphasis mine).
⁸⁹It is plausible that the fusion of the creation and second exodus images led this prophet to the image of a new messiah. See Durham, "Isaiah 40–55," 53.
⁹⁰Lim, *Way of the Lord*, 86.
⁹¹This is more compelling evidence that the exodus motif as a whole should be read as addressing spiritual concerns and not political ones, such as the liberationist reading enjoins.
⁹²Ibid., 86-87.
⁹³Ninow, *Indicators of Typology*, 183.

prophet appears here. There is significant disparity between this chapter and the last and also between this prophet and the representation of Cyrus.[94] Yes, Cyrus did play a role as a servant of Yahweh; however, as Lim says, it is the servant portrayed in Isaiah 49–53 who "truly fulfills the role of the Servant of [chapters] 40–48."[95]

> "It is too small a thing for you to be my servant
>   to restore the tribes of Jacob
>   and bring back those of Israel I have kept.
> I will also make you a light for the Gentiles,
>   that my salvation may reach to the ends of the earth [ʿad-qĕṣēh
>   hāʾāreṣ]."
>
> This is what the LORD says—
>   the Redeemer and Holy One of Israel—
> to him who was despised and abhorred by the nation,
>   to the servant of rulers:
> "Kings will see you and stand up,
>   princes will see and bow down,
> because of the LORD, who is faithful,
>   the Holy One of Israel, who has chosen you."
>
> This is what the LORD says:
>
> "In the time of my favor I will answer you,
>   and in the day of salvation I will help you;
> I will keep you and will make you
>   to be a covenant for the people,
> to restore the land
>   and to reassign its desolate inheritances,
> to say to the captives, 'Come out,' [root: yṣʾ]
>   and to those in darkness, 'Be free!'[96]

---

[94] Lim, *Way of the Lord*, 85.
[95] Ibid.
[96] Literally, "Reveal yourselves!" God addresses those imprisoned in darkness (probably a metaphor for exile), but the reverse will be the case for the daughter of Babylonians (Is 47:5). I am indebted to Paul, *Isaiah 40–66*, 329-30, for this insight.

> "They will feed beside the roads [*derek*]
> and find pasture on every barren hill.
> They will neither hunger nor thirst,[97]
> nor will the desert heat or the sun beat down on them.
> He who has compassion on them will guide them [root: *nhg*]
> and lead them [root: *nhl*] beside springs of water.
> I will turn all my mountains into roads [*derek*],
> and my highways [*məsillāh*] will be raised up.
> See, they will come from afar—
> some from the north, some from the west,
> some from the region of Aswan."[98]
>
> Shout for joy, you heavens;
> rejoice, you earth;
> burst into song, you mountains!
> For the LORD comforts his people
> and will have compassion on his afflicted ones. (Is 49:6-13)

While there is clearly some measure of continuity with what has gone before with regard to the servant, scholars have noted a definite shift in focus: the attention is no longer on Babylon but on the resettlement of Judah. The prophet is like a new Moses, providing deliverance in a new exodus. Yet he will also "reassign its desolate inheritances," something Cyrus never did.[99] In this passage, Yahweh is portrayed as gathering his own people from the farthest reaches of the known world. This servant-prophet will be a light to the nations, to the utter ends of the earth (Is 49:6).[100] Friedbert Ninow, quoting J. A. Motyer, makes the point that this would be near megalomania for the prophet to consider himself

---

[97]This phrase is probably echoed in the last passage we will look at in this book, Rev 21:6. See G. K. Beale, *The Book of Revelation: A Commentary on the Greek Text*, NIGTC (Grand Rapids: Eerdmans, 1999), 1056-57.

[98]This area probably refers to modern-day Aswan in southern Egypt. In ancient times, it was opposite the island of Elephantine and was referred to in the famous Aramaic documents found there (see Paul, *Isaiah 40–66*, 331). What is significant about the geographical descriptions given here is that "the East" is missing. Could it be possible that Isaiah deliberately left this compass point out (as Motyer has argued) so that there would be no confusion that this new thing does not refer merely to the return from Babylon? (See Ninow, *Indicators of Typology*, 186).

[99]Lim, *Way of the Lord*, 86.

[100]See the discussion earlier in the chapter on Is 42:6-7.

Israel, let alone to reckon himself as bringing salvation to the ends of the earth.[101] The only one to whom this utterance of self-aggrandizement could refer (without being such) is the Messiah.[102] After his work on earth is accomplished, that risen and ascended Lord will accomplish his mission to the ends of the earth—without hindrance—through his apostles (cf. Acts 28:25-31).

Isaiah 51:9-11

Important for understanding the "way" metaphor in Isaiah 51:9-11 is Isaiah 51:3:

> The LORD will surely comfort [root: *nḥm*][103] Zion
>   and will look with compassion [root: *nḥm*] on all her ruins;
> he will make her deserts like Eden,
>   her wastelands like the garden of the LORD.
> Joy and gladness will be found in her,
>   thanksgiving and the sound of singing.

The "wilderness" does not merely mean the intermediate land that separates the exiles from their home. It is also "the physical condition of Israel as well as the spiritual state of its former and present inhabitants."[104]

Another way this motif is reworked in Isaiah is in the sense of a battle or warfare theme, as well as a re-creation theme. This use is common in the Psalms, as we have seen. The exodus theme is related to the so-called combat motifs in Babylonian and Ugaritic mythology, which the biblical writers echo and adapt for their own purposes and sometimes even polemicize against.[105] Clearly this is what is going on in Isaiah 51:9-11 where the exodus motif is evoked.[106] The text depicts the surrounding

---

[101] Ninow, *Indicators of Typology*, 183.
[102] The fourth Servant Song (Is 52:13–53:12) has clear boundary markers. A declaration at both ends is framed by "my servant" (*ʿabdî*, Is 52:13 and Is 53:11-12) and the verb "to raise" (*nāśāʾ*). The New Testament applies the messianic principle to Christ Jesus (e.g., Mt 5:18; Acts 3:13; 1 Pet 2:22-25).
[103] The reader should note the intertextual link with Is 40:1.
[104] Lim, *Way of the Lord*, 58.
[105] See Jeremy Hutton, "Isaiah 51:9-11 and the Rhetorical Appropriation and Subversion of Hostile Theologies," *JBL* 126 (2007): 271-303.
[106] For various opinions on how these themes are working here and for bibliography, see Jan L. Koole, *Isaiah*, part 3, vol. 2, *Isaiah 49–55*, trans. Anthony P. Runia, Historical Commentary on the Old Testament (Leuven: Peeters, 1998), 162-69.

nations as the sea monster that God defeated at the beginning of creation, together with reference to God delivering his people at the Sea of Reeds (*yam-sûp*).[107] In this morning call, woven as a complex tapestry of allusions, the power of "the divine warrior triumphs over cosmic as well as human adversaries."[108] God is invoked to testify to the people that the God whose power was so magnificently displayed in the past can achieve similar ends to liberate Israel in the present.

> Awake, awake, arm of the LORD,
> > clothe yourself with strength!
> Awake, as in days gone by,
> > as in generations of old.
> Was it not you who cut Rahab [*rahab*] to pieces,
> > who pierced that monster [*tannîn*] through?
> Was it not you who dried up the sea,
> > the waters of the great deep,
> who made a road [*derek*] in the depths of the sea
> > so that the redeemed might cross over?
> Those the LORD has rescued will return.
> > They will enter Zion with singing;
> > everlasting joy will crown their heads.
> Gladness and joy will overtake them,
> > and sorrow and sighing will flee away. (Is 51:9-11)

"Rahab" looms large in the Israelite epic tradition and the literature of contiguous cultures of the time.[109] Furthermore, "the name Rahab (רהב [*rahab*]) serves as a poetic sobriquet for Egypt in Ps 87:4. . . . It, along with תנין [*tannîn*] (immediately following), serve as literary markers for the subsequent allusion to the splitting of the Reed Sea"

---

[107]See John Wright, "Spirit and Wilderness: The Interplay of Two Motifs Within the Hebrew Bible as a Background to Mark 1:2-13," in Conrad and Newing, *Perspectives on Language and Text*, 269-98. Wright comments, "Further, there have survived in the Old Testament many mythical passages where the Divine overruns the 'monsters of the deep' in order to bring about the creative act (e.g., Job 26:12-13; Ps 34:13-14), which is in turn connected with the crossing of the 'Red Sea' and applied to the New Exodus though the 'wilderness' (Isa 51:9-10)" (277).
[108]Tremper Longman III and Daniel G. Reid, *God Is a Warrior*, Studies in Old Testament Biblical Theology (Grand Rapids: Zondervan, 1995), 102.
[109]For the derivation from Akkadian and Ugaritic parallels to the words used in this context, see Paul, *Isaiah 40–66*, 368.

[*yam-sûp*].[110] As we saw in the Psalms, so also in the Prophets, the sea in which the Egyptians have been drowned is recognized as embodying evil powers. Meredith Kline comments, "With Moses as his messianic agent, Yahweh triumphed over Egypt and its gods in acts of judgment, which Scripture figures as a divine slaying of the satanic dragon.... The Egyptian sea is also identified with the draconic powers whom the Lord defeats in redemptive judgment for the salvation of his people."[111] The passing away of the sea is metaphorically equivalent to the passing away of those things that cause pain and sorrow, all of which may itself be an echo of Psalm 114:3, a passage discussed in detail in the last chapter.[112]

This defeat cannot be accomplished through some mere earthly ruler (e.g., Cyrus); rather, God himself must arise and transform the wilderness, defeating the powers of chaos.[113] In this passage, so "mythically embroidered" with images of Yahweh defeating the sea monster, Israel is quickly reminded (Is 51:13-15) that she need not fear, because God has power over the waves, is concerned for his people, and will set the prisoners free.[114] Isaiah is speaking of deliverance here and moors his consolation in the original exodus. Nevertheless, although this new exodus will parallel the first in some respects, this deliverance will be far greater than the former one, as will be demonstrated in the chapters on the Gospels.[115] Moreover, the ripples continue beyond the Gospels. Isaiah 51:10-11 may even be echoed in the last biblical passage to be considered in this book, Revelation 20:1-7.

Isaiah 52:11-12

In a fascinating echo of the imminent haste of the original exodus, Isaiah 52:11-12 opens with the urgent beckoning of Israel to depart

---

[110]Ibid.
[111]Meredith G. Kline, *Glory in Our Midst: A Biblical-Theological Reading of Zechariah's Night Visions* (Overland Park, KS: Two Age Press, 2001), 161.
[112]Beale, *Book of Revelation*, 1049.
[113]Lim, *Way of the Lord*, 58.
[114]Longman and Reid, *God Is a Warrior*, 114.
[115]See Vern Poythress, *The Shadow of Christ in the Law of Moses* (Brentwood, TN: Wolgemuth & Hyatt, 1991), 253.

Babylon. Here the text starts to bring to closure the announced comfort proclaimed in the prologue.

> Depart, depart, go out [root: $yṣ'$] from there!
> Touch no unclean thing!
> Come out [root: $yṣ'$] from it and be pure,
> you who carry the articles of the LORD's house.
> But you will not leave [root: $yṣ'$] in haste [*bəhippāzôn*],[116]
> or go in flight;
> for the LORD will go [root: *hlk*] before you,
> the God of Israel will be your rear guard. (Is 52:11-12)

There is a clear textual linkage here with Isaiah 48. Both passages recall the exodus event, as the repetition of the Hebrew word *yāṣā'* demonstrates.[117] There is a debate as to whether this passage refers to the new exodus from Babylon, which far exceeds the original exodus,[118] or whether the flow of thought suggests that the treatment of Cyrus and Babylon has been left behind and a far larger picture is in mind.[119] Regardless, in this passage there is a direct innerbiblical allusion to Exodus 12 signaled by the word "in haste" (*bəhippāzôn*). The exiles are told they will not depart in haste, which contrasts Exodus 12:11, where the Israelites are told that they will eat the Lord's Passover "in haste" (*bəhippāzôn*).

In this passage, the vessels of the Lord (*nōśa'ê kəlê yhwh*) in verse 11 probably refer to the sacred vessels that had been confiscated by the Babylonians. By invoking the sacred vessels, Isaiah may be subtly alluding to the temple vessels with institutional realities harkening all the way back to the exodus period.[120] If so, the point here is to establish the connection and continuity with cultic purity enjoined on their ancestors in faith.[121]

---

[116]A clear allusion is made here to Ex 12:11-12, where the Hebrews are commanded to eat in haste as they prepare to escape Egypt.
[117]Daube, *Exodus Pattern*, 31.
[118]See, e.g., Paul, *Isaiah 40–66*, 395.
[119]See Ninow, *Indicators of Typology*, 191.
[120]A point made by Peter R. Ackroyd, "The Temple Vessels—a Continuity Theme," in *Studies in the Religion of Ancient Israel*, VTSup 23 (Leiden: Brill, 1972), 180. Ackroyd directs the reader to 1 Chron 9, where the Levitical orders are described with links all the way back to the exodus.
[121]Ibid., 181.

Previously in the Egyptian exodus, the Israelites were protected by the pillar of cloud and fire, sometimes expressed as an angel, sometimes as the ark of the covenant.[122] Often in scriptural discourse this is represented as the Spirit's presence and protection.[123] What is significant for our discussion of the second exodus is that the Lord himself will lead them, as attested in Isaiah 63:8-9 (a passage immediately preceding another clear reference to the exodus tradition in Isaiah 63:11-14), with Spirit guidance in their midst.[124]

Isaiah 55:12-13

Isaiah 55:6-13 forms the conclusion to the Book of Consolation.[125] Here the Babylonian captivity provides the background once again. The exiles are called on to leave and sojourn back home. In a grand finale contrast between God's ways and their ways, verses 5-9 (with a high frequency of *derek*) provide the background to this final Isaianic passage we will consider:

> "Surely you will summon nations you know not,
>   and nations you do not know will come running to you,
> because of the LORD your God,[126]
>   the Holy One of Israel,
>   for he has endowed you with splendor."
> Seek the LORD while he may be found;
>   call on him while he is near.
> Let the wicked forsake their ways [*derek*]
>   and the unrighteous their thoughts.

---

[122]See, e.g., Ex 13:21; 14:9, 20; 23:20, 23; 32:34; Num 10:33-34; 14:14; Deut 1:33; Ps 78:14; Neh 9:12.

[123]See Meredith G. Kline, *Images of the Spirit* (Grand Rapids: Baker, 1980), chap. 1.

[124]See Timothy S. Laniak, *Shepherds After My own Heart: Pastoral Traditions and Leadership in the Bible*, New Studies in Biblical Theology 20 (Downers Grove, IL: InterVarsity Press, 2006), 127-28.

[125]Lim, as previously pointed out, argues for Is 52:7-10 as the conclusion to Is 40–52; however, he notes that an argument can indeed be made for Is 55:6-13 as another conclusion to this section of Isaiah. See Lim, *Way of the Lord*, 96.

[126]The syntax here is important for the theological constructions made below. Shalom Paul comments, "In the syntactical construction (למען ... לקדוש), the ל denotes 'for the sake of,' e.g., Ezek 36:22: 'Thus said the Lord God: "Not for your sake (למענכם) will I act, O House of Israel, but for the sake of My holy name (קדשי לשם), which you have caused to be profaned among the nations to which you have come"'" (*Isaiah 40–66*, 439).

> Let them turn to the Lord, and he will have mercy on them,
>> and to our God, for he will freely pardon.
> "For my thoughts are not your thoughts,
>> neither are your ways [*derek*] my ways [*derek*],"
>> declares the Lord.
> "As the heavens are higher than the earth,
>> so are my ways [*derek*] higher than your ways [*derek*]
>> and my thoughts than your thoughts." (Is 55:5-9)

This is the undoing of the conditional elements in the Mosaic covenant.[127] It is striking in light of the constant appeal to the exodus. Sinai, with all its conditional obligations on Israel, would have to be rethought. In other words, despite the constant allusions to the exodus motif, the second exodus will be accomplished apart from mere human efforts. Westermann, commenting on verse 5 says, "The new, lasting covenant with Israel is made 'because of Yahweh, your God.' The covenant is altogether an act of God's grace towards Israel; there is no suggestion of Israel's being laid under any obligation."[128] The thought is sublime. It is not merely for their sakes but for the sake of God's holy name.

The climactic section, Isaiah 55:12-13, deals with the second exodus. A great dramatic reversal of the curse on Israel is described here. This will be a reversal of the curse discussed earlier in the vineyard song of Isaiah 5. It may even be a fulfillment of the "pleasant vineyard" theme in the other vineyard song in Isaiah 27.[129] Indeed, this reversal is going to be so magnificent that creation itself breaks forth in praise:

> You will go out [root: *yṣʾ*] in joy
>> and be led forth in peace;
> the mountains and hills
>> will burst into song before you,
> and all the trees of the field
>> will clap their hands.

---

[127] See chap. 2, n. 96, which defines the Sinai covenant-administration.
[128] Westermann, *Isaiah 40–66*, 285.
[129] See Christopher R. Seitz, "Isaiah 40–66: Introduction, Commentary, and Reflections," in *The New Interpreter's Bible*, ed. Leander E. Keck (Nashville: Abingdon, 1994), 6:482.

Instead of the thornbush will grow the juniper.
and instead of briers the myrtle will grow.
This will be for the LORD's renown,
for an everlasting sign,
which will not be destroyed. (Is 55:12-13)

This passage seems to bring to full flower the eschatological quality of the new exodus that has been present throughout Isaiah and now reaches consummation.[130] The first vineyard song of Isaiah 5 should be seen in the context of God's choice of Israel. As Kline says, "The ancestral line of Israel was being singled out in the midst of the diaspora of the nations for its special vocation as the Lord's holy covenant community."[131] Deuteronomy 32:10-11 declares that God found Israel in the desert, in the barren and howling waste of Jeshimon. The vineyard song of Isaiah 5 must be understood in the light of its preceding chapters. Isaiah 1, 3, and 5 are a covenantal lawsuit indictment against Israel. Isaiah 2 and 4 look beyond the indictment to the messianic kingdom. Kline notes:

> The song of the vineyard in Isaiah 5:1ff., on which our Lord's parable is an evident variation, is structured according to the pattern of the covenant lawsuit. The judicial character of the song [chap. 5] is plainly indicated by Yahweh's summons: "And now, O inhabitants of Jerusalem, and men of Judah, judge, I pray you, betwixt me and my vineyard" (v. 3). The parallel between this song and Jesus' parable of the vineyard penetrates beyond the common figure of the vineyard to a common covenantal crisis and judicial process.[132]

In Isaiah 5:1 we are immediately introduced to the song imagery. God planted them on the "hill of fatness," in a good spot. Israel had every chance for success and prosperity. However, instead of bringing forth

---

[130] Lim, *Way of the Lord*, 100; Lim is interacting with Klaus Kiesow, *Exodustexte im Jesajabuch: Literarkritische und Motivgeschichtliche Anaylsen* (Frieburg: Universitiatsverlag, 1979). Kiesow apparently believes that in Isaiah this is the first time that an eschatological quality has appeared in a new exodus text. That is not what Lim thinks.

[131] Meredith G. Kline, *Kingdom Prologue: Genesis Foundations for a Covenantal Worldview* (Overland Park, KS: Two Age Press, 2000), 21.

[132] Meredith G. Kline, *By Oath Consigned: A Reinterpretation of the Covenant Signs of Circumcision and Baptism* (Grand Rapids: Eerdmans, 1968), 53.

good grapes, they brought forth nothing good. Verse 5 and 6 describe the curse on Israel. Verse 6 declares that God will make his vineyard (Israel) into a wasteland (*bātāh*, a pun on *tōhû*). Now God is going to turn his suzerainty protection away from them.

We recall that this imagery was used in Deuteronomy 32:10-11 for describing the creation and care of the apple of Yahweh's eye (see discussion on pages 65-66). Isaiah 5 now evokes a de-creation! God is turning back creation into desolation, a state like Genesis 1:2, in which "the earth was formless and empty." Now, however, God describes in this second exodus passage of Isaiah 55 that there will be a reversal of this curse, bringing forth a new creation, a new exodus, and a new messiah.[133] Nature itself is enjoined to participate in the festal celebration of restoration. What is the connection between the closing of this section (Is 40–55) and the last major section of Isaiah (Is 56–66)? It is possible that the new creation themes evidenced in Isaiah 55 open the way for the eschatological orientation of the final chapters.[134]

Conclusion

In this chapter we have traced in some detail how the exodus theme is incorporated into Isaiah's introduction of a second exodus. How should we understand the use of mythological language in this poetic section of Isaiah? First, could it be that the focus here is not so much on cosmology or creation but rather on God as the divine Sovereign?[135] In other words, by using older material in new, creative, and even formative ways, the

---

[133] Durham, "Isaiah 40–55," 55, says: "I think this much is clear: to an Israel who had suffered so cruelly that they thought creation had been turned to destruction, exodus had been turned to enslavement, and that only a David successor could rescue them, this great prophet-poet declared that: 1) a New Creation, one that reversed the negative outcomes of the former creation, was about to begin in Israel; 2) a New Exodus, one that would ultimately be effective for all people, was about to start with Israel; and 3) a New Messiah, one who would incarnate a drastic redefinition and redirection of what service is and what service brings, was about to emerge in/as Israel."

[134] Lim, *Way of the Lord*, 102. This claim could be stated even more strongly, especially when Is 63:9-13a is examined closely, which teaches that God himself directly provided for the Israelite's redemption. Therefore, the Book of Consolation (Is 40–55) generated an eschatological orientation in the latter chapters of Isaiah.

[135] A point made by Bernard F. Batto in his unpublished paper "The Motif of Exodus in Deutero-Isaiah," 12. See also Bernard F. Batto, *Slaying the Dragon: Mythmaking in the Biblical Tradition* (Louisville, KY: Westminster John Knox, 1992).

author is helping the community of faith with new theological understanding. In short, the author of Isaiah is taking pains to show that Yahweh, the God of Israel, is the divine Sovereign. By recounting the divine Sovereign's past actions and events, a surety is given to the people that their Suzerain will do new and wonderful things on their behalf.

A second function of the exodus motif in Isaiah 40–55 is the opening up of a new universalism. By this I mean that the promises of the covenant of grace revealed to Abraham are coming true, that through him all nations would be blessed. This is in contrast to the particularism of the theocracy in Israel, which largely favored ethnic Israel and Judah alone as the apple of God's eye. Now it is not just ethnic Israel who will be restored, but in some new, amazing way, the nations will see the light of salvation through Israel.[136] This was seen, for example, in Isaiah 49:6 discussed above. In terms of where we are in redemptive history, this is clearly the notion of *complexus* (discussed in chap. 1) describing the new covenant fulfillment of the Abrahamic promises.

A third function of the exodus motif in Isaiah is that the New Testament, at least in part, receives its hermeneutical cue from this reworking of the foundational salvific event of the Old Testament.[137] Indeed, the exodus event is actually the paradigm by which a couple of the Gospel writers organized their books. More recently, it has been demonstrated that the exodus and the wanderings in the wilderness are important frames of reference for the apostle Paul. It is not surprising, then, that advanced periods in the Old Testament revelation are already dealing with earlier revelation in a manner that will inform the New Testament method of interpretation. Thus, the relation between the Old and the New will be understood in terms of historical typology.[138] According to the rule of faith, the Old Testament will shape the New Testament witness. It is no wonder that in discussing Paul's use of the exodus motif in 1 Corinthians 10, for example, Earle Ellis writes, "Exodus 'typology' was not original with Paul or even the early Church. The

---

[136] A point emphasized by Pao, *Acts*, 57.
[137] Another example of the rule of faith.
[138] A point made by Anderson in "Exodus Typology," 195.

concept arises in the OT prophets who 'came to shape their anticipation of the great eschatological salvation through the Messiah according to the pattern of the historical Exodus under Moses.'"[139]

Once again, the rule of faith (discussed in chap. 1) governs the New Testament writers. Did exilic and postexilic books in the Hebrew Bible view the return from exile and resettlement of Jerusalem in this second exodus as described in this chapter as the fulfillment of Isaiah's prophecy? This is the subject to which we will turn in the next chapter.

---

[139] Earle Ellis, *Paul's Use of the Old Testament* (Edinburgh: Oliver & Boyd, 1957), 131, quoting Harald Sahlin, "The New Exodus of Salvation According to St Paul," in *The Root of the Vine*, ed. A. J. Fridrichsen (Westminster: Dacre, 1953), 81.

Six

EXILE AND POST-EXILE

The Second Exodus Revisited

Ha, banishment? Be merciful, say "death";
For exile hath more terror in his look,
Much more than death. Do not say "banishment"! . . .
O friar, the damned use that word in hell;
Howling attends it.

SHAKESPEARE, *ROMEO AND JULIET*

> *In many ways, Ezekiel is the grandfather of intertextual*
> *composition, consciously attempting to echo the language of*
> *earlier prophetic tradition, deuteronomic themes, priestly*
> *concerns, and the cosmic imagery of the temple liturgy.*
>
> LAWRENCE BOADT

The prophetic hopes did not die with Isaiah. They stayed alive in the exilic and postexilic period. The dream of a second exodus lived on as well. Indeed, it provides the foundation for the typological fulfillment that we observe in the Gospels and the rest of the New Testament. There cannot be a mere return to theocracy. That dream is a nightmare. What we observe in the prophets of the latter days of Israel is a new dream: the Davidic covenant must be repristinated with a royal messiah that will truly match the job description.

In this chapter we will look briefly at two more prophets, Jeremiah and Ezekiel. Both are prophets during the time of the exile. Ezekiel was exiled with the people; Jeremiah stayed in the land. After observing the exodus motif in these prophets, we will turn our attention to the books of Ezra and Nehemiah, which show significant influence from both Jeremiah and Ezekiel.

Jeremiah

Jeremiah's hometown was in Anathoth (Jer 1:1). He was a priest, commanded by God not to marry or have children. His ministry carried a tone of doom (Jer 16:1-4). He has been called the "weeping prophet" because the narrative reveals more to us about his inner anguish than just about any other biblical writer.[1] Many of these laments turn on the surprising commands from God not to intercede on behalf of the people. Although Jeremiah is a prophet in the succession of Moses (like all true prophets), he is unlike Moses.[2] At this time in redemptive history, the office of prophet is starting to break down. Why? For "a divine purpose: that Israel might be judged, wholly and completely, and a new beginning set in motion."[3]

Jeremiah prophesied during the reigns of the last kings of Judah: Josiah (640–609 BCE), Jehoahaz II (609), Jehoiakim (609–598), Jehoiachin (598–597), and Zedekiah (597–586). He observed the fall of Judah in 586 BCE. The kingdom ended in the exile of most of its people to Babylon, chiefly as a result of two invasions by King Nebuchadnezzar (597 and 586), though the first deportations occurred as early as 605, the same year that Nebuchadnezzar had decimated the Egyptians at the battle of Carchemish.[4] Until recently, many modern biblical scholars have assumed the prophet's oracles against the nations are *vaticinium ex eventu* (prophecy after the fact). The reasoning has been that the destruction of Babylon by the Persians had not yet occurred in Jeremiah's time. But more recent

---

[1] E.g., Jer 4:19; 9:1; 10:19-20; 11:18-23; 12:1-4; 15:10-21; 17:12-18; 18:18-23; 20:7-18; 23:9.
[2] The theme is insightfully treated by Christopher R. Seitz, "The Prophet Moses and the Canonical Shape of Jeremiah," *Zeitschrift für die alttestamentliche Wissenschaft* 101, no. 1 (1989): 3-27.
[3] Ibid., 11.
[4] Amélie Kuhrt, *The Ancient Near East, c. 3000–300 B.C.* (New York: Routledge, 1995), 2:590-97.

studies, treating the rhetoric of the book as a received whole, have opted to locate these oracles in a more narrow window of 586–550.[5]

We will focus on Jeremiah 23, 31, and 50. But first we must situate those passages in the context of the book as a whole. After the call of the prophet in Jeremiah 1, chapter 2 enters a long description of how Israel had forsaken her God. Even the reform under godly king Josiah had failed. God lamented Israel's apostasy:

> I remember the devotion of your youth,
>   how as a bride you loved me
> and followed me though the wilderness,
>   through a land not sown.
> Israel was holy to the LORD,
>   the firstfruits of his harvest. (Jer 2:2-3)

No longer, however, did they remember their faithful Shepherd.

> They followed worthless idols
>   and became worthless themselves.
> They did not ask, "Where is the LORD,
>   who brought us up out of Egypt [*'ayyēh yhwh hammaʿăleh 'ōtānû mēʾereṣ miṣrāyim*]
>   and led us through the barren wilderness." (Jer 2:5-6)

Priests, shepherds (i.e., leaders), and prophets are all to blame (Jer 2:8).

Chapter 23 is where we start examining the exodus motif in Jeremiah. It continues with the indictment (vv. 1-2) against Judah's shepherds (i.e., kings), but the tone shifts toward promises of a return from exile (vv. 3-4) to a pasture where they will be fruitful and multiply (*ûpārû wərābû*), echoing conditions in the Garden of Eden and therefore suggesting a connection with creation.[6] This seems to suggest that the promise will go the way of a mere return to the land of Palestine.[7] Moreover, a new Davidic king who

---

[5] Martin Kessler, *Battle of the Gods: The God of Israel Versus Marduk of Babylon; A Literary/Theological Interpretation of Jeremiah 50–51* (Assen, Netherlands: Van Gorcum, 2003), 206.
[6] See Gen 1:22, where God "blessed them and said, 'Be fruitful and increase in number [*pərû ûrəbû*],'" and Gen 1:28, where God once again said to them, "Be fruitful and increase in number [*pərû ûrəbû*]."
[7] Friedbert Ninow, *Indicators of Typology Within the Old Testament: The Exodus Motif* (Frankfurt: Peter Lang, 2001), 197.

will be worthy of the name and the office will be reinstated. This is reinforced by a chiastic structure emphasizing the reversal between verses 1 and 4:[8]

> "I will place shepherds over them who will tend them, and they will no longer be afraid or terrified, nor will any be missing," declares the LORD.
>
> "The days are coming," declares the LORD,
> "when I will raise up for David a righteous Branch,
> a King who will reign wisely
> and do what is just and right in the land.
> In his days Judah will be saved
> and Israel will live in safety.
> This is the name by which he will be called:
> The LORD Our Righteous Savior.
>
> "So then, the days are coming," declares the LORD, "when people will no longer say, 'As surely as the LORD lives, who brought the Israelites up out of Egypt [*heʿĕlâ ʾet-bənē yiśrāʾēl mēʾereṣ miṣrāyim*],' but they will say, 'As surely as the LORD lives, who brought the descendants of Israel up out of the land of the north [*mēʾereṣ ṣāpôwnâ*] and out of all the countries where he had banished them [*hāʾărāṣôt ʾăšer hiddaḥtîm šām*].' Then they will live in their own land." (Jer 23:4-8)

Here we see God will provide faithful shepherds for his people. Another chiasm (vv. 5-6) demonstrates and emphasizes the fact that God will raise up a king who will rule according to righteousness and justice.[9] God is not going to merely reconfigure or reconstitute the Sinai covenant, which began with similar words (cf. Ex 19 and esp. Ex 20:1). God is going to bring about a new covenant. In a moment of "raw courage and greatness of heart," Jeremiah is saying that everything will yet be well and that "the return from Babylon will *exceed in greatness* the exodus from Egypt!"[10] The age of this new messianic king will outstrip the former exodus experience.[11]

---

[8]See Timothy S. Laniak, *Shepherds After My Own Heart: Pastoral Traditions and Leadership in the Bible*, New Studies in Biblical Theology 20 (Downers Grove, IL: InterVarsity Press, 2006), 136.
[9]Ibid., 137.
[10]Kenneth E. Bailey, *The Good Shepherd: A Thousand-Year Journey from Psalm 23 to the New Testament* (Downers Grove, IL: IVP Academic, 2014), 73.
[11]Ninow, *Indicators of Typology*, 200. Interestingly, Irenaeus believed that this greater exodus would not occur at the first advent of Christ; rather, it will occur at the end of the age with the general resurrection. See *Against Heresies* 5.34.1 (*ANF* 1:563-64).

Another crucial passage in the development of the exodus motif in Scripture is Jeremiah 31:31-34 (= 38:31-34 LXX). Chapters 30–31 (perhaps 32–33 as well) comprise Jeremiah's Book of Consolation:

> "The days are coming," declares the Lord,
>   "when I will make a new covenant
> with the people of Israel
>   and with the people of Judah.
> It will not be like the covenant
>   I made with their ancestors
> when I took them by the hand
>   to lead them out of Egypt [*ləhôṣi'ām mē'ereṣ miṣrāyim*],[12]
> because they broke my covenant,
>   though I was a husband to them,"
>   declares the Lord.
> "This is the covenant I will make with the people of Israel
>   after that time," declares the Lord.
> "I will put my law in their minds[13]
>   and write it on their hearts.
> I will be their God,
>   and they will be my people.
> No longer will they teach their neighbor,
>   or say to one another, 'Know the Lord,'
> because they will all know me,
>   from the least of them to the greatest,"
>   declares the Lord.
> "For I will forgive their wickedness
>   and will remember their sins no more." (Jer 31:31-34)

This passage is clearly alluding to the Mosaic covenant with its reference to the making of the covenant with their forefathers when the Lord "led them out of Egypt." The Hebrews had broken the covenant shortly after

---

[12]The use of the *hiphil* of this verb is frequent in the book of Exodus to describe the people coming out of Egypt, as will be discussed below.

[13]Many people think that some OT descriptions of a redemptive internalization of God's law (especially here at Jer 31:33-34) is proof that Paul is not talking about universal natural law in Rom 2:14-15. For clarification and rebuttal of this issue, see David VanDrunen, *Divine Covenants and Moral Order: A Biblical Theology of Natural Law* (Grand Rapids: Eerdmans, 2014), 255.

it was first made. Indeed, it is as if they committed adultery on their very wedding night (cf. Ex 32)! Nevertheless, God was patient and merciful toward them, even throughout their long and stubborn history. God would have been just to punish them early on, but he did not.

This is one of the great mysteries of the old covenant. Why did God not punish Israel immediately according to her just deserts? Israel had made him cuckold even though he was the one who tenderly allured her and brought her out of the land of Egypt (cf. Hos 1–2). God was heartbroken—he moaned over Israel more than a parent over a prodigal son (cf. Hos 11). Yet God's people behaved like animals in heat (cf. Jer 2), and Judah acted more like the whore than even Israel (Jer 3:11). Nevertheless, God was patient and merciful toward them. They stretched God's patience thin like a rubber band, until there was no more remedy for their sin-sick lust after other gods:

> The LORD, the God of their ancestors, sent word to them through his messengers again and again, because he had pity on his people and on his dwelling place. But they mocked God's messengers, despised his words and scoffed at his prophets until the wrath of the LORD was aroused against his people and there was no remedy. He brought up against them the king of the Babylonians, who killed their young men with the sword in the sanctuary, and did not spare young men or young women, the elderly or the infirm. God gave them all into the hands of Nebuchadnezzar. (2 Chron 36:15-17)

So how will God act? He will establish a new covenant. He will bring a messiah. The categories that Jeremiah uses are drawn from the exodus and Moses. In the words of W. D. Davies, it is

> not merely homiletical but also theological, in that the first redemption from Egypt became the prototype of the future redemption. Thus although Jeremiah contrasts the New Covenant with that ratified at the Exodus, nevertheless, it was that same Exodus which, were it only by contrast, supplied him with the very categories with which to describe the new redemption that he desired.[14]

---

[14] W. D. Davies, *Torah in the Messianic Age and/or the Age to Come*, SBLMS 7 (Philadelphia: Society of Biblical Literature, 1952), 7-8.

While this passage is worthy of extended discussion,[15] for our present purposes it is sufficient to say that in language reminiscent of the typology discussed in chapter one of this book, the "Exodus from Egypt is the Vorbild [type] for the eschatological Nachbild [antitype]."[16]

Finally, we turn to Jeremiah 50:33-38, part of the prophet's oracles against the nations.[17] The Septuagint actually places these oracles of Jeremiah 46–51 immediately after Jeremiah 25:13b. Almost without exception, modern commentators prefer this arrangement.[18] The issues are complex, and I will accept the Masoretic Text as it has been passed on to us. I only note that recent rhetorical studies have demonstrated that these chapters are not ancillary to the book as a whole but are integral to the whole design of Jeremiah.[19]

> This is what the LORD Almighty says:
>
> The people of Israel are oppressed,
>   and the people of Judah as well.
> All their captors hold them fast,
>   refusing to let them go [root: šlḥ].[20]
> Yet their Redeemer [gōʾālām] is strong [ḥāzāq];[21]
>   the LORD Almighty is his name.
> He will vigorously defend their cause [rîb yārîb ʾet-rîbām]
>   so that he may bring rest [hirgîaʿ [22]] to their land,
>   but unrest [hirgîz] to those who live in Babylon.

---

[15]See my "Leviticus 18:5 and Deuteronomy 30:1-14 in Biblical Theological Development: Entitlement to Heaven Foreclosed and Proffered," in *The Law Is Not of Faith: Essays on Works and Grace in the Mosaic Covenant* (Phillipsburg, NJ: P&R, 2009), 129-31.
[16]Ninow, *Indicators of Typology*, 206.
[17]Although he does not deal with our passage specifically, for a helpful general introduction to this subject, see VanDrunen, *Divine Covenants*, 164-208. His chapter titled "Crimes Against Humanity: Natural Law in the Prophetic Judgments Against the Nations" gives a good overview of this type of literature elsewhere in the Hebrew Bible.
[18]Seitz, "Prophet Moses," 19.
[19]Kessler, *Battle of the Gods*, 7-35, argues for the importance of Jer 50–51 to the overall structure of the book. His reading is primarily literary (see 30-31).
[20]The verb in the *piel* occurs over forty times in the exodus for "to dismiss" or "let go."
[21]Another nice ironic echo since in exodus the verb is used typically to refer to Pharaoh's hardening.
[22]This verb and the one in the following line obviously constitute a brilliant wordplay.

"A sword [MT = *ḥereb*] against the Babylonians!"
   declares the LORD—
"against those who live in Babylon
   and against her officials and wise men!
A sword [MT = *ḥereb*] against her false prophets!
   They will become fools.
A sword [MT = *ḥereb*] against her warriors!
   They will be filled with terror.
A sword [MT = *ḥereb*] against her horses and chariots
   and all the foreigners in her ranks!
   They will become weaklings.
A sword [MT = *ḥereb*] against her treasuries!
   They will be plundered.
A drought [MT = *ḥōreb*] on her waters!
   They will dry up.
For it is a land of idols,
   idols that will go mad with terror." (Jer 50:33-38)

This passage has retrospective allusions and echoes to the exodus narrative and describes the freeing of the exiles and their implied return as a second exodus.[23] A few points will illustrate this.

First, this passage is based on the well-known lawsuit (*rîb*) pattern in the Prophets.[24] This is made obvious by the word choice, especially in verses 33-34. The use of "redeemer" instead of more expected language (e.g., Ps 103:6) reflects legal phraseology deriving from family law.[25] This form of legal invective reflects the role God often plays of prosecutor and judge.[26] The violated right being prosecuted by the Lord, according to Alice Ogden Bellis, is that Israel-Judah has not been manumitted from

---

[23] Alice Ogden Bellis, "The New Exodus in Jeremiah 50: 33-38," in *Imagery and Imagination in Biblical Literature: Essays in Honor of Aloysius Fitzgerald, F.S.C.*, ed. Lawrence Boadt and Mark S. Smith, CBQMS 32 (Washington, DC: Catholic Biblical Association, 2001), 157-68. Bellis wrote a dissertation under Fitzgerald: "The Structure and Composition of Jeremiah 50:1–51:18" (PhD diss., Catholic University of America, 1986).
[24] See Kirsten Nielsen, *Yahweh as Prosecutor and Judge: An Investigation of the Prophetic Lawsuit (Rib-Pattern)*, JSOTSup 9 (Sheffield: JSOT Press, 1978).
[25] Kessler, *Battle of the Gods*, 97. See R. L. Hubbard, "The *Go'el* in Ancient Israel: Theological Reflections on an Israelite Institution," *Bulletin for Biblical Research* 1 (1991): 3-19.
[26] Nielsen, *Yahweh as Prosecutor and Judge*, 74-83.

its slavery (*piel* of *šlḥ*). A scrutiny of pentateuchal slave laws leads Bellis to conclude, "It is fairly probable that the exodus traditions about Yahweh's bringing Israel out of Egypt, the 'house of bondage' (Exod 20:2), are the basis of the argument in Jer 50:33-38."[27]

Bellis uncovers more subtle allusions and echoes to the exodus motif as well. The last reference in verse 38 to *ḥōreb* (a drought, or dry heat) is customarily revocalized by scholars to conform with the repeated references previously (*ḥereb*, "sword").[28] But Bellis may be more in tune with the intentions of the ancient poet than modern text criticism, noting that the "dry heat" (MT = *ḥōreb*) of verse 38 results in the drying up of the Babylonians, water supply (*wəyābēšû*).[29] The wind is the dry sirocco. The point is reinforced by the effects that follow immediately in Jeremiah 50:39-40: Sodom and Gomorrah and the desolate wasteland inhabited by wild beasts.[30] Moreover, Jeremiah 51:36 may provide the final commentary when it presumes Babylon will be dried up like a desert.

When the Lord sweeps the hot east wind (*rûaḥ qādîm ʿazzāh*) over the sea in Exodus 14:21, it turns the sea into dry ground (*ḥārābâ*). The waters were divided, and the Israelites entered the sea on dry ground (*yabbāšā*, Ex 14:22).[31] What was a great salvation for Israel will be a judgment for Babylon, since she will be attacked by sword and judged by the Lord's wrath through a dry, hot wind. As Bellis puts it, "The east wind is an image drawn from the exodus tradition, which makes the expected return from exile typologically a new exodus."[32] Through a playful yet serious pun, Jeremiah has announced judgment on Babylon and salvation for God's people by means of a second exodus.

---

[27] Bellis, "New Exodus," 165.
[28] See Aloysius Fitzgerald, *The Lord of the East Wind*, CBQMS 34 (Washington, DC: Catholic Biblical Association, 2002), 130-31.
[29] Ibid., 109n8. Fitzgerald mentions that the noun *ḥōreb* "generally occurs in contexts where weather is being discussed. In Gen 31:40 and Jer 36:30 '*parching heat*' (*ḥōreb*) is opposed to *qeraḥ*. In Isa 4:6 '*parching* heat' is opposed to *zrm* and *mṭr*. In Judg 6:37, 39, 40 the presence of dew on Gideon's fleece is contrasted with *ḥōreb* on the ground."
[30] Ibid., 131.
[31] In addition to Ex 14:21; cf. Ex 14:16, 29; 15:19.
[32] Bellis, "New Exodus," 167.

Martin Kessler has joined Jeremiah 31 and 50–51 by first noting how 50:33 deliberately compares the exiles with Jacob's descendants in Egypt and Pharaoh's refusal to let the captives go. Then he notes the repeated use of the verb "go out" (*yṣ'*, especially in the *hiphil*) to describe Israel's exodus out of Egypt.[33] However, the verb is used in Jeremiah 51:4 to describe the Babylonians having to spew out the Israelites. Kessler summarizes:

> The exodus out of Egypt was the prologue to the Sinai covenant where Israel was constituted as YHWH's covenant people. In Jeremiah 50-51, Israel/Judah fleeing (from Babylon to Zion) may be seen as analogous to the exodus out of Egypt and the wilderness wandering to Sinai, where the covenant was ratified. A return to Sinai would be irrelevant in the Babylon oracles; Sinai was the locus of revelation, but Zion was YHWH's chosen sanctuary, his city, the place where the people would once again join themselves to YHWH in a ברית עולם [eternal covenant], never to be forgotten (cf. Jer 31:31-34). The prophets repeatedly charged that the Sinai covenant had been ignored, forgotten or violated (Jer 11:1-8; 25:3-8). Exile was YHWH's punishment for Judah's sin. But the time was coming when YHWH decided to liberate Judah so that she might return to her own land. With some justice we may therefore speak of a "second exodus." Just as the exodus out of Egypt was the preface to the covenant (at Sinai), so the "exodus" out of Babylon was the preparation for another covenant (a new covenant!), to reestablish the former covenant which the people had broken.[34]

We again see the pattern of Zion as the final goal, not Sinai. Additionally, the "exodus" leads to covenant, in this case the new covenant.

Ezekiel

Ezekiel, like his contemporary Jeremiah, develops many thematic connections with Exodus as well.[35] As a member of Judah's intelligentsia, he was probably among the first wave of deportees carried off

---

[33] The reader should recall the discussions on Is 48; 49; 52 in the last chapter, where the same verb repeatedly shows up under similar circumstances.
[34] Kessler, *Battle of the Gods*, 164-65.
[35] See Rebecca G. S. Idestrom, "Echoes of the Book of Exodus in Ezekiel," *JSOT* 33, no. 4 (2009): 489-510.

in Nebuchadnezzar's campaigns against Judah (see 2 Kings 24:14-15). As a Zadokite priest, Ezekiel is intimately aware of the need for holiness and Judah's lack of it. The house of Israel and Judah had become sin-sick and believed that "the LORD does not see" (Ezek 9:9). So the Lord declared that he would no longer have compassion on the people, and his glory departed from the temple (Ezek 10; 11:22-23), and his presence from the land. Ezekiel is a good example of the prophetic role of savage indictment against the people and the shepherds of the people on the basis the Sinaitic covenant.[36] Ezekiel 1–24 is mostly about this judgment on Judah. Chapter 20 is a summary of this bleak history of Israel and the focal point of our discussion of Ezekiel.

Many parallels have been drawn between Moses and Ezekiel.[37] Likewise, many parallels between the exodus and a new exodus have been seen in the prophecy of Ezekiel.[38] One recent study asks, what happens when we intentionally read Ezekiel alongside the book of Exodus?[39] "Moses and the exodus become a type for Ezekiel and the new exodus," claims Rebecca Idestrom.[40] Consider first a few of the parallels between Moses and Ezekiel: both minister to a people in exile; both receive the divine call; both reluctantly receive that call; both proclaim judgment and redemption in their message; both are mediators between God and the people; both repeatedly see the glory of the Lord.[41] In other cases, terminology from the exodus is picked up and transformed in Ezekiel.[42]

Ezekiel's repeated saying the people "will know that I am the LORD" (Ezek 6:14; 7:27; 12:15; etc.), sometimes called his "recognition formula," occurs numerous times in the book and is a connecting link with the

---

[36]See Michael Walzer's laconic statements in *Exodus and Revolution* (New York: Basic Books, 1985), 91.
[37]Nevada Levi Delapp, "Ezekiel as Mosel—Israel as Pharaoh: Reverberations of the Exodus Narrative in Ezekiel," in *Reverberations of the Exodus in Scripture*, ed. R. Michael Fox (Eugene, OR: Pickwick, 2014), 56-60.
[38]See the dissertation (hard to acquire in North America) of John Frederick Evans, "An Innerbiblical Interpretation and Intertextual Reading of Ezekiel's Recognition Formulae with the Book of Exodus" (ThD diss., University of Stellenbosch, 2006), 191-98.
[39]Ibid., 490.
[40]Ibid., 491.
[41]Ibid., 492-96.
[42]See ibid., 198-201.

book of Exodus.⁴³ This phrase, *wîdaʿtem kî-ʾănî yhwh* (you shall know that I am Yahweh [Ezek 7:4]), or phrases very similar to it, is repeated over seventy times in Ezekiel.⁴⁴ In both Exodus and Ezekiel, God is the key knowledge revealer, which is especially clear from the recognition formula used in both books.⁴⁵ From the perspective of innerbiblical interpretation, it seems plausible that "Ezekiel alludes to the book of Exodus in some authoritative recension."⁴⁶ Consequently, Ezekiel is not merely reflecting an Exodus tradition or motif but the very book of Exodus itself.⁴⁷ The best-known statement of the recognition formula entailing the proscription of idolatry is Exodus 20:2-3, "I am the LORD your God, who brought you out of Egypt, out of the land of slavery. You shall have no other gods before me." This is evoked in Ezekiel many times, but especially in Ezekiel 20.

Throughout Exodus, and in Ezekiel as well, divine action in judgment and salvation leads to knowledge of God. What is most striking is that Egypt and Pharaoh continued to be addressed in some of Ezekiel's oracles against the nations.⁴⁸ Ezekiel's use of the recognition formula is somewhat unique in the Hebrew Bible: there is an emphasis on judgment rather than salvation and, moreover, a judgment on Israel that is similar to judgment on the foreign nations (although some scholars have noted the recognition formula used in the context of covenantal mercy as well).⁴⁹ We saw this dynamic of biblical reading in two directions in chapter one. In other words, reading Ezekiel's recognition formula in light of Exodus and vice versa is mutually illuminating.

A second-exodus motif is introduced in Ezekiel 11:14-21 (there are others but these verses are representative):⁵⁰

---

⁴³Daniel I. Block, *The Book of Ezekiel: Chapters 1–24*, NICOT (Grand Rapids: Eerdmans, 1997), 39.
⁴⁴See Evans, "Inner-biblical Interpretation," 1.
⁴⁵Delapp, "Ezekiel as Moses," 53.
⁴⁶Evans, "Inner-biblical Interpretation," 66. This thesis is argued in detail on 175-215.
⁴⁷Ibid., 67.
⁴⁸See Ezek 29:6, 9, 16; 30:8, 19, 25, 26; 32:15.
⁴⁹Evans, "Inner-biblical Interpretation," 206. For the dual emphasis on judgment and covenantal mercy, see Delapp, "Ezekiel as Moses," 63-65.
⁵⁰See John Wright, "Spirit and Wilderness: The Interplay of Two Motifs Within the Hebrew Bible as a Background to Mark 1:2-13," in *Perspectives on Language and Text: Essays and Poems in Honor of Francis I. Andersen's Sixtieth Birthday, July 28, 1985*, ed. Edgar W. Conrad and Edward G. Newing

The word of the LORD came to me: "Son of man, the people of Jerusalem have said of your fellow exiles and all the other Israelites, 'They are far away from the LORD; this land was given to us as our possession.'

"Therefore say: 'This is what the Sovereign LORD says: Although I sent them far away among the nations and scattered them among the countries, yet for a little while I have been a sanctuary for them in the countries where they have gone.'

"Therefore say: 'This is what the Sovereign LORD says: I will gather you from the nations and bring you back from the countries where you have been scattered, and I will give you back the land of Israel again.'

"They will return to it and remove all its vile images and detestable idols. I will give them an undivided heart and put a new spirit in them; I will remove from them their heart of stone and give them a heart of flesh. Then they will follow my decrees and be careful to keep my laws. They will be my people, and I will be their God. But as for those whose hearts are devoted to their vile images and detestable idols, I will bring down on their own heads what they have done, declares the Sovereign LORD."

Here we note several significant developments of the exodus motif. The central concern of the text is with the exiles.[51] In the response to the arrogant claim of the Jerusalemites, God makes a striking statement without parallel elsewhere in the Old Testament: he declares that he himself will stand in for them during that exile, to be for them what the temple had formally represented for them.[52] Ezekiel 11:17-20 has the "flavor of a salvation oracle" and continue to describe in a remarkably concise manner the nature of the restoration.[53] There will be a new exodus (v. 17), a new land (v. 18), and a new covenant (vv. 19-20). In the latter verses (vv. 19-20), there seems to be clear influence from Jeremiah with

---

(Winona Lake, IN: Eisenbrauns, 1987), 269-98. Wright notes, "In the exilic and post-exilic literature, the spirit, like the life-giving spirit, given to man and animals at creation, will come again, after the people of Israel had been punished, and purged, after they had been driven into the symbolic wilderness, and traveled back over the wilderness in the New Exodus, and they will be given new life, a new breath, new power, transformation, a new *rûaḥ*. This is seen in Ezek 11:19; 18:36; 36:26 (cf. 36:27; 37:14), and the whole parable of the Valley of Bones symbolizes this" (284).
[51]Block, *Book of Ezekiel*, 346.
[52]Ibid., 349.
[53]Ibid., 351.

innerbiblical exegesis of Jeremiah 32:39.[54] The salvation oracle ends with a reminder not to take this promise for granted (v. 21).

Even more significant is that Ezekiel 20:1-44 brings together two key themes: a new exodus promise and the theme of covenant renewal.[55] However, chapter 20 also forms a core in the prophet's overall argument that Israel's history had been one of unbroken infidelity.[56] As Walther Zimmerli recognized, "the tradition of the exodus dominates the theology of ch. 20, which in the first half speaks of the first exodus and in the second half of the second exodus in typological fashion."[57] Focusing on just the last fourteen verses, we read:

> Therefore say to the Israelites: "This is what the Sovereign LORD says: Will you defile yourselves the way your ancestors did and lust after their vile images? When you offer your gifts—the sacrifice of your children in the fire—you continue to defile yourselves with all your idols to this day. Am I to let you inquire of me, you Israelites? As surely as I live, declares the Sovereign LORD, I will not let you inquire of me.
>
> "You say, 'We want to be like the nations, like the peoples of the world, who serve wood and stone.' But what you have in mind will never happen. As surely as I live, declares the Sovereign LORD, I will reign over you with a mighty hand and an outstretched arm [$bizrô'a\ n\partial tûyâ$] and with outpoured wrath. I will bring you [$w\partial hôṣē'tî$ (root: $yṣ'$) $'etkem$] from the nations and gather you from the countries where you have been scattered—with a mighty hand and an outstretched arm [$bizrô'a\ n\partial tûyâ$] and with outpoured wrath. I will bring you into the wilderness of the nations and there, face to face, I will execute judgment upon you. As I judged your ancestors in the wilderness of the land of Egypt, so I will judge you, declares the Sovereign LORD. I will take note of you as you pass under my rod, and I will bring you into the bond of the covenant. I will purge you of those who revolt and rebel against me. Although I will bring them out of the land where they are living, yet they will not enter the land of Israel. Then you will know that I am the LORD.

---

[54] Ibid., 352-54.
[55] Idestrom, "Echoes," 500.
[56] Evans, "Inner-biblical Interpretation," 256.
[57] Walther Zimmerli, *Ezekiel 1*, trans. Ronald E. Clements, Hermeneia (Philadelphia: Fortress, 1979), 41.

> "As for you, people of Israel, this is what the Sovereign Lord says: Go and serve your idols, every one of you! But afterward you will surely listen to me and no longer profane my holy name with your gifts and idols. For on my holy mountain, the high mountain of Israel, declares the Sovereign Lord, there in the land all the people of Israel will serve me, and there I will accept them. There I will require your offerings and your choice gifts, along with all your holy sacrifices. I will accept you as fragrant incense when I bring you out from the nations and gather you from the countries where you have been scattered, and I will be proved holy through you in the sight of the nations. Then you will know that I am the Lord, when I bring you into the land of Israel, the land I had sworn with uplifted hand to give to your ancestors. There you will remember your conduct and all the actions by which you have defiled yourselves, and you will loathe yourselves for all the evil you have done. You will know that I am the Lord, when I deal with you for my name's sake and not according to your evil ways and your corrupt practices, you people of Israel, declares the Sovereign Lord." (Ezek 20:30-44)

Ezekiel has prophesied here that there will be a new exodus. God will lead them back to the land of their fathers, but first they must know a new exodus will reveal his judgment, so that they may know him.[58] The language here, especially in verses 33-42, is mimicking God's speech to Moses in Exodus 6:6-8:[59]

> Therefore, say to the Israelites: "I am the Lord, and I will bring you out [*wəhôṣē'tî* (root: *yṣ'*) *'etkem*] from under the yoke of the Egyptians. I will free you from being slaves to them, and I will redeem you with an outstretched arm [*bizrôʿa nəṭûyâ*] and with mighty acts of judgment. I will take you as my own people, and I will be your God. Then you will know that I am the Lord your God, who brought you out from under the yoke of the Egyptians. And I will bring you to the land I swore with uplifted hand to give to Abraham, to Isaac and to Jacob. I will give it to you as a possession. I am the Lord."

---

[58]Evans, "Inner-biblical Interpretation," 268.
[59]See Michael Fishbane, *Text and Texture: Close Readings of Selected Biblical Texts* (New York: Schocken, 1979), 131-33. For further detail on correspondences between Ex 6 and Ezek 20, see Evans, "Inner-biblical Interpretation," 177-83.

Michael Fishbane notes that because of the Ezekiel passage's "intentional reuse" of the Exodus passage, "its sarcasm and bitterness were undoubtedly not lost on his first audience."[60] The Ezekiel passage is a "radical inversion" of the exodus language.[61] Such a sarcastic quip may have been anticipated by the use of irony in Ezekiel 20:25: "So I gave them other statutes that were not good and laws through which they could not live." If recent interpretations of this verse are correct about the irony communicated here, it represents Judah's thoughts about God and his laws, placing them back in this previous oracle.[62] Therefore, although there is strong continuity in Ezekiel's use of the recognition formula, there is also jarring discontinuity.[63]

In chapter three and four, we spoke of the pattern of the cosmic mountain ideology. There the narrative pattern motivated by the ancient Near Eastern cosmic mountain ideology was set forth, waiting for further detail to fill in: Egypt–waters–wilderness–sanctuary (symbolized by the mountain).[64] The Israelites constantly failed; however, now God will accomplish a second exodus on their behalf in the future. Although they were unfaithful to the covenant, God will not be.

Ezekiel 20:32 indicates their idolatry: "You say, 'We want to be like the nations, like the peoples of the world, who serve wood and stone.'" Although the pull toward idolatry must have been strong for these exiles, this one verse, as J. F. Evans has shown, is an "excellent key for understanding the background to the incessant refrain" so common in Exodus and Ezekiel: "I am Yahweh, your God." Ezekiel demonstrates a pattern among the people: from the exodus all the way up to the exile, these people have shown a bias for idolatry. Notice Ezekiel 20:5: "This

---

[60] Fishbane, *Text and Texture*, 133.
[61] Evans, "Inner-biblical Interpretation," 263.
[62] See Ronnie Sim, "Revisiting Ezk 20.25-26: Echo Question, Denial, or Echo of a Third Kind" (paper presented at the International Meeting of the Society of Biblical Literature, Tartu, July 2010).
[63] Evans, "Inner-biblical Interpretation," 260. This is not to imply that all of Ezekiel's uses of the recognition formula are in the context of judgment. According to Evans, 75 percent of Ezekiel's recognition formulae occurs in the context of judgment while the remaining formulae occur in contexts of restoration and mercy (see ibid., 275).
[64] L. Michael Morales, *The Tabernacle Pre-figured: Cosmic Mountain Ideology in Genesis and Exodus*, Biblical Tools and Studies 15 (Leuven: Peeters, 2012), 209.

is what the Sovereign LORD says: On the day I chose Israel, I swore with uplifted hand to the descendants of the house of Jacob and reveled myself to them in Egypt. With uplifted hand I said to them, 'I am the LORD your God.'" As Evans says laconically, "To serve idols was to profane Yahweh's holy name (Ezekiel 20:39); contrariwise, to worship God on his holy mountain was to know him by name as Yahweh (vv. 40-44)."[65]

Ezekiel's use of the recognition formula would have been shocking to its audience. Previously in Israel's history, the formula sounded a note of triumphant encouragement. Now in Ezekiel, however, the recognition formula often occurs in the context of judgment. Israel will be given in judgment to her neighbors. As Evans notes, "Nowhere else in all the Bible does the recognition formula appear in an oracle of judgment against Israel."[66] This "Exodus-laced rhetoric" is a perennial call to Israel for repentance.[67]

Ezra-Nehemiah

Assigning a date to the final form of the book of Ezra raises complex literary, chronological, and historical questions. All that can confidently be said is that sometime following the events described in the book, various sources were compiled and brought together into their present form.[68] Additionally, the chronological relationship between Ezra and Nehemiah is one of the most "controversial and vexing problems in Old Testament research."[69] Regarding the actual mission of Ezra, the dates of either 458 or 398 BCE are both viable alternatives from the perspective of the text alone. Kenneth G. Hoglund, through a careful examination of the archaeological, historical, and textual evidence, has

---

[65] Evans, "Inner-biblical Interpretation," 259.
[66] Ibid., 262.
[67] Delapp, "Ezekiel as Moses," 73.
[68] H. G. M. Williamson, *Ezra, Nehemiah*, WBC 16 (Waco, TX: Word, 1985), xxi-lii. Also see his earlier monograph, *Israel in the Books of Chronicles* (Cambridge: Cambridge University Press, 1977); particularly instructive on the possible composition of Ezra 1-6 is his article "The Composition of Ezra i-vi," *JTS* 34 (1983): 1-30.
[69] Geo Widengren, "The Persian Period," in *Israelite and Judean History*, ed. John H. Hayes and J. Maxwell Miller (London: SCM Press, 1977), 503.

convincingly argued that a fundamental change in the status of the Yehud province ushered in the missions of Ezra and Nehemiah occurred in the mid-fifth century BCE.[70] The primary purpose of the change was to enhance the political and military status of the Persian Empire. This change in Persian policy was precipitated by the revolt in Egypt that occurred shortly after the death of Xerxes in 464 BCE. This seems to have tipped the scales in favor of the traditional view (Ezra's mission preceding that of Nehemiah) and its traditional date (458 BCE).[71]

In order to understand the missions of Ezra and Nehemiah, we must set them against the backdrop of Achaemenid imperial history during the mid-fifth century BCE and after.[72] After the successful revolt in Egypt, the opportunistic Delian League in the Mediterranean began looking eastward. The Persian Empire assumed a keen interest in the province of Yehud as a buffer zone in the Levant against the threatening interests of Egypt and, possibly, of Greece. Because of these military and political considerations, Ezra and Nehemiah were commissioned to rebuild Jerusalem and so provide a strong inland fortification against the expanding interests and potential threats from these outside nations.

Against this historical backdrop we can view some of the texts of Ezra that advance the exodus motif. Two formulas are of particular interest: the "go forth" (*hôṣîʾ*, *hiphil* from *yṣʾ*) formula and the "go up" (*heʿĕlāh*, *hiphil* from *ʿlh*) formula. They each have fixed elements: both formulas have the object (Israel or its equivalents) and the determination ("I liberated you from Egypt" or its equivalents).[73] Of the 277 times that the verb *hôṣîʾ* occurs in the Hebrew Bible, over a quarter of those occurrences have to do with the exodus.[74] Moreover, often the

---

[70]Kenneth G. Hoglund, *Achaemenid Imperial Administration in Syria-Palestine and the Missions of Ezra and Nehemiah*, SBLDS 125 (Atlanta: Scholars Press, 1992). Michael W. Duggan, *The Covenant Renewal in Ezra-Nehemiah (Neh 7:72b–10:40): An Exegetical, Literary, and Theological Study*, SBLDS 164 (Atlanta: Society of Biblical Literature, 2001), 4, calls Hoglund's work a "groundbreaking treatment of the social and political background of the missions of Ezra and Nehemiah."

[71]For a very good summary of the issues, see Williamson, *Ezra, Nehemiah*, xxxv-xliv.

[72]For a history of the Achaemenid Empire (c. 550–330), the reader should consult Kuhrt, *Ancient Near East*, 2:647-701.

[73]J. Wjingaards, "A Twofold Approach to the Exodus," *VT* 15 (1965): 91-102.

[74]Ibid., 91.

word serves to recall the historical prologue of treaty relationships, "which is meant to establish the sovereign's right to his vassal's fidelity."[75] The historical prologue gives "the reason motivating stipulations"[76] so when children ask, "Why do we observe these laws?," they have a historical record of God's goodness to them. The "go up" (*heʿĕlāh*) formula distribution is also pervasive, occurring in forty-one cases to the exodus from Egypt.[77] Usually it is in the *hiphil*, for example, in Exodus 17:3 and Exodus 33:12. However, sometimes the *niphal* is used, such as in Ezekiel 1:11, to emphasize divine activity, since it is passive. The verb "to bring up" (*ʿlh*) is often deliberately chosen to echo the exodus. This verb echoes "bring out" (*hôṣîʾ*, hiphil from *yṣʿ*) so that statements about "bringing up" from Babylon to Jerusalem directly echo the exodus, for example, "brought up out of the land of Egypt, unto the land" (Ex 33:1 KJV).[78] Indeed, source-critical scholars see it as pervasive throughout the material of various alleged literary strands.[79] The formula is often mentioned in the context of "coming to the land."[80]

Often the terms have to do with a liturgical character. We might construct the original as "I made you come (here) out of Egypt" (*heʿĕlêtî ʾitkem mimiṣrayim*). This seems to function within the land-giving schema from the very start,[81] but the question remains, what was Ezra's understanding of the restoration? "Ezra's march from Babylonia to Jerusalem was a cultic procession which Ezra understood as a second Exodus and partial fulfillment of prophetic expectation."[82] This is shown in the fact that Ezra insists that followers go along with him in the restoration. As K. Koch notes, even though Ezra takes some five thousand people for this second exodus, that is a relatively small number compared to the first exodus.[83] This action was probably a pre-eschatological step, "a sign

---

[75]Ibid., 92.
[76]Ibid., 95.
[77]Ibid., 98.
[78]See Williamson, *Ezra, Nehemiah*, 19.
[79]Ibid.
[80]Ibid., 99.
[81]Ibid., 100.
[82]K. Koch, "Ezra and the Origins of Judaism," *Journal of Semitic Studies* 19 (1974): 184.
[83]Koch (ibid., 189) points out that Numbers records more than six hundred thousand (cf. Num 26:51).

of a coming fulfillment and not the eschatological fulfillment itself." This was probably what Ezra had in mind in the prayer recorded in Ezra 9:8-9, where he says, "Our God . . . has given us a little renewal . . . for slaves we are."[84] In other words, there is no theology of glory here. This is the wilderness wandering of a pilgrim people, who are expecting something greater than the reestablishment of the theocracy.

Then there is the edict of Ezra 7:12-26, which begins:

Artaxerxes, king of kings,

To Ezra the priest, a teacher of the Law of the God of heaven:

Greetings.

Now I decree that any of the Israelites in my kingdom, including priests and Levites, who volunteer to go to Jerusalem with you, may go. You are sent by the king and his seven advisers to inquire about Judah and Jerusalem with regard to the Law of your God, which is in your hand. Moreover, you are to take with you the silver and gold that the king and his advisers have freely given to the God of Israel, whose dwelling is in Jerusalem, together with all the silver and gold you may obtain from the province of Babylon, as well as the freewill offerings of the people and priests for the temple of their God in Jerusalem. (Ezra 7:12-16)

The main part of the edict shows that the primary concern is for the "establishment of a permanent and effective worship in favour of the people of Israel and in favour of the king of Persia."[85] These considerations lead to the following conclusion: "We find here a further fulfillment of Israel's prophetic hopes for a return from exile, which had themselves drawn on the language and imagery of the Exodus for their expression."[86] Therefore, even in the beginning of the book, we see the formula and the opening of the new exodus:

In the first year of Cyrus king of Persia, in order to fulfill the word of the LORD spoken by Jeremiah, the LORD moved the heart of Cyrus king of Persia to make a proclamation throughout his realm and also to put it in writing:

---
[84]Ibid.
[85]Ibid., 185.
[86]Ibid.

"This is what Cyrus king of Persia says:

"'The Lord, the God of heaven, has given me all the kingdoms of the earth and he has appointed me to build a temple for him at Jerusalem in Judah. Any of his people among you may go up [wəyaʿal] to Jerusalem in Judah and build the temple of the Lord, the God of Israel, the God who is in Jerusalem, and may their God be with them. And in any locality where survivors may now be living, the people are to provide them with silver and gold, with goods and livestock, and with freewill offerings for the temple of God in Jerusalem.'"

Then the family heads of Judah and Benjamin, and the priest and Levites—everyone whose heart God had moved—prepared to go up [laʿălôt] and build the house of the Lord in Jerusalem. All their neighbors assisted them with articles of silver and gold, with goods and livestock, and with valuable gifts, in addition to all the freewill offerings.

Moreover, King Cyrus brought out the articles belonging to the temple of the Lord, which Nebuchadnezzar had carried away from Jerusalem and had placed in the temple of his god. Cyrus king of Persia had them brought by Mithredath the treasurer, who counted them out to Sheshbazzar the prince of Judah.

This was their inventory:

gold dishes	30
silver dishes	1,000
silver pans	29
gold bowls	30
matching silver bowls	410
other articles	1,000

In all, there were 5,400 articles of gold and silver. Sheshbazzar brought all these along with the exiles when they came up from Babylon to Jerusalem. (Ezra 1:1-11)

The book of Ezra develops the previously stated ideas in elaborate detail: the language of "bring up from Babylon to Jerusalem" is meant to deliberately echo "brought up from the land of Egypt, unto the land," and furthermore, the restoration from exile is viewed as a second exodus. This return from exile was freighted with hope and expectation. "Thus we find here a further fulfillment of Israel's prophetic hopes for a return from exile, which had themselves drawn on the language and imagery of the Exodus for their expression."[87]

Nehemiah 9

The prayer of Nehemiah 9, with its echo of Leviticus 18:5, is a masterpiece.[88] Viewed from the standpoint of innerbiblical exegesis and innerbiblical allusion, it is an elaborate discourse that weaves themes into a new construction that demonstrates the fundamental integrity of the parts. Not a word is wasted.[89] Michael W. Duggan offers a masterful reading of the text that encompasses its literary data and its historical progression.[90] Duggan's approach has been simplified by Jacques Vermeylen in the following outline of Nehemiah 9:[91]

A. God and Israel throughout the past (vv. 6-31)
  1. YHWH's foundational activity (vv. 6-8)
    a. The creation of the universe (vv. 6-8)
    b. The election of Abraham (v. 6)
  2. The wilderness period (vv. 9-21)
    a. The era of harmony (vv. 9-15)
      (1) The exodus (vv. 9-11)
      (2) God's gifts in the wilderness (vv. 12-15)
    b. The people's rebellion and God's mercy (vv. 16-21)
      (1) The people's rebellion (vv. 16-17b)
      (2) God's mercy (v. 17cd)
      (3) The people's rebellion (v. 18)
      (4) God's demonstration of mercy (vv. 19-21)[92]

---

[87] Williamson, *Ezra, Nehemiah*, 111.
[88] Estelle, "Leviticus 18:5," 121-22.
[89] See the exquisitely written analysis of Jacques Vermeylen, "The Gracious God, Sinners and Foreigners: How Nehemiah 9 Interprets the History of Israel," in *Deuterocanonical and Cognate Literature: Yearbook 2006*, ed. Friedrich V. Reiterer et al. (New York: De Gruyter, 2006), 77-114.
[90] Duggan, *Covenant Renewal*, 157-233.
[91] Vermeylen, "Nehemiah 9," 80-81.
[92] An alternative to seeing this as a second exodus—that is, interpreting this positively as a return through the desert from Babylon—may be precluded as an interpretation in light of v. 17 and if the context here is Palestinian, as suggested by J. Wright, "Spirit and Wilderness," 288. Others have emphasized the pilgrimage motif as most prominent. See Joshua E. Williams, "Promise and Failure: Second Exodus in Ezra-Nehemiah," in Fox, *Reverberations*, 74-80.

3. The occupation and subsequent life in the land (vv. 22-31)
      a. The era of harmony: the occupation of the land (vv. 22-25)
      b. Rebellion and mercy: life in the land (vv. 26-31)
         (1) Rebellion, oppression, outcry, deliverance (vv. 26-27)
         (2) Rebellion, oppression, outcry, deliverance (v. 28)
         (3) Rebellion, oppression (vv. 29-31)
 B. God and Israel in the present (vv. 32-37)
   1. Petition (v. 32)
   2. Confession (vv. 33-35)
   3. The present distress (vv. 36-37)

In an amazing performance of literary artistry, the writer has emphasized the people's constant rebellion through virtually every period of redemptive history, including the present. Yet the author has also demonstrated that God has kept his word and promises despite the people's recalcitrance.

The prayer reinforces what we have seen earlier: the exodus motif includes liberation from Egypt and Pharaoh, wilderness wandering up to Sinai and beyond, and possession of the Promised Land. It also shows how the remembrance of the exodus is "wholly integrated into a confession of sin."[93] The prayer answers (to some degree) the mystery of God's justice despite the people's constant stubbornness. God has been merciful. He has not treated the people as they deserve. Rather, he has been faithful.

Return from Exile and Prophetic Fulfillment

We have examined Isaiah's prophetic promises in Isaiah 40–55, and we have seen how those same themes emerge in the exilic and postexilic literature of the Hebrew Bible. But a significant question remains. Do the return from exile and the resettlement of Jerusalem fulfill Isaiah's prophecies and his view of a second exodus?[94] Did Cyrus really lead any kind of new exodus? Or do those promises far outstrip anything that can

---

[93]Markus Witte, "History and Historiography in Psalm 78," in *Deuterocanonical and Cognate Literature Yearbook 2006* (New York: De Gruyter, 2006), 30.

[94]Bo H. Lim, *The "Way of the Lord" in the Book of Isaiah*, Library of Hebrew Bible/OT Studies 522 (New York: T&T Clark, 2010), 106.

be measured in the historical record? These questions are crucial for our development of a biblical theology of the exodus motif generally but also because certain answers to those questions have been forcefully asserted by New Testament scholars in recent years. In other words, when we arrive at the New Testament period, is there a notion among the Jews of the time of a "continuing exile"? N. T. Wright, for example, in his recent treatment of this issue, argues that the prayer of Nehemiah 9 maintains that the Jews are still in exile.[95] A detailed discussion of the mindset of Jews at the time of the New Testament will have to await the next chapter. However, I will venture into answering this question in preliminary manner now.

As noted above, Koch sees a genuine fulfillment of prophetic promises and expectations but sees the restoration as only a partial one, a pre-eschatological step. Not all agree with him. For example, Paul D. Hanson recognizes that the early postexilic period is crucial for understanding how biblical movements had turned during this era and as part of the puzzle for grasping how parties would develop in the Hellenistic and Roman periods, as well as being valuable in their own right.[96] Even so, I cannot follow him when he asserts, "There is no hint any longer of hope for the restoration of an indigenous Davidic kingdom.... Eschatological expectations have disappeared."[97] Rather, I find Bo Lim's comments to be more on the mark: "The period in which Ezra and Nehemiah ministered is then to be understood within a continuum of an inaugurated prophetic eschatology."[98]

J. Gordon McConville and H. G. M. Williamson have both taken up Koch's ideas and developed them, although in different manners.[99] McConville asserts that the postexilic community's expectations far

---

[95]N. T. Wright, *Paul and the Faithfulness of God*, Christian Origins and the Question of God 4 (Minneapolis: Fortress, 2013), 151. For his broader discussion of continuing exile, see 139-63.
[96]Paul D. Hanson, "Israelite Religion in the Early Postexilic Period," in *Ancient Israelite Religion: Essays in Honor of Frank Moore Cross*, ed. Patrick D. Miller Jr., Paul D. Hanson, and S. Dean McBride (Philadelphia: Fortress, 1987), 506.
[97]Ibid., 499.
[98]Lim, *Way of the Lord*, 107.
[99]J. G. McConville, "Ezra-Nehemiah and the Fulfillment of Prophecy," *VT* 36, no. 2 (April 1986): 205-24. All references to Williamson are from his *Ezra, Nehemiah*.

exceeded fulfillment, according to the prayers of Ezekiel 9 and Nehemiah 9. He also notes many similarities between Jeremiah 31 and Ezra 7–9. Both passages emphasize repentance as necessary for restoration, and therefore applying prophecy to Ezra's time "is to suggest that act [restoration] is in the process of happening, rather than that it has happened once and for all."[100] Williamson believes that the restoration is a fulfillment of the prophecies in Isaiah (particularly Is 41:2, 25; 44:28; 45:1; and esp. 45:13). He concludes, because of the close lexical allusions, "It is difficult not to suppose that the writer of Ezra indeed had such passages in the forefront of his mind, so close is their language and context to that which he is describing as the fulfillment of prophecy."[101] Joseph Blenkinsopp adds Jeremiah's prophecies (Jer 29:10-14; 25:11-14) to the mix of Isaiah's and concludes about the opening of Ezra that it "marks therefore a very special moment of grace, the historical realization of a new dispensation brought about by divine agency in fulfillment of the prophecies."[102]

At this point in the book, therefore, we can conclude that there was a fulfillment of prophetic hopes. Although this was *a* fulfillment, it was not *the* fulfillment. Rather, it was typological and pre-eschatological. This restoration is not fully realized. The historical restoration community cries out for further realization since the prophetic promises of return far outstripped anything realized in the postexilic community.

Conclusion

In this chapter we have examined exilic and postexilic literature for the continuation of the exodus motif in the form of a second exodus. First, we saw that Jeremiah 23 draws a correspondence between the first exodus out of Egypt and the second exodus out of Babylon. In Jeremiah 31 we saw the exodus motif in the classic passage about God establishing a new covenant in which he will write his covenantal law on his people's heart. Finally, in Jeremiah 50 we noted the theme of a new exodus arising out of a central passage from Jeremiah's oracles against the nations.

---

[100]McConnville, "Ezra-Nehemiah," 217.
[101]Williamson, *Ezra, Nehemiah*, 10.
[102]Joseph Blenkinsopp, *Ezra-Nehemiah*, OTL (Philadelphia: Westminster, 1988), 74-75.

Turning to Ezekiel, we found a new exodus in chapter 11, but judgment prevails in chapter 20, which is permeated by exodus allusions. Finally, in Ezra–Nehemiah we observe how the notion of a second exodus is invoked in stock phrases and alluded to by means of the many prophecies being evoked as background to understanding the postexilic situation. We briefly looked at the prayer of Nehemiah 9, which is a masterful web of innerbiblical allusion. That prayer emphasizes the constant rebellion on the part of the Hebrews in contrast to God's tenacious mercy and faithfulness.

Last, we considered whether the prophetic promises understand the postexilic period as *the* fulfillment of a glorious restoration or whether it is only *a* fulfillment with a much more glorious and profound realization yet to come. Peter Ackroyd, in his classic study on the Babylonian exile, noted that the notion of exile had become enlarged beyond historical and temporal boundaries in the postexilic age:

> It is in this that we may see the truth of that type of interpretation of the post-exilic age which points out that the exile came to be seen as of paramount importance, a great divide between the earlier and later stages, but one which it was necessary to traverse if the new age was to be reached. Only those who had gone through the exile—whether actually or spiritually—could be thought of as belonging.[103]

We affirmed that in the events of the return from exile there is *a* fulfillment but not *the* fulfillment. However, a fuller answer to those biblical theological questions remains for the next chapter.

It should be clear by this point that we have ascended to a high point of anticipation. The exodus motif has shown constant development, but we have not reached the pinnacle of its fulfillment.

---

[103]Peter R. Ackroyd, *Exile and Restoration: A Study of Hebrew Thought of the Sixth Century B.C.*, OTL (Philadelphia: Westminster Press, 1968), 243.

Seven

JESUS AS THE NEW EXODUS IN MARK AND MATTHEW

The coming of Jesus is the new definitive Exodus—this is the burden of the Gospels' message. The New Testament used the Exodus, the decisive divine act of the Old Testament period, to set forth its own meaning.... The Exodus tradition then seems to be one of the most fundamental in Scripture. All stages of redemptive history subsequent to this first event used the Exodus to explain its own meaning. If modern readers no longer feel completely at home with it, this is only because they have lost their Scriptural heritage to a large degree.

Augustine Stock

The Gospels and Acts describe Jesus, the anticipated Messiah, as the agent of the eschatological new exodus. The Old Testament anticipates a glorious new beginning for Israel, a turn in the plot described in a grammar shaped by the exodus. That grammar includes deliverance from tyranny, meeting at the mountain of Sinai, wilderness wanderings, and entrance into the Promised Land. As Michael Walzer says, "The final redemption is the original redemption writ large."[1] However, this new creative and redemptive event marked by the presence of the long-awaited Servant-Messiah—the new Moses—has been cloaked in shadows up to this point in redemptive history.[2] Jesus will guide his

---

[1] Michael Walzer, *Exodus and Revolution* (New York: Basic Books), 1985.
[2] See Aage Bentzen, *King and Messiah* (London: Lutterworth, 1955). Bentzen is the one who has most closely connected the expectation of the *'ebed Yahweh* (servant of the Lord) with the "new Moses" tradition and anticipation of that time. Also see Meredith G. Kline, "The Old Testament Origins of

people to a new mountain in order to establish a new covenant. He is the one who, by his work of suffering and perfect obedience, will merit salvation for all those who have faith, and he will constitute a new people: Israel is to be reborn, even resurrected. A new creation, with good grapes, will issue from the vine that was God's people.

The Gospel of Mark, through its prologue, its use of "wilderness" and "way" (Greek *hodos*) terminology, and indeed its overall structure, clearly shows Jesus as the new exodus. In Matthew, Jesus is presented as the new Moses, not in a manner that diminishes the importance of Moses for the Old Testament theocracy, but surely in a manner that transcends Moses.[3] We will turn our attention to Jesus as the obedient Son, which Israel was not.[4] Christ takes up the vocation of Israel in his earthly ministry; however, nothing should eclipse the fundamental distinction between Christ the redeemer and Israel the redeemed. All the Gospels use the grammar of Old Testament events to describe the arrival of Jesus, but the Gospel writers especially use the exodus motif to announce the coming of King Jesus. Each Gospel writer develops this in his own style. The exodus is recast along worldwide, earthshaking lines. The *new exodus* is a creative event answering the question, who is the true Israel?

The Exodus Motif in Mark

Richard Hays comments that the "full impact of Mark's Christology can be discerned only when we attend to *the poetics of allusion* imbedded in Mark's intertextual narrative strategy."[5] Hays says that Mark is "thunderstruck" with a "fresh encounter with Israel's Scripture in light of the story of Jesus."[6] Mark is full of allusive subtlety.

Mark's Gospel begins on an evocative note:

---

the Gospel Genre," *WTJ* 38, no. 1 (1975): 1-37. A slightly revised version appears in the second edition of *The Structure of Biblical Authority* (self-published, 1989), 172-203, esp. 181.
[3]Dale C. Allison Jr., *The New Moses: A Matthean Typology* (Minneapolis: Fortress, 1993).
[4]This will necessarily maintain the proper distinctions between the typological son, i.e., Israel, and the true Son of Israel, i.e., Christ. There are many distinctions between Israel as a typological son (either corporately or individually as in, say, the case of the king) and Christ as the true Son of God.
[5]Richard B. Hays, *Reading Backwards: Figural Christology and the Fourfold Gospel Witness* (Waco, TX: Baylor University Press, 2014), 28.
[6]Ibid., xi.

The beginning of the good news about Jesus the Messiah, the Son of God, as it is written in Isaiah the prophet:

"I will send my messenger ahead of you,
    who will prepare your way"—
"a voice of one calling in the wilderness,
'Prepare the way for the Lord,
    make straight paths for him.'" (Mark 1:1-3)

Mark attaches brief paragraphs to unified sections in his Gospel in order to draw attention to his point. Mark 3:7-12 and 4:33-34 are two examples. When Mark quotes Isaiah 40:3 in the prologue, he sets in motion the powerful metaphor of "the way" in the wilderness.[7]

The cultural and religious context of Judaism "energized" this theme. The soil was prepared. The community at Qumran saw itself as the true Israel, preparing themselves "for the eschatological denouement in the desert."[8] Such ideas were in the cultural air, part of how people naturally generated metaphors in their communication.[9] For Mark, *the wilderness* (read "desert") *becomes a unifying theme through his prologue*.[10] Indeed, for the whole of Mark's Gospel, the wilderness theme is essential and central.[11]

The concept of wilderness attracted the attention of twentieth-century New Testament scholars because of the parallel importance attributed to Isaiah 40 in the New Testament and at Qumran.[12] Although in the ancient

---

[7]Basil Robert Bater, "The Church in the Wilderness: A Study in Biblical Theology" (ThD diss., Union Theological Seminary, 1962), 71. Not just Is 40:3 but the entire prologue, especially Is 40:9-10, should be seen as backdrop for "the beginning of the gospel" if we understand Mark correctly. See Robert A. Guelich, "'The Beginning of the Gospel': Mark 1–15," *Biblical Research* 27 (1982): 5-15, and Guelich, *Mark 1–8:26*, WBC 34A (Dallas: Word, 1989), 3-46. Bo Lim comments, "Guelich views 1:1 as an introduction to vv. 1-15, Marcus sees it as introducing much more." Bo H. Lim, *The "Way of the Lord" in the Book of Isaiah*, Library of Hebrew Bible/OT Studies 522 (New York: T&T Clark, 2010), 163.
[8]Bater, "Church in the Wilderness," 92 and 98.
[9]"Wilderness" in the Bible may carry negative or positive connotations. The analysis of this symbol is complex and variegated. For a survey, see John Wright, "Spirit and Wilderness: The Interplay of Two Motifs Within the Hebrew Bible as Background to Mark 1:2-13," in *Perspectives on Language and Text: Essays and Poems in Honor of Francis I. Andersen's Sixtieth Birthday, July 28, 1985*, ed. Edgar W. Conrad and Edward G. Newing (Winona Lake, IN: Eisenbrauns, 1987), 269-98.
[10]Augustine Stock, *The Way in the Wilderness: Exodus, Wilderness and Moses Themes in the Old Testament and New* (Collegeville, MN: Liturgical Press, 1969), 70.
[11]Stock, *Way in the Wilderness*, 89-90.
[12]Robert W. Funk, "The Wilderness," *JBL* 78 (1959): 205-14.

Near East the term *wilderness* often denotes an abstract and nonlocal meaning (e.g., "uninhabited land"), that is not the case generally in the New Testament. Even so, what becomes important for New Testament writers is the symbolic sense they derive from references to this wilderness.[13] The importance of the wilderness for the New Testament was demonstrated by Ulrich W. Mauser in *Christ in the Wilderness*.[14]

Most commentators have assumed that Mark 1:1-13 makes up Mark's prologue with a new section beginning at verse 14. However, the prologue proper actually extends all the way through Mark 1:15.[15] This is crucial for a correct understanding of Mark's Gospel in my judgment.[16] The prologue introduces the notion of "*a way* in the wilderness." Often in the Old Testament tradition, the wilderness was a place that evoked memories of testing, murmuring, and disobedience. At the time of the writing of Mark's Gospel, some in Israel had fled to the desert wilderness to set up monastic-like communities, especially at Qumran.

For the community at Qumran, the wilderness had much more positive connotations than much of the Old Testament tradition. In Second Temple Judaism, the wilderness was a place where profound religious and communal experiences were to be expected.[17] "A way in the wilderness" evoked positive anticipation.[18] Josephus testifies to a popular expectation of a second Moses/messiah figure who would deliver in the

---

[13] See esp. Dale C. Allison Jr., "Mountain and Wilderness," in *Dictionary of Jesus and the Gospels*, ed. Joel B. Green, Jeanine K. Brown, and Nicholas Perrin, 2nd ed. (Downers Grove, IL: IVP Academic, 2013), 615-18.

[14] Ulrich W. Mauser, *Christ in the Wilderness: The Wilderness Theme in the Second Gospel and Its Basis in the Biblical Tradition* (London: SCM Press, 1963). Mauser sees the "green grass" on which the people sit at the feeding of the five thousand as signifying the eschatological transformation of the wilderness as part of Isaianic new exodus (see 136-37). Lim, *Way of the Lord*, 20-24, agrees he is probably right and also cites Joel Marcus as approving. I am not sure I agree. This seems a little far-fetched.

[15] The editors of my UBS Greek text betray their understanding by inserting the paragraph heading "The Beginning of the Galilean Ministry" before verse 14.

[16] Leander E. Keck, "The Introduction to Mark's Gospel," *NTS* 12 (1966): 352-70. See also Richard J. Dillon, "Mark 1:1-15: A 'New Evangelization,'" *CBQ* 76, no. 1 (January 2014): 1-18, esp. 17.

[17] See Tremper Longman III and Daniel G. Reid, *God Is a Warrior*, Studies in Old Testament Biblical Theology (Grand Rapids: Zondervan, 1995), 92-93, for bibliography on primary and secondary literature.

[18] For more evidence of the significance of the *hodos* theme at Qumran, see S. Vernon McCasland, "The Way," *JBL* (1958): 222-30. McCasland was one of the first to provide a sustained engagement of the new material from Qumran in order to understand the "way" language in the book of Acts.

wilderness.[19] Mark has his own agenda and underscores the wilderness as a place of covenant making.[20] For the Israelites, the wilderness was the place where God singled them out as his people and made his will known to them in the form of a covenant. Indeed, as one scholar says, "the whole phenomenon of the community of the Dead Sea Scrolls must be set within the hermeneutical framework of an Exodus–New Exodus typology."[21] Rikk E. Watts contends that the exodus motif, or more precisely Isaiah's new exodus, was paradigmatic for the entire Gospel of Mark[22] and makes a legitimate case for its importance in the shaping of Mark.[23] My comments follow the contours of Watts's book.[24]

Watts discusses the role of language in shaping ideology and calls this the "Mediatorial Tole of Ideology." This can be seen in how the founding event of Israel shapes and directs a community's ethos.[25] Working from material developed by Jacques Ellul and Paul Ricoeur, Watts comments, "'Ideology is always more than a reflection on the past,' it is also 'justification and project.'"[26] This makes words formative with respect to

---

[19]P. W. Barnett, "The Jewish Sign Prophets—A.D. 40–70: Their Intentions and Origin," *NTS* 27 (1981): 679-97.

[20]Kline, "Old Testament Origins," 13.

[21]David P. Moessner, *The Lord of the Banquet: The Literary and Theological Significance of the Lukan Travel Narrative* (Minneapolis: Fortress, 1989), 89.

[22]Rikki E. Watts, *Isaiah's New Exodus in Mark* (Grand Rapids: Baker, 1997). See also Watts, "Exodus Imagery," in *Dictionary of the Old Testament Prophets*, ed. Mark J. Boda and J. Gordon McConville (Downers Grove, IL: IVP Academic, 2012), 205-14. In addition to Watts's work on how the way of the Lord/"Isaianic new exodus" theme shaped a New Testament book, see also David W. Pao, *Acts and the Isaianic New Exodus* (Grand Rapids: Baker Academic, 2002); Joel Marcus, *The Way of the Lord: Christological Exegesis of the Old Testament in the Gospel of Mark* (Louisville, KY: Westminster John Knox, 1992); and Kenneth D. Litwak, *Echoes of Scripture in Luke–Acts: Telling the History of God's People Intertextually*, JSNTSup 282 (New York: T&T Clark, 2005).

[23]See R. T. France, *The Gospel of Mark: A Commentary on the Greek Text*, NIGTC (Grand Rapids: Eerdmans, 2002), 20-23. France rejects all attempts at finding an Old Testament model for the Gospel or a single motivation for the writing of the Gospel such as Marxsen's view that Mark was encouraging Christians to flee Galilee or Watts's identifying the influence of the exodus on Mark.

[24]Some scholars, e.g., Rodrigo J. Morales, *The Spirit and the Restoration of Israel: New Exodus and New Creation Motifs in Galatians*, WUNT 2.282 (Tübingen: Mohr Siebeck, 2010), 14, question whether Second Temple Jews "read the Prophets as narrative wholes, such that they would have discerned a clear program, such as 'Isaiah's New Exodus,' in the pages of Scripture." The question is too broad to consider here; however, even if New Testament authors read only parts of Isaiah (e.g., Is 40–55), they could have easily discerned an "Isaianic new exodus" motif.

[25]Watts, *Isaiah's New Exodus*, 36.

[26]Ibid., 38.

influence and a community's ethos, according to Watts. He sees Mark's allusion to Isaiah 40:3 as fitting under this rubric.[27] After developing these foundational concepts, Watts proceeds to apply the principles to the opening words of Mark's Gospel.

The Function of Citation in Mark's Prologue

Interpreters of the Gospel of Mark have always recognized the opening words, especially Mark 1:1-3, as crucial for understanding Mark's intentions. Irenaeus and Origen, for example, stressed the structural cohesiveness and importance of these verses. However, very few up until the modern period have understood how the opening words of Mark are connected to the structure of the entire Gospel.[28] The opening allusions to Old Testament passages are texts whose essential message is judgment. Moreover, the passage plays an innerbiblical role, providing a framework for Mark as a whole.[29] This "thick" interpretive framing is made up of Isaiah, Malachi, and the whole pattern of Israel's redemptive history as it is thematized by the exodus, exile, and return.[30] This is Mark's "poetics of allusion," of which Richard Hays has written.[31]

The prologue of Mark provides the key to the entire book since it introduces the Gospel's main figure.[32] Although Mark says, "It is written in Isaiah the prophet," the prologue's opening words join together several Old Testament allusions, forming a composite quotation probably including Exodus 23:20 and Malachi 3:1 together with

---

[27]Ibid., 42.
[28]Willard M. Swartley, "A Study in Markan Structure: The Influence of Israel's Holy History upon the Structure of the Gospel of Mark" (PhD diss., Princeton Theological Seminary, 1973), 161.
[29]However, see Thomas R. Hatina, *In Search of a Context: The Function of Scripture in Mark's Narrative*, JSNTSup 232 (Sheffield: Sheffield Academic Press, 2002), 138-83. Contrary to recent trends that have tended to import the Old Testament contexts of this composite quotation, Hatina argues that Mark is primarily concerned with John the Baptist and that Is 40:3 does not play a programmatic role for the entire Gospel, nor does the quotation announce the fulfillment of a long-awaited new exodus.
[30]See Peter Phillips, "Biblical Studies and Intertextuality: Should the Work of Genette and Eco Broaden Our Horizons?," in *The Intertextuality of the Epistles: Explorations of Theory and Practice*, ed. Thomas L. Brodie, Dennis R. MacDonald, and Stanley E. Porter (Sheffield: Sheffield Phoenix Press, 2006), 35-40, esp. 40.
[31]Richard B. Hays, *Echoes of Scripture in the Gospels* (Waco, TX: Baylor University Press, 2016), 19, 40, 45, 50, 63, 79, 84 (esp.), 97, 98.
[32]William L. Lane, *The Gospel According to Mark*, NICNT (Grand Rapids: Eerdmans, 1974), 39.

Isaiah 40:3. This conflating of two or more scriptural passages into one passage is characteristic of Mark.[33] The use of *hodos* (way) in the quotations from Malachi and Isaiah is significant. Nowhere else in the New Testament are these Old Testament texts associated with each other. Mark alone among the Gospel writers does this,[34] orienting the reader to the structural function of the term *hodos* later in Mark 8:27–10:52. There is some verbatim agreement between Mark's words and the Septuagint of Exodus 23:20a.[35] The Septuagint reads, "And behold, I send my angel before your face, that he may keep you in the way, that he may bring you into the land I have prepared for you." This passage represents the divine messenger-angel prophetically charging Israel to obey lest they incur the curse sanctions of the covenant.[36] It also marks the transition from the exodus to the way-conquest narratives in Israel's history.[37] The second part of the citation comes from the Hebrew of Malachi 3:1 rather than the Septuagint, but it differs from both in that it reads, *tēn hodon sou* (your way). The Septuagint reads, *pro posōpou mou*, or quoting more fully in translation, "Behold, I send forth my messenger, and he shall survey the way *before me*: and the Lord, whom you seek, shall suddenly come into his temple, even the angel of the covenant, whom you take pleasure in."

For Watts, these matters are pregnant with meaning. Mark's version, argues Watts, contains allusions and a conflation from different Old Testament books in a kind of reinterpretation of the prophet Malachi in a messianic sense.

> In the larger context of the delay of Yahweh's NE [new exodus] coming, Israel accuses him of dereliction of duty since he has not dealt with evildoers. Yahweh's response is that, after sending a messenger to prepare his way, he will indeed come but his coming may not inaugurate the blessing

---

[33]Joel Marcus, *The Way of the Lord: Christological Exegesis of the Old Testament in the Gospel of Mark* (Louisville, KY: Westminster John Knox, 1992), 15.

[34]Swartley, "Study in Markan Structure," 141.

[35]I will not enter into a detailed discussion of Mark's textual source at this point. Most hold to the LXX as a source, although some consider Mark's textual source to be a Greek translation of a Targum.

[36]See Meredith G. Kline, *Images of the Spirit* (Grand Rapids: Baker, 1980), 75.

[37]Willard M. Swartley, "Israel's Scripture Traditions and the Synoptic Gospels: Story Shaping Story" (Peabody, MA: Hendrickson, 1994), 47. See also Marcus, *Way of the Lord*, 12-17.

his people expect since they themselves may well be the ones who are purged in the judgment.[38]

Mark's composite quotation, according to Watts, serves as a corrective to ancient and modern readers who neglect the influence of Exodus 23, with its final warning, in the opening of Mark.[39] Moreover, it is apparent that one of Malachi's fundamental concerns is the threat associated with Yahweh's coming, and the composite quote from Exodus highlights Malachi's thrust.

Even so, the text also communicates a nuanced message of consolation through its reference to Isaiah 40:3. Three factors are significant in the rest of the prologue of Mark, and this composite citation focuses on what was important to the Evangelist: the herald, the Lord, and the wilderness.[40] Nevertheless, as Watts concludes, Mark's application of these texts to Jesus suggests that he is to be identified not only as the Messiah but also as none other than "the Lord" (*hā'ādôn*) and the "angel of the covenant" (*mal'ak habbrît*) from Malachi, or "in terms of Isaiah 40:3, [Jesus is] the presence of Yahweh himself."[41] What is the upshot of this?

> Thoroughly integrated within the Exodus/NE schema—on the one hand it looks back to the first Exodus in its ironic use of Exodus 23:20 and on the other it concerns the delay of the INE [Isaianic new exodus]—it implies not only that Israel is not ready for Yahweh's coming, but also that a right response to John as Malachi's Elijah is imperative if the nation is to avoid the specter of Yahweh's purging judgment which hangs over Jerusalem's *raison d'etre*, the temple.[42]

For Mark, the long-awaited Isaianic new exodus had begun, bringing hope; however, some of Mark's audience who would have heard Mark's opening words may have been living in a fool's paradise.[43] Anticipating

---

[38] Watts, *Isaiah's New Exodus*, 71.
[39] The fact that this is a composite quotation but that Mark attributes it to Isaiah is not problematic. See G. K. Beale, *The Erosion of Inerrancy in Evangelicalism: Responding to New Challenges to Biblical Authority* (Wheaton, IL: Crossway, 2008), 141.
[40] Lane, *Gospel According to Mark*, 46.
[41] Watts, *Isaiah's New Exodus*, 87.
[42] Ibid., 90.
[43] It is plausible that Mark preserved Peter's preaching to the church at Rome, a mixed audience of Jews and Gentiles.

blessing, they were destined to be cursed—if they did not bow the knee to the incarnate Messiah.

In short, the prologue of Mark is "replete with [new exodus] imagery."[44] When we read in Mark 1:1 ("The beginning of the good news [*euangeliou*] about Jesus the Messiah") and Mark 1:15 ("'The time has come'... 'The kingdom of God has come near. Repent and believe the good news [*euangeliou*]!'"), a link is forged by the keyword *euangeliou*. Other keywords also serve as links in this chapter, which is marked as "the programmatic beginning of Jesus' ministry proper."[45]

The Beloved Son

With the baptism of Jesus and the approbation as the beloved son of God, God's voice is heard announcing the true son of Israel who comes in the wilderness fulfilling all righteousness. The agent of the eschatological new exodus trumpeted loudly at the Jordan River. Mark's prologue introduces John the Baptizer's ministry in Mark 1:4: "And so John the Baptist appeared in the wilderness, preaching a baptism of repentance for the forgiveness of sins." The "wilderness" or "desert region" that Mark invokes is a deliberate disruption of the original text.[46] Isaiah 40:3 had used *midbār* and *ʿărābâ*, "which in general refers to desert, waterless region," in parallel to one another.[47] Mark omits the latter.[48] By doing so, John Wright argues, he is deliberately changing the thrust of Isaiah 40:3 in that Mark's text "stresses the placing of John's ministry in the wilderness. But in contrast, by implication, and by reading 'his paths' (i.e., the Lord's) ["make straight paths for him" (Mk 1:3)] instead of the 'paths of our God' [Is 40:3] Mark is interpreting the role of Jesus in a messianic manner, not being tied to one place."[49] Mark is giving new meaning to

---

[44]Watts, *Isaiah's New Exodus*, 117. Hatina, *In Search of a Context*, 163, would allow for the presence of the exodus motif at some level but not as a controlling paradigm for Mark.
[45]R. H. Lightfoot, *The Gospel of St. Mark* (Oxford: Oxford University Press, 1950), 20, quoted in Watts, *Isaiah's New Exodus*, 99.
[46]On this concept involved in intertextuality, see chap. 1.
[47]See Wright, "Spirit and Wilderness," 272.
[48]Mark is followed by Lk 3:4, Mt 3:3, and Jn 1:23 in this.
[49]Wright, "Spirit and Wilderness," 291.

the old exodus motif.[50] The motif of the wilderness as "wilderness trek" now becomes the wilderness as the place where the voice of the Lord will be heard. The symbol has triggered an updated meaning.[51] The Jordan has now become the place of new beginnings.[52]

The baptism and desert scene in Mark 1:9-13, which occurs in the "very waters that parted for Israel's original entry into the land,"[53] relates its story in a catena of Old Testament texts influencing Mark's Gospel:

> At that time Jesus came from Nazareth in Galilee and was baptized by John in the Jordan. Just as Jesus was coming up out of the water, he saw heaven being torn open and the Spirit descending on him like a dove. And a voice came from heaven: "You are my Son, whom I love; with you I am well pleased."
>
> At once the Spirit sent him out into the wilderness, and he was in the wilderness forty days, being tempted by Satan. He was with the wild animals, and angels attended him.

In Jesus' baptism as Mark narrates it,[54] the allusion to the voice in Mark 1:10-11 is likely a reference to Isaiah 63:19 (MT; ET 64:1), "Oh, that you would rend the heavens and come down, / that the mountains would tremble before you!"[55] Regardless of their date of composition, the later chapters of Isaiah are representative of the people's disappointment at the delay of the promises. But they also contain echoes of many of the hopeful and joyously unrestrained prophecies found in Isaiah 40–48.

The upshot of this for Mark is that "the descent through the rent heavens of the Spirit upon Jesus is entirely in keeping with the last great lament of the book of Isaiah. For Mark, Jesus is Yahweh's answer to that cry: he has indeed come, 'in strength,' to announce and to effect Israel's long-awaited [new exodus]."[56] Jesus is the one who reverses the judgment

---

[50]Ibid.
[51]Ibid.
[52]Ibid., 293.
[53]Longman and Reid, *God Is a Warrior*, 93.
[54]For an excellent technical discussion, see Marcus, *Way of the Lord*, 48-79.
[55]I will reserve my comments on the temptation narrative for the discussion on the Gospel of Matthew.
[56]Watts, *Isaiah's New Exodus*, 107.

on Israel. It is well known that Mark suppresses Jesus' identity as divine Son (sometimes called the "messianic secret"). However, as Joel Marcus puts it, "By the references to Isaiah 63 in Mark 1:9-11, Mark's community is let in on the vital secret that in Jesus' baptism the eschatological theophany foretold in the Old Testament has occurred."[57] The approbation from heaven announces to Mark's auditors that Jesus is *the* Son.[58] Israel failed; Christ prevailed.

The pronouncement from heaven after the baptism with the approbation "You are my Son, whom I love; with you I am well pleased" (*su ei ho huios mou ho agapētos, en soi eudokēsa*) (Mk 1:11) is most likely a conflated allusion to Psalm 2:7 ("He said to me, 'You are my son; / today I have become your father'") and Isaiah 42:1 ("Here is my servant, whom I uphold, / my chosen one in whom I delight; / I will put my Spirit on him / and he will bring justice to the nations").[59] The Septuagint of Isaiah 42:1 contains an explicit interpretation of the prophecy concerning Jacob, which is to be understood as a "*corporate designation* for 'Israel, my chosen one' (ὁ ἐκλεκτός μου)."[60] The strongest evidence of the allusion to Psalm 2 is the shared second person language in both Psalm 2:7 (*huios mou ei su*) and Mark 1:11. Indeed, the prediction formula "you are" is only here combined in the Old Testament with the title "Son of God."[61] Israel's sonship is in the background, the most prominent allusion being Exodus 4:22-23, "Then say to Pharaoh, 'This is what the Lord says: Israel is my firstborn son, and I told you, "Let my son go, so he may worship me." But you refused to let him go; so I will kill your firstborn son.'" This is evocative language applied to Adam in Genesis 5:3 and Genesis 1:26.[62]

---

[57]Marcus, *Way of the Lord*, 58.
[58]Wright develops more than anyone I have discovered the nuanced development of Is 63 as a background for the approbation (see "Spirit and Wilderness," 281, 287, 288, 295).
[59]Stock, *Way in the Wilderness*, 24, says we have evoked here "the profound theology of the suffering Servant poems of Second Isaiah."
[60]Richard B. Hays, *Reading Backwards: Figural Christology and the Fourfold Gospel Witness* (Waco, TX: Baylor University Press, 2014), 60-61.
[61]Marcus, *Way of the Lord*, 50n10, building on the work of Steichele. Some scholars have also noted a possible allusion to Gen 22; however, that is less firm.
[62]Rikki E. Watts, "The New Exodus/New Creational Restoration of the Image of God: A Biblical-Theological Perspective on Salvation," in *What Does It Mean to Be Saved? Broadening Evangelical Horizons of Salvation*, ed. John G. Stackhouse Jr. (Grand Rapids: Baker Academic, 2002), 24.

Looking in the other direction, there has been some debate as to whether Jesus stands in this trajectory later in redemptive history.[63] This question about Jesus' and Israel's sonship seems significant since the idea that God is a father to his people is relatively rare in the Old Testament.[64]

At this point Matthew differs slightly in his formulation. Recently it has been vigorously argued that Matthew has in mind Deuteronomy 32:5, 20: "They are corrupt and not his children; / to their shame they are a warped and crooked generation"; "'I will hide my face from them,' he said, / 'and see what their end will be; / for they are a perverse generation, / children who are unfaithful.'" These passages address the corporate disobedience of Israel as children.[65] It seems plausible that Matthew has in mind national Israel's sonship.[66] In contrast to the disobedient nation, baptism marks out Jesus as his obedient Son. Indeed, as Brandon Crowe has argued, this background of sonship from Deuteronomy emphasizes not so much status as obligation.[67] In short, Jesus' baptism has perplexed New Testament scholars for years; however, what comes from the analysis above is to ask why it occurred in the wilderness.[68] One answer offered by Wright is that the "spirit giving life has been noted, as has the inauguration of the new age and the endowment of the man Jesus."[69] As was noted in the prophets (Hos 11:1; Jer 2:2), God met Israel in the wilderness and cared for her; however, the prophets also speak of a second return to the wilderness (Hos 11:11; 2:16-25 [ET 14-23]) in which the marriage will be restored and the relationship healed.[70] If C. Kavin

---

[63]The debate about Jesus' standing in the tradition of Israel's sonship at this point has to do with whether he is "considered the new Israel of the [new exodus]" and thus representative of Israel or whether he is designated in this passage "as both King-Messiah and Servant of the Lord." See Jay Smith Casey, "Exodus Typology in the Book of Revelation" (PhD diss., Southern Baptist Theological Seminary, 1981), 60-61. Relevant here is the high proportion of explicit references in the exodus/Sinai events, in comparison to the few explicit references to God as father in the Scriptures. See Allen Mawhinney, "Baptism, Servanthood, and Sonship," *WTJ* 49 (1987): 35-64.
[64]See Robin Routledge, "The Exodus and Biblical Theology," in *Reverberations of the Exodus in Scripture*, ed. R. Michael Fox (Eugene, OR: Pickwick, 2014), 190.
[65]Brandon D. Crowe, *The Obedient Son: Deuteronomy and Christology in the Gospel of Matthew*, BZNW 188 (Boston: De Gruyter, 2012), 186-200.
[66]Ibid., 200.
[67]Ibid., 117. What German scholarship names *Verpflichtungsverhältnis*.
[68]Wright, "Spirit and Wilderness," 296-97.
[69]Ibid., 297.
[70]See ibid., 297.

Rowe is correct in his analysis of Luke's Christology (discussed below), then Jesus' baptism is with reference not merely to the man Jesus but also to the Lord Jesus.

Returning to Mark's Gospel, what are we to conclude from these allusions to Isaiah and the Psalms in Mark's prologue? Watts asserts, "The matrix of baptismal setting with the coming up out of the water, the descent of the Spirit, and the subsequent forty days in the wilderness, seems to be a conscious echo of Israel's Exodus experience. Thus Jesus is apparently presented, if not explicitly then implicitly, as 'true Israel.'"[71] Moreover, in contrast to the disobedience of Israel, Jesus is the one who prevails in his probation-keeping righteousness in the "called-proved-obedient" pattern that emerges in the parallel narratives of Matthew and Luke.[72] To get "behind" Israel, I add that Jesus is also presented as the true Adam. Here is how Tremper Longman and Dan Reid express it:

> Mark introduces Satan, the archenemy, in his thumbnail sketch of the temptation (Mk 1:12-13). The Spirit drives (*ekballō*) Jesus into the desert, where Satan tempts him for forty days, wild beasts accompany him, and angels come to his aid. Old Testament typology is clearly alive here, recalling Israel in the desert. Mark's previous use of New Exodus typology suggests that his temptation narrative, like that of Matthew and Luke, portrays Jesus as God's faithful Son who prevails over temptation where Israel failed. Israel too was driven out of Egypt into the desert (note *ekballō* in LXX Ex 12:33, 39), where she spent forty years and was tested (Ex 15:25; 16:4; Dt 4:34; 8:2) before marching into the land and driving out its occupants.[73]

The authors add in a footnote on the same page, "But this typology could well include remembrances of Adam in Eden, which even in its Genesis account seems to be rendered as a paradigm of the experience of Israel." This is significant theologically since Jesus, as the true Israel and the second Adam, will fulfill the role of an obedient son. The different

---

[71]Watts, *Isaiah's New Exodus*, 114.
[72]See, e.g., the excellent article by G. H. P. Thompson, "Called-Proved-Obedient: A Study in the Baptism and Temptation Narratives of Matthew and Luke," *JTS* 11 (1960): 1-12.
[73]Longman and Reid, *God Is a Warrior*, 95-96.

outcomes between the first and second Adam could not be any clearer.[74] Christ will earn the anticipated legal outcome for his people by his own meritorious work, a point I have been developing throughout this book and which is now carried forward in our analysis of the exodus motif in the New Testament.[75] God had been preparing Israel for the realization of what is revealed in the prologue of Mark. Jesus is Yahweh's answer to the perfect obedience needed by his Son in order to win the approbation of a heavenly God. As Mike Higton has eloquently stated, "The Gospels themselves require of us the acknowledgment that the significance of Jesus is unlimited: that the whole of history, the whole of creation, is caught up in the story told here."[76]

The desert had been a place of testing in which Israel failed time and time again. But now a true Son of Israel has emerged in the wilderness. He is the giver of life (Mk 1:8, "I baptize you with water, but he will baptize you with the Holy Spirit") and one who is humble (Mk 1:9, "At that time Jesus came from Nazareth in Galilee and was baptized by John in the Jordan"). As Augustine Stock says, "Jesus' mission is one of enduring God's judgment for the sake of others, culminating in his crucifixion. What is begun in his baptism will be continued throughout his ministry and will be resolved in his death."[77] All Israel had failed in the wilderness; however, the true Son of Israel will prevail as *the* obedient one. Unlike the corporate people of Israel, who failed from the beginning and who again and again were faithless, Jesus alone was determined and resolute to provide the obedience necessary in the face of temptation in the wilderness.[78]

---

[74]Meredith G. Kline, *Kingdom Prologue: Genesis Foundations for a Covenantal Worldview* (Overland Park, KS: Two Age Press, 2000), 145, comments: "Against the first Adam, the angels stood as adversaries, preventing his return from the wilderness to the garden. Now they minister to the needs of the second Adam in the wilderness (Mark 1:12). Following the unsuccessful probation in Eden, the Glory-Spirit had appeared in terrifying storm-theophany to pronounce condemnation. Now, before leading Jesus to the temptation crisis, the Spirit appears in the theophanic form of the dove above the waters, evocative of the Creator-Spirit of Genesis 1:2 and bespeaking the divine favor."

[75]For Christ as the true paschal Lamb who provides the forensic basis of deliverance through his sacrificial act, see Meredith G. Kline, "The Feast of Cover-Over," *JETS* 37, no. 4 (1994): 501, 509.

[76]Mike Higton, *Christ, Providence and History: Hans W. Frei's Public Theology* (London: T&T Clark, 2004), 8.

[77]Stock, *Way in the Wilderness*, 67.

[78]Mauser, *Christ in the Wilderness*, 96.

Likewise, early in the Gospel of John, the Baptizer declares, "Look, the Lamb of God, who takes away the sin of the world!" (Jn 1:29). John the Baptist is the "personification of the witness of the Old Testament" at this point.[79] Christ is indeed the "true Israel." Mark wanted his audience to think "iconically" (i.e., invoking a hermeneutical framework), and that hermeneutical framework within which he wanted them to think was in terms of an Isaianic new exodus for which the entire Old Testament had been preparing them.[80]

Literary Structure and the "Way" in Mark 8:27–10:52

We have seen that the prologue of Mark is crucial for understanding Mark's use of the exodus motif. It also demonstrates that "the way of the Lord" is Mark's parlance for the fulfillment of the Isaianic new exodus. Furthermore, the prologue is a structuring device that bears implications for understanding Mark's Gospel as a whole.

The "way" theme is advanced in Mark 8:27–10:52, where we can observe a cohesive *hodos* (way) section.[81] The focus is on anticipating the Lord's passion, the confession about the Messiah, and especially discipleship. Mark's structure reinforces his teaching: entrance into the kingdom of God entails a life similar to the Messiah's, that is, one of suffering along the way to our final destination. Werner Kelber concludes, "The Markan entrance formula is ultimately derived from a translation of Deuteronomy's entrance tradition into an eschatological key. Modeled after Israel's first entrance, the present journey into the Kingdom constitutes a second entry into the Promised Land."[82] This insight grasps the contribution of the Gospel of Mark in discerning the pattern of redemptive history. And it underscores an important theme we have been developing: the salvation complex involves liberation, presence with God, sanctification in wilderness wanderings, and entry into the Promised Land.[83] The proper human response is a cruciform

---

[79]Stock, *Way in the Wilderness*, 113.
[80]Watts, *Isaiah's New Exodus*, 120.
[81]Swartley, *Story Shaping Story*, 98–115.
[82]Quoted in Swartley, "Study in Markan Structure," 184.
[83]Kelber, who was so influential for Swartley's position, suggested that the "way" theme (*hodos*),

response to the Messiah's great salvation event.[84] The practical ramifications of Mark 8:27–10:52's teaching on "the way" abound.

The journey to Jerusalem has been transformed from the idyllic goal testified to in the Old Testament prophets. Now it is the way of persecution and death for the Messiah. Some interpreters have noted the significant subtle continuity between Isaiah's use of the way and its function in Mark's Gospel, especially in light of Mark's collision of "apocalyptic eschatology" with his theology of the cross. This intertextual collision results in something brand-new.[85] It is clear that in Mark, the way of victory is not through military might but through the trek to Jerusalem, where the apparent defeat of Jesus becomes God's means of victory.[86] Marcus writes, "The main point of this portrayal is to show that Jesus' journey up to suffering and death in Jerusalem is, in the strange logic of a cruciform apocalyptic theology, the victorious assault of the divine warrior on the resistant cosmos."[87] Marcus puts the accent on Jesus' salvation event rather than the journey as a human response of discipleship. However, Marcus offers great insights regarding the transformation of the way of the Lord at this point in redemptive history.

Against the backdrop of the way of the Lord in Isaiah, Marcus notes that

> Mark pictures exactly the opposite of human beings preparing the Lord's way; the earthly Jesus, acting in the power of God, *goes before* the disciples (10:32, 52) and prophesies that this precedence will continue even after his resurrection (14:28; cf. 16:7). Christian discipleship is a matter of following Jesus in the way of the cross (8:34; 10:52) or of being with him (cf. 3:14), not of going before him or of preparing his way.[88]

---

which controls 8:27–10:52, is modeled after the Old Testament's "way" theme which took the Israelites from the wilderness or from Sinai (Ex 23:20) to the Promised Land. This point, of course, is integrally connected to major points made previously about Mark's prologue. I am in basic agreement with Swartley that "the cumulative weight of these observations on the parallelism between 8:27–10:52 and the Old Testament exodus—and entrance—events is indeed convincing." See Swartley, "Structural Function," 81.

[84] See J. Gresham Machen's classic treatment, *Christianity and Liberalism* (Grand Rapids: Eerdmans, 1923), 126-28.
[85] Lim, *Way of the Lord*, 164.
[86] See ibid.
[87] Marcus, *Way of the Lord*, 40.
[88] Ibid., 42-43.

This insight reinforces the practical and ongoing relevance of the exodus and the way of the Lord for disciples today. In Judaism the ritualized act of remembering the exodus in the daily recitation of the Shema was meant to reinforce the certainty of God's care for his people.[89] Likewise, the Christian community should remember the exodus event and its manifestation in the way of the Lord for Christian discipleship. The way does not end with the Messiah. Nevertheless, there is a shift in the content of the message at this point in redemptive history. Rather, in Bo Lim's words, "it continues to possess an eschatological import since Jesus will come again, this time on the clouds of heaven. The Church's preaching of the gospel 'prepares the way' for Jesus' return."[90] So while Marcus (above) emphasizes that Christian discipleship does not prepare for the Messiah's way, once Christ is crucified, buried, resurrected, and ascended into heaven, it becomes the responsibility of the church to herald his second advent.

Hermeneutically speaking, this is not mere analogy; it is typological or figural heightening. Mark does not call us simply to return to a Hebrew pattern of life and discipleship but calls us to follow the path of the new exodus opened up by the new Moses, *the way* of discipleship blazed by Christ Jesus himself. As David Pao points out, the new exodus involves a change in identity of the people of God as well as the themes of persecution and rejection.[91]

The previous analysis about the literary structure of Mark 8:27–10:52 underscores what we saw in our study of Exodus in chapter three: the exodus is a synecdoche for the entirety of salvation; it includes deliverance

---

[89]B. M. Bokser, "Messianism, the Exodus Pattern, and Early Rabbinic Judaism," in *The Messiah: Developments in Earliest Judaism and Christianity*, ed. James H. Charlesworth (Minneapolis: Fortress, 1992), 239-58.

[90]Lim, *Way of the Lord*, 164-65.

[91]See G. K. Beale, review of *Acts and the Isaianic New Exodus*, by David W. Pao, *Trinity Journal* 25 (2004): 93-101. Lim, *Way of the Lord*, 173-74, highlights a significant disagreement. He criticizes Pao for following Zimmerli's interpretation of Is 40:3 (i.e., that it initially referred to a literal highway and was later reinterpreted) and for following Hanson's view that Second Isaiah's prophecy seemed to not be fulfilled following the exile and was later reinterpreted. However, Lim's greatest critique comes in the form of alleging that Pao fails to address the relationship between Is 40–55 and Is 56–66 (especially the transfer of leadership from Servant to community of servants). Lim says a unique contribution of Pao is finding the anti-idol polemic in Acts to be rooted in Is 40–55 (ibid., 169, referring to Pao, *Acts*, 182-216).

from Egypt, God's leading the people into his presence at Mount Sinai, the wilderness wanderings, and—importantly—the conquest of the Promised Land, which is used typologically of the world-to-come itself. In Mark's Gospel the exodus motif has been transposed: Christ has introduced a new thing, a way of salvation through his own suffering and crucifixion that leads to the path of pilgrim discipleship, a theology of the cross that leads to the new Promised Land, the kingdom of God, ultimately the new Jerusalem.

Conclusion on Mark's Use of the Exodus Motif

Several strands of evidence show the significance and pervasive use of the exodus motif in Mark's Gospel.[92] Various Old Testament patterns as well as individual texts profoundly influenced Mark's description of Jesus as the new exodus. The new exodus provides a framing device for Mark's structure and content and a significant means of describing the advent of the Messiah. In Mark's understanding of the advance of redemptive history and revelation, Christ is the agent of the new exodus and a new creation. Michael W. Martin has argued that the influence of Isaiah's new exodus on Mark's Gospel signals that salvation for Mark, as it was for Isaiah, is a matter of grace from start to finish.[93] Christ is the captain of a host of captives who now herald the Messiah's second coming.

The exodus is not just an incidental background of the Gospel but a dominant one. Meredith Kline has argued that the Gospel genre had its origins in the exodus motif.[94] Recent scholarship has confirmed this view. The Isaianic paradigm of a new exodus is the exodus motif "eschatologized," a future event based on God's past action in delivering his people. As Willard M. Swartley remarks, "To understand the present by the past is to announce the future."[95]

---

[92] See Casey, "Exodus Typology," 71.
[93] Michael W. Martin, "Salvation, Grace, and Isaiah's New Exodus in Mark," in *Getting "Saved": The Whole Story of Salvation in the New Testament*, ed. Charles H. Talbert and Jason A. Whitlark (Grand Rapids: Eerdmans, 2011), 119-54.
[94] See Kline, "Old Testament Origins."
[95] Swartley, "Study in Markan Structure," 227.

The Exodus Motif in Matthew

Matthew is overt about his use of the Old Testament, which is perhaps one reason his Gospel comes first in canonical position.[96] One explanation for this is that Matthew intends to write the concluding chapter to the complex story of the Hebrew Bible. Building on the work of N. T. Wright, Martin C. Spadaro has made a persuasive case.[97] Often Matthew will say, "This took place to fulfill what had been spoken through the prophet, saying . . ." Not only does he introduce scriptural citations directly; he also makes numerous allusions to the Hebrew Scriptures.[98] Matthew's use of the Old Testament has undoubtedly had a sweeping impact on how people have read the Old Testament throughout history, but it is wise not to let Matthew's quotation practice dominate our understanding of how the Old Testament is to be read.[99]

By moving away from Matthew's use of quotations and allusions and thinking about how Matthew's Gospel, even in its genealogy, is integrated with and transforms the Old Testament narrative, we see that the Gospel "constructs itself as a continuation and fulfillment of Israel's Scriptures."[100] Matthew 1:1–4:11, roughly the first four chapters of the New Testament, teaches the church from the very opening of the Gospels that the story of Jesus is a recapitulation of Israel's history.[101] Matthew works backward from the story of Jesus to the Garden of Eden, which "typologically corresponds to the history of Israel."[102] Job Y. Jindo writes, "Just as Adam and Eve were expelled from the Garden of Eden for not keeping God's command (Gen 3:11), so too the people of Israel were

---

[96] A point made by Hays, *Reading Backwards*, 37.
[97] See Martin C. Spadaro, *Reading Matthew as the Climactic Fulfillment of the Hebrew Story* (Eugene, OR: Wipf & Stock, 2015).
[98] See Hays, *Echoes of Scripture in the Gospels*, 106.
[99] Ibid., 108.
[100] See Gil Rosenberg, "Hypertextuality," in *Exploring Intertextuality: Diverse Strategies for New Testament Interpretation of Texts*, ed. B. J. Oropeza and Steve Moyise (Eugene, OR: Cascade, 2016), 17. Rosenberg applies Gérad Genette's theory of intertextuality to the genealogy of Matthew.
[101] This thesis, which has been sadly neglected by New Testament scholars, has nevertheless been argued at length recently by Joel Kennedy (among others) in *The Recapitulation of Israel: Use of Israel's History in Matthew 1:1–4:11*, WUNT 2.257 (Tübingen: Mohr Siebeck, 2008).
[102] See, for one example, Job Y. Jindo, *Biblical Metaphor Reconsidered: A Cognitive Approach to Poetic Prophecy in Jeremiah 1–34*, HSM 64 (Winona Lake, IN: Eisenbrauns, 2010), 160.

exiled from the Land of Promise for the same reason (cf., e.g., Lev 26:14, 27-33; Deut 28:15, 64-68; Jer 7:28)." When these and numerous other related images are taken into consideration, there emerges the biblical concept "that the land of Israel is Yhwh's royal garden."[103] What is significant is that "the elected people of Israel appear as a collective Adam bearing the royal task of cultivating the divine garden (= the Land of Promise)."[104] Indeed, sometimes the whole Old Testament paradigm of exodus and settlement is portrayed as God transplanting his beloved plant (the people of Israel) in their divine manor (Land of Promise).[105] Many Old Testament passages present this biblical theological image (e.g., Ex 15:17; 2 Sam 7:10; Ps 80:9; Num 24:5-7; Hos 9:10; Jer 2:3). Jesus' ministry is in some sense a reexhibition of the history of Israel, and the history of Israel is in some sense a recapitulation of the history of Adam in the garden. But where Adam failed, Jesus prevailed.[106]

In order to explain Matthew's use of the exodus motif, we need to return briefly to the Prophets, namely, Hosea. The exodus motif looms large in Hosea, as do the themes of covenant and the giving of the law.[107] The clearest exodus reference is Hosea 13:4 ("But I have been the LORD your God / ever since you came out of Egypt. / You shall acknowledge no God but me, / no Savior except me"), but there are other references as well.[108] In Hosea 2:14-16 (MT = 2:16-18), the prophet also alludes to the exodus motif, declaring:

> "Therefore I am now going to allure her;
> I will lead her into the wilderness
> and speak tenderly to her.
> There I will give her back her vineyards,
> and will make the Valley of Achor a door of hope.

---

[103]Ibid., 160-61.
[104]Ibid., 162.
[105]Ibid.
[106]Similar patterns are pointed out by Westminster Theological Seminary professors G. K. Beale and Brandon D. Crowe. See Beale, *A New Testament Biblical Theology: The Unfolding of the Old Testament in the New* (Grand Rapids: Baker Academic, 2011); Crowe, *The Obedient Son: Deuteronomy and Christology in the Gospel of Matthew*, BZNW 188 (Boston: De Gruyter, 2012).
[107]Crowe, *Obedient Son*, 120.
[108]See, e.g., Beale's discussion in *New Testament Biblical Theology*, 408-12.

There she will respond [*ʿānâ*] as in the days of her youth,
    as in the day she came up out of Egypt.

"In that day," declares the LORD,
    "you will call me 'my husband';
    you will no longer call me 'my master [*baʿlî*].'"

This passage is shot through with exodus imagery. However, it comes in a section that is looking forward to what is going to take place in the new covenant period, the time of the New Testament.

The Valley of Achor was the valley where God had brought judgment and cursing; however, Hosea is saying that in the period of the new covenant this will be reversed, and God declares he will bring hope instead of curse. There is an ambiguity in the text signaled by the Hebrew word *ʿānāh*, which can carry more than one meaning. It could mean "sing" or "respond." If it means "sing," then we have a development of the exodus imagery here with an echo of the Song of the Sea. If it is intended to mean "respond," then the reference is to the response of the covenant work of God (cf. Ex 24). This also fits the context. Not only is it difficult to decide, but Hosea is a punster and may even intend a double entendre. Either way, we are confronted with the exodus motif. The narrator in Hosea represents God as not only a heartbroken lover but also a heartbroken parent.[109]

In Hosea 11:1 we return to this theme: "When Israel was a child, I loved him, / and out of Egypt I called my son." This verse is cited by direct quotation in the second chapter of Matthew, but with application to Jesus following the escape from Herod: "And so was fulfilled what the Lord had said through the prophet: 'Out of Egypt I called my son'" (Mt 2:15). This is meant to demonstrate that Jesus brings to a climax the exodus motif.[110] A former student of mine eloquently captures the theological significance: "What is at work theologically in Matthew 2:15 then is that Jesus, God's son, the *new* Israel of God, goes into Egypt-exile and

---

[109] Sylvia C. Keesmaat, *Paul and His Story: (Re)Interpreting the Exodus Tradition*, JSNTSup 181 (Sheffield: Sheffield Academic Press, 1999), 117, building on Fretheim.

[110] See Douglas J. Moo, "The Problem of the Sensus Plenior," in *Hermeneutics, Authority, and Canon*, ed. D. A. Carson and John D. Woodbridge (Grand Rapids: Zondervan, 1986), 179-211, esp. 191.

comes out again to show that he will bear exile-judgment for his people."[111] However, allusions to the exodus permeate Matthew's passage even apart from this direct quotation. In the verses that follow Hosea 11:1, the narrator's pathos is evident as God is portrayed as the tender father who taught his son how to walk (Hos 11:3) and yet aches with compassion over his straying son.

Often New Testament writers intend for us to examine a whole context when they quote an Old Testament passage.[112] So when we advance to Hosea 11:10-11, there is an eschatological expectation for Yahweh's sons to return home from east and west. The "restoration is described as a new exodus event."[113] As Crowe suggests, perhaps it is this combination of eschatological expectation and hope for Israel's sons that attracted Matthew to this passage.[114] This quotation has become a hermeneutical test case for the New Testament use of the Old Testament in recent years.[115] The reader will recall our discussion in chapter one about New Testament "perturbation" or "disruption" in its use of the Old Testament. There is an *intertextual identity* here between the quote in the pretext (Q^2) and the quote in the later text (Q^1);[116] however, there is modification of the quote, and therefore there is a secondary grammar occurring here in the intertext ($Q^1 \neq Q^2$).[117]

Matthew does not follow the Septuagint reading, "Out of Egypt have I called *his children*" (*ta tekna autou*); rather, Matthew seems to follow a Greek text that more closely follows the MT here by reading, "Out of Egypt I called *my son*" (*ton huion mou*).[118] Matthew seems to be

---

[111] Adam Phillips, "A Figural Reading Through the 'Rule of Faith': The Message of Hosea 11:1 and Matthew's Hearing of It" (unpublished paper, April 30, 2015).
[112] See C. H. Dodd, "The Old Testament in the New," in *The Right Doctrine from the Wrong Texts?*, ed. G. K. Beale (Grand Rapids: Baker, 1994), 176.
[113] Ibid., 39.
[114] Crowe, *Obedient Son*, 124.
[115] See, e.g., Stanley E. Porter and Beth M. Stovell, eds., *Biblical Hermeneutics: Five Views* (Downers Grove, IL: IVP Academic, 2012), where each contributor was asked to take their particular hermeneutical stance and apply it to Mt 2:7-15, which quotes Hos 11:1.
[116] See the appendix for further explanation.
[117] The reader should recall the discussion of intertext in chap. 1 and also consult the appendix at the rear of the book. See also Wright, "Spirit and Wilderness."
[118] For a detailed explanation of the textual issues here, see W. D. Davies and Dale C. Allison Jr., *The Gospel According to Saint Matthew*, ICC (Edinburgh: T&T Clark, 1988), 1:262n8.

transcending a choice between the corporate or individual accent on Son.[119] The focus on a youthful figure, a son, is critical for Hosea and Matthew, for "it is the only christological title of the entire chapter."[120] Hays summarizes well, although perhaps his accent on a "retrospective" reading could be better stated under the rubric of a rightly construed notion of the rule of faith:[121]

> In context in Hosea, the "son" is clearly the people Israel as a whole; the sentence is not a prediction of a future messiah but a reference to past events of the exodus. Thus, Hosea's metaphor, referring to Israel corporately as God's "son," evokes a tradition that goes all the way back to God's instructing Moses to tell Pharaoh that "Israel is my firstborn son" (Exod 4:22-23). Matthew, however, transfigures Hosea's text by seeing it as a prefiguration of an event in the life of Jesus. Reading backwards, Matthew now sees the fate of God's "son" Israel recapitulated in the story of God's Son, Jesus: in both cases, the son is brought out of exile in Egypt back to the land.[122]

It is not merely Matthew's retrospective reading that leads to the insight, although this is important, but the manner in which Hosea had already expressed himself exerted theological pressure on Matthew's construal. As we saw in Mark, so here also, both Hosea and Matthew are inspired by Exodus 4:22.[123] Matthew is evoking the immediate and larger context of Hosea here. A reader's understanding of Matthew's intent is dependent on the reader's recognition of the original context of the verse quoted from Hosea. This is a superb example of the necessity for "allusion competence." Hence, both the author and reader are crucial in this interpretation. In other words, the original words of Hosea must be tethered

---

[119] Richard B. Gaffin Jr., "The Redemptive-Historical View," in Porter and Stovell, *Biblical Hermeneutics*, 107, sums up well: "This singular, collective here for Israel as God's chosen son-nation is linked to references elsewhere to a royal individual, to a chosen son set apart from the rest of the nation yet in solidarity with it (e.g., Ps 2:2, 6-7, 12; 80:15, 17; 89:26-27)." See also G. K. Beale, "The Cognitive Peripheral Vision of Biblical Authors," *WTJ* 76 (2014): 263-93, esp. 277.

[120] Garrett Galvin is quoting Ulrich Luz, *Matthew 1–7: A Commentary*, trans. James Crouch, rev. ed., Hermeneia (Minneapolis: Fortress, 2007) in *Egypt as a Place of Refuge*, FAT 2.51 (Tübingen: Mohr Siebeck, 2011), 177.

[121] See comments in chap. 1 under "The Rule of Faith: Reading Forward."

[122] Hays, *Reading Backwards*, 40.

[123] Galvin, *Place of Refuge*, 177.

to the exodus story for the meaning to be conveyed clearly.[124] This type of approach respects the original author's intent. Did Hosea have this interpretation immediately in mind when he wrote? This question has dominated so much of the cut and thrust of debates over this passage.[125] A better approach, as mentioned in chapter one, is not to overestimate the intentionality of the human author (e.g., John Sailhamer) or to underestimate the intentionality of the divine author (e.g., Dan McCartney and Peter Enns).[126] Rather, the prophets don't always know how the divine author is going to use their words in the future.[127] However, it seems clear to me that Matthew is not changing Hosea's words; rather, he is respecting the original context in its fullness, both the immediate context and the canonical context. As G. K. Beale states, "*History is unified* by a wise and sovereign plan so that the earlier parts are designed to correspond with and point to the latter ones."[128] As the subsequent reader engages the text, all factors come into play: the original words of the human author, the divine author's subsequent instantiation of the text in a new context after further organic development, and the Gospel writer's realization in light of the rule of faith. A former student captures the dynamic:

> An unread text . . . is a dead text. It means nothing without a mind to engage it. Only when a reader comes to the text, seeking to be addressed by something outside of himself, can the meaning inchoate be made manifest. Meaning is lithified within the words and vivified by human interaction. Meaning lies neither completely in the text, as there the words are only ink, nor in the reader, as the ideas of the text are extrinsic to him. Before reading, the reader has no knowledge of the subject matter before him. Upon reading, his thoughts may grasp the meaning he assimilated. The words came alive to him, and they might transform the way he thinks.[129]

---

[124]See Hays, *Reading Backwards*, 41.
[125]See the interchange between John H. Sailhamer, "Hosea 11:1 and Matthew 2:15," *WTJ* 63 (2001): 87-96, and Dan McCartney and Peter Enns, "Matthew and Hosea: A Response to John Sailhamer," *WTJ* 63 (2001): 97-105.
[126]The author is indebted to Phillips, "Figural Reading," for the precise formulation.
[127]See Beale, "Cognitive Peripheral Vision," especially his citation and development of Machen on 293.
[128]Ibid., 285. Also see his fine summary in G. K. Beale, "The Use of Hosea 11:1 in Matthew 2:15: One More Time," *JETS* 55, no. 4 (2012): 697-715, esp. 710.
[129]Elizabeth VanDyke, "Born Back into Hope: A Hermeneutical, Exegetical, and Theological Reflection on Matthew's Remembrance of Hosea 11:1" (unpublished paper, April 30, 2015).

But one might ask, did Matthew, in using this exodus typology, have in mind Jesus as a new Israel or a second Moses? This likely poses a false dichotomy, as Dale Allison maintains: "Jesus' experience of another Exodus made him both like Israel and like Moses."[130] The two motifs, Moses and Israel, should not be played off against each other. The new Moses is also the new Israel.[131] As John Wright suggests, "It is in the wilderness that God met Israel and cared for him/her (Hos 11:1; Jer 2:2) as a child or as a bride. It is in the return to the desert that this relationship will be recreated a second time (Hos 11:11; 2:16-17), the sonship will be renewed, the marriage will take place. In Jesus, this relationship is cemented, in the wilderness."[132] Beale summarizes, "Instead of going from the one to the many, Matthew goes from the many (Israel) to the one (Jesus), but he analyzes the same kind of 'one and many' corporate hermeneutical approach to interpreting and applying Scripture as did Hosea."[133] Much more could be said about this passage, but now we must move on to the temptation narrative in Matthew, a passage with broad implications for the unfolding nature of the exodus motif.[134]

The Temptation Narrative: Matthew 4:1-11

Not only Hosea but especially the book of Deuteronomy reverberates in the background of Matthew's Gospel.[135] Matthew has a much more expanded narrative of the temptation in the wilderness than Mark does.[136] Although this section could be considered the climax of the first four

---

[130]Allison, *New Moses*, 142.
[131]Ibid., 199.
[132]Wright, "Spirit and Wilderness," 297.
[133]Beale, *New Testament Biblical Theology*, 411-12.
[134]For an extensive treatment of the scholarship on the influence of Moses and Moses traditions on New Testament Christology (inside and outside Scripture), see John Lierman, *The New Testament Moses: Christian Perceptions of Moses and Israel in the Setting of Jewish Religion*, WUNT 173 (Tübingen: Mohr Siebeck, 2004), 258-88.
[135]See Crowe, *Obedient Son*, chaps. 1–4, esp. chap. 5, "Deuteronomic Sonship in Matthew: Part 1: Strong Allusions," 158-80.
[136]This is not to suggest that Matthew is not consistent in tone and content with Mark; rather, there is a great deal of continuity between the two Gospels with Matthew complementing and developing Mark's message for the ongoing needs of the Christian community with whom he had to deal. See J. Andrew Doole, *What Was Mark for Matthew?*, WUNT 344 (Tübingen: Mohr Siebeck, 2013).

chapters of Matthew, Crowe argues that Matthew 3:15 with its reference to "fulfill all righteousness" (*plērōsai pasan dikaiosynēn*) is the "*key* to understanding these chapters."[137] The temptation narrative is the most significant location in Matthew where the sonship of Jesus vis-à-vis the sonship of Israel comes to the fore.[138] As Allison notes, "If in Matthew 2 the evangelist glossed the traditional Moses typology with an Israel typology, in Matthew 4 just the opposite occurred: the evangelist overlaid the existing Israel typology with specifically Mosaic motifs."[139] There is an "unmistakable linkage to Exodus typology" here.[140]

The resemblance of Jesus' wilderness temptations to those of Israel is obvious from even a superficial reading of the account.[141] And its evocation is enhanced by the Hosea quotation by Matthew in 2:15.[142] But there are numerous other echoes comparing Christ and Moses here. Among these are Israel's wilderness wanderings evoked in Jesus' forty days and forty nights of fasting, a possible reminiscence of Moses atop Pisgah and the Nebo tradition triggered in Matthew 4:8, with its many verbal parallels with Deuteronomy 34:1-4. Finally, there is ancillary support coming from contemporary extrabiblical literature for the notion of echoes here as well.[143]

In the second temptation (Mt 4:5; cf. Lk 4:9), the testing, according to G. H. P. Thompson, is an echo of Deuteronomy 6:16, where the notion of "testing" (either *peirazein* or *ekpeirazein*) means "to require evidence whether he can provide and carry out his purposes."[144] There may be further allusions to Psalm 90:12 and Deuteronomy 1:31.[145] In the third test (Mt 4:8; cf. Lk 4:6), Thompson argues that "Jesus' answer is in fact a

---

[137] Crowe, *Obedient Son*, 184.
[138] Ibid., 159.
[139] Allison, *New Moses*, 166.
[140] Casey, "Exodus Typology," 75.
[141] Allison, *New Moses*, 166.
[142] As J. Wright suggests, normally the spirit is interpreted along theological lines, i.e., in such a way that recipients receive some kind of vision or revelation in God's very presence, but in Jesus' case "the movement is for a different reason, namely to be tested. But, in this very temptation, when he wins through, by so overcoming, God reveals himself" ("Spirit and Wilderness," 298).
[143] Allison, *New Moses*, 166-72.
[144] Thompson, "Called-Proved-Obedient," 4.
[145] Crowe, *Obedient Son*, 162-64.

summary of the teaching of the whole book of Deuteronomy."[146] Once again, similar to the first two temptations, there is a clear focus on Jesus' Sonship.[147]

What begins to emerge in these innerbiblical allusions is that "Jesus is commissioned by God and is then put to the test in the wilderness to see whether he will remain true to his vocation, just as Israel was commissioned by God and then proved in the wilderness."[148] The upshot of this narrative is that Jesus is proved to be the obedient Son whereas Israel was not. Moreover, "Jesus demonstrates himself to be the true Israel who completes and fulfills Israel's history."[149] Additionally, his obedience in his Sonship to God is probably the key to understanding all three temptations in the narrative.[150] Luke's rendition of the temptation narrative invokes a typology that stretches back to Adam as well as Israel. Luke (evoking a similar Pauline theme) is driving home the point in his temptation narrative that Jesus, the second Adam, undoes the damage wrought by the first Adam.[151] Jesus' obedience as the second Adam and true Son of Israel calls for an ethical conformity that flows from the grateful hearts of disciples, who must resist their own temptations (*peirasmos*) (cf. 1 Cor 10:12-13).[152] Jesus' great victory over Satan entails his people's striving for ethical conformity to his commands.[153]

The conclusion of this evidence is clearly stated by Jay Smith Casey: "All the failings of Israel in the original Exodus experience are rejected and overcome by the representative of new Israel in his wilderness

---

[146] Thompson, "Called-Proved-Obedient," 4.
[147] Crowe, *Obedient Son*, 164.
[148] Thompson, "Called-Proved-Obedient," 6.
[149] Crowe, *Obedient Son*, 165.
[150] Ibid., 164.
[151] Thompson, "Called-Proved-Obedient," 8.
[152] Ibid., 11.
[153] Daniel Reid, "The Christus Victor Motif" (PhD diss., Fuller Theological Seminary, 1982), summarizes Paul's insight well: "The life of the believer as he struggles though life with the power of sin, the flesh and the supernatural powers can be cast in the language of the battlefield or an athletic contest. Paul speaks of his own life as a race being run or as a boxing match with an opponent (1 Cor 9:25-27). He runs to win, he fights with well-delivered blows and he trains rigorously. All of this is indicative of his own effort to master himself in order that having preached to others, he might not disqualify himself" (343).

testing."[154] Matthew 2 and 4 suggest a larger pattern in the Gospel. The opening chapters of Matthew's Gospel (particularly Mt 1–8) offer an extensive typology that undergirds what we have examined here: Matthew's story of Jesus is the story of a new exodus. In this, Matthew is no innovator but stands in a long chain of witnesses, including Hosea, Isaiah, and Ezekiel. The eschatological new exodus outstrips the old.[155] The patterns already in place in the Hebrew Bible provide the typological grid that Christ fulfills. Christ as the Son of God has fulfilled a righteousness that Israel as son of God failed to exhibit.

Conclusion

Just as the book of Exodus is the record of the life and work of a covenant mediator, so also are the Gospels a record of the life of the Mediator of a new covenant. And just as the latter part of the book of Exodus is principally about the inauguration of the Sinai covenant, with its profound ramifications for the polity of the newly minted people of God, so too the Gospels witness a new covenant that is fulfilled with polity ramifications for the newly minted people of God.

---

[154]Casey, "Exodus Typology," 77.
[155]See Allison, *New Moses*, 194-99.

Eight

THE EXODUS MOTIF
IN LUKE–ACTS

As a matter of fact, He has not merely paid the penalty of Adam's first sin, and the penalty of the sins which we individually have committed, but also He has positively merited for us eternal life. He was, in other words, our representative both in penalty paying and in probation keeping. He paid the penalty of sin for us, and He stood the probation for us.

J. GRESHAM MACHEN

In Luke's two-part work of Luke–Acts, he develops the "way" terminology from the beginning of his Gospel through its duration. Luke freights the word (*hodos*) in such a manner that it takes on a technical meaning as a name for a Christian movement in Acts. Luke's Gospel is clearly influenced by the exodus motif and the Isaianic new-exodus motif in describing the life of Jesus. Luke takes great pains to develop a positive connection between Moses and Jesus.[1] He also presents Jesus as the deliverer who will usher in the eschatological new exodus.[2]

---

[1] Jindrich Mánek, "The New Exodus in the Books of Luke," *Novum Testamentum* (January 1957): 8-23. See also Alan Richardson, *An Introduction to the Theology of the New Testament* (New York: Harper & Row, 1958), 181-85.

[2] See Mark L. Strauss, *The Davidic Messiah in Luke–Acts: The Promise and Its Fulfillment in Lukan Christology*, JSNTSup 110 (Sheffield: Sheffield Academic Press, 1995), 301. Bo H. Lim, *The "Way of the Lord" in the Book of Isaiah*, Library of Hebrew Bible/OT Studies 522 (New York: T&T Clark, 2010), says that if Isaiah is read as a unity, then the leader of the new exodus may be viewed as a king, the Davidic king in particular. On this see also Carl Judson Davis, *The Name and Way of the Lord: Old Testament Themes, New Testament Christology*, JSNTSup 129 (Sheffield: Sheffield Academic Press, 1996). Davis concludes that this kingship is about God's glory (70) and connects it with Cyrus, but unfortunately (according to Lim) does not take it "one step further and relate this way of Cyrus and the people to the eschatological 'way of the Lord'" (Lim, *Way of the Lord*, 162n).

While the exodus motif cannot account for all of Luke's use of Israel's Scriptures, it can illuminate many portions of Luke–Acts.³ Indeed, some scholars who have recognized the significant influence of Isaiah and the new exodus on Luke's Gospel nevertheless think that the "dual mission of the servant, as expressed in Isa. 49.6," provides a "better hermeneutical framework for understanding the *entire* narrative."⁴ David Pao has argued that the Isaianic new-exodus paradigm is evoked and transformed in Luke's writings.⁵ His work is the most extensive treatment of Luke's use of the Isaianic new-exodus motif in Luke–Acts.⁶ We have already seen how the exodus motif was "eschatologized" in a couple of ways. First, the exodus became a "future event promised on the basis of God's action in the past."⁷ This is pronounced in Isaiah 43, where we see the distinction between the "former things" and the "new things" (see chap. 5). Additionally, there is a reformulation of the exodus motif with a cosmogonic theme, emphasizing the "(new) Exodus as a creative event."⁸ This naturally leads to a universalistic emphasis.⁹ The redefinition of the people of God is now left open. Moreover, the means by which God's creative acts are performed is now transformed. In the original exodus, the mighty acts of God were central. Now, Paul argues, it becomes the Word of God, as Acts 19:20 recounts: "In this way the word of the Lord spread widely and grew in power." Richard Hays detects a nuance in the quotation of Isaiah 40:3-5 in Luke 3:4-6, noting that it is clearly intended as a reference to the proclamation of the new exodus that is Jesus himself, not merely the word of God.¹⁰

---

³Kenneth D. Litwak, *Echoes of Scripture in Luke–Acts: Telling the History of God's People Intertextually*, JSNTSup 282 (New York: T&T Clark, 2005), 31.
⁴Peter Mallen, *The Reading and Transformation of Isaiah in Luke–Acts*, Library of New Testament Studies 367 (New York: T&T Clark, 2008), 188.
⁵David W. Pao, *Acts and the Isaianic New Exodus* (Grand Rapids: Baker Academic, 2002). For an extensive critique of Pao's work, see Joshua L. Mann, "The (New) Exodus in Luke and Acts: An Appeal for Moderation," in *Reverberations of the Exodus in Scripture*, ed. R. Michael Fox (Eugene, OR: Pickwick, 2014), 94-120.
⁶Mallen, *Reading and Transformation*, 16.
⁷Pao, *Acts*, 56, quoting Watts.
⁸Ibid.
⁹Ibid., 57.
¹⁰See Richard B. Hays, *Reading Backwards: Figural Christology and the Fourfold Gospel Witness* (Waco, TX: Baylor University Press, 2014), 125n25. Hays argues for a corrective to Pao's focus on

We will begin by looking at a few passages from Luke's Gospel before proceeding to Acts. Along the way we will discuss the function of "continuing exile" and how it helps us understand the Gospels.

Luke 3:2-6, Framing Discourse, and the "End of Exile"

The main elements of the theme of a new exodus in Luke–Acts can be noted in the following manner:

> A "way" is to be prepared for the Lord in the wilderness (Isa. 40:3-5; 43:19); God will come as a warrior to defeat Israel's oppressors (40:10; 42:13; 49:24-25); the Lord will lead his people out of captivity and shepherd them along "the way" (51:12-16; 52:11-12; 40:11); God will pour out his Spirit on them and teach them (44:3; 48:17); and finally God will be enthroned in a restored Zion/Jerusalem (40:9; 52:1-10).[11]

Luke's citation of Isaiah 40 (Lk 3:2-6) offers at least one "hermeneutical key for the Lukan program."[12] First, notice how Luke narrates his account of John the Baptizer with an extended citation of Isaiah:

> During the high-priesthood of Annas and Caiaphas, the word of God came to John son of Zechariah in the wilderness. He went into all the country around the Jordan, preaching a baptism of repentance for the forgiveness of sins. As it is written in the book of the words of Isaiah the prophet:
>
> "A voice of one calling in the wilderness,
> 'Prepare the way for the Lord,
>   make straight paths for him [lit., "make straight *his* paths" (*autou*)].

---

the word as the agent of the new exodus by claiming that Luke 3:1-6 conveys the idea that this passage "would suggest that however much the proclaimed message may have an instrumental role in implementing the new exodus, the true *agent* of the new exodus is Jesus the Lord himself. (This is also the implication of Acts 1:1.)"

[11]See Mallen, *Reading and Transformation*, 14. He acknowledges that the list is taken from Max Turner, *Power from on High: The Spirit in Israel's Restoration and Witness in Luke–Acts* (Sheffield: Sheffield Academic Press, 1996), 247.

[12]Pao, *Acts*, 38. However, Mallen, *Reading and Transformation*, 187-89, would demur from such a strong claim. For Mallen, although he thinks that the notion of a new exodus would have resonated with diverse groups in Second Temple Judaism and that the new-exodus paradigm has some explanatory power for reading Luke and Acts, the Achilles heel of Pao's claim according to Mallen is that the new exodus (as Mallen defines it) fails to account for the divergence from the new-exodus motif in the second half of Acts (i.e., Acts 15–28).

Every valley shall be filled in,
> every mountain and hill made low.
The crooked roads shall become straight,
> the rough ways smooth.
And all people will see God's salvation.'" (Lk 3:2-6)

In verses 2 and 4 above, the word translated "wilderness" (*erēmō*) is significant. For some New Testament scholars, this alone in the narrative (especially given the importance of Isaiah 40) would be enough to "evoke a whole Isaianic constellation of New Exodus hopes."[13] Luke extends Mark's allusion to Isaiah 40:3 by adding Isaiah 40:4-5 as well. This is not the first mention of John the Baptizer in Luke's Gospel (see Lk 1:17; 1:76). As C. Kavin Rowe notes, "Narratively speaking, 1:16-17 and 1:76 prepare us for 3:4-6."[14] There is an identification between John and Elijah based on these citations earlier in the narrative.[15]

Strikingly, Luke also applies the Elijah typology to Jesus as well "without any sense of logical impropriety."[16] George L. Balentine, for example, thinks it is likely that Luke has fused two prophets, Moses and Elijah, into one image, "that of the eschatological Prophet of Deuteronomy 18:15."[17] Evidence for this point may be seen in the transfiguration scene (Lk 9:30-35).[18] More significant yet are the clear references to Christ as the eschatological Prophet in Acts 3:17-26. Peter testifies that he had grasped the significance of the transfiguration, and he understood that the "ultimate application of the Deuteronomic requirement

---

[13] See Turner, *Power from on High*, 171.
[14] C. Kavin Rowe, *Early Narrative Christology: The Lord in the Gospel of Luke* (Grand Rapids: Baker Academic, 2006), 56.
[15] For further discussion, see I. Howard Marshall, *Luke, Historian and Theologian* (Grand Rapids: Zondervan, 1989), 145-47.
[16] Ibid., 147.
[17] See, e.g., George L. Balentine, "The Concept of the New Exodus in the Gospels" (ThD diss., Southern Baptist Theological Seminary, 1981), 323. There was a tendency to assimilate Elijah to Moses within Jewish interpretation. For further analysis, see Turner, *Power from on High*, 238-40. It seems possible that Matthew was doing something similar in the temptation narrative; see Dale C. Allison Jr., *The New Moses: A Matthean Typology* (Minneapolis: Fortress, 1993), 166.
[18] Balentine, "New Exodus," 325: "In the Lukan account of the transfiguration Jesus is identified as the Mosaic Prophet of Deuteronomy 18:15, but at the same time both Moses and Elijah, the combined prototype of the Mosaic Prophet, appear on the mountain with Jesus."

that Israel obey God's prophet" (cf. Deut 18:18) was being applied to Jesus as *the* antitypical prophet figure.[19]

It is also important to note how Luke's Gospel begins with a resonance with Israel's Scriptures. Kenneth Litwak has explored the many intertextual echoes of Israel's Scriptures. Among them are echoes of the Abrahamic narratives and the Abrahamic covenant in Luke 1, the importance of past deliverers and prophets, and Mary's Magnificat.[20] Litwak understands these as providing a "framing discourse" that develops expectations for readers and auditors, setting a register for how they should hear statements throughout Luke's two-part narrative.[21] Litwak explains, "The concept of framing in discourse tells readers how to read, how to make sense of the narrative, i.e., what kind of narrative the audience in encountering. . . . The purpose of Luke's discursive framing is primarily to show continuity between the early Christians and Israel in the past."[22] Moreover, this framing function serves "for a story about God's servant, someone whose life is marked by faithfulness to God and obedience to his word."[23]

When we ask what Luke expects his audience to hear in his citation of Isaiah 40:3-5, it is undoubtedly an expectation for a new exodus for the people of God.[24] In Second Temple Judaism, as evidenced by the Qumran scrolls, "wilderness is a common metaphor used to characterize a variety of ideological exiles."[25] Furthermore, the Isaianic passage is often used across early Jewish literature to refer to the judgment of God against Jewish enemies or Gentiles.[26] Primarily, however, the theme of

---

[19]Meredith G. Kline, *Images of the Spirit* (Grand Rapids: Baker, 1982), 81-82.
[20]Litwak, *Echoes of Scripture*, 82-111.
[21]The reader should not pass quickly over the importance of the primary role of the author here and the reader's ethical responsibility to give heed to the cues of previous texts (see further chap. 1).
[22]Ibid., 32.
[23]Litwak, *Echoes of Scripture*, 114.
[24]For a good summary of evocations of Is 40:3 in the New Testament and in extracanonical Jewish literature, as well as Qumran and post-Christian Jewish literature, see Davis, *Name and Way*, 61-102.
[25]Michael E. Fuller, "Isaiah 40.3-5 and Luke's Understanding of the Wilderness of John the Baptist," in *Biblical Interpretation in Early Christian Gospels*, vol. 3, *The Gospel of Luke*, ed. Thomas Hatina, Library of New Testament Studies 376 (New York: T&T Clark, 2010), 49 (emphasis mine).
[26]Ibid.

judgment is placed within the context of God's coming as judge to vindicate his people and restore them to the land.[27] Exile, specifically the return from exile, is crucial to a correct interpretation of the New Testament.[28] A major question in current New Testament scholarship is whether Jews of the first century regarded themselves as continuing in exile. As Rikki E. Watts says, "It is now increasingly recognized among New Testament scholars that Jesus cannot properly be understood apart from Israel's restorationist hopes," by which he means "Jesus is the one who inaugurates Israel's new exodus/new creation return from exile."[29] But did the restoration to the land after the Babylonian exile exhaust the notion of exile and restoration, or are we to think in categories of "continuing exile"?

N. T. Wright is the preeminent proponent of the notion that Jews of the Second Temple period regarded themselves as living in a continuing exile. Wright says, "One of the main kingdom-themes informing Jesus' retelling of Israel's story was his belief that the real return from exile, and the real return of YHWH to Zion, were happening in and through his own work. The major symbols of his work strongly reinforce and illuminate this."[30] This is a major theme in Wright's work, and he goes so far as to associate the return from exile with forgiveness of sins.[31] This

---

[27]Ibid.

[28]See, e.g., Brant Pitre, "The 'Ransom for Many,' the New Exodus, and the End of Exile: Redemption as the Restoration of All Israel (Mark 10:35-45)," *Letter & Spirit* 1 (2005): 41-68, and Pitre, *Jesus, the Tribulation, and the End of Exile: Restoration Eschatology and the Origin of the Atonement*, WUNT 2.204 (Tübingen: Mohr Siebeck; Grand Rapids: Baker Academic, 2005), esp. 41-130, who sees the understanding of "return from exile/end of exile" as well as the theme of tribulation as providing some of the greatest explanatory power for future research in New Testament studies in the context of early Jewish background.

[29]Rikki E. Watts, "The New Exodus/New Creational Restoration of the Image of God: A Biblical-Theological Perspective on Salvation," in *What Does It Mean to Be Saved? Broadening Evangelical Horizons of Salvation*, ed. John G. Stackhouse Jr. (Grand Rapids: Baker Academic, 2002), 31.

[30]N. T. Wright, *Jesus and the Victory of God*, Christian Origins and the Question of God 2 (Minneapolis: Fortress, 1996), 428. Wright had already set forth his view on continuing exile in *The New Testament and the People of God*, Christian Origins and the Question of God 1 (Minneapolis: Fortress, 1992), 268-70. Furthermore, in that work Wright identifies that what the early church was saying by announcing Jesus' resurrection "to the world as the summons to obedient faith, is that in his death he had taken the exile as far as it could go, and that in his resurrection he had inaugurated the real return from that real exile" (400).

[31]Wright, *Victory of God*, 268-74, esp. 272. In his subsequent work, he makes similar statements about the connection between death and resurrection, which "function as the moment of the new exodus,

view has its critics[32] and has sparked a good deal of debate.[33] Research has demonstrated that there was indeed a Second Temple Jewish notion of Israel still being in exile at the time of Jesus.[34] This cannot be denied. Nevertheless, how we interpret this data is another matter.

"End of exile" is only the presenting problem in my view. The more seismic issue beneath the surface is the arc of tension that the narratives of the patriarchs and, moreover, the prophetic corpus introduce into the flow of redemptive history. As Walther Zimmerli demonstrated, there is a kind of excess of promises embedded in the Old Testament, a desire for future resolution that cannot be contained within the Hebrew Bible alone.[35] The tension is not fully resolved even with the collapsing of the Mosaic covenant, the initiation of the new covenant, the advent of Christ, and the inauguration of his kingdom. Only the category of a fully developed already/not-yet principle, an eschatological principle of inauguration/consummation, can do justice to the tensions introduced by this nexus of exile, advent, and partially realized promises of the Old Testament.[36] In my view, everything is moving toward Christ and his

---

of the 'return' from the long exile of sin and death, of the overthrow of all the powers that enslaved the world, and those who now belong to the Messiah share in the benefits of all this." Wright, *The Resurrection of the Son of God*, Christian Origins and the Question of God 3 (Minneapolis: Fortress, 2003), 239.

[32]See, e.g., James D. G. Dunn, review of *Jesus and the Victory of God*, *JTS* 49, no. 2 (October 1998): 727-33.

[33]For an excellent introduction to the issues as well as updated bibliography, see James M. Scott, "Exile and Restoration," in *Dictionary of Jesus and the Gospels*, ed. Joel B. Green, Jeanine K. Brown, and Nicholas Perrin, 2nd ed. (Downers Grove, IL: IVP Academic, 2013), 251-58. For an evaluation of Wright's thesis from various perspectives, see James M. Scott, ed., *Exile: A Conversation with N. T. Wright* (Downers Grove, IL: IVP Academic, 2017); even if the exile is not to be interpreted in a purely negative manner, as Kiefer's chapter in this book may suggest, my hesitations expressed below still stand.

[34]See the excellent chapter by Craig A. Evans, "Jesus and the Continuing Exile of Israel," in *Jesus and the Restoration of Israel: A Critical Assessment of N. T. Wright's 'Jesus and the Victory of God*,'" ed. Carey C. Newman (Downers Grove, IL: InterVarsity Press, 1999), 77-99. Also see Thomas R. Hatina, *In Search of a Context: The Function of Scripture in Mark's Narrative*, JSNTSup 232 (London: Sheffield Academic), 156-57.

[35]See Walther Zimmerli's masterful essay "Verheissung und Erfüllung," *Evangelische Theologie* 12 (1952-53): 34-59. ET: "Promise and Fulfillment," *Int* (1961): 310-38. Reprinted in *Essays on Old Testament Hermeneutics*, ed. Claus Westermann (Richmond, VA: John Knox Press, 1971), 89-122.

[36]I am indebted to Dr. Lee Irons at this point for conversations on this knotty issue and for his helpful suggestions with regard to wrestling with the evidence brought to the surface by recent scholarship in this complex area. See his unpublished paper "Walther Zimmerli as Biblical Theologian," The Upper Register, January 2001, www.upper-register.com/papers/zimmerli.pdf.

penalty-paying substitution as well as his probation-keeping obedience in order to satisfy the just demands of God's holy law and end the curse of the exile. I remain unconvinced "that the thought of Israel as still in exile formed the principal metanarrative governing either the thought of the time or Jesus' understanding of his own ministry," especially the latter point.[37] As we will observe in what follows, Jesus' understanding of his own ministry primarily involved setting people free from the bondage and tyranny of Satan (who is the antitype of Pharoah), releasing people from the slavery of sin, and announcing jubilee, which, as Robert B. Sloan suggests, is by no means "merely socio-economic in character, but decidedly *cultic*."[38]

Returning to Luke's Gospel, we see that he has skillfully developed his account of John the Baptist. Luke's effective use of ambiguity can be seen by comparing his citation of the Isaiah text and the Septuagintal text, which he was undoubtedly relying on.[39] The Greek text of Isaiah 40:3 reads, "Make straight the paths of our [*hēmōn*] God," which leaves no doubt that the path in the wilderness is that of Israel's God. However, Luke says "make straight his [*autou*] paths" (Lk 3:4, author's translation). The effect of this, as it was in Mark's Gospel, is to leave it somewhat ambiguous. Earlier John the Baptist was said to be "going before" and "preparing the way" of the Lord (Lk 1:16-17, 76). Taking these allusions

---

[37]Dunn, review of *Jesus and the Victory of God*, 730. In my view, "end of exile" is resolved for Christians at the cross—or, more precisely, through our Lord's whole life and work as mediator, both his human and divine work, leading up through his death, resurrection, ascension, and exaltation. Although the blessings of the Abrahamic covenant are not fully manifest in this age and will not be fully realized until the second advent and the new Jerusalem descends from above, the work of Christ and his obedience are sufficient to end the curse represented by Israel's exile for Christians. How can Christians still be under the curse of sin and exile in any way? It is true that the blessings of Abraham come in a two-stage, inaugurated/not-yet-consummated way. Indeed, there is an interval between Christ's exaltation and the subjugation of all his enemies. Christ has not yet completed building his church by bringing believing Christians into the church regardless of ethnicity. But the bondage of Satan, the curse of sin, and exile are resolved without remainder for Christians in Christ's work accomplished. This is why the second advent will be the manifestation of his mercy for Christians, whereas the second advent will be a manifestation of his justice for the wicked (cf. Mt 25:31-46; Rom 2:5-6; 9:22-23; 2 Thess 1:7-10). This is the eschatological tension about which I think N. T. Wright needs to be more precise when speaking of the curse of continuing exile.

[38]Robert B. Sloan Jr., "The Favorable Year of the Lord: A Study of Jubilary Theology in the Gospel of Luke" (PhD diss., University of Basel, 1977; published in Austin: Schola Press, 1977), 172.

[39]For an extended discussion of the details, see Rowe, *Early Narrative Christology*, 70-77.

together, we may ask whether Luke intends a subtle switch to make Jesus the referent of *kyrios* (Lord) in 3:4. Or is the ambiguity intentional in the way Rowe claims, as follows?

> Looking back from 3:4-6 through 1:76 to 1:16-17 we can discern both the ambiguity in terms of the referent of κύριος and how such ambiguity shifts in referential probability from God to Jesus as we move from 1:17 back out to 3:4. In 1:17 we find only an intimation of Jesus' coming. In 1:76 the weight is more balanced, particularly as Jesus now exists in the Lukan text as κύριος. By Luke's final repetition in 3:4, Jesus' coming as the Lord and John's preparation for him are no longer intimations but events in the process of being fulfilled.[40]

It does seem that Luke has allowed ambiguity to serve his purpose: there is a shared identity "between Jesus the κύριος and the κύριος of Israel."[41] By invoking Isaiah 40:3-5, Luke has announced Jesus as the agent of the new exodus. None other than the Lord of Israel himself has come to deliver his people. Additionally, Luke takes pains to suggest that this was not only the understanding of John the Baptist but our Lord's self-understanding also.

Luke 4: Temptation and the Messiah's Announcement of New Exodus Liberation

Luke's temptation narrative in 4:1-13 is the first time in Luke's Gospel that Jesus quotes from Israel's Scriptures. Litwak notes that many who are working within a promise-fulfillment hermeneutic miss the importance of this passage for Jesus' use of Israel's Scriptures and skip over it to concentrate on Jesus' reading of Isaiah in Luke 4:18-19.[42] When we compare Jesus' temptation in Luke with that of Matthew, we find some important Lukan nuances that inform our understanding of the exodus motif. Jesus is in the desert for forty days and tempted by the devil. In his refusal to give in to the alluring word of the adversary, Jesus quotes from Deuteronomy 8. Many have seen the correspondence between the

---

[40]Ibid., 74.
[41]Hays, *Reading Backwards*, 63.
[42]Litwak, *Echoes of Scripture*, 111.

forty days of temptation and forty years in the wilderness in Israel's Scriptures (cf. Num 14:34; Ezek 4:6) and the similarity between Jesus' temptation and that of Israel. Litwak notes many other correspondences in Israel's Scriptures between forty years and forty days (e.g., Noah, the exodus event, Moses on Sinai) and concludes that "no one familiar with the Scriptures of Israel, especially of Deuteronomy, ... could fail to catch the intertextual echo of forty."[43]

Similar to Matthew but in his own manner, Luke presents Jesus as the obedient One through his scriptural framing of this discourse (Luke's order of temptations differs, and Luke ends with showing him Jerusalem).[44] Luke begins the story with echoes of the exodus and its aftermath, which sets the reader's expectation for how to understand Jesus' words and actions. These next verses (Lk 4:16-30) are tremendously significant for Luke's Gospel and can even be considered a "programmatic sermon."[45] The citation here follows the Septuagint. Even so, Pao notes four significant changes from the Septuagint.[46] Max Turner summarizes the details: (1) "to heal the broken hearted" has been omitted, (2) "to set the oppressed at liberty" from Isaiah 58:6 has been added, (3) the original "to announce" has been changed to "to proclaim," and (4) "and the day of recompense of our God" has been omitted.[47] The background that helps explain the passage may have been understood originally as the eschatological messianic Jubilee (Lev 25:10 LXX: *eniautos apheseōs*) with new exodus hopes.[48] If this is the case, then this reading by Jesus may be the realization of the hope/expectation of Daniel 9.

Luke's quotation of Isaiah 61:1-2 demonstrates that a new age of salvation, one that includes the Gentiles, is announced and also effected. This is a "performative utterance" that was "probably inherent in the originally kingly language of Isa. 61:1-2" but is strengthened by "the

---

[43]Ibid., 114.
[44]Ibid.
[45]Turner, *Power from on High*, 231.
[46]Pao, *Acts*, 72.
[47]Ibid., 220-21.
[48]Ibid., 226-32. Also see Richard B. Hays, *Echoes of Scripture in the Gospels* (Waco, TX: Baylor University Press, 2016), 229.

inclusion of the interpretive line 'to set the captives at liberty' from Isa. 58.6d."[49] If Luke's audience *metaleptically* recalled the fuller context of Isaiah 58, then an allusion to the exodus would already have been activated ("the glory of LORD will be your rear guard" [Is 58:8]).[50] Note the repetition of the word *aphesis* (a release) in the conflated citation of these two passages from Isaiah: "He has sent me to proclaim freedom [*aphesin*] for the prisoners / and recovery of sight for the blind, / to set the oppressed free [*aphesei*]" (Lk 4:18). Jesus understands his own work here in terms of a "release" to the oppressed. Of course, this raises the question: To whom are they captive? I will argue below that they are being freed from the tyranny of Satan.

But if new-exodus liberation is being announced, an important issue here is precisely how Jesus and Moses are connected according to Luke. This passage also anticipates Luke's claims in his second volume. Jesus actually provokes rejection by citing examples of Elijah and Elisha reaching out graciously to non-Israelites (cf. 1 Kings 17:1-16; 2 Kings 5:1-14).[51] Therefore, Christians, who belong to the Way (cf. Acts 9:2), will become the new people of God. Moreover, other New Testament scholars have claimed that the Isaianic servant himself has inaugurated the new exodus.[52] The point is that this brings great offense to the Jews. Mark had registered such an offense as well in his Gospel (Mk 6:3), but Luke has radically intensified the offense.[53] Hays summarizes, "No other story illuminates more clearly the way in which Luke's Jesus carries forward the story of Israel's redemption while at the same time transforming that story into something different and surprising—and thereby arousing opposition and division."[54]

In order to understand the influence of the exodus motif on Luke's writing, even here in this programmatic passage of Luke, we need to

---

[49]Turner, *Power from on High*, 261.
[50]Hays, *Echoes of Scripture in the Gospels*, 225-26.
[51]Ibid., 229.
[52]Turner, *Power from on High*, 249.
[53]Jacob Elias, "The Furious Climax in Nazareth (Luke 4:28-30)," in *The New Way of Jesus: Essays Presented to Howard Charles*, ed. William Klassen (Newton, KS: Faith and Life Press, 1980), 87-90, esp. 89.
[54]Hays, *Echoes of Scripture in the Gospels*, 230.

fast-forward to Stephen's speech, the longest speech in Acts (7:2-53). Stephen says in Acts 7:6-7, "God spoke to him [Abraham] in this way: 'For four hundred years your descendants will be strangers in a country not their own, and they will be enslaved and mistreated. But I will punish the nation they serve as slaves,' God said, 'and afterward they will come out of that country and worship me in this place.'" Moses and the exodus actually occupy about 60 percent of Stephen's speech.[55] Nils A. Dahl draws our attention to the purpose of the Israelite exodus for Luke: he concludes that the purpose of the Israelite exodus was not merely to enter the land; it was to worship God in Jerusalem.[56] Dahl notes subtle but important differences in the Septuagint citation of Acts 7:6-7:

> The Septuagint text of Genesis 14:14b reads: "But afterwards they shall come out hither with much baggage." For this, Acts 7:7b substitutes: "And afterwards they shall come out and worship me in this place." This phrase is taken from Exodus 3:12: "And you (the Israelites) shall worship God upon this mountain," and adapted to Genesis 15:14b and 16, "and they shall come back here." Thus, according to Stephen's quotation of Scripture, the goal of the Exodus is neither the worship of God at Mount Sinai, nor the possession of Canaan itself but, much more, worship of God in the land promised to Abraham and his posterity. This means that just as Acts 7:6-7b is a prediction of Israel's coming to Egypt and the Exodus (Acts 7:9-23), so the final clause in 7:7b points forward to the events in the time from Joshua to Solomon and even later. The correspondence is clear; it is not so much the conquest of Canaan as the worship performed there which is center of interest (Acts 7:44ff.).[57]

Susan R. Garrett, accepting and following Dahl's conclusions, has convincingly argued for the crucial connection between Acts 7 and Luke 4. In Stephen's speech, the original Israelite exodus was followed by a lapse into idolatry: "That was the time they made an idol in the form of a calf" (Acts 7:41). Therefore, there was a need for a second exodus.

---

[55]David P. Moessner, *Lord of the Banquet: The Literary and Theological Significance of the Lukan Travel Narrative* (Minneapolis: Fortress, 1989), 301-2.
[56]This is Dahl's thesis as developed in Nils Alstrup Dahl, *Jesus in the Memory of the Early Church: Essays by Nils Alstrup Dahl* (Minneapolis: Augsburg, 1976), 66-86, esp. 74.
[57]Ibid.

Garrett links the message of that passage back to Luke 4:16-20. For her, Luke presents Jesus as similar to Moses, the one "who through death and resurrection led an exodus from bondage to Satan; and one of Christ as the second Adam, whose death and resurrection removed the curse of death put on the first Adam and his descendants."[58] Her interpretation seems to be confirmed by the fact that Jesus' ministry in subsequent chapters is a liberation from demon possession and death. Furthermore, "those who confess faith in Christ have been released from all the bonds that the law of Moses could not break" (cf. Acts 13:37-39; Heb 2:14-15).[59]

Garrett claims that Jesus' understanding of this synagogue reading in Luke 4 is that he is fulfilling a new exodus, which can especially be understood as release from the bondage of Satan in light of Luke's Gospel (cf. Lk 4:6). She argues,

> Luke regarded the death, resurrection, and ascension as an "exodus" because *in these events Jesus, "the one who is stronger," led the people out of bondage to Satan.* Luke believed that Satan had long exercised authority over the peoples of the world (Luke 4:6; cf. Acts 26:18). Like Pharoah, the devil was an arrogant and relentless tyrant. He had oppressed even Jesus, bringing about the death on the cross (Luke 22:3, 53), but death and Hades had been unable to hold Jesus (Acts 2:24, 27, 31-32). Luke supposed that at Jesus' resurrection and ascension to the right hand of God, Satan has been cast out from his place of authority in heaven.[60]

Garret continues to argue that Christians can now participate in this new exodus since they have been released from the domain of darkness and brought into their inheritance: the goal of the first exodus has truly been achieved (cf. Acts 20:32; 26:18; Col 1:13; see below).[61] The antitype of the first exodus has been achieved in the new exodus: the resurrection and ascension of Christ, along with the subsequent fall of Satan.[62]

---

[58]Susan R. Garrett, "The Meaning of Jesus' Death in Luke," *Word and World* 12 (1992): 11-16, quotation on 11.
[59]Ibid., 16.
[60]Susan R. Garrett, "Exodus from Bondage: Luke 9:31 and Acts 12:1-24," *CBQ* 52, no. 4 (1990): 659.
[61]Ibid., 670.
[62]Ibid.

All of the former argumentation is strengthened by Luke's explanation of Jesus' own *exodos* (exodus) as described in the transfiguration scene.

Luke 9: The Transfiguration

Immediately preceding Luke 9, Jesus delivers several from impurity and death. This strengthens the previous argument that Jesus understood his own ministry as a liberation from sin, a deliverance from bondage to Satan and all the afflictions of this evil age. As we turn to the transfiguration, a question presents itself. Why would Jesus, at his transfiguration (9:28-36), discourse with Elijah and Moses about his own exodus (*exodon*, cf. 9:31)?[63] The narrator could have chosen other ways to express himself if he had merely meant to talk about Jesus' "departure" (which *exodos* can mean as some translations indicate) or his death. Therefore, this seems to be a deliberate allusion, at least recalling theophanies on Mount Sinai but probably communicating even more.[64] This is the case especially since it is the object of *plēroun* ("which he was about *to bring to fulfillment* [*plēroun*] at Jerusalem" [Lk 9:31]) and therefore may sound to "biblical ears" like "a mighty act of redemption."[65] This evidence may also militate against a date for the commencement of the new exodus beginning with the travel narrative (which will be discussed below), since *ēmellen plēroun* (he was about to fulfill) assumes that the new exodus is already underway.[66] Luke 9:31 seems to be a confluence of many other Old Testament passages. Many options have been suggested for the interpretation of *exodon* at this point in the chapter; it may at the very least be said that Luke is deliberately connecting the work of Jesus with God's earlier deeds in the exodus.[67] However, Garrett has offered compelling reasons for a maximal connection between Israel's

---

[63] This same word is used in 2 Pet 1:15 as well.
[64] Tremper Longman III and Daniel G. Reid, *God Is a Warrior*, Studies in Old Testament Biblical Theology (Grand Rapids: Zondervan, 1995), 120.
[65] Craig F. Evans, "The Central Section of St. Luke's Gospel," in *Studies in the Gospels: Essays in Memory of R. H. Lightfoot*, ed. D. E. Nineham (Oxford: Basil Blackwell, 1967), 51.
[66] A point driven home by Strauss, *Davidic Messiah*, 304.
[67] I. Howard Marshall, *The Gospel of Luke: A Commentary on the Greek Text*, NIGTC (Grand Rapids: Eerdmans, 1978), 384-85.

exodus and Luke's description of the transfiguration and the work of Jesus as a second exodus.

As discussed previously, Garrett offers a tight connection between the exodus of Israel and the exodus of Jesus by appealing to Acts 7 and then rereading Luke's description of the transfiguration in light of Stephen's speech. If Jesus is announcing release from bondage in Luke 4, then it invites the question, to whom are they in bondage? Without squeezing Luke–Acts into a "wooden typological framework," Garrett argues plausibly from a wide array of relevant Lukan passages for a particular meaning of *exodon* ("departure" or "exodus") in the transfiguration scene (Lk 9:31): Jesus is providing a "new exodus" that results in a release from the bondage of Satan, who has exercised authority over the inhabited world (Lk 4:6; cf. Rev 14:7-8).[68] She claims that this new exodus allows Christians to finally worship God truly, for they have received their inheritance (Acts 20:32). Daniel Smith, who has researched recent uses of "new exodus" topics in New Testament scholarship finds Garrett's argument "particularly persuasive" by her appeal to Acts 26:18 (where Paul is describing his Damascus road experience to Agrippa and why he received his apostolic commission).[69] Paul is sent by Jesus "to open their [the Gentiles'] eyes and turn them from darkness to light, and from the power of Satan to God, so that they may receive forgiveness [*aphesis*] of sins and a place [an inheritance] among those who are sanctified by faith in me [Jesus]" (Acts 26:18).

Jesus' own understanding of his ministry according to Luke 4, as well as the strong links between the Israelite exodus and Luke's presentation of the transfiguration, where Moses and Elijah discuss with Jesus his own upcoming "exodus," demonstrates that liberation from the bondage of Satan and sin and release from the curse of death so that Christians could receive their inheritance are primary categories for Luke's presentation of what new exodus is all about.

---

[68] Garrett, "Exodus from Bondage," 666.
[69] Daniel Lynwood Smith, "The Uses of 'New Exodus' in New Testament Scholarship: Preparing a Way Through the Wilderness," *CurBS* 14, no. 2 (2016): 207-42, esp. 229.

Lukan Travel Narrative

In 1989 David P. Moessner published a very important study on the middle section of Luke's Gospel.[70] For Moessner, Luke 9:1-50 functions as a "preview to the journey of 9:51–19:44."[71] Particularly, he argues that Jesus is a prophet like Moses (a suffering mediator) but bound for Jerusalem.[72] His journey to Jerusalem is "signally announced" in Luke 9:51, "As the time approached for him to be taken up to heaven, Jesus resolutely set out for Jerusalem." As we have seen, Luke gives intimations of the exodus motif early on in his Gospel, so it stands to reason that further adumbrations would be noticed later in his Gospel. Indeed, Joel B. Green states that while Luke 9:51–19:48 is "painted with hues of Israel's exodus journey, Jesus' journey to Jerusalem is especially concerned with the formation of his disciples."[73] Moessner's method is literary, and he notes two significant Deuteronomic patterns or motifs that he thinks helped Luke in the construction of what has been characterized as heterogeneous. He asserts that Jesus' new exodus is a "going out" and a "departure" from Jerusalem, a kind of dual exodus.[74] As Moses' death brought about the children of Israel's entrance into the land, so Jesus' death brings about the blessing of the covenant promised to Abraham.[75] Moessner draws attention to many illuminating parallels between Deuteronomy, Luke 9, and Luke–Acts, where Jesus is portrayed as the ultimate Moses-like prophet, whose journey culminates in Jerusalem as a new exodus.[76] The notion of Jesus as a journeyer-guest prophet, which is an integrating motif, looms large in Luke according to Moessner. Luke uses "the home-meal imagery of the Kingdom and its banquet to announce that he is host. Only those who receive him as guest in their home can receive him as Lord and host of the Banquet of the Kingdom

---

[70]Moessner, *Lord of the Banquet*.
[71]Ibid., 46.
[72]Ibid., 60.
[73]Joel Green, "Luke, Gospel of," in Green, Brown, and Perrin, *Dictionary of Jesus*, 544.
[74]Moessner, *Lord of the Banquet*, 66.
[75]Ibid., 68-69.
[76]See, e.g., Rikki E. Watts's article, "Triumphal Entry," in Green, Brown, and Perrin, *Dictionary of Jesus*, 980-85, esp. 981, which describes how the triumphal entry occurred on Passover, a feast in which many expected a repetition of the exodus deliverance.

of God."⁷⁷ The disciples then are to continue the journey following Jesus' resurrection-ascension-exaltation.

Moessner's book is an ambitious project that will no doubt factor into many works in the future that wrestle with the structure, form, and meaning of the middle section of Luke. The number of reviews is emblematic of this fact.⁷⁸ Even so, the project has received some significant criticism. One critic says that "the author finds too much coherence in the Lucan travel narrative, now and then forcing the data to fit the interpretive grid being placed upon Luke's story."⁷⁹ Another critic claims that Moessner's thesis is unconvincing for the main reason that "it takes the form of a somewhat forced combination of several elements which do not find a sufficient basis in the text of the OT itself" and it is overdependent on previous secondary literature (i.e., Steck).⁸⁰ Hays, in his recent volume, thinks that by the time we arrive at Luke 9:51-62, the forthcoming intertextual echoes have more to do with the cycle of Elijah narratives than with the exodus.⁸¹ Furthermore, as I demonstrated from Luke 3:4-6, it seems that the inauguration of Jesus' public ministry is a better commencement point for the new exodus.⁸² I appreciate Moessner's massive study for many reasons, especially since it comes to the completely opposite position of Hans Conzelmann's influential thesis: that Luke imparts no atoning significance to Jesus' death.⁸³ Rather, Luke maintains that "without Jesus' death there is no forgiveness (ἄφεσις) of sins."⁸⁴ Consequently, although I find Moessner's monograph suggestive, I think it needs to be handled with critical care given the significant amount of reviews and their criticisms of it.

---

⁷⁷Moessner, *Lord of the Banquet*, 158.
⁷⁸For a list of reviews, see A. Denaux, "Old Testament Models for the Lukan Travel Narrative," in *The Scriptures in the Gospels*, BETL 131 (Leuven: Leuven University Press, 1997), 284.
⁷⁹J. T. Carroll, review of *The Lord of the Banquet*, by David P. Moessner, *Journal of Biblical Literature* 110 (1991): 166.
⁸⁰Denaux, "Old Testament Models," 284.
⁸¹Hays, *Echoes of Scripture in the Gospels*, 202.
⁸²A point also made by Strauss, *Davidic Messiah*, 303.
⁸³Moessner, *Lord of the Banquet*, 322.
⁸⁴Ibid., 323.

Luke 24:44-49

The Isaianic themes introduced in Luke 4 are advanced further in this passage with its concern for the inclusion of the Gentiles: the active role of the Spirit ties Luke and Acts together. Moreover, *"beginning with Moses and all the Prophets*, [Jesus] explained to them what was said in all the Scriptures concerning himself"* (Lk 24:27). Moessner (not surprisingly) sees the key to the Emmaus road episode and all of Luke as "the recognition of the journeying guest who is revealed at table as the Lord (v. 35) and as Lord, the host of the banquet in the Kingdom of God."[85] I will give a translation below and then proceed to discuss the passage in greater detail in order to bring to light Luke's distinct and additional contribution to the development of the exodus motif at this point. This passage, it should be noted, belongs to the larger pericope of Luke 24:36-53, and the main themes can be summarized in the following Greek words: *metanoia, aphesis, hamartiōn*, and *martys* (repentance, release, sin, and witness).

Pao begins his discussion by making a literary point: just as the beginning of Luke provides a link with the story of Jesus, so too does the end of Luke.[86] When Jesus says, "This is what is written" (Lk 24:46), the reference is not literally to "Scripture" but most likely alludes to totality, Pao argues. Here *gegraptai* (it is written) is followed by three infinitive clauses in Luke 24:46-47 (notice Luke's use of *pathein*, "to suffer," *anastēnai*, "will rise," and *kērychthēnai*, "will preach"). "The extension of the message of salvation to the gentiles now becomes part of the Christological program," Jacques Dupont asserts.[87] This becomes most clear at Luke 24:44 with *peri emou* (i.e., "about me" = Jesus). In Luke 24:47 *aphesin* (forgiveness) now characterizes the message of the early Christians. The same term is used to characterize the message of Jesus in Luke 4:18 (i.e., "release" from the bondage of Satan). The point is clear: there is unity and continuity between the ministry of Jesus and that of the apostles.

---

[85]Ibid., 184.
[86]Pao, *Acts*, 84.
[87]Quoted in ibid., 87.

Luke 24:44 reveals the divine plan (*dei plērōthēnai*), which "must be fulfilled." This sets forth the whole idea of prophecy fulfillment. When Jesus in Luke 24:46 begins with *gegraptai* (it is written), this reference to prophecy fulfillment, in combination with Luke 4:16-30, sets the stage for the ministry of Jesus while anticipating the ministry of the apostles: he "will suffer and rise from the dead on the third day," and they will be "witnesses of these things." It is true that *martyres* (witnesses) only occurs twice in Luke; however, in the book of Acts it becomes a significant designation (Act 1:8, 22; 2:32; 3:15; 5:32; 10:39, 41; 13:31; 22:15, 20; 26:16).

In short, it may be said that in "the ministry of Jesus, Luke 24:44-49 pushes the Isaianic program as announced in Luke 4:16-30 a step forward with the introduction of the theme of the Gentiles."[88] The concern for the Gentiles that we saw in Luke 4 is now made even more explicit in Luke 24:47. Now that the connection has been made between Jesus' ministry and the ongoing ministry of his disciples, the next step is to turn to Luke's other writing: the book of Acts.

Luke's Second Book: Who Is the True Israel?

Pao maintains that a central question now emerges: Who is the "true Israel"? To answer this question, he turns to Luke's use of *hodos* (way) terminology, a concept that played an important role in Watts's analysis of the Gospel of Mark also. In our discussion of Luke's Gospel, we argued that the citation of Isaiah 40:3-5 in Luke 3:2-6 demonstrates that Luke expected his audience to lean forward with the announcement of a new exodus for the people of God. We noted that the temptation of Jesus narrated in Luke 4 has many parallels with Israel's wilderness temptations and that Jesus' reading of Isaiah in the synagogue (Lk 4:16-20) was a kind of programmatic sermon for the rest of his Gospel: Jesus had come to enact a new exodus that proclaimed release from the bondage of Satan and sin. When we turned to the transfiguration in Luke 9, we saw that Jesus' "exodus" (*exodon*, Lk 9:31) discussed with Elijah and Moses

---

[88]Ibid., 89-90.

indicated (in light of Garrett's research and comparison with Stephen's speech in Acts 7) that Jesus was fulfilling a new exodus that especially meant that God's people could be freed from bondage to Satan in order to offer worship to God. The Lukan travel narrative commenced at Luke 9:51 with Jesus setting himself resolutely toward Jerusalem. Green has stated that the "way to Jerusalem" in Luke is painted with "hues of Israel's exodus journey."[89] That seems correct not only because the exodus motif plays such a significant role early in Luke's Gospel but also because this appears to be the denouement of the Song of the Sea (Ex 15:17, "You will bring them in and plant them / on the mountain of your inheritance— / the place, LORD, you made for your dwelling, / the sanctuary, LORD, your hands established," as discussed in chap. 3).

The term *hodos* (way) occurs in numerous places in Acts. In each case, "the way" is used in a polemical context where the identity of the "true" people of God is at stake. In short, the phraseology is used in establishing the church as the true heir of the ancient traditions in Israel.[90] Furthermore, all the contexts show conflict and challenge to the early Christian movement.[91]

For example, Acts 9:1-2 (Saul dealing with Christians) says, "Meanwhile, Saul was still breathing out murderous threats against the Lord's disciples. He went to the high priest and asked him for letters to the synagogues in Damascus, so that if he found any there who belonged to *the* Way, whether men or women, he might take them as prisoners to Jerusalem." Another example occurs in Acts 22:3-5. Here the credentials of Saul as a Jew and the authority of Jewish high priests are set in contrast to the Way: "I am a Jew, born in Tarsus of Cilicia, but brought up in this city. I studied under Gamaliel and was thoroughly trained in the law of our ancestors. I was just as zealous for God as any of you are today. I persecuted the followers of *this* Way to their death, arresting both men and women and throwing them into prison." Yet another example occurs in Acts 19:8-9, where the

---

[89]Green, "Luke, Gospel of," 544.
[90]Pao, *Acts*, 60.
[91]Ibid., 61.

opposition against Paul can be felt: "Paul entered the synagogue and spoke boldly there for three months, arguing persuasively about the kingdom of God. But some of them became obstinate; they refused to believe and publicly maligned *the Way*." Yet again, in Acts 19:23: "About that time there arose a great disturbance about *the Way*." It seems that the context in Acts 19 demands for conflict between the Christian and Ephesian worshipers of Artemis, but the reader should take notice of the curious appearance of the Jew Alexander: "The Jews in the crowd pushed Alexander to the front, and they shouted instructions to him. He motioned for silence in order to make a defense before the people. But when they realized he was a Jew, they all shouted in unison for about two hours: 'Great is Artemis of the Ephesians!'" (Acts 19:33-34).

A definitive passage is Paul's speech before Felix in Acts 24:10-23. Paul says, "However, I admit that I worship the God of our ancestors as a follower of *the Way*, which they call a sect" (Acts 24:14). Noteworthy here is the use of "the Way" as a clear identity marker.[92] What is the upshot of all this evidence? Pao comments,

> The term [*way*] is not a remnant of Luke's source accidentally appearing in Acts (and nowhere else in early Christian literature). In the narrative of Acts, it is a term that functions as a symbol that defines the identity of the early Christian movement over against the competing claims of the majority culture. Only with this understanding can the conceptual context of this term be examined. The use of the term should be understood against the background of the Isaianic New Exodus.... The term "Way" [*derek*]... in Isaiah 40–55 became a term that evoked the Exodus tradition and signaled the presence of the new salvific act of God.[93]

Pao concludes that Isaiah 40:3-5 serves as a hermeneutical principle for understanding narrative in Luke–Acts: "The use of the term should be understood against the background of the INE [Isaianic new exodus]."[94]

---

[92]Ibid., 65.
[93]Ibid., 65-66.
[94]Ibid., 66. See G. K. Beale, *Handbook on the New Testament Use of the Old Testament: Exegesis and Interpretation* (Grand Rapids: Baker Academic, 2012), 80-89, for other examples in which a New Testament author takes over a large Old Testament context as a model for creative patterning.

Furthermore, the national story of the people of Israel is evoked in order to demonstrate that the church is the redefinition of the people of God. As we have seen earlier, the Qumran scrolls offer further evidence. There, "way" terminology functions as an identity marker for a sectarian Jewish community of the Second Temple period. Pao demonstrates that "specific Isaianic statements are used at critical points in the narrative of the Lukan writings to provide meaning for the development of the story in Acts."[95] We will now look at some of the evidence that Pao has gathered from Luke's writings.

Acts 1:8

Acts 1:8 is programmatic for the entire structure of the book of Acts: "You will receive power when the Holy Spirit comes on you; and you will be my witnesses in Jerusalem, and in all Judea and Samaria, and to the ends of the earth."[96] Luke could envision the new exodus as leading to the spiritual "conquest" of the nations for the name of Christ.[97]

Here too there are allusions to the prophet Isaiah. Dennis Johnson outlines some of the allusions and differences, as seen in table 8.1.[98]

Table 8.1. Acts 1:8 and Isaiah (LXX): allusions and differences

Acts 1:8 (NIV)	Isaiah (LXX)
"when the Holy *Spirit comes upon you*"	"until the *Spirit comes upon you* from on high" (Is 32:15)
"*you shall be my witnesses*"	"*Become witnesses for me*, and I myself am witness, says the Lord God, and my servant whom I have chosen." (Is 43:10) "*You are witnesses for me*, and I myself am witness, says the Lord God." (Is 43:12) "*You are witnesses*, whether there is any god besides me." (Is 44:8)

---

[95] Green, "Luke, Gospel of," 70.
[96] Pao, *Acts*, 91.
[97] Davis, *Name and Way*, 101.
[98] Cf. Dennis E. Johnson, *The Message of Acts in the History of Redemption* (Phillipsburg, NJ: P&R, 1997), 35-36.

Acts 1:8 (NIV)	Isaiah (LXX)
"to the ends of the earth"	"Is it a great thing for you to be called my servant to cause Jacob's tribes to stand and Israel's dispersion to return? I will appoint you for a covenant of the people, for a light to the Gentiles, that you may be for salvation *to the ends of the earth.*" (Is 49:6)
	"Turn to me and be saved, you who are from *the ends of the earth;* for I myself am God, and there is no other." (Is 45:22)

Source: Dennis E. Johnson, *The Message of Acts in the History of Redemption* (Phillipsburg, NJ: P&R, 1997), 35-36.

Johnson has identified three themes from his analysis of the Isaiah allusions:

1. The *Spirit of God* is poured out upon God's people.

2. God's people are *his witnesses*, testifying on the basis of the saving acts that they have seen that he alone is God and Savior.

3. Their witness extends *to the ends of the earth*, calling pagan nations to abandon their idols and turn to the Lord for salvation.[99]

The "ends of the earth" in this passage is not just geographical, argues Pao. It is "theopolitical."[100] That is, in the first part of Acts 1:8, we find a reference to a city and two regions, and the final phrase "to the ends of the earth" does not refer to a city or a specific region. The four geographical terms—Jerusalem, Judea, Samaria, ends of the earth—may refer to three theopolitical categories.[101] Jerusalem needs no explanation. Judea and Samaria may evoke the theopolitical notions of the two regions. And the final phrase, "ends of the earth," has its theological significance established by allusion to Isaiah 49:6 ("I will also make you a light for the Gentiles, / that my salvation may reach to the ends of the earth"). These three categories correspond to three stages of the Isaianic new exodus: (1) the dawn of salvation on Jerusalem, (2) the reconstitution

---

[99] Johnson, *Message of Acts*, 36.
[100] Pao, *Acts*, 94.
[101] Ibid., 95.

and reunification of Israel, and (3) the inclusion of the Gentiles in the people of God.[102]

Acts 13:46-47

In Acts 13:46-47 we have a citation from Isaiah 49:6. There are some slight differences from the Septuagint, but the meaning is not significantly affected.

> Then Paul and Barnabas answered them boldly: "We had to speak the word of God to your first. Since your reject it and do not consider yourselves worthy of eternal life, we now turn to the Gentiles. For this is what the Lord has commanded us:
>
> "I have made you a light for the Gentiles,
>   that you may bring salvation to the ends of the earth."
>   (Acts 13:46-47)

This subtle citation of Isaiah 49:6, which we discussed in chapter five, is a further transformation of the Isaianic new-exodus motif: the redefinition of the people of God.[103] First, we saw the inclusion of the Gentiles (Luke 24; Acts 1:8; etc.), and now there is a new element, the rejection of the message by the Jews, which is said to motivate the change. Second, the context of Acts 13–14 is the sustained effort to take the gospel beyond the territories of the land of Israel.[104] Third, in Acts 13:46-47 we have a strategic turning point. The quotation of Isaiah 49:6 (Acts 13:47) and the rejection by the Jews (Acts 13:46) make it clear that Luke is emphasizing "for the first time in the Lukan narrative the connections between the two important themes of Luke and Acts: the rejection by the Jews and the offer of the salvation to the Gentiles."[105] Fourth, it is noteworthy that the role of the servant is transferred from the Savior Jesus to the early Christian missionaries. In short, this passage confirms that the Isaianic new-exodus motif has taken a refined meaning. As Pao puts it, "Isaiah is not used in a narrow

---
[102]Ibid., 95.
[103]Ibid., 98.
[104]Ibid.
[105]Ibid., 99.

Christological sense. Instead, it serves to construct the identity of the early Christian movement."[106] Jesus is integrally bound to his church.

Acts 28:25-28

At the conclusion of the book of Acts, we find an extended quotation from Isaiah 6:9-10, with perhaps an echo of Isaiah 40:5 in the phrase *to sōtērion tou theou* (the salvation of God).

> They disagreed among themselves and began to leave after Paul had made this final statement: "The Holy Spirit spoke the truth to your ancestors when he said through Isaiah the prophet:
>
> "'Go to this people and say,
>   "You will be ever hearing but never understanding;
>   you will be ever seeing but never perceiving."
> For this people's heart has become calloused;
>   they hardly hear with their ears,
>   and they have closed their eyes.
> Otherwise they might see with their eyes,
>   hear with their ears,
>   understand with their hearts
> and turn, and I would heal them.'
>
> "Therefore I want you to know that God's salvation [*to sōtērion tou theou*] has been sent to the Gentiles, and they will listen!" (Acts 28:25-28)

Given the recalcitrance of the audience, it is significant that in citing Isaiah 6:9-10 and possibly echoing Isaiah 40:5, Luke is alluding to one Isaianic passage announcing judgment and another announcing salvation to the Gentiles. If this is the case, then Luke is both showing continuity and demonstrating that the people of God may include Jews and Gentiles, those "who understand his words and those who do not, and between those in whom his word brings fruit and those in whom it does not."[107]

Just as in Acts 13:46-47, there is a turning to the Gentiles after an unfavorable response on the part of the Jewish people.[108] In both texts,

---

[106]Ibid., 100.
[107]Litwak, *Echoes of Scripture*, 194.
[108]Pao, *Acts*, 104.

the quotation from Isaiah is medial and the context is the unfavorable response of the Jews. However, there has been a dramatic reversal. In Luke 3, Isaiah 40 is quoted. In Acts 28, Isaiah 6 is quoted, and yet with no mention of the remnant mentioned in the latter part of Isaiah 6. The original order of judgment-salvation leading to consolation has become salvation-judgment. This is a profound reversal. Pao states,

> The similarities between Isa 6:1-12 and 40:1-11 highlight the one critical contrast between the two passages. In Isa 6:1-12, emphasis is placed on the themes of judgment and destruction and the impossibility of the people of God to respond to the message of the prophet. In Isaiah 40, however, a dramatic reversal of the previous indictment is introduced. This is a section written by one who has "the task of proclaiming salvation, and nothing but salvation, to his people."[109]

Isaiah 40:1-11 contains the unequivocal announcement of the dawn of salvation and the reversal of the previous oracles of doom.[110]

The upshot of this reversal is that the dawn of the new age has come (Luke 4). However, this has been qualified in two ways according to Luke–Acts. First, there is the rejection of prophetic movement to the Jews (Is 6). Second, there is the inclusion of Gentiles (using Is 49:6). The people of God now have a new, distinctive identity, but one that has continuity with the past.[111] Throughout the history of redemption and evident throughout the Bible, there are two distinct levels of promise and fulfillment. We see this pattern well illustrated here:

1. On one level, the typological is provisional and prototypical.

2. On another level, the fulfillment of the typological is messianic and eternal and in this case "churchly."

Once again, the issue with regard to hermeneutics is the relationship between these two levels, the typological and the fulfillment of the typological. Covenant theology sees a relationship: there is continuity and unity, but also a measure of discontinuity. The first level is a promise; the

---

[109]Ibid., 107. Pao quoting Westermann at the end of the quotation.
[110]Ibid.
[111]Ibid., 109-10.

second is fulfillment. The Isaianic new exodus is pervasive in Mark, Matthew, and Luke–Acts. It is not mere repetition of the Old Testament pattern but an advancement and supplementation within the progress of redemption.

Conclusion: The Exodus Motif in the Synoptic Gospels

We have seen how pervasive and significant the exodus motif is for the Synoptic Gospels. Sometimes this influence goes into the very marrow of the organizing structure of the Gospels, such as for Mark. In Mark's Gospel, through his prologue and his use of "way" terminology and his allusion to the wilderness with all its contemporary resonance, Jesus is the agent of the new exodus. Matthew's innerbiblical echoes of Hosea's exodus themes, along with his accent on Jesus as the second Moses who fulfills Israel's history and on Jesus' obedience in contrast to Israel's disobedience, showcases Christ as the faithful Son who has come to fulfill all righteousness.

Luke–Acts, by means of its unique use of framing discourse and by touching on the "end of exile" theme, demonstrates that Jesus is also the Messiah who fulfills the Old Testament Scriptures. Luke uses Isaiah 40:3-5 to announce Jesus and the new exodus, a new era of redemptive history. The temptation of Jesus in Luke 4 and the programmatic sermon that Jesus makes from his reading of Isaiah demonstrate that he has come as the agent of the new exodus, broken the bondage of Satan, and released the oppressed from his tyranny, especially in light of Stephen's speech in Acts 7. The transfiguration scene of Luke 9 confirms that Jesus is fulfilling his exodus and is a prelude to the travel narrative announced in Luke 9:51: Jesus resolutely sets out on a journey, destined to die in Jerusalem, and provides liberation for his people in the process. The continuity between Luke and Acts demonstrates that the Isaianic new exodus is coming into its own: salvation is now for all those who will receive the life-giving word of the Messiah, Jew and Gentile alike.

THE EXODUS MOTIF IN PAUL

I was so much moved by my memories that I wrote a sonnet to the cheese. Some critical friends have hinted to me that my sonnet is not strictly new; that it contains "echoes" (as they express it) of some other poem that they have read somewhere. . . . I confess I feel myself as if some literary influence, something that has haunted me, were present in this otherwise original poem; it is hopeless to disentangle it now.

G. K. Chesterton

*Exiles feed on empty dreams of hope.
I know it. I was one.*

Aeschylus

The nerve-centre of all that happens in history consists in the fact that, when God's holiness has been wounded, things cannot go on as they are.

Claus Westermann

So many have commented on the Pauline corpus that it is difficult to choose your conversation partners. I am not first and foremost a Pauline scholar. So I have deliberately chosen conversation partners that are familiar and unfamiliar, sympathetic and unsympathetic with my views. Consequently, we have a very interesting dinner party. There is N. T. Wright, from whom I have benefited so much and yet differ from in many ways. Nevertheless, his massive work on Paul is a project to be reckoned with. Next, there is one of his students, Sylvia Keesmaat, who appreciates her mentor's work yet is willing to stand against him out of strong conviction. Then there is Richard Hays, who has been so influential in seeing "story" and "echo" as essential to understanding Paul. Finally, there are those who are closer to home: those old perspective on Paul adherents such as Douglas Moo and Stephen Westerholm, and also confessional Presbyterians such as Guy Waters. I think we can learn from this dialogue. We will first look at the narrative dynamics in Paul. Then we will examine 1 Corinthians, Galatians, Romans, and a brief passage from Colossians, looking for evidence of the exodus motif in Paul's writing.

The influence of the exodus in Paul's letters is not as immediately evident as it is in Psalms or Isaiah. Nevertheless, as many as forty references or allusions to the exodus have been identified in the Pauline corpus.[1] Before Harald Sahlin made this claim, W. D. Davies had already introduced the concept of new exodus into the conversation on Paul's theology.[2] Regrettably, part of his reasoning was that Jesus instituted a "new Passover" with the Lord's Supper. This, however, is too simplistic. The Supper was instituted on the occasion of the Passover, but it is not a new Passover.[3] But Davies also concluded that Paul was "the preacher of a New Exodus wrought by the 'merit' of Christ, but this New Exodus like the Old was constitutive of a community, it served to establish the New Israel."[4] For Davies, Jesus was not the new Moses; rather, he was the new Torah. And while E. P. Sanders could rejoice that Davies had introduced the new exodus so that Judaism was seen as the fulfillment rather than the antithesis of Judaism,[5] the Jewish pattern of covenantal

---

[1] See Harald Sahlin, "The New Exodus of Salvation According to St. Paul," in *The Root of the Vine*, ed. A. J. Fridrichsen (Westminster: Dacre, 1953), 84.
[2] See W. D. Davies, *Paul and Rabbinic Judaism: Some Rabbinic Elements in Pauline Theology* (London: SPCK, 1948), 146. Also see discussions on 251-52, 313, and esp. 323.
[3] See my "Passover: Continuity or Discontinuity?," in *Children and the Lord's Supper*, ed. Guy Waters and Ligon Duncan (Fearn, UK: Mentor, 2011), 31-57.
[4] Davies, *Paul and Rabbinic Judaism*, 323.
[5] E. P. Sanders, *Paul and Palestinian Judaism: A Comparison of Patterns of Religion* (Minneapolis: Fortress, 1977), 9.

nomism, according to him, should not be determined by the exodus typology.⁶ The difficulty of uncovering echoes of the exodus event in Paul's writings is that they lie more beneath the surface. However, that does not mean they do not exist. Keesmaat, for example, in her monograph about the exodus tradition in Romans 8, claims that "not just images associated with the exodus, but the very narrative of the exodus seems to have provided the framework for Paul's discussion."⁷ Therefore, in this chapter we will begin to trace some of the scholarly views on the exodux motif in Paul in order to build a link with Peter's ecclesial and ethical use of the exodus motif. That will come in the next chapter.

Continuing Exile

This issue of a continuing exile is integrally related to the concept of the new exodus.⁸ I introduced Wright's thesis in *Jesus and the Victory of God* about continuing exile in the last chapter: Wright contends that Jesus was declaring the end of exile for the Jews and that as the Christ (Messiah) he was the agent bringing about that end in the midst of a people with a mindset of continuing exile. He laments that Protestants often skip over this major issue and retrospectively go right back to Moses.⁹ Integrally related to this is the notion expressed early in Wright's writings that the curse described in Galatians 3:10-14 is not to be construed along the lines of "*post mortem* damnation which hangs over the heads of sinners" but rather as involving exile of corporate Israel as a covenant people.¹⁰ Recently, Wright has carried this thesis through in his analysis of Paul as well.¹¹ To be fair to Wright's views, he is trying to provide a corrective to an overemphasis on the individual categories of soteriology that miss the grand

---

⁶Ibid., 511-13, esp. his comments on 513.
⁷Sylvia C. Keesmaat, *Paul and His Story: (Re)Interpreting the Exodus Tradition*, JSNTSup 181 (Sheffield: Sheffield Academic Press, 1999), 89.
⁸See Daniel Lynwood Smith, "The Uses of 'New Exodus' in New Testament Scholarship: Preparing a Way Through the Wilderness," *CurBS* 14, no. 2 (2016): 218.
⁹See N. T. Wright, *Paul and the Faithfulness of God*, Christian Origins and the Question of God 4 (Minneapolis: Fortress, 2013), 141.
¹⁰For Wright, the curse of the covenant as expressed in Deut 27–28 refers to divine judgment of Israel for a national curse rather than a curse on individuals. See N. T. Wright, *The Climax of the Covenant: Christ and the Law in Pauline Theology* (Minneapolis: Fortress, 1992), 142, 146, 148.
¹¹See Wright, *Paul and the Faithfulness of God*, 145 and esp. 428.

story of redemptive history, categories that from his vantage point have given a thin description of sin (since the important category of idolatry is sometimes absent).[12] Moreover, I agree with Wright that we must avoid an exaggerated spiritualism, which understands there to be nothing more after the judgment than spirits in an uncreated heaven.[13] I agree with Wright that we must avoid an abstract supernaturalism and a view of salvation that becomes purely transcendent, which may engender an ascetic view of life that leads to monasticism. We need to avoid a Platonized view of heaven that is focused on the redemption merely of individuals, or disembodied souls.[14] The exodus motif does not engender such a reductionism. Although Wright's rhetoric may seem at places like he is dismissing the individual aspects of salvation, a careful reading of his interactions with the flourishing interpretations of the school of "Apocalyptic Paul" interpreters (e.g., J. Louis Martyn) actually reveals that he polemicizes against their tendency to avoid the necessity of individual responses to the gospel.[15] He says:

> Partly with Beker but more particularly with Martyn and his followers, "apocalyptic" interpretations aim to highlight the "cosmic," global and supraglobal dimensions of Paul's thought, over against individualistic and even privatized readings. Here is the irony: in Martyn at least . . . one sometimes has the impression that the main thing to be avoided is the kind of fussy, who's-in-who's-out sort of Christianity one finds in—popular American religion![16]

We are now postured to pull some threads together, connecting Wright's ideas of continuing exile with the biblical material and the new exodus.

---

[12]See, e.g., ibid., 163, 182-83, 248, 754-55, 841, 1169.
[13]This was Origen's position, according to Herman Bavinck, *Reformed Dogmatics*, vol. 4, *Holy Spirit, Church, and New Creation*, ed. John Bolt, trans. John Vriend (Grand Rapids: Baker Academic, 2008), 718.
[14]See esp. his most recent book, N. T. Wright, *The Day the Revolution Began: Reconsidering the Meaning of Jesus's Crucifixion* (San Francisco: HarperOne, 2016).
[15]See, e.g., N. T. Wright's response to recent critiques in *The Paul Debate: Critical Questions for Understanding the Apostle* (Waco, TX: Baylor University Press, 2015), 41-64. For Wright's clearest and fullest statements on "apocalyptic," see N. T. Wright, "The Challenge of Dialogue: A Partial and Preliminary Response," in *God and the Faithfulness of Paul*, ed. Christoph Heilig, J. Thomas Hewitt, and Michael F. Bird, WUNT 2.413 (Tübingen: Mohr Siebeck, 2016), 711-70, esp. 743-54.
[16]N. T. Wright, *Paul and His Recent Interpreters: Some Contemporary Debates* (Minneapolis: Fortress, 2015), 142.

Many have offered critiques of Wright's understanding of continuing exile. Clearly there was some notion of continuing exile in many Second Temple Jewish texts, but there are also texts that testify to the end of the exile in some sense.[17] And surely, as Greg Beale claims, there is some sense in which "Paul views Christians in Rom. 6-8 to be the actual beginning fulfillment of the prophesied resurrection of Israel that was to transpire in the later days at the time of their restoration from exile."[18] Yet others have critiqued Wright's view of continuing exile as being the one lens through which some view the New Testament documents, with a result of over-interpretation of biblical data along corporate rather than individualistic lines.[19] We must exercise extreme care not to deny that there is this corporate dimension in Scripture in regard to the categories of sin and redemption and consequently in the typological patterns developed in Scripture as evidenced in the last chapter.[20] But when this notion is extended to say that Paul's well-stocked mind, with its concepts of overthrowing sin, servitude, and slavery to the tyrant of Egypt, is best captured mostly or primarily along corporate lines rather than individual categories, then one must ask if Wright has overinterpreted the data according to this highly complex scheme—a concern raised by more than a few New Testament scholars.[21] It seems to me that Paul has in mind, especially in the early chapters of Romans, individual sinners (Rom 1:18), including individual Gentiles (Rom 1:18-32) and individual

---

[17]See the evidence cited, e.g., by Mark A. Seifrid, *Christ, Our Righteousness: Paul's Theology of Justification*, New Studies in Biblical Theology 9 (Downers Grove, IL: InterVarsity Press, 2000), 22-25.

[18]See G. K. Beale, *A New Testament Biblical Theology: The Unfolding of the Old Testament in the New* (Grand Rapids: Baker Academic, 2011), 254.

[19]See, e.g., Douglas J. Moo, "Israel and the Law in Romans 5–11: Interaction with the New Perspective," in *Justification and Variegated Nomism*, vol. 2, *The Paradoxes of Paul*, ed. D. A. Carson, Peter T. O'Brien, and Mark A. Seifrid (Grand Rapids: Baker Academic, 2004), 200-205.

[20]However, the category of corporate election recently discussed in the academy does not seem to cohere with what we have argued here or elsewhere in Scripture. For a good survey, see Stephen M. Baugh, *Ephesians*, Evangelical Exegetical Commentary (Bellingham, WA: Lexham Press, 2016), 165-70.

[21]See, e.g., Moo, "Israel and the Law," 188, 194-95. Also Guy Prentiss Waters, "Covenant Theology and Recent Interpretation of Paul: Some Reflections," *Confessional Presbyterian* 6 (2010): 167-79, esp. 177-78. This criticism would extend to other New Testament scholars who essentially encourage a corporate interpretation to the exclusion of the more individual paradigm typical of Reformation exegesis. Here I have in mind Tom Holland, *Contours of Pauline Theology: A Radical New Survey of the Influences on Paul's Biblical Writings* (Fearn, UK: Mentor, 2004), or more recently Holland's commentary, *Romans: The Divine Marriage* (Eugene, OR: Pickwick, 2011).

Jews (Rom 2:1–3:8), for which "the wrath of God is each offender's due."[22] In my reading of Paul, both the plight of sin and the solution for sin are construed primarily along individual lines rather than corporate ones. Paul characteristically starts with the one (the individual) and then moves to the many (the corporate),[23] although sometimes the Scriptures move from the many (Israel) to the one (Christ). Finally, following some recent treatments of Paul and the law, we see that the ultimate curse of the law in Galatians (alluding to Deut 27:26 in Gal 3:10) is probably connected to the category of death in Paul's mind and not to exile.[24]

It may be more fruitful to take an "intertextual" approach to these issues rather than a "narrative" approach.[25] In chapter one we saw that echoes are crucial resonances in biblical literature.[26] While some maintain that echoes are less explicit than allusions,[27] Christopher Beetham sees a distinction between allusion and echo in regard to an "essential interpretive link." If such a link is located, the text should be identified as an allusion. If it is not, then the text is an echo.[28] I am committed to the distinction that "echo" be used where there is a less sustained, less distinguishable reference.[29] Israel's story indeed lies behind Paul's formulations, but the critical question is at what level.[30]

---

[22]Waters, "Covenant Theology," 177.
[23]Pace Holland, *Contours of Pauline Theology*, 110.
[24]See Rodrigo J. Morales, *The Spirit and the Restoration of Israel: New Exodus and New Creation Motifs in Galatians*, WUNT 2.282 (Tübingen: Mohr Siebeck, 2010), 86-87.
[25]R. Barry Matlock, "The Arrow and the Web: Critical Reflections on a Narrative Approach to Paul," in *Narrative Dynamics in Paul: A Critical Assessment*, ed. Bruce W. Longenecker (Louisville, KY: Westminster John Knox, 2002), 53.
[26]Stanley E. Porter, "Further Comments on the Use of the Old Testament in the New Testament," in *The Intertextuality of the Epistles: Explorations of Theory and Practice*, ed. Thomas L. Brodie, Dennis R. MacDonald, and Stanley E. Porter (Sheffield: Sheffield Phoenix Press, 2006), 109.
[27]See Christopher A. Beetham, *Echoes of Scripture in the Letter of Paul to the Colossians*, Biblical Interpretation 96 (Leiden: Brill, 2008), 20.
[28]Ibid., 20-24.
[29]A similar categorical distinction is used by John Frederick Evans, "An Inner-biblical Interpretation and Intertextual Reading of Ezekiel's Recognition Formulae with the Book of Exodus" (ThD diss., University of Stellenbosch, 2006), 70.
[30]See Doug Moo's review of *Paul and the Faithfulness of God*, The Gospel Coalition, November 6, 2013, www.thegospelcoalition.org/article/paul_and the_faithfulness_of_god. Moo comments, "I'm not convinced we can make this story—or, indeed, any 'story'—as basic as Wright wants, especially when the alleged narrative framework is privileged over the framework supplied by explicit textual evidence (e.g., Rom 5–8)."

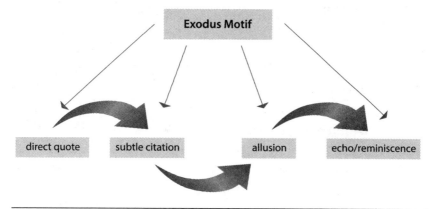

Figure 9.1. Biblical authors' use of the exodus motif

If we take the exodus motif as the overarching category, we should understand quotation, subtle citation, allusion, and echo as tools by which an author "works" the motif. This arrangement allows all three categories of agency to stay active: the author, the text, and the audience or subsequent readers. Consider the illustration again from chapter one (fig. 9.1). This grouping gives us four broad categories for identifying how any biblical author is using the exodus motif or any other motif. My suggestion is that the exodus and the Isaianic new exodus and their subsequent expression in the new exodus brought about by Christ—the meganarrative salvation events of the Old Testament and the Gospels—have influenced the apostle Paul in significant and substantial ways. How could they not come out in his writings? This may happen in an allusive or echoic manner. Allusions are more likely to provide an interpretive link, such as numerous connections to the Septuagint, which the apostle undoubtedly used. In other places, we may come up short when hunting for explicit interpretive links for the reader, and therefore we may opt for an echoic reference. Colossians 1:12-14, discussed below, is an example of an echoic reference with possible allusions to Exodus 6:6-8. Given the frequency of the keywords used by Septuagint translators for redemption and inheritance in these passages, the passage in Colossians may be a montage of passages that ultimately find their moorings in Exodus 6:6-8.

In such instances, the interpreter bears a greater burden to argue a plausible case for alleged echoes. Additionally, the interpreter should sit lightly on cherished echoic identifications since they rest on a less firm foundation and should consequently only be set forth on a scale of more or less plausibility. This becomes important for recognizing echoes in Paul, who may not have consciously intended to refer to the exodus but nevertheless does.[31] In other words, sometimes authors make references without direct, immediate conscious awareness. This is a viable claim given the apostle's profound and extensive education, especially within a culture that depended on orality more than our own. If this is the case for the Prophets, as we have suggested, then it might surely be the case with Paul as well. Ultimately, the divine author is where we search for authorial intent. This process is constrained by the canon of Scripture. Even so, given the apostle's richly stocked mind, we must allow that the apostle was fully aware of what he is consciously doing at times! Francis Watson cautions us not to bend the concept of story to the breaking point.[32] For Watson, Paul should not be reduced to a storyteller; rather, the apostle is an interpreter of the grand story that draws from Old Testament Scripture, especially Genesis and Exodus.[33] The upshot for Watson is that "Paul is certainly a theological interpreter of scriptural narrative, but it is a mistake to understand him as a 'narrative theologian.'"[34] It bears repeating that this is all constrained by the canon of Scripture, both Old Testament and New Testament. It is not open-ended.

My theoretical claims above can in part be justified by reminding the reader of Paul's extensive preparation for his divinely appointed vocation. Paul was a yeshiva boy and a gymnasium boy.[35] In other words, he received the best of Jewish education and to a lesser degree

---

[31] See Keesmaat, *Paul and His Story*, 49. Also see Morales, *Restoration of Israel*, 9.
[32] Francis Watson, "Is There a Story in These Texts?," in Longenecker, *Narrative Dynamics in Paul*, 231-39.
[33] Ibid., 234.
[34] Ibid., 239. Watson must have struck a nerve in N. T. Wright, who deliberately mentions Watson's trenchant criticism as the triggering point for devoting many pages of response in his recent tome on Paul. See Wright, *Paul and the Faithfulness of God*, 462-68.
[35] I think I picked up this phrase from novelist Larry Woiwode, although I have not been able to locate where in his books I read it.

Gentile education in his day. More precisely, he probably received a relatively good Greek education and a superior education in Judaism. Probably beginning at the age of six or seven, he memorized huge sections and possibly even entire books of the Hebrew Bible (probably more in Greek than Hebrew).[36] Raised in Tarsus, a city that was no backwater, he was brought up at the feet of Gamaliel, one of the leading rabbis of the day. He probably was not, however, moved to Jerusalem as a young child.[37]

Christian Dispensation as New Exodus: 1 Corinthians 10:1-10

Davies argues that the Christian dispensation is to be understood in the apostle Paul's mind as a new exodus: "There is much to indicate that a very significant part of the conceptual world in which Paul moved, *as a Christian*, was that of the Exodus."[38] Davies continues, "It is clear that, as for Matthew and other New Testament writers, so for Paul, there was a real correspondence between the Christian Dispensation and the Exodus of Israel from Egypt. The redemption of the Old Israel was the prototype of the greater redemption from sin wrought by Christ for the New Israel."[39]

Davies takes as his starting point 1 Corinthians 10:1-10:

> I want you to know, brothers, that our fathers were under the cloud, and all passed through the sea, and all were baptized into Moses in the cloud and in the sea, and all ate the same supernatural food and drank the same supernatural drink.[40] For they drank from the Supernatural Rock which

---

[36] See E. P. Sanders, "Paul Between Judaism and Hellenism," in *St. Paul Among the Philosophers*, ed. John D. Caputo and Linda Martin Alcoff (Bloomington: Indiana University Press, 2009), 74-90.
[37] Ibid., 77.
[38] W. D. Davies, *The Setting of the Sermon on the Mount* (Cambridge: Cambridge University Press, 1964), 349. See also Davies, "Paul and the New Exodus," in *The Quest for Context and Meaning: Studies in Biblical Intertextuality in Honor of James A. Sanders*, ed. Craig A. Evans and Shemaryahu Talmon (New York: Brill, 1997), 443.
[39] Davies, "Paul and the New Exodus," 444.
[40] Tertullian, interestingly, had a well-developed notion of baptism being prefigured by the waters of the Red Sea, which included delivery from the tyrannical powers of sin and the devil. See *On Baptism* 9 (*ANF* 3:673). See Cyprian as well for similar typological development; e.g., *Epistles* 62.8 (*ANF* 5:360); *Treatises* 12.1.12 (*ANF* 5:511).

followed them, and the Rock was Christ. Nevertheless with most of them God was not pleased; for they were overthrown in the wilderness. Now these things are warnings for us, not to desire evil as they did. Do not be idolaters as some of them were; as it is written, "The people sat down to eat and drink and rose to dance." We must not indulge in immorality as some of them did, and twenty-three thousand fell in a single day. We must not put the Lord to the test, as some of them did and were destroyed by serpents; nor grumble, as some of them did and were destroyed by the Destroyer.[41]

As Davies says, the understanding of the Christian life in this passage as an experience of a new exodus is explicit. Davies continues to root the imperative of the Christian life in passages he sees as describing a new exodus that the Christian is undergoing (1 Thess 2:10-11; 4:7, 8; 5:5-11; Gal 5:1, 25; 2 Cor 8:7; Rom 6:2-4; Col 3:1). William Wilder has likewise drawn significant parallels between 1 Corinthians 10:2-4 and 1 Corinthians 12:13, "For we were all baptized by one Spirit so as to form one body—whether Jews or Gentiles, slave or free—and we were all given the one Spirit to drink."[42] Davies also suggests that 1 Corinthians 5:7 owes something to the exodus motif, as does Romans 6:2-11, and he finds other passages more generally alluding to the exodus. For example, in 2 Corinthians we find Paul speaking of the Christian life in terms of a new covenant (2 Cor 3:1-18) and a sojourn in the wilderness (2 Cor 5:1-5).[43] Whereas Jesus is seen as the "new Moses" in 1 Corinthians, in 2 Corinthians he is viewed as the "new Torah." Additionally, Paul's language of inheritance is possibly related to the Christian life as a new exodus.[44] Finally, Davies suggests that the life of a Christian is a new exodus in the sense that when Paul speaks of imitating Christ, he may be thinking of following Jesus as a new Torah that is to be copied in words and deeds.[45] "To be 'in Christ' was for Paul

---

[41]The translation is by Davies, *Setting of the Sermon on the Mount*, 350.
[42]William N. Wilder, *Echoes of the Exodus Narrative in the Context and Background of Galatians 5:18*, Studies in Biblical Literature 23 (New York: Peter Lang, 2001), 100-104. See also P. Lundberg, *La typologie baptismale dans l'ancienne eglise* (Leipzig: Lorentz, 1942).
[43]Davies, "Paul and the New Exodus," 446.
[44]Ibid.
[45]Ibid., 447-63.

to have died and risen with Christ in a new exodus and this in turn meant that one is to be subject to the authority of the words and Person of Christ as a pattern."[46]

Echoes of the Exodus in Galatians

The language of adoption (*huiothesia*) looms large in the apostle Paul's writing. Interpreters have investigated whether Paul is referring to the Hellenistic background and its legal practices of adoption, or whether the Old Testament/Jewish background is in the foreground. Many New Testament commentators have opted for a Greco-Roman background of adoption and guardianship.[47] Yet there are significant incongruities between Paul's statements in Galatians 4 and what we know about the Greco-Roman practices.[48]

James Scott has argued on the basis of six criteria that the background for Paul's statements on adoption should be located in a conceptual framework of Israel's status in Egypt at the time of the exodus and their subsequent deliverance and adoption as God's children.[49] The four strongest arguments include the following.[50] First, the term *heir* refers to the sons of Abraham, not an abstract legal principle. Second, there is no evidence for *nēpios* (child) as a technical term for a minor in the Greco-Roman literature. Third, the use of the phrase *kyrios pantōn* (Lord of all) as a legal concept connected with the secular practice of adoption is highly dubious, with only slender support from the papyri.[51] Finally, the notion that *prothesmias* (time, date) is a technical legal term associated with adoption is also highly dubious.[52] Paul states,

---

[46]Ibid., 460.
[47]For some examples, see Morales, *Restoration of Israel*, 115.
[48]Ibid., 115-16.
[49]For an exhaustive analysis, see James M. Scott, *Adoption as Sons of God*, WUNT 2.48 (Tübingen: Mohr Siebeck, 1992), 126-49. See the entirety of chaps. 1 and 2 for lengthy discussion of the Greco-Roman institution and Old Testament background and the practices of early Judaism, particularly the importance of 2 Sam 7:14-17.
[50]Here I am following Morales, *Restoration of Israel*, 115-16, by only listing four of the strongest points. The reader may consult Keesmaat, *Paul and His Story*, 158-63, for a summary of Scott's position.
[51]See Scott, *Adoption*, 120-35.
[52]Following Morales, *Restoration of Israel*, 116-17.

> What I am saying is that as long as an heir is underage [*nēpios*], he is no different from a slave [*doulou*], although he owns the whole estate [*kyrios pantōn ōn*]. The heir is subject to guardians and trustees until the time [*prothesmias*] set by his father. So also, when we were underage [*nēpioi*], we were in slavery under the elemental spiritual forces [*stoicheia*] of the world [*tou kosmou*]. But when the set time had fully come, God sent his Son, born of a woman, born under the law [*hypo nomon*],[53] to redeem those under the law, that we might receive adoption to sonship [*huiothesian*]. Because you are his sons [*huioi*], God sent the Spirit of his Son into our hearts, the Spirit who calls out, "*Abba,* Father." So you are no longer a slave [*doulos*], but God's child [*huios*]; and since you are his child [*huios*], God has made you also an heir.
>
> Formerly, when you did not know God, you were slaves [*edouleusate*] to those who by nature are not gods. But now that you know God [*gnontes theon*]—or rather are known by God [*mallon de gnōsthentes hypo theou*]—how is it that you are turning back to those weak and miserable forces [*stoicheia*]? (Gal 4:1-9)

Paul has been using the imagery of slavery and sonship extensively throughout this letter.[54] Scott argues that the language of sons and slaves in Galatians 4:1-7 echoes the exodus. More precisely, he argues that 4:1-2 demonstrates first-exodus typology while 4:3-7 exemplifies new-exodus typology. Moreover, he demonstrates that the language of restoration and sonship resonates with new-exodus associations in a number of texts in the Jewish tradition of the time.[55]

In this passage, Paul is speaking of Israel as a whole under the law.[56] In verses 3 and 9, he speaks of the "*stoicheia* of the world," the meaning of

---

[53] Strangely, Barclay and Dunn note that the interpretation that sees this reference as condemnation in existence "under the law" as being excluded by Gal 4:4 is puzzling since "it does not fit the description of Christ himself being ὑπὸ νόμον," as noted by Wilder, *Exodus Narrative*, 259-60. Better is Wilder's explanation: "Actually, the reverse seems to be true. The way in which Christ '[redeemed] those who were under the law' (ἵνα τοὺς ὑπὸ νόμον ἐξαγοράσῃ, Gal 4:5) is the same way in which 'Christ redeemed us [Jews] from the curse of the law' (Χριστὸς ἡμᾶς ἐξηγόρασεν ἐκ τῆς κατάρας τοῦ νόμου, Gal 3:13): 'by becoming a curse on our behalf' (γενόμενος ὑπὲρ ἡμῶν κατάρα)." The translation is Wilder's. He goes on to argue further for other corroborative scriptural support that supports the notion that Gal 4:3 here, pace Dunn and Barclay, does contain overtones of condemnation and that such overtones are carried on in Gal 5:18 occurrence of the phrase as well.
[54] See Scott, *Adoption*, 167-69, for a helpful listing of all the passages.
[55] Ibid., 149-55.
[56] Morales, *Restoration of Israel*, 121.

which is disputed.⁵⁷ In Galatians 4:3, he identifies it with the Mosaic law. In many respects, this passage revisits what was said in Galatians 3:23-29:⁵⁸

> Before the coming of this faith, we were held in custody under the law, locked up until the faith that was to come would be revealed. So the law was our guardian until Christ came that we might be justified by faith. Now that this faith has come, we are no longer under a guardian.
>
> So in Christ Jesus you are all children of God through faith,⁵⁹ for all of you who were baptized into Christ have clothed yourselves with Christ. There is neither Jew nor Gentile, neither slave nor free, nor is there male and female, for you are all one in Christ Jesus. If you belong to Christ, then you are Abraham's seed, and heirs according to the promise.⁶⁰

In comparing these passages and observing that Paul refers to his audience's pre-Christian condition in Galatians 4:8, one is immediately struck by the fact that the "*stoicheia* of the world" can also refer to something that bound pagans. But *stoicheia* is used as well to characterize the Israelites in a condition in which they were bound as children: "Jews under Moses were children enslaved under the *stoicheia*."⁶¹ Notice how Paul reasons in Galatians 4:9: he is not concerned that they will return to paganism; rather, he is concerned that by returning to the Mosaic law, they will return to the "same pitiful condition they experienced as pagans."⁶² Life under paganism and life under the Mosaic law for the Israelites are described as being under the "*stoicheia* of the world."⁶³ This means that "Gentiles' experience before coming to Christ was broadly analogous (though not identical) to the pre-messianic condition of the Jews."⁶⁴

---

⁵⁷In what follows, I am agreeing with and expounding David VanDrunen's treatment in *Divine Covenants and Moral Order: A Biblical Theology of Natural Law* (Grand Rapids: Eerdmans, 2014), 358-65.
⁵⁸For further details on the relationship between these two passages, see Morales, *Restoration of Israel*, 117-18.
⁵⁹As Wright, *Climax of the Covenant*, 42-44, demonstrates, this reference to "sons of God" carries strong echoes of the exodus.
⁶⁰For details, see Wilder, *Exodus Narrative*, 86-98.
⁶¹VanDrunen, *Divine Covenants*, 359.
⁶²Ibid., 360.
⁶³Ibid.
⁶⁴Wilder, *Exodus Narrative*, 253.

What does *stoicheia tou kosmou* mean? Of all the various interpretations, two hold out some plausibility: the "*stoicheia* of the world" refer either to the elemental principles of the world (e.g., air, fire, water, earth) or to just basic principles.[65] The crucial issue for either option remains: "Paul speaks of the *stoicheia* of the world in Galatians 3:9 in order to refer both to a moral standard that obligates humanity and to the things of this present created order."[66] In short, it refers to the *protological* character of the Mosaic law, "the life under the confines of the original creation."[67] Paul takes pains throughout Galatians to dissociate himself from the world. Those who are in Christ and are identified as a new creation through the cross of Jesus have made a radical break with the world. To return merely to this *protological* standard is to regress rather than to identify with the *eschatological* moral standard associated with the new creation in Christ.[68] Israel was a picture of the human race written in miniature: Israel's plight, which was their being destined to failure from the beginning (cf. Deut 31:16-18), is the world's plight without God, lost in the world in an estate of sin and misery.[69] Paul understood that Israel's existence "under the law" was a condition of Egypt-like bondage.[70] This does not mean that a believing Hebrew was not saved by trusting in the Messiah to come. Old Testament saints were saved in the same manner as New Testament saints, by faith through grace. Nor is this to deny what is taught elsewhere in Scripture, that the need for grateful obedience (the so-called third use of the law) was always there in the old covenant.[71] So too were all the other blessings of Christian liberty.[72] However, that is not Paul's point here. Paul does not

---

[65]VanDrunen, *Divine Covenants*, 360-61.
[66]Ibid., 361. This interpretation fits well with Paul's assertion in Gal 4:3, 9, and with the closing section of Galatians more broadly (see ibid., 363).
[67]Ibid., 362.
[68]Ibid., 363. See 363-64 for further corroborating evidence from Col 2:8-23; 3:1-4.
[69]Ibid., 365.
[70]Wilder, *Exodus Narrative*, 252.
[71]See Westminster Confession of Faith 19.6-7; Westminster Larger Catechism 97; Heidelberg Catechism 115. See, e.g., Ps 119:1-6, 101, 104, 128; Mic 6:8.
[72]E.g., Rom 4:6-8; 1 Cor 10:3-4; Heb 11:1-40. See the Westminster Confession of Faith 20.1, which goes on to say that all these blessings "were common also to believers under the law. But, under the new testament, the liberty of Christians is further enlarged, in their freedom from the yoke of

want these Gentile believers to be entangled with a yoke of bondage (see Gal 5:1; Acts 15:10-11).

What is needed, according to Paul, is a new exodus, one in which a divine warrior will liberate humans (individually and corporately as a church) from the tyranny of sin and the devil, lead them through the chaotic death waters of this life, and then ascend the mountain of God (the true Mount Zion) with a host of willing captives in the Victor's train. Paul says that God had delivered them from bondage to a new sonship, and now they are in danger of returning to such a yoke of bondage if they follow the path laid out by the Judaizers. Paul has reminded them laconically (in Gal 4:4) of Christ's redemptive work: Christ was born "under the law," the very estate from which we have been redeemed and the very condition to which we must not return (Gal 4:21; cf. Rom 6:14-15). Christ voluntarily put himself under the curse of the law (Gal 3:10, 13), where he must do the law (Gal 3:12) and perform all its requirements by perfectly obeying (Gal 5:3-4). This he did, as Galatians 4:5 says, in order "to [*hina*] redeem those under the law, that [*hina*] we might receive adoption to sonship [*huiothesian*]."[73]

Galatians 4:1-9 provides an echo of Hosea. Previously, I noted Hosea's use of the exodus motif and its influence on Matthew's understanding of Jesus as the agent of the new exodus. Scott argues that *nēpios* in Galatians functions as an allusion to Hosea 11:1 to refer to the first exodus.[74] Rodrigo J. Morales, taking his cue from Scott, suggests that the more appropriate allusion may be to cognate "childhood."[75] Like Hosea 11:1, Hosea 2:17 (LXX) describes the time of Israel's exodus from Egypt as the "days of her childhood [*tas hēmeras nēpotētos*]." Moreover, this occurrence is in a context in which "an oracle of judgment ... leads eventually to the redemption of Israel." By this divine intervention, God "will

---

the ceremonial law, to which the Jewish church was subjected; and in greater boldness of access to the throne of grace, and in fuller communications of the free Spirit of God, than believers under the law did ordinarily partake of."

[73] See *Justification Report of the Committee to Study the Doctrine of Justification* (Willow Grove, PA: The Committee on Christian Education of the Orthodox Presbyterian Church, 2007), 35-36.
[74] Scott, *Adoption*, 129-30, 143, 146-49.
[75] See Morales, *Restoration of Israel*, 119.

remove the names of the idols from Israel's lips and make a new covenant with them (Hos 2:17-18)."[76] As a result of God's dealing with them "in righteousness" (*en dikaiosynē*), "in mercy" (*en eleei*), and "in faithfulness" (*en pistei*),[77] Israel will know the Lord (*epignōsē ton kyrion*). Morales claims, "Although Hosea does not explicitly refer to Israel as being in slavery, still less in slavery to the Law, it does associate Israel's status as an infant with sin and punishment."[78] He goes on to say,

> Hosea 11 shares not only the language of "child/childhood" with Hos 2:17 (LXX), but also some of the themes found in Hosea 2 as a whole. As in Hosea 2, when God called Israel as a "child" (νήπιος) out of Egypt, Israel went astray after idols and after the Baals of the land. The idolatry of the nation then leads to punishment (11:6-7), but once again a punishment that eventually ends in mercy. God promises not to destroy Israel, but rather to have compassion on the nation. Moreover, God's mercy results in a relationship of knowledge between God and Israel, though this time it is the former who knows the latter. In contrast to Israel and Judah's lying and wickedness, at the time of their redemption "now God knows them (ἔγνω αὐτοὺς ὁ θεός) and they shall be called the God's holy people" (Hos 11:12). This last phrase is particularly striking in light of Paul's description of the change in status that occurred for the Galatians when they came to believe in Christ: "But now that you know God, or rather have come to be known by God (μᾶλλον δὲ γνωσθέντες ὑπὸ θεοῦ)" (Gal 4:9).[79]

---

[76]Ibid.
[77]Hos 2:21-22 (MT; ET = 2:19-20), says "I will betroth you to me in righteousness [*baṣedeq*], and in justice [*bəmišpāṭ*], in lovingkindness [*bəḥesed*] and compassion [*bəraḥămîm*], and I will betroth you to me in faithfulness [*beʾĕmûnāh*], and you will know the Lord" (author's translation). Since "righteousness" and "faithfulness" are used in parallel fashion here, it may seem at first glance to support the notion that the righteousness of God is God's faithfulness to Israel, a position often taken by those who follow Käsemann, such as many new perspective on Paul proponents, as discussed above. However, "in faithfulness" here means that God will establish this new covenant in an irrevocable bond, one that cannot be broken, not in the subjective genitive sense often argued for in the *pistis christou* as discussed previously (i.e., God's faithfulness to his covenant). See Charles Lee Irons, *The Righteousness of God: A Lexical Examination of the Covenant-Faithfulness Interpretation*, WUNT 2.386 (Tübingen: Mohr Siebeck, 2015), 153-55.
[78]Morales, *Restoration of Israel*, 120.
[79]Ibid. Morales adds corroborating material to his argument from Ezek 16 (LXX) as well, but that I have left to one side due to space. The argument can be easily followed without that evidence.

Both the first exodus and the new exodus resound in Galatians 4. This is well established in New Testament scholarship today.[80]

Galatians 5-6

Wilder takes the insights of Scott into Galatians 4:1-9 and extends them to Galatians 5–6.[81] Wilder argues that Galatians 5:18 ("If you are led by the Spirit, you are not under the law") bears significance "well out of proportion to its length or frequency which its terminology is employed elsewhere in the NT."[82] For Wilder, this verse in Galatians is programmatic for the apostle's understanding of the entirety of the wilderness wanderings in contrast to the new Christian community. Israel was "under the law," whereas Christians in the new exodus are "under the Spirit."[83] Paul is here building on Psalm 143 (MT; LXX = 142). Understanding the exodus motif as mediated through Psalm 143 illuminates the role of the exodus in Paul's thought.

However, Paul's use of the exodus motif should not be construed along *merely* relational lines. Romans 6:17-18 states, "Though you used to be slaves to sin, you have come to obey from your heart. . . . You have been set free from sin and have become slaves to righteousness." Rather, what Paul has done in a "provocative rhetorical shift" is to support his opposition of Spirit and flesh (Gal 5:16-17) by saying, in the language of Galatians 5:18, that "if you are led by the Spirit, you are not under the law." As Wilder puts it, this verse has been shaped by "two central events associated with the exodus: the redemption of the Israelites from Egypt and their subsequent guidance by the theophanic cloud through the

---

[80] I have in mind Keesmaat, *Paul and His Story*, 155-215; Wright, *Paul and the Faithfulness of God*, 698-700, 718-19, and in numerous other places; and the very fine theological article by Scott R. Swain, "'Heirs Through God': Galatians 4:4-7 and the Doctrine of the Trinity," in *Galatians and Christian Theology: Justification, the Gospel, and Ethics in Paul's Letter*, ed. Mark W. Elliott et al. (Grand Rapids: Baker Academic, 2014), 258-67.

[81] See esp. Wilder, *Exodus Narrative*, 75-119. His argument is similar to mine—namely, that "the exodus is a narrative so basic to Paul's understanding of the gospel that, even where it does not actually break through, its storylines may be descried beneath the surface of Paul's argumentation" (75).

[82] Ibid., 1. Wilder notes that "four out of six passages containing 'under the law' (ὑπὸ νόμον) are in Galatians and, we shall argue, each contains distinct connotations of an Egypt-like bondage shared by Jews 'under the law'" (77).

[83] Of course, that does not mean that the New Testament Christian doesn't have an obligation to show grateful obedience to his or her Lord by obeying the law, out of gratitude.

wilderness is an allusion to the Israelites' experience of being guided by the cloud." Wilder goes on to say that Israel's "being 'under the law' is, paradoxically enough, typologically equivalent to the Israelites' bondage in Egypt."[84] This is a major perturbation injected by Paul: he has "associated the law in this book at least with Egyptian bondage, rather than exodus freedom."[85] Perhaps Paul's particular rhetoric was driven especially by the dangers posed by the Judaizers. Wilder finishes by highlighting Paul's answer to his programmatic question from Galatians 3:2: "'Did you receive the Spirit by works of the law, or by hearing with faith?' On the basis of the new exodus narrative Paul is able to draw that self-evident conclusion to which their own experience should testify: 'if you are led by the Spirit, you are not under the law.'"[86]

Echoes of the Exodus in Romans 8:14-23

Adam is all over Romans.[87] Israel is also. Tired of the myopic exegesis of New Testament scholars, Wright states regarding Romans 3–8 that the story of the exodus is influential for the overall shape of Paul's arguments in these chapters of Romans and perhaps even to the beginning chapters.[88] Wright also notes many allusions to Genesis 4 and Cain in Romans 7.[89] Regarding the phrase "led by the Spirit," he concludes that

> Paul treats the Christians as precisely God's new-Exodus people. They are led by God through their present wilderness.... Their guide is the Spirit, who here takes up the role of the pillar of cloud and fire in the wilderness; were there world enough and time, this would be worth exploring in

---

[84] Wilder, *Exodus Narrative*, 75-76.
[85] Ibid., 76. Keesmaat, *Paul and His Story*, 177-79, notes similar disjunctions but overstates the matter when she claims that Paul has essentially redefined the law.
[86] Wilder, *Exodus Narrative*, 276. Daube, once again, is worth quoting for his insight into the legal background of this statement: "That, paradoxically, this change of master follows from a rescue into liberty is already an element in the original scheme: a captive brought back becomes his ransomer's bondman, the Israelites pass under God's rule because it is he who frees them from the Egyptians." David Daube, *The Exodus Pattern in the Bible* (London: Faber and Faber, 1963), 45.
[87] See Wright, *Paul and the Faithfulness of God*, 769.
[88] N. T. Wright, "New Exodus, New Inheritance: The Narrative Substructure of Romans 3–8," in *Romans and the People of God: Essays in Honor of Gordon D. Fee on the Occasion of His 65th Birthday*, ed. Sven K. Soderlund and N. T. Wright (Grand Rapids: Eerdmans, 1999), 26-35. Also see Wright, "Romans," in *The New Interpreter's Bible*, ed. Leander E. Keck (Nashville: Abingdon, 2002), 10:550.
[89] Wright, *Climax of the Covenant*, 226-30.

terms of its implications for Paul's overall view of the Spirit within a Christian vision of God.[90]

Wright also speaks about the new exodus in Romans in a chapter in his most recent book, *The Day the Revolution Began: Reconsidering the Meaning of Jesus's Crucifixion*.[91] What he stated seminally in his book *Surprised by Hope* (2008) he argues further in this new work: "For Paul, exactly in line with Revelation and other early writings, the result of Jesus's achievement is a *new creation*, a new heaven-and-earth world in which humans can resume their genuinely human vocation as the 'kingdom of priests,' the 'royal priesthood.'"[92] For Wright this means that a major aspect of redemption is that the original human vocation of stewardship has been reestablished—"the original project of creation is now at last back on track."[93]

Keesmaat has argued that Paul's use of the Old Testament in Romans 8 demonstrates that "Paul is assuming many Old Testament motifs and trajectories which he alludes to and builds upon in the course of his arguments."[94] Her position is that Paul is wrestling with the notion of "God's faithfulness to Israel," a notion prominent in the new perspective on Paul. He is "drawing on the motif central to Israelite consciousness which revealed God's faithfulness to Israel. He is rooted in the past, yet he transforms the tradition in this passage, extending it beyond the land and people of Israel, to all people in Christ Jesus and to the whole of creation."[95] The familiar text of Romans 8:14-17 reads as follows:

> For those who are led [*agontai*] by the Spirit of God are the children [*huioi*] of God. The Spirit you received does not make you slaves [*douleias*], so that you live in fear again; rather, the Spirit you received brought about your adoption to sonship [*huiothesias*]. And by him we cry, "*Abba*, Father."

---

[90] Wright, "New Exodus," 29.
[91] See Wright, *Day the Revolution Began*, esp. 263-94. Wright also gives fresh attention to the Passover and atonement in chap. 13, which primarily focuses on the beginning chapters of Romans. We will not discuss those ideas since it raises issues too broad to be entered into here.
[92] Ibid., 268.
[93] Ibid., 89.
[94] Sylvia C. Keesmaat, "Exodus and Romans 8:14-30," *JSNT* 54 (1994): 29-49.
[95] Ibid., 49.

The Spirit himself testifies with our spirit that we are God's children [*tekna*]. Now if we are children [*tekna*], then we are heirs—heirs of God and co-heirs with Christ, if indeed we share in his sufferings in order that we may also share in his glory.

In arguing for an exodus background, Keesmaat offers several lines of evidence. First, the verb *agein* (to lead) with its cognates seems to evoke the exodus imagery as it was known in the symbolic world of first-century Judaism.[96] The Song of the Sea (Ex 15) initiated a grammar by which Israel thought of her salvation. There the people sang, "You have led [LXX = *hōdēgēsas*] in righteousness this your people, whom you redeemed."[97] This correlation between the language of "leading" and the exodus is found in a number of psalms, including Psalm 77 (LXX; MT = 78) and Psalm 22 (LXX; MT = 23). They also use the same verbs to refer to the exodus motif.[98]

Perhaps the use of *agein* (to lead) verbs in an exodus context would not be persuasive were it not for the frequent coupling of the language with another concept, sonship. The language of sonship occurs frequently in the Hebrew Bible, coordinated with verbs of leading, and this is seen here in Paul as well. These texts are most often connected with Israel's king, who is also the son of God (e.g., 2 Sam 7:14; Ps 2:7; 89:26-27).[99] Even more notable are the possible echoes of Deuteronomy 32 in our passage.[100] The cry "*Abba*, Father" is often considered by New Testament scholars as a specific kind of cry, an ecstatic cry in the midst of suffering. Or often the reference is moored to Jesus' use of the word at the beginning of the Lord's Prayer. However, it is noteworthy that explicit references to God as father are most often found in the context of the exodus/Sinai events.[101] Additionally, there are other echoes of

---

[96]See Keesmaat, *Paul and His Story*, 56-57. This would include compounds like *exagein* and *eisagein* as well as *hodēgein*. These are frequently used in the context of the exodus. Keesmaat is building on the work of Ignace de la Potterie and remains baffled why other New Testament scholars (e.g., Dunn and Moo) ignore the evidence or are dismissive of it.
[97]The translations of the LXX are by Keesmaat (ibid., 57).
[98]Ibid., 57-59.
[99]Ibid., 60.
[100]Ibid., 61-62.
[101]See Allen Mawhinney, "Baptism, Servanthood, and Sonship," *WTJ* 49 (1987): 35-64.

exodus imagery here. The language of the Spirit as a co-witness providing testimony, the connection of the inheritance with the exodus, the coupling of becoming heirs with being glorified, and the theme of suffering are all comingled to make the apostle's point: the character of the new exodus that Paul has been describing is one of suffering.[102] Last, notice that from the apostle's perspective this new exodus event has been inaugurated; the Christian community has already experienced it, at least in part.[103] According to Romans 8:18 (and following), this new reality entails a hopeful restoration of something even more magnificent than has already been experienced.[104] Many exegetes in the past have written about the resurrection of the sons of God sharing in a renewed creation in the world-to-come.[105] Some have emphasized that the continuity between the former world and the world-to-come is at precisely this point: the resurrection of believers' bodies. It is primarily believers in the Lamb who provide the point of continuity between the former world and the new creation.[106] Precisely what the nature of that restoration is—what part the present cultural activities of Christians play in contributing to this world-to-come and how these activities pertain to the resurrection of the children of God and the possible restoration of the creation, even the renewal of the external (natural) world—is too broad a question to be entered on here. We now move on to another Pauline epistle.

---

[102] See Keesmaat, *Paul and His Story*, 77-96, esp. 88-89. I remain unconvinced that Paul's point is mostly or merely about corporate Israel here.
[103] Wright, *Paul and the Faithfulness of God*, 1069.
[104] Ibid., 96.
[105] See, e.g., Charles Hodge, *Commentary on the Epistle to the Romans* (1886; repr., Grand Rapids: Eerdmans, 1960); Herman Bavinck, *Reformed Dogmatics*, vol. 1, *Prolegomena*, ed. John Bolt, trans. John Vriend (Grand Rapids: Baker Academic, 2003), 445; Bavinck, *Holy Spirit, Church, and New Creation*, 715-24; Douglas J. Moo, *The Epistle to the Romans*, NICNT (Grand Rapids: Eerdmans, 1996), 517; Beale, *New Testament Biblical Theology*, 257.
[106] See, e.g., Meredith G. Kline, "Death, Leviathan, and Martyrs: Isaiah 24:1–27:1," in *A Tribute to Gleason Archer: Essays on the Old Testament*, ed. Walter C. Kaiser Jr. and Ronald F. Youngblood (Chicago: Moody Press, 1986), 229-49, who sees Is 24:1–27:1 as significantly influencing the apostle's discussion in Rom 9–11. A shorter summary of his arguments can be found in Kline, *God, Heaven, and Har Magedon: A Covenantal Tale of Cosmos and Telos* (Eugene, OR: Wipf & Stock, 2006), 24-27, 276-80. Also see David VanDrunen, *Living in God's Two Kingdoms: A Biblical Vision for Christianity and Culture* (Wheaton, IL: Crossway, 2010), 63-71, 102-3.

Colossians

In Colossians 1:12-14, Paul offers a compact statement of the exodus pattern that I have been making repeatedly throughout this book—redemption from slavery to inheritance:[107] "Giving joyful thanks to the Father, who has qualified you to share in the inheritance [*klērou*] of his holy people in the kingdom of light. For he has rescued [*errysato*] us from the dominion of darkness and brought us into the kingdom of the Son he loves, in whom we have redemption [*apolytrōsin*], the forgiveness of sins." Paul has not cited any particular Old Testament passage at this point; rather, he echoes the primary and major Old Testament salvation event.[108] He also has used some of the most frequently occurring vocabulary in the Septuagint for the exodus deliverance.

The parallels are numerous. God has delivered the Colossian believers from the domain of darkness just as he had delivered the Israelites from the iron furnace of the Egyptians. God brought these Colossian Christians into the kingdom of the Son just as God brought the Hebrews into their new land, which would be established as a kingdom. God brought these Colossian Christians out of slavery to sin just as he had secured the redemption of the Israelites from their physical slavery. Keywords in the passage of Colossians echo keywords in the programmatic statement of Exodus 6:6-8 and throughout the Septuagint's translation of passages referring to the foundational salvation event of the Old Testament.[109]

One new concept that Paul has introduced here, which seems somewhat enigmatic but is an important new nuance added to our understanding of our inheritance, is the notion that God has given us a share in the kingdom of light (Col 1:12). The immediate context, which makes a contrast with the "domain of darkness" (Col 1:13) from which we have been rescued, suggests at least that Christians have been delivered into the (realm of) light, a place where God's glory "radiates and

---

[107]Here I am greatly dependent on the arguments for the second exodus in the book of Colossians as demonstrated by Beetham, *Echoes of Scripture*.
[108]Ibid., 82.
[109]See the discussion in chap. 3 under "The Unfolding Meaning of the Exodus."

illuminates all."[110] Paul may have written this in light of his Damascus road experience.[111]

Conclusion

In this chapter we have seen that the influence of the exodus motif on the apostle Paul is pervasive. This is especially the case for two of Paul's most important and doctrinal books, Galatians and Romans, although we find significant echoes in 1 Corinthians and Colossians as well.

We explored the apostle's thinking in 1 Corinthians 10, where a new-exodus theme is conspicuous. In Galatians 4:1-7 we observed the ethically oriented guidance of the Holy Spirit in the New Testament age vis-à-vis the age of theocratic Israel, which was "under the law." We found that the proper context for understanding Paul's allusions to adoption is the exodus rather than Greco-Roman practices of adoption. The exodus motif has profound and far-reaching ramifications for our understanding of Galatians 5–6 as well. Noting the role of the exodus in providing a narrative substructure for Romans 3–8, we examined how the notes of the exodus are sounded in Romans 8:14-17. Finally, we looked briefly at Colossians 1:12-14, a passage replete with exodus motif echoes. This passage well demonstrates that Paul understood the importance of redemption from slavery unto inheritance. Moreover, this inheritance is categorized as an inheritance into a realm of light as opposed to darkness.

We now turn our attention to Peter's contribution to the exodus motif.

---

[110]Beetham, *Echoes of Scripture*, 93.
[111]Ibid., 92.

Ten

THE EXODUS MOTIF IN 1 PETER

We tend very much, with or without the historical-critical methods, to discuss what texts mean without attention to their function, either deliberately or accidentally.

WALTER BRUEGGEMANN

Exegesis is a most complex act, especially when it involves not only the message of the biblical author but also his use of previous source material.

GRANT R. OSBORNE

First Peter demonstrates an extraordinary dependence on the Old Testament, especially considering its size. William Schutter found "forty-six quotations and allusions in all, not counting iterative allusions that would greatly boost the total, or nearly one for every two verses."[1] Moreover, the Old Testament is broadly represented in 1 Peter: four books of the Pentateuch, four books of the Latter Prophets, three from the Writings with a concentration from Isaiah, Psalms, and Proverbs. Beyond the atomistic approach of quotation and citation, the function of metalepsis (evoking the context, message, or story of the previous text) is also an important consideration for rightly understanding 1 Peter.[2]

---

[1] William L. Schutter, *Hermeneutic and Composition in 1 Peter*, WUNT 2.30 (Tübingen: Mohr Siebeck, 1989), 43.

[2] See, e.g., the suggestive article by Jeannine K. Brown, "Metalepsis," in *Exploring Intertextuality: Diverse Strategies for New Testament Interpretation of Texts*, ed. B. J. Oropeza and Steve Moyise (Eugene, OR: Cascade, 2016), 29-41.

Our interest of course is in the exodus motif. But is this a major metaphor for the composition of 1 Peter?[3]

Some interpreters have asked what the controlling metaphor is in 1 Peter.[4] J. H. Elliott set forth the view that *oikou tou theou*, "house of God," refers to the community of Christians, not the temple. The language of *oikos*, "house," is pervasive throughout the book (1 Pet 1:17; 2:5, 11, 18; 3:7; 4:10, 17), as is other household language. Elliott saw these references in contrast to *paroikos* (resident alien), not as figurative terms but actual, literal references to someone that holds the status—politically, legally, and socially—as homeless, whose transience derives from literal migrations of peoples in Asia Minor.[5] "The addressees of 1 Peter were *paroikoi* by virtue of their social condition, not by virtue of their 'heavenly home.' ... [First] Peter was directed to actual strangers and resident aliens who had become Christians. Their new religious affiliation was not the cause of their position in society though it did add to their difficulties in relating to their neighbors," says Elliot.[6] Elliott's view has been criticized.[7] Paul Achtemeier responded by setting forth criteria for determining whether a text is communicating literally or metaphorically.[8] He claims that the metaphor of "the Christians as the new chosen people of God" is actually the controlling metaphor in 1 Peter.[9] My aim is not to establish a new controlling metaphor but to call attention to a significant metaphor (the exodus) for the argument of 1 Peter, especially the first two chapters.

The blood of Christ provides the ransom through which God's elect—the living stones built up to be a royal priesthood—are now rescued to live

---

[3]C. F. D. Moule seems to think it is; see "The Nature and Purpose of 1 Peter," *NTS* 3. no 1 (1956): 1-11, esp. 4-5. Moule's main purpose is to refute the thesis of 1 Peter being a baptismal liturgy.

[4]J. H. Elliott, *A Home for the Homeless: A Sociological Exegesis of 1 Peter, Its Situation and Strategy* (Philadelphia: Fortress, 1981). This book was later republished with a new introduction, in which Elliott qualified his earlier book. Elliott leaves more room for a metaphorical reading by saying here that the number of actual aliens was great enough that it could be applied to the Christians.

[5]See ibid., 39-45.

[6]Ibid., 130, 132.

[7]See, e.g., John W. Pryor, "First Peter and the New Covenant (II)," *RTR* 45 (January/April 1986): 45-46.

[8]Paul J. Achtemeier, "Newborn Babes and Living Stones: Literal and Figurative in 1 Peter," in *To Touch the Text: Biblical and Related Studies in Honor of Joseph A. Fitzmyer*, ed. Maurya P. Itorgan and Paul J. Kobelski (New York: Crossroad, 1989), 207-36.

[9]Ibid., 218.

holy lives and proclaim the excellencies of him who called them to be so. Citing Hosea, Peter takes pains to demonstrate that the church is the new people of God. Previously they were a "no people" (*ou laos*); however, now they are a royal nation, God's own people (*laos theou*) (1 Pet 2:9). Peter trumpets the dignity of Christians.[10] And it is in the first section of the book (1 Pet 1:3–2:10) where images of the exodus from Egypt are clearly echoed,[11] including Passover, the demand to be holy (Lev 11:44; 19:2), the golden calf, ransomed lives, an unblemished lamb. As Raymond Brown comments, Christians are now "like Israel in the exodus on the road to the Promised Land; they should not look back to their former status as did the Israelites (1:14), but press on to their imperishable inheritance (1:4)."[12]

The strong echoes of the exodus suggest that the Gentiles who are being addressed had been catechized in the Hebrew Bible and could appreciate the exodus tradition and the privileges they themselves had inherited.[13] Emphasizing the ethical side of the letter, Bonnie Howe has shown how the metaphors in 1 Peter serve as the basis for analogizing from the world of the original audience toward ethical exhortation for the modern reader.[14]

1 Peter 1:13-21

After commenting at length in the introduction that Christians have been born to a living hope, a hope that grants sure salvation, Peter calls these Christian pilgrims to holiness, and "he paints the whole scene in colours of the Exodus."[15] Here the underlying narrative of 1 Peter comes into sharp relief:[16]

> Therefore, girding up the loins of your minds, be sober-minded [*nēphontes*], fixing your hope unreservedly on the grace that is being brought to you

---

[10]Raymond E. Brown, *An Introduction to the New Testament* (New York: Doubleday, 1997), 709, 713.
[11]Ibid., 709.
[12]Ibid., 714.
[13]Ibid., 720.
[14]Bonnie Howe, *Because You Bear This Name: Conceptual Metaphor and the Moral Meaning of 1 Peter* (Leiden: Brill, 2006).
[15]Pryor, "First Peter," 44.
[16]Joel B. Green, "Narrating the Gospel in 1 and 2 Peter," *Int* (July 2006): 262-77, esp. 269. Green's article (by his own admission) is really mostly about 1 Pet 1:13-21.

in the revelation of Jesus Christ; as obedient children, do not fashion yourselves or do not allow yourselves to be fashioned to the previous lusts, which were yours in ignorance; rather, just as the one who called you is holy—become holy in all you do! Therefore, it is written, "You shall be holy, because I am holy." For if [as you do] you appeal to the Father as One who judges impartially—according to each man's work—in fear conduct yourselves during your time of temporary residence, knowing [*eidotes*] that not with things corruptible like silver and gold were you redeemed [*elytrōthēte*] out of your vanity of life that was passed on from the fathers, but rather with the precious blood of a lamb [*amnou*], blameless and spotless, (the blood) of Christ, for he was foreknown before the foundation of the world, but was made manifest at the end of time for your sake, who through whom are believers in God, who raised him from the dead and gave glory to him, so that your faith may also be your hope in God. (1 Pet 1:13-21, author's translation)

This section begins and ends by enjoining one to hope. Peter actually begins 1:13-21 with the end of the story.[17] This would entail that "the revelation" of verse 13 is taken as the parousia of Christ, when he is revealed.[18] Previously (vv. 18-19) Peter has emphasized that Christians have been redeemed by the blood of the spotless lamb and called from darkness into light. They are freed from the dissolute life that they once lived in paganism and are now obligated to strive to live holy lives. The christological foundation of hope (vv. 17-21) is the indicative that grounds the imperatival exhortations to holiness (vv. 14-16).

The background here is clearly the exodus event and the Passover lamb, whose blood is now the redeeming blood of Christ Jesus.[19] Some have objected to this paschal identification on linguistic grounds, but there are other New Testament texts where Christ is clearly identified in paschal terms.[20] As Howe says, "While some of this expression in

---

[17] Ibid., 273.
[18] The view of numerous New Testament scholars and Calvin; see Karen H. Jobes, *1 Peter*, Baker Exegetical Commentary on the New Testament (Grand Rapids: Baker Academic, 2005), 110.
[19] See Edward Gordon Selwyn, *The First Epistle of St. Peter: The Greek Text with Introduction, Notes and Essays* (London: Macmillan, 1946), 146.
[20] A. R. C. Leany, "1 Peter and the Passover: An Interpretation," *NTS* 10, no. 2 (1964): 238-51, esp. 245-46.

1:18-19 may be about release from 'debt'—the financial domain—the expression is embedded in a text replete with allusions to the salvation history of Israel and to the story of Jesus' life."[21]

Passover plays a central part in Scripture, being described in many key Old Testament texts and referenced or alluded to in many others.[22] Passover was the meal celebrated by those Hebrew families that were delivered from the angel of death after they had marked the doorposts of their houses with blood from a sacrificed lamb. Peter's invoking the Passover evokes the Passover tradition, which had experienced a long evolution and development.[23] How the Passover was celebrated by the first generation of Israelites fleeing out of Egypt differed from how it was practiced in Jesus' day when the preparation of the sacrifice was made at the temple, which in turn differed from the Passover celebrated by Jews outside Jerusalem after the destruction of the temple in 70 CE when there is an absence of the sacrificial animal.

Why would Peter invoke the exodus and Passover here? First, the reference to the Passover enables us to understand nuances of Christ's atonement. Second, this legal act of redemption provides the origin of hope enjoined earlier. Thus, the indicative precedes the imperatives here, so to speak.

In contrast to rabbinic Judaism, the Passover was understood as a kind of atonement offering making the redemption from Egypt possible.[24] Jesus' sacrifice (blood) is *timiō*, "precious." This marks a "profound, if easily overlooked, theological move" on Peter's part.[25] Christ's sacrifice is also *amōmou*, "blameless," and *aspilou*, "spotless." This is what is required in Old Testament sacrifices—they must be *amōmos*, "without

---

[21]Howe, *Because You Bear This Name*, 207.
[22]E.g., Ex 12–13; 34:25; Lev 23:5-8; Num 9:4-6; 28:16-25; 2 Chron 30:1-9.
[23]For a survey of some possible developments (some of which are informed by higher-critical presuppositions), see Anthony J. Saldarini, *Jesus and Passover* (New York: Paulist, 1984), 5-40. For an up-to-date summary of various recent theories about the Passover, see Tamara Prosic, *The Development and Symbolism of Passover Until 70 CE*, JSOTSup 414 (London: T&T Clark, 2004), 19-32.
[24]See Joachim Jeremias, *The Eucharistic Words of Jesus* (New York: Charles Scribner's Sons, 1966), 225-31.
[25]Green, "Narrating the Gospel," 272. Green clarifies, "Reckoned by human criteria, Jesus' death on a cross (2:24) was anything but honorable, so mention of his passion could easily evoke valuations of humiliation and scorn."

blemish," and *aspilos*, "without spot."[26] The writer to the book of Hebrews actually refers to Christ's offering of himself as *amōmon*, "unblemished," to God (Heb 9:14). Leonhard Goppelt sums it up well: "The comparison with the Passover lamb contributes to the understanding of Jesus' death, which God himself makes possible as atonement and thus legally: Jesus' death makes possible the liberating exodus, in accord with God's gracious institution in the Old Covenant."[27] As we have noted repeatedly in this book, this recovery of slaves entails a new domain of coming under God's rule, because it is God who has freed and liberated them. Against the background of the exodus, we can now appreciate the exhortation of 1 Peter 2:13-16, "Submit yourselves to every ordinance of man for the Lord's sake ... as free, and not using your liberty for a cloke [*sic*] of maliciousness, but as the slaves of God."[28] This may be one of the clearest echoes of the exodus from Egypt in Peter's epistle.[29]

Based on this legal foundation of Christ's sacrificial ransom, Peter calls his audience to "gird up the loins of their minds and be soberminded [*nēphontes*]." This is probably an allusion to Exodus 12:11, when the Lord charges the Hebrews to leave Egypt. It is a Semitic idiom for preparing for intentional effort and action.[30] In alluding to the exodus narrative, Peter has provided some perturbation or disruption from the original setting in order to engage his audience. The context seems to suggest self-control, to discipline one's mind in a way that determines conduct.[31] This facilitates prayer and an awareness of the devil's ways (1 Pet 4:7; 5:8, where the aorist imperative is used). As Karen Jobes sums

---

[26]Cf. Lev 22:17-25. Although *aspilos* doesn't occur in the LXX, it is used in a figurative way in Jas 1:27.
[27]Leonhard Goppelt, *A Commentary on 1 Peter*, ed. Ferdinand Hahn, trans. John E. Alsup (Grand Rapids: Eerdmans, 1993), 116.
[28]A point driven home by David Daube, *The Exodus Pattern in the Bible* (London: Faber and Faber, 1963), 46. The legal foundations of the exodus are again and again emphasized in Daube's little book—one only wishes he had written more here. The translation is his.
[29]Paul E. Deterding, "Exodus Motifs in First Peter," *Concordia Journal* 7, no. 2 (March 1981): 62. Note well, however, that Howe, *Because You Bear His Name*, 201-8, holds out the possibility that cognitive domains related to first-century views of debt slavery and ransom, as well as exodus motifs from the story of Israel, may be at play here.
[30]See Jobes, *1 Peter*, 111.
[31]Ibid.

up, "Peter wishes his readers to avoid any form of mental or spiritual intoxication that would confuse the reality that Christ has revealed and deflect them from a life steadfastly fixed on the grace of Christ."[32] Moreover, they are to live a holy life. This is accomplished by the work of the Holy Spirit (1 Pet 1:2).[33]

The injunction to "be holy" (1 Pet 1:16) is from Leviticus 19:2 (LXX).[34] A little later Christians are called the new people of God with an allusion to Exodus 19:6. What is interesting here is that an authoritative passage from Leviticus is applied to the New Testament community but shorn of the specifics of the Levitical code.[35] The rule of faith applies here since Peter accepts the Old Testament as authoritative for his Christian audience. In light of the adoption language that we observed in Paul, it is striking that Peter immediately follows this with a charge to Christians to remember their heavenly Father/child relationship. Peter may have taken his cue from Leviticus itself.[36]

1 Peter 1:22-25

Demonstrable love is inextricably bound up with Christian living for those who have turned their hope toward Christ in an exodus from this world (1 Pet 1:13-21).[37] The third major command in Peter's ecclesial emphasis (following exhortations to holiness and a fear of God based on hope grounded in the true Passover Lamb) is to love each other in this new-exodus community:[38]

---

[32]Ibid.
[33]Deterding, "Exodus Motifs," 61, comments, "Although the second exodus is properly the work of Jesus Christ as an expression of the mercy of God the Father, the implementation of the work of Christ in the lives of individuals is the task of the Holy Spirit, who makes the church holy on the basis of what Christ has done. Thus, the apostle also assigns a role in the new exodus to the Third Person of the Trinity."
[34]The statement is found with some variation four times in Leviticus (Lev 11:44; 19:2; 20:7-8; 20:26).
[35]See Jobes's discussion in *1 Peter*, 114-15.
[36]The next verse in Leviticus following what Peter has quoted says, "Each of you must respect your father and mother" (Lev 19:3).
[37]Goppelt, *Commentary on 1 Peter*, 122.
[38]The exhortation to love in the community is found frequently at Qumran as well; however, there the self-understanding of love is expressed in a dramatically different manner. It is manifested as an inward-facing solidarity among the exodus community. Here in Peter, the parenetic tradition is manifested in conduct toward outsiders as well. See ibid., 122-24.

Now that you have purified yourselves [*hēgnikotes*] by obeying the truth so that you have sincere love each other, love one another [*agapēsate*] deeply, from the heart. For you have been born again [*anagegennēmenoi*], not of perishable seed, but of imperishable, though the living and enduring word of God. For,

> "All people are like grass,
>   and all their glory is like the flowers of the field;
> the grass withers and the flowers fall,
>   but the word of the Lord endures forever."

And this is the word that was preached to you.

The imperative "to love" (*agapēsate*) is surrounded by participial phrases (*hēgnikotes* and *anagegennēmenoi*) that act like motive clauses, reinforcing the command. The second participle is an echo from the opening of the letter in 1 Peter 1:3, when Peter declared, "Praise be to the God and Father of our Lord Jesus Christ! In his great mercy has given us new birth [*anagennēsas*] into a living hope." Embedded in this charge to love one another and reinforcing the second participial phrase is a quotation from Isaiah 40:6-8, an Isaianic exodus motif passage. This has the effect of elevating the style and making a didactic point.[39] The permanence of this newly born life, of which mutual love is a sign, is contrasted with the transience of human life.

As we observed earlier, this Isaianic passage was used in Mark 1:1-3 to proclaim Jesus as the agent of the new exodus. Here in 1 Peter, just as the exiles in Babylon were to derive comfort from the message of the coming Messiah, so also these Christians in Asia Minor should be comforted by their Messiah having come. Considering the larger context of Isaiah 40, the exaltation of God as sovereign above all earthly rulers would surely console this exodus community of Asia Minor facing the mighty Roman Empire.[40]

---

[39] Ibid., 123.
[40] Jobes, *1 Peter*, 130.

1 Peter 2:9-10

After describing how Christians have gone through a new birth and are now to be ethically transformed, Peter cites stone imagery from three Old Testament passages (Ps 118; Is 8:14-15; 28:16) to show that Christ is the living stone, the Messiah, and the chief cornerstone. This section has been called the "fundamental indicative for the entire epistle."[41] Peter says that Christians are living stones, built into a spiritual house, once again emphasizing ecclesial community and solidarity. Now Peter makes a striking, subtle citation of significant passages from Exodus and Hosea, creating an intertext that surely would have caused his audience's ears to tingle. The point is rather simple and yet profound: Christians are now the new people of God.

> But you are a chosen people [*genos eklekton*], a royal priesthood [*basileion hierateuma*],[42] a holy nation [*ethnos hagion*], God's special possession [*laos eis peripoiēsin*], that you may declare the praises [*tas aretas exangeilēte*] of him who called you out of darkness into his wonderful light. Once you were not a people, but now you are the people of God; once you had not received mercy, but now you have received mercy. (1 Pet 2:9-10)[43]

There is no doubt that Peter is making an allusion to Hosea 2:23, from a chapter we have encountered earlier.[44] Another allusion is made to

---

[41] John W. Pryor (quoting Elliott), "First Peter and the New Covenant (1)," *RTR* 45 (January/April 1986): 3. There have been attempts to demonstrate a literary connection between this section of Peter and Qumran, but they have numerous shortcomings. See Klyne Snodgrass, "1 Peter 2:1-10: Its Formation and Literary Affinities," *NTS* 24, no. 1 (1977): 101-2.

[42] The emphasis is on "the collective pedigree and role of the people of God as being royal and priestly" whether the words are taken as substantives or as an adjective with a substantive. See David Hill, "'To Offer Spiritual Sacrifices . . .' (1 Peter 2:5): Liturgical Formulations and Christian Paraenesis in 1 Peter," *JSNT* 16 (1982): 45-46.

[43] This passage and the verses just prior have been the classic proof text for the Protestant doctrine of the priesthood of all believers. See Alex T. M. Cheung, "The Priest as the Redeemed Man: A Biblical-Theological Study of Priesthood," *JETS* 29, no. 3 (September 1986): 265-75, esp. 274. The problems are many here, especially considering that Christ's priestly role cannot be repeated by any individual; it is *ephapax*, "once for all" (Heb 7:27; 10:10). It is important to recognize that the reference in Peter is to a "royal priesthood" and thus in many respects to the nation in its corporate identity. See R. T. France, "First Century Bible Study: Old Testament Motifs in 1 Peter 2:4-10," *Journal of the European Pentecostal Theological Association* 18 (1998): 26-48, esp. 36, 38. One of the fullest and best treatments touching on this subject and priesthood in the New Testament generally is Ernest Best, "Spiritual Sacrifice: General Priesthood in the New Testament," *Int* 14, no. 3 (July 1960): 273-99. Best demonstrates that one must steer the middle way between corporate and individual categories in order to do justice to the biblical material as a whole (see esp. 297).

[44] See chaps. 7 and 9.

Exodus 19:5-6, a passage deserving some discussion at this point. In this text, three statements are connected with the promise of reward: (1) the promise that Israel will be God's treasured possession (*səgullâ*); (2) the promise of God's universal rule; and (3) the promise that Israel will be a "kingdom of priests."[45] This last point must be understood in light of the new exodus provided by Christ.[46] Peter also alludes to Isaiah 43:20-21, a new-exodus passage we explored in chapter five. Peter applies passages to his Christian audience, undoubtedly including Gentiles, that before now had only applied to the nation of Israel.

Isaiah 43:20-21 entails a new exodus and describes God's provision of water for his chosen people. The Septuagint of verse 20 has "my chosen race" as *to genos mou to eklekton*, and the Septuagint of verse 21 describes "the people I formed for myself that they may proclaim my praise" as *laon mou hon periepoisamēn tas aretas mou diēgeisthai*. Peter weaves allusions to Isaiah 43 (with slight modifications) together with Exodus 19:5-6, "Now if you obey me fully and keep my covenant, then out of all nations you will be my treasured possession [MT = *səgullâ*; LXX = "my people," *moi laos periousios*]. Although the whole earth is mine, you will be for me a kingdom of priests [LXX = *basileion hierateuma*] and a holy nation [LXX = *ethnos hagion*]." Peter's syntactical modifications may be due to literary causes.[47]

From a cognitive-metaphorical-analytic perspective, in this brief text Peter collected images from several Old Testament sources in order to "map geo-political and ethnic religious source concepts onto a target domain he names only 'you.'"[48] Peter does this deliberately. He implies through this metaphor of collectivity that the church addressed has "the status and belonging, the communal identity entailed in peoplehood or nationhood."[49] Despite debates over distinctions between the words *genos*, *ethnos*, and *laos*, what is significant from a cognitive-linguistic

---

[45]See Thomas B. Dozeman, *God on the Mountain: A Study of Redaction, Theology and Canon in Exodus 19–24*, SBLMS 37 (Atlanta: Scholars Press, 1989), 94; see 93-98 and 162-63 for a detailed discussion of how Old Testament scholars, especially those committed to notions of distinct traditions, have tried to harmonize these passages.
[46]See Deterding, "Exodus Motifs," 61.
[47]Selwyn, *First Epistle of St. Peter*, 278. All the texts are compared on 279.
[48]Howe, *Because You Bear This Name*, 266.
[49]Ibid., 267.

perspective is that these terms are, as Howe points out, "grounded in the schemas they evoke. What persists, no matter the Greek 'people' word used, is the notion that the Christians' new set of relationship with one another and with God—their group identity—is like that of a distinctive people group."[50]

In employing these concepts and titles from the Old Testament, Peter has in mind not just any people group but *the* nation, the people of Israel.[51] He has transferred certain attributes, responsibilities, and privileges from the people of Israel to the Christians spread abroad in Asia Minor. In a word, the church is the new Israel. This is reinforced by his allusion to Hosea 2:23. In contrast to the Qumran community, which mapped some of these same concepts onto their own community but was inwardly focused, the responsibility of this new exodus community is to "declare the praises of him who called you out of darkness into his wonderful light" (1 Pet 2:9). This new exodus community "has both its identity and its destiny framed in moral terms, in holiness and manifesting the 'virtues' (ἀρετή), the mighty and good acts, of its God."[52] Peter will go on to apply much more moral advice in this letter, but the point is that this advice only makes sense and can only be performed in light of this reframed identity.[53] The indicative precedes the imperative.

Conclusion

We have looked at three significant passages from 1 Peter 1–2 that have obvious innerbiblical connections with the exodus and even new exodus passages. Peter's unique contribution is an "ecclesial" reading of the exodus motif. Christians, who have been purified by the sprinkling of the blood of Christ, now offer God new obedience and spiritual worship. The Christians of Asia Minor are encouraged to think along the lines of a reframed identity.[54] Peter presents us with a timely question: "Whose

---

[50] Ibid.
[51] Ibid., 268.
[52] Ibid., 269.
[53] Ibid.
[54] Deterding, "Exodus Motifs," 63.

guiding narrative, whose grand story do we embody?"[55] Recent studies in neurobiology confirm that as humans we are concerned about making *storied sense* of our lives.[56] Peter points us toward the ultimate story of our liberation in Christ.

There may even be a final reference to the exodus in 1 Peter 5:6, "Humble yourselves, therefore, under God's mighty hand, that he may lift you up in due time." In the Old Testament the deliverance of the Israelites from Egypt is often attributed to God's mighty hand.[57] Perhaps, as Paul E. Deterding suggests, the "Apostle is saying that the Last Day will be a new exodus. For the people of God it will be an act of deliverance and salvation from the Egypt of this world."[58] In the book of Exodus, God reassures Moses that he will be with him: "This will be the sign to you that it is I who have sent you: When you have brought the people out of Egypt, you will worship God on this mountain" (Ex 3:12). As Michael Morales says, "all of the subsequent narrative, including the refrain, 'Let my people go so they may worship me' ([Ex] 5.1; 7.16; 8.1, 20; 9.1, 13; 10.3), has been driving to Exod 19, to the shadow of the mount equated by YHWH with worship."[59] However, as we observed earlier in this study, it is not Sinai but Jerusalem that is the ultimate resting place for God's people. Zion, not Sinai, will be the ultimate gathering place where the bride of Christ will worship the lamb forever. That is what John reminds us of in the next chapter.

---

[55] Joel B. Green, "Identity and Engagement in a Diverse World: Pluralism and Holiness in 1 Peter," *Asbury Theological Journal* 55, no. 2 (Fall 2000): 88.
[56] Green, "Narrating the Gospel," 266.
[57] Ex 3:19-20; 13:3, 9, 14, 16; Deut 4:34; 5:15; 6:21; 7:8, 19; 9:26; 11:2; 26:8; etc.
[58] Deterding, "Exodus Motifs," 64.
[59] L. Michael Morales, *The Tabernacle Pre-figured: Cosmic Mountain Ideology in Genesis and Exodus*, Biblical Tools and Studies 15 (Leuven: Peeters, 2012), 205.

Eleven

THE EXODUS MOTIF IN REVELATION

Redemption, Judgment, and Inheritance

It was inevitable then that the consummation of all things should be presented in Exodus terminology as well and that consequently it would figure prominently in the book of Revelation.

AUGUSTINE STOCK

The Apocalypse of John takes a viewpoint similar to that of 1 Peter.[1] However, by extending complex images the book of Revelation is a rebirth of Old Testament imagery. And while there are many themes woven into the Apocalypse, the exodus motif is pervasive and multifaceted.

By the blood of the Lamb, saints have been freed from a world subjected to Satan and are now a kingdom of priests (Rev 5:9-10). This is a renewal of the ancient covenant (cf. Rev 11:19) written in a time of persecution and evoking memories of the Red Sea (cf. Rev 15:3). Viewed from a broad perspective, the book of Revelation has a tripartite characterization of the exodus that involves redemption, judgment, and inheritance. Jay Casey Smith maintains that this "not only establishes an inclusive framework within which to examine the use of the typology in Revelation, but also is an accurate outline of John's perception of the meaning of the Exodus."[2] Revelation recalibrates the Jewish

---

[1] Xavier Léon-Dufour, *Dictionary of Biblical Theology*, trans. P. Joseph Cahill and E. M. Stewart, 2nd ed. (Boston: St. Paul, 1967), 155.
[2] Jay Smith Casey, "Exodus Typology in the Book of Revelation" (PhD diss., Southern Baptist

understanding of the exodus and finds its fulfillment in Christ. As Smith elucidates, "God remains his people's redeemer, the judge of their oppressors, the guarantor of their eternal inheritance."[3] Before looking at specific passages, we will explore the archaeology of allusion hunting and how John uniquely makes allusions.

Tracing Allusions in the Apocalypse

A familiarity with the Old Testament helps us read the Apocalypse well.[4] Greg Beale says, "To what degree has the author consciously selected ideas and material from his 'learned' past? This is an essential question in attempting to discern genuine OT allusions and in trying to isolate 'associational threads' between various allusions found in a passage."[5] In a similar vein, Steve Moyise points out that Revelation is "an ideal text to explore notions of intertextuality because it does not quote Scripture but utilizes its language and imagery for a variety of rhetorical purposes."[6] Tracing the threads of an allusion in Revelation is a challenge, but it is possible.

Beale helpfully lays out several criteria for tracing allusions in the Apocalypse, each yielding a different level of certitude: (1) a *clear allusion* is where the "the wording is almost identical to the OT source, shares some common core meaning, and could not likely have come from anywhere else"; (2) a *probable allusion* is where "though the wording is not as close, it still contains an idea or wording that is uniquely

---

Theological Seminary, 1981), 134. Casey provides the most thorough analysis of exodus typology in the book of Revelation. He has been criticized, however, for suggesting that exodus typology is the framework for the entire book. See David Mathewson, *A New Heaven and a New Earth: The Meaning and Function of the Old Testament in Revelation 21.1–22.5*, JSNTSup 238 (Sheffield: Sheffield Academic Press, 2003), 64.

[3] Jay Casey, "The Exodus Theme in the Book of Revelation Against the Background of the New Testament," in *Exodus, a Lasting Paradigm*, ed. Bas van Iersel and Anton Weiler (Edinburgh: T&T Clark, 1987), 34.

[4] Quoted in G. K. Beale, *The Book of Revelation: A Commentary on the Greek Text*, NIGTC (Grand Rapids: Eerdmans, 1999), 97.

[5] G. K. Beale, *The Use of Daniel in Jewish Apocalyptic Literature and in the Revelations of St. John* (Lanham, MD: University Press of America, 1984), 8–9.

[6] Steve Moyise, "Intertextuality and Historical Approaches to the Use of Scripture in the New Testament," in *Reading the Bible Intertextually*, ed. Richard B. Hays, Stefan Alkier, and Leroy A. Huizenga (Waco, TX: Baylor University Press, 2009), 25.

traceable to the OT text or exhibits a structure of ideas uniquely traceable to the OT passage"; and (3) a *possible allusion* is where "the language is only generally similar to the purported source, echoing either its wording or concepts."[7]

Beale notes several issues that arise in detecting allusions in the Apocalypse. One issue is the presence of *combined allusions*. Beale acknowledges the "nonformal character of the OT references in Revelation,"[8] and he deals sympathetically with the difficulty of whether allusions are being made consciously or unconsciously. A related issue is whether John's use Old Testament texts is in harmony with their broad contextual meanings.[9] Beale cites Geerhardus Vos as a "representative of those who argue that John handles OT passages without respect for the OT contexts."[10]

Beale's conclusion has a slightly different nuance from Vos's. He says, "We may viably speak of changes in application, but need not conclude that this means a *disregard* for OT context. . . . It is probable that John is making *intentional allusions* and demonstrates varying degrees of respect for the OT contexts."[11] Beale categorizes the Apocalypse's various uses of allusion to the Old Testament in the following manner. First, Old Testament segments may be used as *literary prototypes*. These Old Testament contexts become models after which John patterns his creative compositions (e.g., Dan 2 and 7 are followed in Rev 1, 4, 5, 13).[12] Second, there are *thematic uses*, in which important Old Testament themes (such as holy wars) are developed. Third, there are *analogical uses*. Here we are concerned with specific well-known persons, places, and events. The reference to the "ancient serpent" in Revelation 12:9 is such an example. Fourth, there is the *universalization* theme. Albert Vanhoye, according to Beale, has described this as a formal use of allusion (e.g., Exodus plague imagery, originally localized in Egypt, is extended to the whole

---

[7]Beale, *Book of Revelation*, 78.
[8]Ibid., 79.
[9]Ibid., 81.
[10]Ibid., 84.
[11]Ibid., 85.
[12]Ibid., 86.

earth in Rev 8:6-12; 16:1-14).¹³ Fifth, there is possible *indirect fulfillment*, in which Revelation cites no formal Old Testament quotations (with introductory formulas), but Old Testament texts are "used as prooftexts to indicate prophetic fulfillment." It is still probably the case, says Beale, "that some OT texts are *informally* referred to in order to designate present or future fulfillment of OT verbal prophecy."¹⁴ For example, Revelation 1:1 seems to be a fulfillment of Daniel 2:28-29 (John's "quickly" is substituted for Daniel's "in the latter days").

There are also so-called inverted uses of allusions. Revelation 3:9, for example, refers to Isaianic prophecies that the Gentiles will come and bow down before Israel and recognize Israel as God's chosen people (e.g., Is 45:14; 49:23). But this is reversed in Revelation 3:9, where "those who are of the synagogue of Satan, who claim to be Jews though they are not," are to come and bow down before the Gentile believers (at the Philadelphian church). There are stylistic uses of Old Testament language as well. Indeed, the Greek of John's Apocalypse is highly unusual and probably heavily influenced by Old Testament Semitisms, Septuagintalisms, and so forth. R. H. Charles writes, "*While [John] writes in Greek, he thinks in Hebrew*, and the thought has naturally affected the vehicle of expression."¹⁵ John probably wrote in this manner to create a "biblical" impression on his audience.¹⁶

We turn now to a couple of passages that illustrate the Apocalypse's use of the exodus motif.

Exodus Typology in Redemption: Revelation 1:4-6

John addresses his letter to the "seven churches," which may serve as a universal identity of the whole church in the ancient world.¹⁷ There quickly follows a threefold clause: "from him who is, and who was, and

---

¹³Ibid., 91.
¹⁴Ibid., 93. Of course, this depends on one's overall view of the book, i.e., whether one is a preterist, futurist, idealist, etc.
¹⁵R. H. Charles, *A Critical and Exegetical Commentary on the Revelation of St. John*, International Critical Commentary (Edinburgh: T&T Clark, 1920), 1:cxliii.
¹⁶Beale, *Book of Revelation*, 96.
¹⁷Ibid., 187.

who is to come" (Rev. 1:4). This may be a reflection of Exodus 3:14, the revelation of God to Moses (*'ehyeh 'ăšer 'ehyeh*, "I AM WHO I AM"), refracted through certain temporal descriptions of God in the book of Isaiah.[18] Already in this salutation John may be signaling to us that we are entering the allusive orbit of the Exodus revelation.

Christ is referred to in this passage as the "faithful witness," "firstborn," and the "ruler of the kings of the earth." This is likely a reference to Psalm 89:27, 37 (Ps 88 LXX), where all these designations are listed. "The faithful witness" may also be an allusion to Isaiah 43:10-13.[19] "Firstborn," as Beale points out, "refers to the high, privileged position that Christ has as a result of the resurrection from the dead," a position demonstrating that he is the "inaugurator of the *new* creation by means of his resurrection."[20]

It is the unambiguous allusion to Exodus 19:6, "you will be for me a kingdom of priests and a holy nation," that stands out as an evocation of the exodus motif. John's wording ("to him who ... has made us to be a kingdom and priests") differs slightly from that of 1 Peter 2:9 as well as the Hebrew of Exodus 19:6. The Septuagint renders the MT *mamleket kōhănîm* as *basileion hierateuma*, which 1 Peter picks up. However, John combined the abstract singular *basileian* with the concrete plural *hiereis*, so it is probably best translated, "and he has made us a kingdom, priests to his God and father." There is no "and" between "kingdom" and "priests" (but cf. Rev 5:10). The title that God had given to Israel is now applied to the church. As Beale notes, this suggests that the end-time temple "has been inaugurated in the church."[21] These important verses open the Apocalypse and signal the new high point that redemptive history has reached: God's glory has been achieved through the work of the incomparable Christ, and he has established his work through the service of his people as kings and priests.[22]

---

[18]Ibid.
[19]Ibid., 191.
[20]Ibid.
[21]G. K. Beale, *John's Use of the Old Testament in Revelation*, JSNTSup 166 (Sheffield: Sheffield Academic Press, 1998), 106. See also Beale, *Book of Revelation*, 194.
[22]Beale, *Book of Revelation*, 194.

Exodus Typology Making Kings and Priests: Revelation 5:9-10

In the previous passage, we saw the integral connection John makes between the church and the kingdom of priests by invoking Exodus 19:6. In Revelation 5:9-10 we see that it is Jesus himself who has formed this band of brothers and sisters, and it is Jesus who is *the* high priest, "who represents his church before the Father (Rev 1:5-6; 5:9-10)."[23] He is the lion and the lamb, images that should be held in tension, not torn asunder (Rev 5:5-6). There is a juxtaposition of images here: "John *hears* of the 'Lion of the tribe of Judah' and *sees* a 'Lamb standing as if it had been slaughtered.'"[24] He is the Lamb being slain, which evokes a memory of the "Paschal Lamb and Israel's exodus and liberation from Egypt."[25] In response to the vision of the Lamb (*arnion*) who is worthy (*axios* [Rev 5:2, 4]) to break the seals and open the scroll, the Lamb "looking as if it had been slain" (Rev 5:6), the celestial audience sings a "new song":

> You are worthy to take the scroll
> > and to open its seals,
> because you were slain,
> > and with your blood you purchased for God
> persons from every tribe and language and people and nation.
> You have made them to be a kingdom [*basileian*] and priests [*kai hiereis*]
> > to serve our God,
> and they will reign on earth.

It seems that the Passover lamb imagery is more influential here than the servant imagery of Isaiah 53.[26] The designation of Jesus as the *arnion* occurs twenty-eight times in Revelation. Interestingly, in rabbinic tradition there

---

[23]Dennis E. Johnson, *Triumph of the Lamb: A Commentary on Revelation* (Phillipsburg, NJ: P&R, 2001), 58.
[24]See Steve Moyise, "Dialogical Intertextuality," in *Exploring Intertextuality: Diverse Strategies for New Testament Interpretation of Texts*, ed. B. J. Oropeza and Steve Moyise (Eugene, OR: Cascade, 2016), 8; see esp. 7-14. Moyise notes how many New Testament scholars have argued that the lamb imagery is to marginalize the "violent" imagery of the lion, but he argues that this is a reduction of John's intention.
[25]Benjamin G. Wold, "Revelation's Plague Septets: New Exodus and Exile," in *Echoes from the Caves: Qumran and the New Testament*, ed. Florentino García Martínez (Boston: Brill, 2009), 280.
[26]Casey, "Exodus Typology," 149.

was the notion that the blood of the Passover lamb shed at the exodus had sufficient merit for effecting the liberation and redemption of Israel at the end of time.[27] John elsewhere uses the imagery of the warrior lamb (cf. Rev 17:14), but here the emphasis is on the *slain* lamb, which demonstrates that his sacrificial death has the power to achieve redemption.[28]

The "new song" is frequently found in the Psalter.[29] In Revelation, the "newness" evokes the themes of the new heavens and earth (Rev 21:1), the new Jerusalem (Rev 3:12; 21:2), the possession of a new name (Rev 2:17; 3:12), and the newness of everything in creation (Rev 21:5). Much more is entailed here than merely chronological newness; rather, something wholly other and miraculous has been wrought by the slain Lamb.[30] "New songs" were sung in the history of salvation to celebrate new events in which God rescued his people.[31] The original "new song" was the Song of the Sea, celebrated at the birth of a particular people. Now the song of the Lamb is sung by an international assembly.[32]

Whereas in Revelation 1:5-6 there was no "and" (*kai*) between "kingdom, priests," here in Revelation 5:10 the text reads, "You have made them to be a kingdom and priests." What is more significant is the addition of "and they will reign on earth." Whereas the focus in 1:5-6 was on individual sin and the acquisition of the dignity and authority of kings and priests, here the focus is on its corporate manifestation.[33]

---

[27] Ibid., 145-46, 151.
[28] Ibid., 152.
[29] E.g., Ps 33:3; 40:3; 96:1-4. In Ps 33:3, the psalmist calls on the congregation to "Sing [masculine plural imperative] to him a new song!" As Vos comments, "The Psalter is wide awake to the significance of history as leading up to the eschatological act of God." See Geerhardus Vos, *Eschatology of the Psalter*, found as an appendix in *The Pauline Eschatology* (Phillipsburg, NJ: P&R, 1930), 335-36. Vos notes numerous phrases throughout the Psalter that demonstrate the continuity of God's plan with its goal of bringing to final fruition the promise of the new heaven and new earth. The notion of a "new song" is especially evocative of the latter part of Isaiah, where the prophet exhorts the exilic community not to look to the wondrous things of old but to the new thing God is doing (cf. Is 42:9-10). Johnson, *Triumph of the Lamb*, 109-10, notes the international dimension of Ps 96 and the linking of the new Song of the Lamb in Revelation.
[30] See discussion in Casey, "Exodus Typology," 143.
[31] Johnson, *Triumph of the Lamb*, 108.
[32] Ibid., 110.
[33] Casey, "Exodus Typology," 146. This demonstrates the close connection between redemption and inheritance; see 194-95.

John's theme of the reign of the saints is clearly sounded.[34] The background for the dual office of priests and kings resides not only in Exodus 19:6 but also in Isaiah 61:6, where the end-time restoration of God's people as an entire nation "will be called priests of the Lord."[35]

Typological Fulfillment of the Exodus-Wilderness-Jericho Pattern: Revelation 11:14-19[36]

The trumpets imagery in Revelation offers many allusions to the physical plagues that befell Egypt.[37] Divine warrior motifs are elicited (cf. Rev 19:11-16) in this scene at the sounding of the last trumpet in Revelation 11:14-19.[38] The Lord is coming to dwell among his people and bring victory to them, for *he is* (cf. Ex 3:14; Rev 11:17; 16:5)! The content of the third woe and the seventh trumpet is probably an "explanation of the consummation of history since [Rev] 10:7" since it has been announced that when the seventh trumpet sounds, "then will be completed God's accomplishment of his plan for history."[39]

Beale comments that in Revelation 11:16-17 the threefold divine name evokes "God of past ('who was'), present ('who is'), and future ('who is coming'). This threefold divine named is used in the OT and Jewish writings in contexts describing God as the incomparable sovereign Lord of history, as he who is therefore able to fulfill prophecy by delivering his people despite overwhelming odds, whether from Egypt, from Babylon, or from the nations."[40]

In verse 19 God's heavenly temple is opened, the ark of the covenant becomes visible, and lightning, thunder, and an earthquake ensue. The passage evokes some of the Song of Moses (cf. Ex 15:13-18).[41] In

---

[34] Ibid., 148.
[35] Beale, *Old Testament in Revelation*, 377.
[36] I am indebted here to Beale, *Book of Revelation*, 619.
[37] Johnson, *Triumph of the Lamb*, 143.
[38] See Josephine Massyngbaerde Ford, "Shalom in the Johannine Corpus," *Horizons in Biblical Theology* 6, no. 2 (1984): 67-89, especially the first half of the article where she deals with the divine warrior image in the book of Revelation.
[39] Beale, *Book of Revelation*, 609.
[40] Ibid., 612-13.
[41] Ex 15:13 speaks of "guid[ing] them to your holy dwelling," and the nations becoming enraged. The LXX has *ethnē . . . ōrgisthēsan* in Ex 15:14.

Exodus 15:17 God brings his people to his habitation, a "sanctuary." The phrase in Revelation 11:15 "He will reign for ever and ever" is a verbatim parallel of Exodus 15:18. With the first six trumpets clearly modeled on the Exodus passages, this is an appropriate way to conclude the trumpets section. Beale sums it up: "Rev. 11:15-19 notes the end of the evil world kingdoms and the church's reward in escalated typological fulfillment of the Exodus-wilderness-Jericho pattern."[42] The exodus motif has been transformed to demonstrate the completion of God's grand redemptive plan. He has delivered his people from the tyranny of oppression. He has brought them through their pilgrimage, their wilderness wanderings. And finally, he has granted them entitlement to the Promised Land.

Exodus Typology in Inheritance: Revelation 15:1-4

Revelation 15:1-4 is especially important for the exodus motif since it links the Song of the Sea with the Song of the Lamb.[43] It is "equally as pivotal in understanding the plague septets as part of a new exodus theme" as is Revelation 5:9-11.[44] By way of introduction, up through Revelation 14:20, only six visions of the sevenfold series have been presented (beginning in Rev 12:1). The seventh vision does not begin with 15:1 but with 15:2. The presentation of the seventh vision is interrupted by the introduction of the seven angels with bowls of plagues in 15:1, though the new series is not picked up until verse 5. "The best explanation of verses 2-4 is that they serve both as a conclusion to 12:1–14:20 and as part of the introduction to the bowls."[45] Revelation 15:1-4 reads as follows:

> I saw in heaven another great and marvelous sign: seven angels with the seven last plagues—last, because with them God's wrath is completed. And I saw what looked like a sea of glass glowing with fire and, standing beside the sea, those who had been victorious over the beast and its image and over the number of its name. They held harps given them by God and sang the song of God's servant Moses and of the Lamb:

---

[42]Beale, *Book of Revelation*, 619.
[43]Casey, "Exodus Typology," 150; Johnson, *Triumph of the Lamb*, 108.
[44]Wold, "Revelation's Plague Septets," 280-81.
[45]Beale, *Book of Revelation*, 784.

> "Great and marvelous are your deeds,
>   Lord God Almighty.
> Just and true are your ways,
>   King of the nations.
> Who will not fear you, Lord,
>   and bring glory to your name?
> For you alone are holy.
> All nations will come
>   and worship before you,
> for your righteous acts have been revealed."

Dale C. Allison sees the new and final exodus clearly evoked in this passage. He writes, "Here those who have conquered the beast and its image and the number of its name stand beside a sea of glass and 'sing the song of Moses' (cf. Exodus 15; Deuteronomy 32). Clearly the deliverance from the Red Sea is here the typological equivalent of the eschatological deliverance, and the song in Revelation 'celebrates a new and greater exodus.'"[46] The seven bowls of 15:1 are modeled on the plagues, and the song in 15:3-4 is an imitation of the Song of Moses (Ex 15). As Beale points out, "The reference to a new, final exodus victory in Rev. 15:2-4, which concludes the segment of 12:1–14:20, inspires a recall in chapter 16 of the latter-day exodus plagues leading up to the final victory."[47]

The "last things" of Revelation 15:1 are sometimes viewed as "futurist"—that is, the seven bowls come at the end of history after the events narrated in the seals and trumpets. More likely is Beale's view that the phrase "indicates the order in which John saw the visions and not necessarily the chronological order of their occurrence in history."[48] Both the Old Testament and Jewish contemporary literature seem to provide this interpretation, that "last" with respect to plagues means "that they occur in the latter days . . . in contrast to the former days when the Egyptian plagues occurred."[49]

---

[46]Dale C. Allison Jr., *The New Moses: A Matthean Typology* (Minneapolis: Fortress, 1993), 198, quoting at the end J. P. M. Sweet, *Revelation* (Philadelphia: Westminster, 1979), 239.
[47]Beale, *Book of Revelation*, 785.
[48]Ibid., 786.
[49]Ibid., 787.

Revelation 15:2-4, therefore, is a prophecy of the coming of God's kingdom and not a mere anticipation or prolepsis of the later chronological presentation of it in Revelation 19–21.[50] Uppermost in John's mind is Exodus 15, the Song of the Sea.[51] Jewish exegetical tradition depicts the Red Sea as becoming a "sea of glass."[52] The sea has become the place where the Lamb has judged the Beast. There is advancement of the image, however. In the old exodus, Israel could only stand by and watch. Here, however, they are "involved in combat with the sea beast." John has extended the development we saw in Revelation 5—the reign of the saints. Just as Israel praised God in the Song of the Sea for delivering them from Pharaoh, so the church praises God in the Song of the Lamb for "defeating the beast on their behalf."[53]

In verse 3 Moses is "God's servant," which is probably an allusion to Exodus 14:31. Here as well there has been advancement, since they do not sing the Song of Moses but the Song of the Lamb. The incomparability formula does not derive just from Exodus 15; rather, it is woven from passages throughout the Old Testament. As the God of the exodus generation was praised because "his works are perfect" and "all his ways are just" (Deut 32:4), likewise he is praised here.

The theme of God's reign over the nations is evident in Revelation 11:15-18. Here in Revelation 15:4 there is a clear allusion to Jeremiah 10:7, "Who should not fear you, / King of the nations?" Most of the other language in verse 4 is based on Psalm 86:9-10. "All nations" is probably a metonymy, by which the whole world is substituted for a part of it in order to emphasize that many will worship. The theme of divine incomparability is seen as well in Jeremiah 10 and Psalm 86 and clearly appears in the Song of the Sea (Ex 15:11): "Who among the gods / is like you, Lord? / Who is like you— / majestic in holiness, / awesome in glory, / working wonders?" The final lines of Revelation 15:4 are clearly a reference to Psalm 98:2, "The Lord has . . . revealed his righteousness to the nations." Interestingly, this follows on the heels of a

---

[50]Ibid., 789.
[51]In the analysis, I am following Beale.
[52]Beale, *Book of Revelation*, 789.
[53]Ibid., 792.

reference to the exodus in Psalm 98:1, "Sing to the LORD a new song, / for he has done marvelous things; / his right hand and his holy arm / have worked salvation for him." The same transition of thought is seen in Revelation 15.

The upshot of these allusions is this: "The use of the OT in vv. 3-4 is not the result of random selection but is guided by the theme of the first Exodus and the development of that theme later in the OT. This is but a continuation of the latter-day Red Sea setting in 15:2. The main point of vv. 2-4 is the adoration of God and the Lamb's incomparable act of redemption and judgment."[54] The theme of inheritance, which is so prominent in Revelation, is also present here but receives a fuller treatment in Revelation 20–22.[55] Once again, the exodus is biblically defined as involving more than mere liberation from sin. The end game in this passage is the community of God singing the Lord's praises together, turfed in their inheritance: the Promised land, the world-to-come.

The Climax of Exodus Typology— New Creation: Revelation 21:1-8

Although other passages from the final chapters of Revelation could be engaged at this point, Revelation 21:1-8 demonstrates clear antecedents in new-exodus passages we have examined earlier in this book. The inheritance theme, which has played a crucial role in our development of the exodus motif, is clearly evoked here. The text reads as follows:

> Then I saw "a new heaven and a new earth," for the first heaven and the first earth had passed away, and there was no longer any sea. I saw the Holy City, the new Jerusalem, coming down out of heaven from God, prepared as a bride beautifully dressed for her husband. And I heard a loud voice from the throne saying, "Look! God's dwelling place is now among the people, and he will dwell with them. They will be his people, and God himself will be with them and be their God. 'He will wipe every tear from their eyes. There will be no more death' or mourning or crying or pain, for the old order of things has passed away."

---

[54]Ibid., 799.
[55]Casey, "Exodus Typology," 231.

> He who was seated on the throne said, "I am making everything new!" Then he said, "Write this down, for these words are trustworthy and true."
>
> He said to me: "It is done. I am the Alpha and the Omega, the Beginning and the End. To the thirsty I will give water without cost from the spring of the water of life. Those who are victorious will inherit all this, and I will be their God and they will be my children. But the cowardly, the unbelieving, the vile, the murderers, the sexually immoral, those who practice magic arts, the idolaters and all liars—they will be consigned to the fiery lake of burning sulfur. This is the second death."

In chapter five we looked at Isaiah 43:14-21 as a new-exodus text. David Mathewson has made a persuasive case that Isaiah 43:18-19 ("Forget the former things; / do not dwell on the past. / See, I am doing a new thing! / Now it springs up; do you not perceive it? / I am making a way in the wilderness / and streams in the wasteland") is alluded to by John in Revelation 21:5 ("I am making everything new!"). The effect, says Mathewson, is to provide "a new exodus context for this final eschatological scenario."[56] This fits with the corroboratory evidence seen already in John's treatment of exodus themes, as well as other material we have not discussed.[57] Mathewson claims that Isaiah 65:17-20, a passage that focuses on the new heavens and new earth, is also influential for John in Revelation 21:1-5. The significance of mixing Isaiah 65 with Isaiah 43 results in John's conceiving "of eschatological salvation, where God will recreate heaven and earth and dwell with his people in a renewed covenant relationship in a new Jerusalem, as the climax and goal of the new exodus motif."[58]

Mathewson also argues for the influence of the new exodus on the cryptic statement in Revelation 21:1, "there was no longer any sea."[59] How are we to understand this statement? First, we need to ask what the sea represents in the book of Revelation. The sea is actually used in about five different ways: (1) the origin of cosmic evil (Rev 4:6; 12:18; 13:1; 15:2);

---

[56]Mathewson, *New Heaven*, 63.
[57]See ibid., 63-64.
[58]Ibid.
[59]Ibid., 64-69; Mathewson, "New Exodus as a Background for 'The Sea Was No More' in Revelation 21:1c," *Trinity Journal* 24 (2003): 243-58.

(2) unbelieving, rebellious nations that bring about tribulation for God's people (Rev 12:18 [Greek text]; 13:1; 17:2, 6); (3) the place of the dead (Rev 20:13); (4) the location of the idolatrous world's trade activity (Rev 18:10-20); and (5) a literal body of water sometimes in conjunction with the earth. "Sea" is a kind of synecdoche, a part for the whole. The sea is used to describe an old part of creation that represents the totality of creation.[60] To one degree or another, the reference to "there was no longer any sea" in Revelation 21:1 is probably informed by all these previous meanings in Revelation.

Expanding our investigation to the entirety of Scripture, we see more generally that the sea is often a symbol of chaos and evil. That is the case here as well. But the point here is that Christ has conquered the sea. Mathewson traces the theme of God drying up the sea in the Old Testament (e.g., Ps 106; 114; Is 51:9) and claims, "By conceiving of the sea of Rev. 21.1c within the new exodus-exilic return framework as the Red Sea of hostility and affliction, the sea no longer constitutes a barrier to entrance into the new heavens and earth and new Jerusalem, but has been removed with their establishment."[61]

Earlier in our study we saw that the Song of the Sea describes Israel's deliverance within the framework of the archetypal journey: through the waters → to the mountain → for worship. Now John has demonstrated that God is not only Creator but also Consummator, and a new pattern emerges: *destroy* the waters → to Zion, the new Jerusalem → for worship. The reader will recall that the waters are an indicator of chaos and a symbol of death in the broader picture of Scripture; however, now this motif takes on cosmic dimensions: "The disappearance of the sea provides a passage into a renewed cosmos."[62]

The disappearance of the sea in Revelation 21:1 gives way to new imagery of complete union and communion with God: the intimacy of marriage and God tabernacling among his people appear in Revelation 21:2-3. The old order has passed away, and the new creation emerges. For

---

[60]See Rev 5:13; 7:1-3; 8:8-9; 10:2, 5-6, 8; 14:7; 16 (?). All references are cited by Beale, *Book of Revelation*, 1041-42.
[61]Mathewson, *New Heaven*, 68.
[62]Ibid.

the second time in the book of Revelation, God himself is represented as speaking directly. This is probably to assure the listener of the gravity of what is about to be spoken, "for these words are trustworthy and true" (Rev 21:5). The statement "It is done" (Rev 21:6) further emphasizes the assurance of the things described. Next, God says, "I am the Alpha and the Omega, the Beginning and the End" (Rev 21:6), adding further reassurance to the words spoken by the literary instrument of a merism (opposites meant to communicate totality). The implication: God is an absolute Sovereign over history, and he will indeed bring creation to its consummated end with salvation and judgment.[63]

The new exodus clearly emerges in Revelation 21:7. John summarizes the inheritance theme: "Those who are victorious will inherit all this."[64] "This" includes "dwelling with God, the absence of tears, sorrow, and pain, and sustenance from God's living water, vv. 3-4, 6."[65] Of course, the consummate blessing is the filial relationship that God's people will enjoy, a theme we saw inaugurated in Paul, now consummated in John. The adopted people of God enjoy full union and communion with their Savior. Revelation 21:3 affirms the whole people's destiny as God's people, and "this fulfillment of the individual's redemption in sonship thus becomes a feature of that corporate inheritance."[66] Revelation 21:8 stands as a grave warning to all who would hear this glorious message, especially those outside Christ but also those who seek by God's grace to persevere, so that we should not be excluded from the presence of God. To those in Christ, to the overcomers who seek to persevere, belongs the inheritance described here, the sure promises of David. We, like Christ (David's greater Son), shall be included in the full inheritance of adoption as sons of God.[67] The exodus motif has experienced its coming-home day.

---

[63]Ibid., 1055.
[64]Casey, "Exodus Theme," 40-42.
[65]Ibid., 40.
[66]Ibid.
[67]Believers were adopted as sons, not because only males were heirs of God, but because in the Greco-Roman world *both* males *and* females were heirs, and thus as a matter of grammatical gender the text designates all as *sons*.

Although some view Revelation 21:1-8 literally as the physical description of the city of God (which includes a transformed earthly world) with the heavenly Jerusalem descending from above, this seems implausible for the following reasons. First, it is literal and it is physical, but in the following way. John is shown the "bride of the Lamb" in Revelation 21:9-10: "'Come, I will show you the bride, the wife of the Lamb.' And he carried me away in the Spirit to a mountain great and high, and showed me the Holy City, Jerusalem, coming down out of heaven from God." But this city is identified in Revelation 21:2 as the bride, the eternal community of the redeemed, which is also the city of God (see vv. 9-10). We read in verse 1, "The first earth had passed away, and there was no longer any sea," and therefore this Scripture teaches the "passing away" of the former natural world (although not its annihilation); nevertheless, it does not teach that there is no continuity whatsoever. The continuity *according to this passage* is primarily to be found at precisely this point: the resurrection of believers' bodies. John emphasizes this: it is primarily believers in the Lamb who provide the point of continuity between the former world and the new creation, for John identifies the community of the redeemed as the new Jerusalem.

God is the Creator and Consummator of his perfectly orchestrated plan. Although his people—beginning with Adam and Eve and continuing throughout redemptive history—have only been unfaithful, he remains faithful.

CONCLUSION

"Why to think of it, we're in the same tale still!
It's going on. Don't the great tales never end?"
"No, they never end as tales," said Frodo.
"But the people in them come, and go when their part's
ended. Our part will end later—or sooner."
"And then we can have some rest and some sleep," said Sam.

J. R. R. TOLKIEN, THE TWO TOWERS

First, . . . wherever you live, it is probably [like] Egypt;
second, . . . there is a better place, a world more
attractive, a promised land; and third, . . . "the way
to the land is through the wilderness."

MICHAEL WALZER[1]

We have come a long way in our study of the exodus motif in Scripture. It is now time to review what we have seen thus far and then discuss some implications for biblical theology and our Christian life today.

Looking Back

In chapter one we reviewed the burgeoning field of intertextuality in biblical studies. Early on I sought to define terms closely and carefully. I sought to revivify what I think is a responsible use of the terms

---

[1] Walzer is citing a short phrase of W. D. Davies.

and methods vis-à-vis irresponsible or less rigorous methods of intertextuality. We also discussed how allusions work and how intertextuality overlaps with typology. Since the Enlightenment, typology has fallen on hard times. Indeed, underrating the typologizing tendencies of the biblical authors may be one reason that people have not recognized the prominence of the exodus motif in Scripture. We explored how the mode of biblical typology was employed by the early Hebrew and Christian writers as a legitimate interpretation of Old Testament and New Testament texts, especially with regard to the exodus motif.

In chapter two we considered the backgrounds of the exodus motif as they are found in the biblical creation account. Our tracing of this motif in the Bible began with first things: creation, particularly the so-called primeval history found in Genesis 1–11, and the immediately following chapters concerning the promises to Abraham. In creation the big themes set the stage and provide the backdrop for so much of the rest of the Bible: cosmic mountain ideology, wilderness, avian (bird) imagery, alienation, and promise. Creation is also important for its connection with covenant.

Having laid the Genesis foundations, we came to the heart of the matter in chapter three with a discussion of the exodus motif as a paradigm. We explored the foundational salvific event of the Old Testament and built a platform for tracing our theme throughout Scripture. We noted that not only were biblical themes interwoven in the book of Exodus but also the themes and ideas of the surrounding cultures became mixed in the biblical message for particular theological purposes. This was especially the case with mythological themes of cosmology.

In dealing with the Song of the Sea (Ex 15), one question kept presenting itself: What is the scope of the exodus motif? I demonstrated that the exodus motif is a much bigger concept than merely the liberation of the Hebrews from Egypt. It is about God crafting a people by bringing them to the very abode of his presence at Mount Sinai. But surprisingly, divine presence is not the most important reality of the exodus event. Just as there was an anticipated goal at the beginning of creation in the Garden of Eden, so also there is an anticipated goal for Israel. The exodus motif is also about the goal of this deliverance, which concluded not at Sinai but with Israel's deliverance to the Promised Land. In the immediate context of the Hebrew Bible, this meant the land of Canaan. However, the ultimate goal transcends Canaan in the grandest gift imaginable: entitlement to the world-to-come itself, the final resting point for the people of God.

In chapter four we observed how the threads of the exodus motif are woven into the tapestry of the Psalms. We began to see the function of the exodus motif: Israel was called to a new level of understanding in light of God's faithfulness in the past. God as the divine warrior conquered the enemies of his people just as he subdued the ancient tumultuous waters of chaos. The patterns recognized earlier in the Bible, especially with regard to what exactly constitutes the exodus motif, were confirmed in a close-grained reading of a number of the psalms.

Chapter five dealt with the exodus motif in Isaiah. The prophet tells us that something "new" is going to take place. From different vantage points and in various ways, the foundational salvific event of the exodus now becomes a paradigm to announce a new salvation event altogether: a new exodus, the Isaianic new exodus. In Isaiah 40–55, we observed a fusion of creation-redemptive themes in over thirteen passages.

In chapter six we turned to the exilic and the postexilic periods, especially dealing with two other prophets, Ezekiel and Jeremiah. Ezekiel speaks of a coming new exodus as having much to say about Israel's disobedience (especially in Ezek 20). Jeremiah is also interested in the typology of disobedience with special interest in the wilderness tradition, which has its moorings in the exodus motif. But mixed with prophetic indictment there was also prophetic hope, for Jeremiah proclaimed the promises of a better covenant yet to come. During the biblical postexilic period, the exodus motif continued to influence the manner in which the authors of Scripture describe redemptive history. In Ezra–Nehemiah's contribution we find an antechamber for the coming agent of the new exodus that would be announced in the Gospels.

In chapter seven the "new thing" that the prophets anticipated was seen to be realized in the coming of the Messiah-King, who inaugurated his kingdom. The paradigm of Isaiah's new exodus was evoked to demonstrate that the exodus motif had now become "eschatologized." That is to say, the exodus had become a presently (partially) realized and future event promised on the basis of God's past action in delivering his people. Chapter seven illustrated how this is developed in Mark and Matthew. Chapter 8 dealt with Luke–Acts.

All this evocation of the exodus event could not possibly have left the apostle Paul untouched. In chapter nine we noted the pervasive influence of the exodus motif in three of the apostle's letters. N. T. Wright has argued that the exodus motif provides a narrative substructure for Romans 3–8 and other places in Paul.[2] While appreciating some of Wright's insights (as well as those of his students), I also engaged some of his ideas critically.

In chapter ten we explored how 1 Peter makes prominent use of the exodus motif, especially in 1 Peter 1–2. I argued that Peter focuses on the exodus motif from an "ecclesial perspective." In other words, in Peter's epistle, Christians are now viewed as redeemed by the spotless blood of the Passover Lamb. They have become the new people of God and the fulfillment of the promise of that royal priesthood (Ex 19:5-6).

In chapter eleven we came to the end of the biblical corpus with an examination of the exodus motif in the Apocalypse of John. Revelation shows similarities to Peter's epistle, but there are advances on Peter's contributions as well. Indeed, Christians are seen as the new kingdom of priests. Here, the strands came together in the expected consummation of the ages. Jesus is repeatedly referred to as the Lamb of God with obvious references to the lamb of Passover. He brings about the consummation of the new exodus. The divine warrior themes became

---

[2]For Wright's most recent and clearest statements on his views of these chapters (at the time of this writing), see *The Day the Revolution Began: Reconsidering the Meaning of Jesus's Crucifixion* (San Francisco: HarperOne, 2016), 263-94 (chap. 12, "The Death of Jesus in Paul's Letter to the Romans: *The New Exodus*"). For a charitable, balanced review of the book, see Mike Horton, "N. T. Wright Reconsiders the Meaning of Jesus's Death," The Gospel Coalition, October, 10, 2016, www.thegospelcoalition.org/article/book-reviews-the-day-the-revolution-began.

prominent again but through the unexpected turn of the warrior lamb looking as if he was slain. The Christians' victory is seen as complete. All the typological adumbrations traced throughout Scripture are now fulfilled, and the consummation of the ages has come. Those who overcome will reign with the Lamb.

Stepping Back

Having traced out our study of Scripture's use of the exodus motif, I would like to step back to see the forest from the trees and briefly analyze what possible contribution this study can make to the discipline of biblical theology. Since the exodus motif is so paradigmatic in the Bible, what are some of the ramifications for the Christian life and systematic theology?

First, I think this study demonstrates that the hermeneutical methods outlined at the beginning of the book (especially chap. 1) can bear fruitful exegesis when applied to a theme or motif. Innerbiblical exegesis and intertextuality are burgeoning areas of work in biblical studies today. Many steer clear of the field, probably in part because of its associations with literary studies and its unfamiliarity, especially with regard to poststructuralist semiotic theorists like Julia Kristeva and Roland Barthes. However, it is not incumbent on interpreters to accept the ideological frameworks of these authors just because we use the term *intertextuality*.[3] In an age that is seeking fresh approaches to the Scriptures, I hope that this study has been of some help in demonstrating the use of such methods in a responsible manner.

Second, the exodus motif in Scripture is an explanation of God's plan to fulfill the original design of creation. It is an excellent rubric for teaching about typology or figural readings of the Scriptures. In the Garden of Eden, Adam had not ascended to the *summum bonum* (the best state): entitlement to the world-to-come. Indeed, because he chose to heed the apocryphal word of Satan instead of the canonical word of God, he was expelled from the sanctuary into the wilderness wanderings

---

[3]See Richard B. Hays, *The Conversion of the Imagination: Paul as Interpreter of Israel's Scripture* (Grand Rapids: Eerdmans, 2005), 173.

of this sin-cursed world. However, God was not done with humanity. He was still going to accomplish the final eschatological goal of entitlement to the world-to-come, where humanity would no longer be able to sin. Christ by his perfect work has attained that destiny, and believers claim all the benefits of his finished work, including the world-to-come, where they may worship him forever.

I have argued elsewhere that entitlement to heaven or the world-to-come is an important but underdeveloped (and sometimes missing) aspect in classical dogmatic constructions of the doctrine of justification by faith.[4] If my previous argument is valid—that is, that entitlement to the world-to-come is the contemplated legal aspect of the garden situation (at least as a semi-eschatological step)—then we are touching on something with wider canonical implications. Had Adam passed his probation, he would have moved from a state of relative perfection to a higher estate of at least being not able to sin (*non posse peccare* in the classical formulation). However, he failed. Consequently, that entitlement to the world-to-come has been proffered by God through the work of Jesus Christ and in no other way. It makes sense, therefore, that the exodus motif is consistent with this teaching. The exodus motif, its development in Scripture along with its attendant goal, is one long argument (in story form) in support of the way in which one may secure entitlement to the world-to-come. The upshot of this study is that the exodus is a synecdoche for the story of salvation as understood by the Christian church for centuries. The Hebrews had divine promises made to them, promises intended to lift their hearts to the hopeful anticipation of something greater than the land of Canaan as an inheritance. John Calvin sums it up nicely:

> The same church existed among them, but as yet in its childhood. Therefore, keeping them under this tutelage, the Lord gave, not spiritual promises unadorned and open, but ones foreshadowed, in a measure, by

---

[4] See Bryan Estelle, "Leviticus 18:5 and Deuteronomy 30:1-14 in Biblical Theological Development: Entitlement to Heaven Foreclosed and Proffered," in *The Law Is Not of Faith: Essays on Grace and Works in the Mosaic Covenant*, ed. Bryan Estelle, J. V. Fesko, and David VanDrunen (Phillipsburg, NJ: P&R, 2009), 109-46.

earthly promises. When, therefore, he adopted Abraham, Isaac, Jacob, and their descendants into the hope of immortality, he promised them the Land of Canaan as an inheritance. It was not to be the final goal of their hopes, but was to exercise and confirm them, as they contemplated it, in hope of their true inheritance not yet manifested to them. And that they might not be deceived, a higher promise was given, attesting that the land was not God's supreme benefit. Thus Abraham is not allowed to sit by idly when he receives the promise of the land, but his mind is elevated to the Lord by a greater promise.[5]

The final goal of the exodus, a goal envisioned and subsumed under the more immediate goal of bringing the people to the foot of the mountain, was to bring the people of God to Sinai, and then to deliver them up to the Promised Land, where they may worship. This goal was the land of Canaan first; however, the eschatological goal was not merely the geopolitical land of Israel. It was far greater. God had his goal for the royal priesthood that he was crafting as his own, that they would ascend to a much greater end: entitlement to the world-to-come itself. This was the ultimate bliss envisioned by the story: union and communion with God as a "turfed" people in the world-to-come, worshiping God forever. Enlandment, conjoined with ethical righteousness and perfected worship, was the ultimate goal. And nothing less than the world-to-come was meant by that land promise. In this respect, there are some striking comparisons between the original goals in the Garden of Eden and the goals that the exodus motif encompasses.

Adam was created in a state of relative perfection. He had not reached his highest estate yet. Although he was created upright, there was the anticipated legal outcome of his probation in the garden, signified by the tree of life itself. He was to offer up the positive obedience required by the probation test and enter into an estate of *confirmed* righteousness. The just and legal outcome of obedience was entitlement to the world-to-come, plain and simple. Life, in the sense of life consummated through eschatological blessing, hence entitlement to the world-to-come, was the

---

[5]John Calvin, *Institutes of the Christian Religion*, ed. John T. McNeill, trans. Ford Lewis Battles, Library of Christian Classics 21-22 (Philadelphia: Westminster, 1960), 2.11.2.

promised reward for fulfilling the command in the garden (Gen 2:16-17).[6] Eschatology, in this sense, preceded soteriology.[7]

In the Garden of Eden, the probation was put in negative terms with an implicit positive promise, eschatological life. In the period covered by the exodus, the Mosaic economy, that was reversed: the probation was put in positive terms (temporal blessings) with an explicitly stated punishment, exile from the land. Additionally, it was obvious that no mere mortal this side of the fall could earn or merit this ultimate life—gain entitlement to the world-to-come, that is—since human beings after the fall are only able always to sin. Nevertheless, God was well-pleased to hold out the promise of life, with its temporal blessings, in order to teach the Israelites that there was an entitlement to a land beyond any geopolitical sphere they could envision, greater even than the monarchy under the peaceful reign of King Solomon. They could enter the rest of the world-to-come, and a greater Joshua could lead them there one day, a true Son of Israel (Heb 4). Entitlement to the world-to-come, however, this side of the fall into sin, can only be secured by grace through faith, not by means of works, not mere human works, that is. Thus, Adam's situation in the garden may be viewed in a manner relative to the exodus motif and the new exodus fulfilled by Christ.

God has given us a grand picture through the exodus motif, a picture that includes liberation from tyrannizing forces, ushering us into his presence and finally into a land. But ultimately this will not be fully realized until the final consummation of the ages. Individual salvation is indeed important, but it is not everything. We must not set the individual over against the corporate. We are saved *as* a people; a royal priesthood worshiping in the heavenly Zion is what God has in mind.

---

[6] See Louis Berkhof, *Systematic Theology*, 4th ed. (Grand Rapids: Eerdmans, 1984), 213; J. Gresham Machen, *The Christian View of Man* (London: Banner of Truth, 1965), 154; Francis Turretin, *Institutes of Elenctic Theology*, trans. George Musgrave Giger, ed. James T. Jennison Jr. (Phillipsburg, NJ: P&R, 1992), 1:585, §8.6.10-13; R. L. Dabney, *Lectures in Systematic Theology* (Grand Rapids: Zondervan, 1972), 303; Herman Witsius, *Economy of the Covenants Between God and Man: Comprehending a Complete Body of Divinity*, trans. William Crookshank (1822; repr., Phillipsburg, NJ: P&R, 1990), 1:75, §1.4.7.

[7] Geerhardus Vos, *The Pauline Eschatology* (Phillipsburg: P&R, 1979), 325n1; Vos, *Biblical Theology* (Grand Rapids: Eerdmans, 1948), 22; Witsius, *Economy*, 1:75, §1.4.7.

The upshot of all this is that the exodus story line is the salvation story line in miniature.

One very important point that emerges from this structural analysis is that the central thrust of the Song of the Sea and of the exodus motif, as represented in the Psalms, Prophets, and throughout this book, is that it is about more than mere liberation. It is not merely a political liberation, as some would have it in contemporary political readings of Exodus. It is about God accomplishing the redemption of his people so they may commune with him and worship him in the wilderness at the foot of Sinai. But it is about more even than that. As we noted in the Gospels, Jesus understood his own ministry as primarily liberation from Satan, sin, and death. Ultimately, the goal is to lead the people into a holy abode, a place where they may worship God. The holy abode, as seen in Revelation, is the new Jerusalem, a realm in which God's name will be placed above every other name and every tear will be wiped away. There will be peace.

Our postmodern culture cries out for a space where injustice is resolved, where meaning and significance can be discovered, and where passions poured into causes will make a difference. Young people yearn for a better world than the one presented by political parties, power-hungry politicians, greedy moneymongers, and the previous generation that raised them. They pine for a space they define as a better world than the one they observe. They imagine a better story. Like a diamond's many facets reflecting beautiful shafts of color when held and turned just right, so the Bible's presentation of the exodus motif through its various genres may generate a glimpse of a beautiful yet unrealized kingdom.

Third, I would like to make some suggestions with regard to systematic theology and the Christian life. I have argued throughout the book that the exodus motif is a synecdoche for the whole salvation complex. It is perhaps possible that the claims made here provide a way of talking about salvation that bridges a chasm created by many recent debates in the academy and the church, particularly the issue of participationist schemes versus juridical understandings of salvation.[8] By now it should be obvious

---

[8] For a helpful, terse outline of the debate, see N. T. Wright, *Paul and the Faithfulness of God*, Christian Origins and the Question of God 4 (Minneapolis: Fortress, 2013), 779. See, on the ecclesiastical

that I am not proposing to compromise the necessary legal and juridical foundations of salvation. Nevertheless, by taking up a large motif like the exodus, perhaps there can be some rapprochement between frequently divided camps in order to enter into more constructive discussion.

I made the claim repeatedly throughout this book that discussing the whole complex of salvation is necessary if we are to fairly present God's plan of redemption. This project has provided a big-picture response to any who would suggest that mere participationist schemes or union with Christ is a way to avoid the issues. It is not. The biblical data has to be faced. What is helpful about the kind of approach I am taking in this book is that it avoids the common battle lines drawn between the constant concern over participation versus forensic (legal) accounts of salvation. I am not using "forensic" in the same sense as the new "apocalyptic" school does in their interpretation of Paul.[9] Rather, I am using the term in the more traditional sense in which the "old perspective" on Paul did. In my view this is not a retroversion to a bygone, exhausted paradigm.

The exodus story, rather, is definitely construed along the lines of enforcing legal claims. As David Daube claimed years ago, it is exemplified in "God's demand to Pharaoh 'Israel is my son. . . . Let my son go'" (cf. Ex 4:22-23).[10] This is clearly legal terminology.[11] As I have demonstrated, studying the exodus motif necessarily brings us into contact with the divine warrior motif. Consequently, juridical, military, and forensic terms and categories cannot be neglected through redemptive history.[12] We have been rescued, and the conquering King expects his due.

---

side of things, Mark A. Garcia, "*Sic et Non: Views in Review*: Westminster Seminary California Distinctives? Part III," *The Confessional Presbyterian* 10 (2014): 171-86.

[9]See N. T. Wright's response to recent critiques in *The Paul Debate: Critical Questions for Understanding the Apostle* (Waco, TX: Baylor University Press, 2015), 41-64. For Wright's clearest and fullest statements on "apocalyptic," see N. T. Wright, "The Challenge of Dialogue: A Partial and Preliminary Response," in *God and the Faithfulness of Paul*, ed. Christoph Heilig, J. Thomas Hewitt, and Michael F. Bird, WUNT 2.413 (Tübingen: Mohr Siebeck, 2016), 711-70, esp. 743-54.

[10]David Daube, *The Exodus Pattern in the Bible* (London: Faber and Faber, 1963), 13. Daube's aim is a very narrow one, "to call attention to the social and legal affiliations of the pattern generally neglected, and to say something about their antecedents and effects" (14).

[11]Ibid., 29.

[12]See Daniel Reid, "The Christus Victor Motif" (PhD diss., Fuller Theological Seminary, 1982), 4-5, who states, "Military and juridical functions both belong to the sphere of a king and thus are often intermingled. This is true in the OT pictures of God and Messiah and carries over into the NT.

The one greater than Moses, the true Son of God, has become the agent of a new exodus. He has brought an end to the exile and has brought about the new creation in the lives of Christians: "If anyone is in Christ, the new creation has come: The old has gone, the new is here!" (2 Cor 5: 17). David VanDrunen describes the profound implications this has for the Christian life:

> The Christian life should *not* follow the pattern that the first Adam was supposed to follow. Christians are not to pursue righteous obedience in the world and then, as a consequence, enter the world-to-come. Instead, Christians have been made citizens of the world-to-come by a free gift of grace and now, as a consequence, are to live righteous and obedient lives in this world. Christians do not pick up and continue the task of Adam. Thanks be to the finished work of Christ, Christians should view their cultural activities in a radically different way from the way that the first Adam viewed his. We pursue cultural activities in response to the fact that the new creation has already been achieved, not in order to contribute to its achievement.[13]

Knowing that one is forgiven, knowing that Christ is the agent of the new exodus who has procured all the benefits of this liberating act on behalf of his people, has profound ramifications for how we live our lives.

But being brought into God's presence by his marvelous victory also cannot leave the subject of union with Christ alone since the only way a sinner can approach God and come into his presence is through Christ. Nor can union with Christ be substituted as an escape hatch to avoid the debate as if relational and transformative participation could replace or cancel the legal side of justification.[14] This is a false dichotomy.

In the book of Revelation Jesus is both judge and warrior, in John the conflict may be pictured as a cosmic trial between the Church and Christ on the one hand, and the devil on the other. In Paul it is translated into the analogy of 'how a conqueror makes the defeated enemies his slaves.' Both military and forensic terms are thus combined in Rom. 5–8 and man's liberation from sin is expressed as a deliverance from guilt and bondage."

[13]David VanDrunen, *Living in God's Two Kingdoms: A Biblical Vision for Christianity and Culture* (Wheaton, IL: Crossway, 2010), 56-57.

[14]See Geerhardus Vos, "The Alleged Legalism in Paul's Doctrine of Justification," in *Redemptive History and Biblical Interpretation: The Shorter Writings of Geerhardus Vos*, ed. Richard B. Gaffin Jr. (Phillipsburg, NJ: P&R, 1980), 384.

My view is best summarized by the Westminster divines, who indicate that justification is not prior to or the basis of union with Christ; however, justification is prior to sanctification.[15] To wit, it is prior to sanctification in the order of salvation (*ordo salutis*) as traditionally conceived (i.e., calling, faith, justification, adoption, sanctification, and glorification) in classic Reformed theology.[16] The Westminster divines wrote in the following question in their larger catechism (Q. 69), "What is the communion in grace which the members of the invisible church have with Christ?" The answer they gave is, "The communion in grace which the members of the invisible church have with Christ, is their partaking of the virtue of his mediation, in their justification, adoption, sanctification, and whatever else, in this life, manifests their union with him." Third, a major claim that must be maintained here is that "justification is *the necessary prerequisite* of the sanctified moral life."[17] Knowing that one is forgiven, completely and freely, matters greatly for demonstrable, grateful obedience in the Christian life. Demonstrated holiness is necessary for entitlement to the world-to-come, but this should not be construed in such a manner as to endanger the doctrines of free grace. The bias of all humans is to seek salvation not by means of faith alone in our Lord Jesus Christ alone but by relying in some sense on their own works as contributing to their eternal happiness.[18]

Finally, I will conclude with some comments on Christian prayer and piety. The language of the exodus and God leading his people by the pillar of cloud and fire to their inheritance was never far from Paul's mind and the minds of the early Christians. The liberation that the early Christians experienced through Jesus, especially the resurrected Jesus, pushed them into new patterns of prayer.[19] Therefore, tracing the exodus motif and its

---

[15]See Westminster Confession of Faith 10.1-2.
[16]This is the sense in which there is a prioritization of the forensic over the transformative elements in salvation. See, e.g., J. V. Fesko, "Vos and Berkhof on Union with Christ and Justification," *Calvin Theological Journal* 47 (2012): 50-71.
[17]See the excellent discussion in David VanDrunen, *Divine Covenants and Moral Order: A Biblical Theology of Natural Law* (Grand Rapids: Eerdmans, 2014), 437-40.
[18]See esp. Edward Fisher, *The Marrow* (Fearn, UK: Christian Focus, 2009), 358-61.
[19]Wright, *Paul Debate*, 38-39.

fulfillment in the new exodus may have ramifications for our use of the Lord's Prayer. For example, N. T. Wright published a brief article on the Lord's Prayer years ago that considered the prayer in light of the new exodus.[20] Wright proposes that the Lord's Prayer is now the "true Exodus" prayer for God's people, which reflects that Jesus viewed his own ministry as a "New Exodus" and that the Lord's Prayer itself encapsulates this. In short, according to Wright, the Lord's Prayer should be viewed from a new exodus perspective. He suggests several lines of thought for how God's "people of the New Exodus" might see with fresh eyes how to incorporate the Lord's Prayer into their pilgrim lives.

More recently, Brant Pitre published a brief piece on the same subject.[21] Pitre sees his article as building on and strengthening Wright's proposal for the Lord's Prayer. Most significantly, Pitre argues that the Lord's Prayer is best understood by exploring the OT context of the language and imagery in the prayer itself for the actions of the God portrayed in the events of the exodus becomes a prototype of how God will save his people in the end times. Each line of the Lord's Prayer, according to Pitre, is a prayer for the new exodus and everything that entails. Other ramifications of the exodus motif for our piety and practice in the church may occur by exploring the connections between Israel's baptism and the Christian's. Since baptism is painted with exodus hues in Scripture, Wright, for example, thinks that the Lord's Prayer should appropriately take place with the liturgy of baptism, and the Eucharist as well.[22] This may strengthen our understanding of the relationships between 1 Corinthians 10:1-4, for example, and Isaiah 63:11 and following. There is much grist for the biblical, theological, and ecclesiological mill here.

Maranatha!

---

[20] N. T. Wright, "The Lord's Prayer as a Paradigm for Christian Prayer," in *Into God's Presence: Prayer in the New Testament*, ed. Richard N. Longenecker (Grand Rapids: Eerdmans, 2001), 132-54.
[21] Brant Pitre, "The Lord's Prayer and the New Exodus," *Letter & Spirit* 2 (2006): 69-96.
[22] Wright, "Lord's Prayer," 148.

Appendix

INTERTEXTUALITY

In this appendix I identify how allusions work in biblical literature.¹ The purpose here is to drill deeper into the issues presented in chapter one. Texts often form allusive and perhaps dictional links with other texts. In other words, many texts use the same concepts and words. This raises the question of whether "quotation" is bare citation of words and phrases or whether it may be incorporated into the category of intertextuality along with the use of images or literary form. In short, what constitutes influence of one text on another? In what follow, we will overview the history of intertextuality studies, focusing on two theorists, Julia Kristeva and Mikhail Bakhtin, together with linguist Ferdinand de Saussure. Then we will discuss author-oriented and reader-oriented forms of intertextuality and their influence on biblical studies, followed by a close look at the definition of a text and precision in terminology.

History of Intertextuality Studies

The term *intertextuality* and the practice of its method in all its various forms is widespread in current scholarly discourse, including biblical studies.² As Michael Schneider states, "Since Julia Kristeva introduced the concept into debates in the fields of linguistics and literature, it has

---

¹See, e.g., Udo J. Hebel, "Towards a Descriptive Poetics of *Allusion*," in *Intertextuality*, ed. Heinrich F. Plett (New York: De Gruyter, 1991), 135-64.

²George Aichele, Peter Miscall, and Richard Walsh, "An Elephant in the Room: Historical-Critical and Postmodern Interpretations of the Bible," *JBL* 128, no. 2 (2009): 383-404. For historical criticism, the term *intertextual* is used rather sloppily to refer to the so-called comparative method (the Bible's interaction with extrabiblical texts) or innerbiblical influence of an earlier text on a later one. Contrary to this designation, postmodern approaches tend to use the term to describe the relationship between texts (regardless of chronological order) that readers establish.

steadily gained importance beyond these fields."[3] Kristeva emphasized the reuse of previous texts instead of the autonomy of texts.[4] Until recently, except among a very small group of biblical exegetes and theologians, there has been a significant absence of theoretical reflections on the matter of intertextuality. Simultaneously, an unprecedented amount of confusion has arisen over the hermeneutical status of intertextuality.[5] Seismic movements are occurring in literary analysis, and they are profoundly influencing biblical studies.[6]

As mentioned in chapter one of this book, Julia Kristeva was the first to coin the word *intertextual*.[7] Her influence is profound because she is largely responsible for mediating to the West the semiotic ideas of one of the leading Russian thinkers of the twentieth century, Mikhail Bakhtin. Kristeva and Bakhtin are arguably two of the most influential figures in modern literary critical theory.

For Kristeva, Western culture is in a crisis concerning values and meaning as conveyed in language.[8] Her definitions of intertextuality were meant to demonstrate that any text is a mosaic of quotations from other texts and that any given text is in some sense absorbing other texts. The primary question is, who determines meaning in the text and what controls that meaning? Is it controlled by the original author's intent and horizon of understanding, or are meaning and sense in a text determined by subsequent readers and their interpretations based on what the signs in a text mean for them in their subsequent horizon of understanding?

---

[3]Michael Schneider, "How Does God Act? Intertextual Readings of 1 Corinthians 10," in *Reading the Bible Intertextually*, ed. Richard B. Hays, Stefan Alkier, and Leroy A. Huizenga (Waco, TX: Baylor University Press, 2009), 41.
[4]Daniel Estes, "The Psalms, the Exodus, and Israel's Worship," in *Reverberations of the Exodus in Scripture*, ed. R. Michael Fox (Eugene, OR: Pickwick, 2014), 37.
[5]G. D. Miller, "Intertextuality in Old Testament Research," *CurBR* 9 (2010): 283-309, esp. 305.
[6]Some scholars even speak of a "structural turn," by which they mean the intellectual environment following the structural revolution in linguistics, anthropology, and literary studies—indeed all across the social and human sciences—and involving such names as Saussure, Peirce, Barthes, Derrida, Foucault, and Kristeva.
[7]This is not to suggest that the concept of intertextuality has not been present as a rhetorical category for centuries. On this, see Heinrich F. Plett, "Rhetoric and Intertextuality," *Rhetorica* 17, no. 3 (Summer 1999): 313-29.
[8]See Hans-Peter Mai, "Bypassing Intertextuality: Hermeneutics, Textual Practice, Hypertext," in *Intertextuality*, ed. Heinrich F. Plett (New York: De Gruyter, 1991), 47.

Like Kristeva, Bakhtin had a deep concern over values and meaning communicated in language, as well as what he considered a profound and all-pervasive alienation from self and the world that marked the West.[9] As a practicing psychoanalyst, Kristeva utilized the findings of Sigmund Freud and Jacques Lacan, weaving the disciplines of linguistics, psychoanalysis, and philosophy into an integrated approach and bringing it to bear on literature, art, and poetry. Her simple recognition, as noted, is that any text is a mosaic of quotations from other texts.

Kristeva saw Bakhtin's work as crucial for its incorporation of insights from Russian formalism, an influential theory of literary criticism in Russia during the early twentieth century, but she also viewed Bakhtin's work as crucial for moving beyond those theories to address Western culture and the crisis in meaning she perceived.[10] Bakhtin had written provocatively about Fyodor Dostoyevsky's novels, attempting to broaden the traditional concept of authorship by suggesting that the characters represented in Dostoyevsky's works speak with their own voices in addition to the traditionally emphasized author's (i.e., narrator's) voice. Bakhtin claimed that Dostoyevsky created the "polyphonic novel," in which "polyphony means that the characters have real voices, and this entails a radical revision [or rethinking] of the author's role and position."[11] Dostoyevsky, according to Bakhtin, had developed a dialogical way of writing in which "the characters represent different views of the world that are not resolved into *one* truth."[12] *Dialogical* here focuses on the notion that "different textual surfaces intersect in a literary work."[13]

---

[9] See Katerina Clark and Michael Holquist, *Mikhail Bakhtin* (Cambridge, MA: Harvard University Press, 1984), 77. In the late 1960s, the cultural function of the humanities, especially literature, was at stake with a broad consensus, especially in Europe, that the intellectual community was falling apart. See Mai, "Bypassing Intertextuality," 33.

[10] For Bakhtin's distinctions from the Russian formalists, see Tzvetan Todorov, *Literature and Its Theorists: A Personal View of Twentieth-Century Criticism*, trans. Catherine Porter (Ithaca, NY: Cornell University Press, 1987), 70-88, esp. 72-74.

[11] Kevin J. Vanhoozer, *Remythologizing Theology: Divine Action, Passion, and Authorship* (Cambridge: Cambridge University Press, 2010), 311.

[12] Stefan Alkier, "Intertextuality and the Semiotics of Biblical Texts," in Hays, Alkier, and Huizenga, *Reading the Bible Intertextually*, 5.

[13] Antti Laato, *History and Ideology in the Old Testament Literature: A Semiotic Approach to the Reconstruction of the Proclamation of the Historical Prophets*, Coniectanea Biblica: Old Testament Series 14 (Stockholm: Almquist & Wiskell International, 1996), 302. For Bakhtin, this notion was as

For Bakhtin, every word spoken is freighted and delivered with a history behind it, a network of meaning that is assumed; every word is a response that is part of an ongoing chain of interactions that anticipate a future response. Dialogue for Bakhtin is more than mere literary influence. When Kristeva discovered this Bakhtinian notion, it seemed an apt fit for what she was suggesting with regard to intertextual influences. She extended Bakhtin's dialogical analysis from voices to texts. For Kristeva, it is not just a matter of what text influenced another; rather, the author has intruded himself or herself into a complex dialogue that includes the writing subject, the addressee, and a whole series of exterior texts. For Kristeva, this means the text is *transfinite*. That is to say, it is a plural dialogue between multiple factors: the subject that enunciates his or her own identity, the addressee (i.e., the reader), and the whole realm of language in all that it takes for granted in its "infinitely open 'set' that it constitutes," or the cultural norms and ideas that influence any writer composing a text.[14]

Kristeva generalized and broadened the Bakhtinian concept of dialogue.[15] For her the text is not defined as "the actualization of the verbal sign system nor as the verbal sign system itself. Rather, it is regarded as a 'transsemiotic universe'—that is, as a conglomerate of all systems of meaning and cultural codes, both in its synchronic and its diachronic networking."[16] What does Kristeva mean by this? An intertext is

---

revolutionary at the aesthetic level as Copernicus and Einstein had been for knowledge of the physical world (see Todorov, *Literature and Its Theorists*, 76). Todorov criticizes Bakhtin at just this point, however, suggesting that "Dostoevsky is not just one voice among others within his novel, he is the unique creator, privileged and radically different from all his characters, since each of them after all has a single voice, whereas Dostoevsky is the creator of this plurality" (80).

[14] Julia Kristeva, *Desire in Language: A Semiotic Approach to Literature and Art*, ed. Leon S. Roudiez, trans. Thomas Gora, Alice Jardine, and Leon S. Roudiez (New York: Columbia University Press, 1980), 173. No wonder she is characterized negatively by Porter as invoking the entire textual universe! See Stanley E. Porter, "Further Comments on the Use of the Old Testament in the New Testament," in *The Intertextuality of the Epistles: Explorations of Theory and Practice*, ed. Thomas L. Brodie, Dennis R. MacDonald, and Stanley E. Porter (Sheffield: Sheffield Phoenix Press, 2006), 98-110, esp. 99. In other words, taken to its logical end, such efforts in full discovery of the thickest possible meaning of a text could involve an interpreter in an infinite regress, let alone a fit of insanity.

[15] Magdolna Orosz, "Literary Reading(s) of the Bible: Aspects of a Semiotic Conception of Intertextuality and Intertextual Analysis of Texts," in Hays, Alkier, and Huizenga, *Reading the Bible Intertextually*, 192.

[16] Alkier, quoting Holthuis, "Intertextuality," 6.

never completely explicable.¹⁷ For our purposes, how does this apply to biblical studies?

There is a danger at just this point with regard to using intertextual methods, if intertextuality is not defined carefully and used conservatively.¹⁸ Although he appreciates intertextual methods as an important supplement to hear the unique voice of a text within a chorus of supporting voices, James H. Charlesworth has leveled a serious criticism against literary intertextuality without constraints when applied to other methods used in biblical studies. The danger is that we will lose focus on *particular* texts.¹⁹ Let me explain.

Kristeva wrote an important proposition in her groundbreaking book Σημειωτική [*Sēmeiōtikē*]: "Tout texte est absorption et transformation d'un autre texte" (Every text absorbs and transforms another text).²⁰ Charlesworth criticizes this as nonsense for two reasons. First, whenever one says "tout" (all), there is the danger of misrepresenting what one is trying to describe as a result of generalization (what he calls the "all fallacy"). Second, according to Charlesworth, Kristeva's saying "creates an abstract world divorced from phenomenal reality; that is, it reduces all texts to an imagined norm that may well be false to the author we are eager to understand."²¹ In other words, texts must be studied according to their own uniqueness, integrity, and identity. Nevertheless, despite these concerns, one cannot deny that human beings make meaning with words and sentences within social and cultural structures, a realization

---

¹⁷Heinrich F. Plett, "Intertextualities," in Plett, *Intertextuality*, 3-29, esp. 7. Also see Laurent Jenny, "The Strategy of Form," in *French Literary Theory Today*, ed. Tzvetan Todorov (Cambridge: Cambridge University Press, 1982), 34-63, esp. 48-49.

¹⁸See, e.g., Charles Lee Irons, *The Righteousness of God: A Lexical Examination of the Covenant-Faithfulness Interpretation*, WUNT 2.386 (Tübingen: Mohr Siebeck, 2015), 303-8, where he dismantles the methodology of Hays and Campbell for their combination of a "subjective theory of intertextuality" with Cremer's relational view of righteousness in their treatments of Gen 15:6, Hab 2:4, and Ps 143.

¹⁹See James H. Charlesworth, "Intertextuality: Isaiah 40:3 and the Serek Ha-Yaḥad," in *The Quest for Context and Meaning: Studies in Biblical Intertextuality in Honor of James A. Sanders*, ed. Craig A. Evans and Shemaryahu Talmon (Leiden: Brill, 1997), 197-224.

²⁰Julia Kristeva, Σημειωτική [*Sēmeiōtikē*]: *Recherches pour une sémanalyse* (Paris: Editions du Seuil, 1969), 146, 255.

²¹Charlesworth, "Intertextuality," 203-4.

that has been worked out responsibly without granting all structuralist and poststructuralist presuppositions.[22]

Jonathan Culler has also polemicized against Kristeva.[23] He concludes—somewhat wrongly, I believe—that Kristeva's theory is an enterprise that can't be performed or mastered since it sets out a discursive space of unmasterable precursor texts. Nevertheless, if we are wholly dismissive of Kristeva's insights, might we lose potentially significant insights by not paying attention to the kind of poetics of allusions and intertextual connections that Kristeva's claims point out? In other words, making painstaking efforts to understand echoes and concatenated references between, among, and to other texts, traditions, and motifs may provide a much thicker and richer appreciation for what a particular text is intending to mean. Therefore, I am most interested in the mutual relationships between texts. Developing greater "allusive competence"— that is, developing an appreciation for the influence of one text on another—can greatly enhance our appreciation of the meaning of a text. The impact of Ferdinand de Saussure, the father of modern linguistics, is significant in this regard.

Saussure more than any linguist or philosopher has influenced how the modern world thinks about language study.[24] His influence on the wider cultural context, especially on the human sciences, is also profound. He made scholars aware that the content of words (lexemes) is determined by what exists outside words. That is to say, words stand for either concepts or objects. They do not have meaning in isolation but in relation to one another and to the environment in which they appear. Saussure is considered by many to have initiated the modern discipline of semiotics. The purpose of this special branch of linguistics is to "investigate the

---

[22]E.g., from a sociolinguistic perspective, see J. L. Lemke, who builds on notions of "register" and meaning as developed by M. A. K. Halliday, in "Ideology, Intertextuality, and the Notion of Register," in *Systemic Perspectives on Discourse*, vol. 1, *Selected Theoretical Papers from the 9th International Systemic Workshop*, ed. James D. Benson and William S. Greaves, Advances in Discourse Processes 15 (Norwood, NJ: Ablex, 1985), 275-93. Also see Lemke, "Thematic Analysis: Systems, Structures, and Strategies," *Recherches Sémiotiques* 3, no. 2 (1983): 159-87.

[23]See Jonathan Culler, *The Pursuit of Signs: Semiotics, Literature, Deconstruction* (Ithaca, NY: Cornell University Press, 1981).

[24]With the possible exception of Ludwig Wittgenstein (1899–1951).

production of the sign constitution of the text of enabled text senses."[25] Saussure suggested two approaches or perspectives on language and time, the aforementioned synchronic and diachronic approaches.

For Saussure, synchrony is described as "the axis of simultaneities," which considers the "relations of things which coexist, relations from which the passage of time is entirely excluded." Diachrony, by contrast, is "the axis of successions," in which "one may consider only one thing at a time. But here we find all the things situated along the first axis, together with the changes they undergo."[26] These divergent approaches markedly influence the debate about what constitutes literary influence and intertextuality in biblical studies.[27] Consider, for example, an intertextual exercise of comparing Psalm 113 with the Song of Hannah (1 Sam 2:1-10). Scholars pursuing a diachronic approach would ask questions and study factors that may lead to determining which text preceded the other. Scholars pursuing a synchronic approach (i.e., accepting the text as it has been received and is now) would recognize that it is extremely difficult, if not impossible, to determine with certainty which text preceded the other.[28]

It was my claim in this book that if biblical scholars already engaged in the cut and thrust of debate over intertextuality and its methods can pause to recognize terminological distinctions and the different questions

---

[25] Alkier, "Intertextuality," 251-52. There are different approaches to semiotics: the *structuralist* approach, which depends on Saussure, who studied the closed structure between syntactic and semantic relationships in terms of intratextuality; the *poststructuralist* approach, which is also dependent on Saussure, but because of criticisms of structuralism and because of Kristeva's work (among others), this second approach inquires about intertextuality that is opened to a wider field of sign/signified relations but is still based on a Saussure's binary sign model; and finally, the *categorical* approach, which is a triadic scheme (a text's sign system is worked out on the basis of syntactic concerns, semantics, and pragmatics). This last approach, which seems to be the method that yields the most explanatory power of texts, was first worked out by Charles Sanders Peirce and then made more accessible through the works of Umberto Eco and Charles Morris.

[26] Ferdinand de Saussure, *Course in General Linguistics*, ed. Charles Bally and Albert Sechehaye, trans. Roy Harris (Chicago: Open Court, 1983), 80.

[27] For a brief history of the development of these two approaches in biblical studies, see Martin Kessler, *Battle of the Gods: The God of Israel Versus Marduk of Babylon; A Literary/Theological Interpretation of Jeremiah 50–51* (Assen, Netherlands: Van Gorcum, 2003), 31-35.

[28] See, e.g., the stimulating study of Marianne Grohmann, "Psalm 113 and the Song of Hannah (1 Samuel 2:1-10): A Paradigm for Intertextual Reading?," in Hays, Alkier, and Huizenga, *Reading the Bible Intertextually*, 119-35.

being asked by their respective approaches, then they may realize that Kristeva and her followers have a point worth listening to. We need to recognize not only that texts interact with other texts but also that "texts have an interactive relation to cultures of various kinds."[29] One of the benefits of studying recent trends in literary studies and particularly intertextuality is that it forces the "scholar out into other texts and into other manifestations of culture to explore the deep-seated manifestations of foundations of which the text is a part."[30] Such an approach forces the reader not only into other particular texts but also into traditions, customs, and cultural ideas that had a formative influence on the biblical text.[31] Furthermore, by recognizing that authors may be influenced by common cultural concepts or traditions, we are safeguarded against identifying echoes between texts as intentional or deliberate allusions; that is, two biblical texts could be alluding to a common cultural concept and not to each other.[32] Subsequent texts may be, to borrow Vincent Skemp's language, "echo[es] within cultural intertexture."[33] This should help us understand the complex intertexture of ideas that may be woven throughout an ancient text.[34]

French structuralism, an important movement that began in the early 1900s, emphasized these kinds of complex interrelations.[35] It

---

[29]Vincent Skemp, "Avenues of Intertextuality Between Tobit and the New Testament," in *Intertextual Studies in Ben Sira and Tobit*, ed. Jeremy Corley and Vincent Skemp, CBQMS 38 (Washington, DC: Catholic Biblical Association, 2005), 43-70, esp. 46-47.

[30]A point developed eloquently by Peter Phillips in "Biblical Studies and Intertextuality: Should the Work of Genette and Eco Broaden Our Horizons?," in Brodie, MacDonald, and Porter, *Intertextuality of the Epistles*, 36.

[31]This point is nicely stated by Sylvia C. Keesmaat, *Paul and His Story: (Re)Interpreting the Exodus Tradition*, JSNTSup 181 (Sheffield: Sheffield Academic Press, 1999), 49.

[32]Skemp, "Avenues of Intertextuality," 47.

[33]Ibid., 54.

[34]Christopher A. Beetham, *Echoes of Scripture in the Letter to Paul to the Colossians*, Biblical Interpretation 96 (Leiden: Brill, 2008), 24-27. He calls this dynamic "parallel" based on his interaction with Richard Altick's *The Art of Literary Research*; however, he uses the term more broadly to also refer to themes and even doctrines rather than just textual relationships. In other words, there may be echoes in a later text that allude retrospectively to something that is extratextual or extralinguistic—e.g., a motif not anchored in a single text, a social practice commonly known.

[35]For a very good introduction to structuralism (including poststructuralism), see Ann Jefferson, "Structuralism and Post-structuralism," in *Modern Literary Theory: A Comparative Introduction*, ed. Ann Jefferson and David Robey, 2nd ed. (London: B. T. Batsford, 1986), 92-121.

rejected the longstanding notion that the author had sole authority over the text, substituting instead the concept of thought in relation. This concept has been alarming, to say the least, to scholars with a conservative bent and a desire to protect authorial intentions.[36] Only speaking of authorial intent, especially the psychology of authorial intent, without due regard for the reader has its own pitfalls.[37] Regardless, the important point for the modern reader to grasp is that the reigning concept in literary theory up to the early twentieth century—intersubjectivity—has been replaced with a notion of texts in relation with one another, "broadly understood as a system of codes or signs."[38] As Kristeva noted, "What allows a dynamic dimension to structuralism is his [Bakhtin's] conception of the 'literary word' as the *intersection of textual surfaces* rather than a *point* (a fixed meaning), as a dialogue among several writings: that of the writer, the addressee (or the character), and the contemporary or earlier cultural context."[39]

Texts, especially biblical texts, are to be interpreted in light of subsequent biblical texts. An appreciative reading of Kristeva's insights (without sharing all of Kristeva's ideological premises) performed in cross-disciplinary fashion may indirectly help Old Testament and New Testament biblical scholars recognize not only ancient Near Eastern and classical influences in the biblical text but also how those cultural echoes have been transposed by the biblical text in both testaments. This is one of the great dividends to be paid to the student of the Bible who becomes sensitized to intertextual reading. The reader is driven into the culture behind the text. We will now look at the influence of these trends on biblical studies.

---

[36]These reactions are responding to some juiced-up reader-oriented approaches that demonstrate little respect for what the author of an ancient text meant to say.

[37]For the famous essay that made the "intentionalist fallacy" an important part of modern theoretical interactions, see W. Wimsatt Jr. and M. Beardsley, "The Intentional Fallacy," *Sewanee Review* 54 (1946): 468-88. This essay was later published by Wimsatt in *The Verbal Icon: Studies in the Meaning of Poetry* (London: Methuen, 1954). Wimsatt and Beardsley were not against authorial intent; they merely wanted it properly nuanced.

[38]Steve Moyise, "Intertextual and Historical Approaches to the Use of Scripture in the New Testament," in Hays, Alkier, and Huizenga, *Reading the Bible Intertextually*, 23.

[39]Kristeva, *Desire in Language*, 65.

Synchronic Intertextuality: Reader Oriented

As discussed in chapter one, scholars interested in intertextuality studies usually divide the field into two major trends: synchronic or diachronic approaches. The synchronic approach has produced a heightened awareness of how quotation and allusion work. Let me address the complex issue of what is involved in the grammar of quotation, and then I will address synchronic versus diachronic concerns.[40]

In every use of quotation (or allusion), the following elements must be considered in order to explain an intertextual relation: intratextual coherence and intertextual coherence. First, texts in which quotations or allusions occur have an *intra*textual coherence. In other words, the most immediate integrity of the text coheres without reference to the quoted pretext: the text which incorporates a quotation from a previous text may stand alone and be understood as a self-contained unit. However, understanding the pretext (the text from which the quotation originally came) may enrich an interpreter's understanding. Second, all texts have structural relations with other texts and are therefore *inter*textual, especially when quotations or allusions are made in a text.[41] A quotation text (the text in which the quotation actually occurs) we will call T^1. Next, the previous text, from which the quotation is taken, we will simply call Q. As Heinrich Plett explains, "The form we usually call quotation [or we might add, allusion] possesses a twofold existence."[42] The quotation belongs to the pretext T^2 (this we can label Q^2) and then becomes a part of the quotation text T^1 (this we can label Q^1). In other words, the quotation belongs to two spheres. In this relationship, as Plett maintains, $Q^1 = Q^2$ and signifies the *intertextual identity*. However, what if you have an intertextual deviation? In other words, what if the quotation text is changed in some manner in the subsequent quoting text, that is to say, the quoted text from Q^2 is changed in some manner in Q^1?[43] Perhaps *modification* is

---

[40]For the following discussion on the grammar of quotation, I am indebted to Plett's essay "Intertextualities."
[41]Ibid., 5.
[42]Ibid., 10.
[43]Actually, any quotation by occurring in a new context is a kind of distortion of the source text. See the excellent article by Carmela Perri, "On Alluding," *Poetics* 7 (1978): 289-307, esp. 303-4.

a better word since it carries less pejorative implications and is present in theoretical discussions of allusion.[44] This can be explained as a "secondary grammar." Two levels are distinguished here. "Expression and content, or, to use a different terminology, surface and deep structure."[45]

Consider the following biblical example of intertextual deviation. In Romans 10:6-8, Paul quotes the Septuagint of Deuteronomy 30:11-14:

> "Do not say in your heart, 'Who will ascend into heaven?'" (that is, to bring Christ down), "or 'Who will descend into the deep?'" (that is, to bring Christ up from the dead). But what does it say? "The word is near you; it is in your mouth and in your heart," that is, the message concerning faith that we proclaim.[46]

In this passage, Paul has suppressed all language about "doing" from the quote as it occurred in its original context of Deuteronomy. In other words, Paul did not quote Deuteronomy 30 verbatim; he dropped verbs having the notion of "doing" in order to make his point in Romans 10: you can't add any of your own works to the calculus of salvation—it's God's initiation and work. Paul has suppressed something. Moreover, he has interpreted the original quote in light of Christ's incarnation and resurrection. Paul is not rewriting Moses at this point; rather, his position (as an apostle and positioned where he is in the course of redemptive history) dictates that he write from a stance of fulfillment: Christ is the second Adam who has gone through the death passage and fulfilled by his own work what Israel could not on her own (individually or corporately). Paul has added something, and Paul has subtracted something. He is "heightening certain elements ... in order to enhance the experience of the reader."[47] The point: God has taken the initiative and accomplished what no mere human could. Salvation has nothing to do with "doing" on the part of Israel, corporately or individually. It has

---

[44]See, e.g., Hebel, "Descriptive Poetics," 150-51.
[45]Plett, "Intertextualities," 9.
[46]For a more detailed discussion, see my "Leviticus 18:5 and Deuteronomy 30:1-14 in Biblical Theological Development," in *The Law Is Not of Faith: Essays on Works and Grace in the Mosaic Covenant*, ed. Bryan Estelle, John Fesko, and David VanDrunen (Phillipsburg, NJ: P&R, 2009), 109-46.
[47]In the language of Phillips, "Biblical Studies and Intertextuality," 44.

everything to do with faith, which is received as a free gift. In this case, $Q^1 \neq Q^2$ and the thicker level of meaning must be interrelated and understood by Paul's recipients (see fig. A.1).

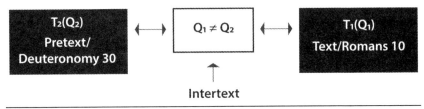

Figure A.1. Intertextual deviation in Romans 10:6-8

The method proposed here may have more explanatory power than quotation theories that look to ancient practices of "loose quotation" as providing answers for discrepancies that we find difficult to square with the modern notion of the inviolability of the author's original text.[48] Rather, this mechanism of intertextuality attempts to explain why an act of perturbation or disruption occurs.[49] In Bakhtin's terms, this dialogue extends well beyond the previous context of Deuteronomy 30. As Plett argues, "The more quotations [or we might add, allusions] are encoded in a . . . text, the more complex will be its intertextual deep structure, the more polyphonic the textual dialogue."[50] The prologue of Mark, which I examined extensively with its concatenated quotations and allusions in chapter seven, is an example of this complex intertextual structure.

In literary studies as well as in biblical studies, synchronic methods are often less concerned with how a text came to be through time. Students of the Bible approaching the text synchronically are primarily concerned with studying the final form of the text irrespective of how that text may have come to be, perhaps even over a long period of time. On the other hand, those who are concerned to study the text using a diachronic methodology will be applying a different set of questions to

---

[48]Here I have in mind Christopher D. Stanley's work *Paul and the Language of Scripture*, SNTSMS 69 (Cambridge: Cambridge University Press, 1992), 274.
[49]Jenny, "Strategy of Form," 59.
[50]Plett, "Intertextualities," 10.

the text to answer the primary question of how this text came to be in its present condition through time.

The influence of structuralism has led devotees of the synchronic approach to understand the meaning of texts apart from chronological concerns. "Diachrony is transformed into synchrony" is the battle cry of advocates of synchrony.[51] However, to demarcate the battle lines and categories as falling merely into "history and ahistorical ('experimental') approaches," as many have done in the past, may be too facile a construction on closer examination (at least in relation to Kristeva), as Christopher Hays points out.[52]

The upshot of the methodology of this synchronic approach is that it is not primarily the chronology of texts with which one is occupied (diachrony), nor the authors of those texts.[53] Rather, according to the synchronic approach, what should occupy the attention of exegetes is "the logical and analogical reasoning of the reader in interaction with the text."[54] Ellen Van Wolde states, "Without a reader a text is only a lifeless collection of words."[55] In other words, language must be responded to in order to generate meaning through communication.

Although historical criticism has raised our understanding of the background in which biblical texts were written, it has yielded disappointing results in interpreting texts. Hence, the proliferation of synchronic studies in biblical studies has arisen in order to understand Scripture in areas that were often neglected. "Structuralism . . . argues that such diachronic (historicist) interests are a barrier to true meaning

---

[51] Kristeva, *Desire in Language*, 65.
[52] Christopher B. Hays, "Echoes of the Ancient Near East? Intertextuality and the Comparative Study of the Old Testament," in *The Word Leaps the Gap: Essays on Scripture in Honor of Richard B. Hays*, ed. J. Ross Wagner, C. Kavin Row, and A. Katherine Grieb (Grand Rapids: Eerdmans, 2008), 28.
[53] Under the structuralist approach, as Jefferson ("Structuralism and Post-structuralism," 98) declares, "The critic's job is no longer to retrieve *the* meaning of a text, but rather, in the full knowledge that the meanings of the text are plural, to produce an interpretation which realizes just one of the possibilities contained in the text."
[54] Ellen Van Wolde, "Trendy Intertextuality?," in *Intertextuality in Biblical Writings: Essays in Honour of Bas van Iersel* (Kampen: Kok, 1989), 43. She integrates some interesting comments from Foucault's *Les mots et les choses* (Paris: Gallimard, 1969) into her discussion.
[55] Van Wolde, "Trendy Intertextuality?," 47.

and that the interpreter must consider only the synchronic (literary) presence of the text as a whole," says Grant R. Osborne.[56] When mere knowledge about an author and his or her background is in question, the synchronic approach's emphasis on the meaning of the text may be a welcome and chastening reduction to the vain attempts of traditional biblical critics with their Enlightenment assumptions.[57]

Even so, there are definite liabilities with the synchronic approach—or at least an extreme synchronic approach—of which we must be aware. First, do we really want to use this approach, which basically compares texts irrespective of any external historical reference or dating system (if such dating is achievable)? In other words, should we see "the benefits of simply reading two texts against each other without regard to historical priority, and the desire of many to play down literary canons, new and old alike"?[58] Do we really wish to concede that "the possibilities [of interpretations] are endless because, indeed, 'there is no end to the making of texts' (Eccles. 12:21b), or to the making of connections"?[59]

A second major problem is that focusing merely on the synchronic approach can lead to escapism with regard to hermeneutical responsibilities. No doubt the problems of intertextuality are many, but that does not warrant shirking our responsibilities as interpreters. For example, if the ancient horizon of the author and original readers is discernable, then it is our duty as readers to factor this into our interpretations. We have an ethical responsibility to do so. An extreme synchronic approach can be a lazy capitulation and at times actually "mask an abdication of critical rigor."[60] I would suggest that the author of a text does maintain certain control over our interpretation of texts.[61]

---

[56]Grant R. Osborne, *The Hermeneutical Spiral: A Comprehensive Introduction to Biblical Interpretation*, 2nd ed. (Downers Grove, IL: IVP Academic, 2006), 472.
[57]Hays, "Echoes of the Ancient Near East?," 42.
[58]Jay Clayton and Eric Rothstein, "Figures in the Corpus: Theories of Influence and Intertextuality," in *Influence and Intertextuality in Literary History*, ed. Jay Clayton and Eric Rothstein (Madison: University of Wisconsin Press, 1991), 12.
[59]Danna Nolan Fewell, "Introduction: Writing, Reading, and Relating," in *Reading Between Texts: Intertexuality and the Hebrew Bible* (Louisville, KY: Westminister John Knox, 1992), 17.
[60]Benjamin D. Sommer, *A Prophet Reads Scripture: Allusion in Isaiah 40–66* (Stanford, CA: Stanford University Press, 1998), 10.
[61]For an excellent, nuanced discussion, see Merold Westphal, "The Philosophical/Theological View,"

Diachronic Intertextuality: Author Oriented

Some would suggest that the diachronic approach should be categorized under the rubric of "influence and allusion."[62] It is concerned with "the affiliative relations between past and present literary texts and/or their authors," says Benjamin D. Sommer. "Influence-study generally entailed the practice of tracing a text's generic and thematic lineage. . . . [Studies of influence focused] on the ways literary works necessarily comprise revision or updating of their textual antecedents."[63]

Just as the synchronic approach has its attendant issues, so the problems with the diachronic approach can be manifold and peculiar to its methods. For example, there is the issue of dating texts. Sometimes we can confidently date biblical texts and identify the authors of those compositions. Other times, we are less sure. Another issue is the problem of hermeneutical horizon. As previously mentioned, we need to consider the author of any given text, the text's original horizon, and the horizon of the reader(s) and subsequent readers. A call to return merely to the text and to the author's intentions will be too simplistic if all these horizons and contexts and their complicated interplay are not brought into the picture, including the interplay of the reader and the patterns that are created (even in the reader's own mind) when reading a text freighted with motifs and allusions. If this is a problem for literary texts generally, it is even more complex when we consider the fact that Scripture is a text with a divine author as well as a human author and the divine author has intentions for further horizons than just the original horizon of the author/narrator of any biblical book.

Can there be no rapprochement between the synchronic and diachronic methodologies of intertextual relations? On the one side of the issue are some, like Sommer, who hold that there is a complete dichotomy between

---

in *Biblical Hermeneutics: Five Views*, ed. Stanley E. Porter and Beth M. Stovell (Downers Grove, IL: IVP Academic, 2012), 70-88, esp. 82-83.

[62]Sommer, *Prophet Reads Scripture*, 6-7.

[63]Ibid., 14. Renza has been very helpful here. See Louis A. Renza, "Influence," in *Critical Terms for Literary Study*, ed. Frank Lentricchia and Thomas McLaughlin (Chicago: University of Chicago Press, 1990), 186-202.

the synchronic and diachronic approaches.[64] On the other side, there have been a few adherents to a possible reconciliation between the methods. M. R. Stead, for example, argues that intertextuality is an umbrella term, encompassing both synchronic and diachronic concerns. He is much more optimistic about bridging what seems to be an impassable gap, that these two approaches are mutually exclusive and that there cannot be any rapprochement between them.[65] Stead incorporates the various approaches into a chart (see fig. A.2), and he delineates the issues along three spectrums.[66] Under the category of mosaic, he lists the different kinds of influence between texts along a spectrum of certainty. Under the category of dialogism, he signifies a spectrum of texts that either contend with each other or nuance each other. Under the category of the reader's role, he signifies a spectrum of the reader's role from generating new meaning to decoding an author's meaning in any given text.

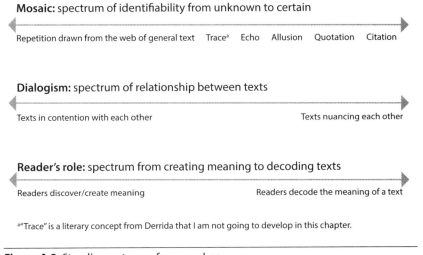

Mosaic: spectrum of identifiability from unknown to certain

Repetition drawn from the web of general text   Trace[a]   Echo   Allusion   Quotation   Citation

Dialogism: spectrum of relationship between texts

Texts in contention with each other   Texts nuancing each other

Reader's role: spectrum from creating meaning to decoding texts

Readers discover/create meaning   Readers decode the meaning of a text

[a]"Trace" is a literary concept from Derrida that I am not going to develop in this chapter.

Figure A.2. Stead's spectrum of approaches

---

[64]Sommer, *Prophet Reads Scripture*, 7. Sommer's position is driven in part by his commitment to a source-critical approach.
[65]M. R. Stead, "Intertextuality and Innerbiblical Interpretation," in *Dictionary of the Old Testament Prophets*, ed. Mark J. Boda and J. Gordon McConville (Downers Grove, IL: IVP Academic, 2012), 355-64.
[66]The chart is reproduced from ibid., 356.

Stead's diagram is helpful in demonstrating the complexity of possibilities and factors that go into interpreting a text. *Furthermore, his diagram indicates that both approaches, synchronic and diachronic, are attempting to obtain meaning by asking different kinds of questions.* In other words, approaching the biblical text with different methods and different sets of questions will necessarily yield different results. Asking historical questions about the original horizon of the text is important and will bring insight to the meaning of the text. Asking questions about how one scriptural passage relates to another is crucial since Scripture interprets Scripture and referencing one text to another often brings clarity. Asking questions about how a reader (either a reader contemporary with the time of composition or a subsequent reader in a later audience) can help us understand how the true and full sense of a scriptural text (illumined by the Holy Spirit) may evoke meaning and understanding.

Stead also argues that "these three sprectra of possibilities mean that there cannot be a single intertextual approach."[67] My own solution is to follow the lead of Kristeva herself by striving for terminological precision. Even she recognized the multiple connotations of intertextuality and attempted careful terminological definitions from the beginning.[68]

Breaching the Impasse: Defining Texts and Terminology

Every hermeneutical problem of meaning communicated in written texts begins and ends with the reader.[69] If we mean, to borrow speech-act categories, that the intended trajectory and aim of a speech utterance or text "hinges on the reader's response," then I could not agree more.[70] In

---

[67] Stead, "Intertextuality and Innerbiblical Interpretation," 356.
[68] A course suggested by Miller, "Intertextuality," 305. Kristeva actually opted for a different term, *transposition*, at one point because of the potential lack of clarification she saw the field of literary hermeneutics generating. By switching to the notion of transposition, Kristeva wanted to communicate "the possibility of passage from one signifying system to another, independently of any literary or aesthetic factors." See Jenny, "Strategy of Form," 43. On Kristeva's frustration with scholars that use *intertextuality* as a trendy label, see Mai, "Bypassing Intertextuality," 68.
[69] See Osborne, *Hermeneutical Spiral*, 465-521. Osborne provides a good introduction to and taxonomy of the major issues and players associated with current debates around meaning in the hermeneutics of texts, especially the biblical text.
[70] Kevin Vanhoozer, *Is There a Meaning in This Text? The Bible, the Reader, and the Morality of Literary Knowledge* (Grand Rapids: Zondervan, 1998), 367.

reality, at least three foci have to be engaged in the hermeneutical enterprise: the author, the text, and the reader.[71] In using the term *author*, I recognize that I am oversimplifying matters.[72] *Author* is a comprehensive and simplified term that includes the narrator or implied author in a text (e.g., Ecclesiastes) or a group of people (e.g., "the sayings of the wise" in Prov 22–24; certain psalms, such as "Of the sons of Korah").[73] Add to this the fact of allusion, citation, and "revision" of quoted Scripture, and we now have more than three foci: the "author" and his or her influences, the text, and reader(s). Readers include especially auditors of the original horizon (if that can be determined) and subsequent readers in future horizons. Hence, interpreting the meaning of any given discourse is a complicated endeavor.

Too often biblical scholars have not paused long enough to consider prolegomenous issues (i.e., first things). With this in mind, we want to give some care to defining our text theory. Let me say a few more words about the discipline called "semiotics," which we discussed previously and which will ultimately have a bearing on how we understand an author's intention and a reader's response in relation to understanding the meaning of a text.

It is best to understand "intertextuality as a subfield of semiotics of biblical texts."[74] Saussure claimed, "It is therefore possible to conceive of a science *which studies the role of signs as a part of social life*. It would form part of social psychology, and hence of general psychology. We shall call it *semiology* (from the Greek, *sēmeion*, 'sign')." Saussure goes on to say, "Linguistics is only one branch of this general science. The laws which semiology will discover will be laws applicable in linguistics, and linguistics will thus be assigned to a clearly defined place in the field of human knowledge."[75]

---

[71] Osborne, *Hermeneutical Spiral*, 465.
[72] For this suggestion of interpretation on "author," I am indebted to a conversation with Rev. Zach Keele, January 18, 2015.
[73] For a good summary of the concept of implied author, see Vanhoozer, *Is There a Meaning*, 238.
[74] Alkier, "Intertextuality," 7.
[75] Ferdinand de Saussure, *Course in General Linguistics*, in *Modern Criticism and Theory: A Reader*, ed. David Lodge (London: Longman, 1988), 8.

Umberto Eco (b. 1932) was a great popularizer of semiotics and intertextuality with his fictional publications.[76] He is often characterized as fitting into the poststructuralist movement. Moreover, a description of Eco's approach to semiotics can be derived from his many works.[77] For Eco, a text "is—according to semiotic terminology—a complex verbal sign (or a verbal sign complex) that corresponds to a given expectation of textuality."[78] Although this definition may seem cumbersome, it helps us cut through the battle between text-centered and reader-centered theories. All the various horizons that factor into the meaning and sense of a text are taken into account. The definition considers "signs and their relations to each other (syntactics), their relations to that which they designate (semantics), and their relations to sign users (pragmatics)."[79] For Eco, therefore, the intention of a given text is the joint responsibility of the author and the reader of the text since the addressee of any given speech utterance (and their context) must be evaluated.[80] Essentially,

---

[76]Eco's fictional works include *The Name of the Rose*, trans. William Weaver (repr., London: Vintage, 1992); *Foucault's Pendulum*, trans. William Weaver (London: Pan Books, 1990); *The Island the Day Before*, trans. William Weaver (repr., London: Mandarin/Reed, 1996); and *Baudolino*, trans. William Weaver (London: Vintage, 2003).

[77]See Umberto Eco, *A Theory of Semiotics* (Bloomington: Indiana University Press, 1976); *The Limits of Interpretation*, rev. ed., Advances in Semiotics (Bloomington: Indiana University Press, 1990); *The Role of the Reader* (London: Hutchinson, 1981); *Travels to Hyperreality*, trans. William Weaver (San Diego: Harcourt, 1986); *The Open Work*, trans. Anna Cancogni (Cambridge, MA: Harvard University Press, 1989); *Six Walks in the Fictional Woods: The Charles Eliot Norton Lectures 1993* (Cambridge, MA: Harvard University Press, 1994); *Mouse or Rat: Translation as Negotiation* (London: Weidenfield & Nicolson, 2003); *Serendipities* (New York: Columbia University Press, 2002); and "Between Author and Text," in *Interpretation and Overinterpretation*, ed. Stefan Collini (Cambridge: Cambridge University Press, 2002), 67-68. See also Stefan Collini, ed., *Interpretation and Overinterpretation: Umberto Eco with Richard Rorty, Jonathan Culler and Christine Brooke Rose; The Tanner Lectures 1990* (Cambridge: Cambridge University Press, 1992); Linda Hutcheon, *A Poetics of Postmodernism: History, Theory, Fiction* (New York: Routledge, 1988); and Norma Bouchard and Veronica Pravadelli, eds., *Umberto Eco's Alternative: The Politics of Culture and the Ambiguities of Interpretation* (New York: Peter Lang, 1998).

[78]Alkier quoting textual theorist János Petöfi, in "Intertextuality," 7.

[79]Alkier, "Intertextuality," 8. Pragmatics is the branch of linguistics especially interested in how language is used by speakers in certain contexts.

[80]Jason T. LeCureux, *The Thematic Unity of the Book of The Twelve* (Sheffield: Sheffield Phoenix Press, 2012), 35-39. Eco wants to understand intentions in a text, and he developed a triad of terms. There are three main axes in interpretation: *intentio auctoris* (author oriented), *intentio operis* (text oriented), and *intentio lectoris* (reader oriented). See Eco, *Limits of Interpretation*, 44-63. Later, Eco developed a fourth level of intention, *intentio intertextualis*. See Phillips, "Biblical Studies and

Eco's understanding of intertextuality is Bakhtinian and therefore also Kristevan.[81]

Scripture is made up of texts; therefore biblical interpretation can be described as "tri-lectic" since it should take into account the "author," the text, and the reader.[82] The divine author must be taken into account as well, as I emphasized in chapter one and throughout the book. This approach is more helpful than dividing interpretation along the customary dichotomous lines of synchronic and diachronic, or reader-oriented and author-oriented, approaches. I am attempting to help readers rethink their hermeneutical position and reexamine their opinions in light of other approaches with which they may not be familiar.[83] Consequently, it is helpful to distinguish two perspectives from which the text may be viewed: the "universe of discourse" perspective, and the encyclopedic relationships of the text (all the ways the text is situated in a cultural framework).[84] Such a theoretical discussion helps with understanding why scholars have reached an impasse: some have focused on authors, others have focused on readers, and still others have focused on the cultural and historical influences on the biblical author. Actually, all this must be considered to the degree such things are discernable.

The need for an allusion theory was addressed in the 1960s.[85] Ziva Ben-Porat has provided some of the most extensive analysis of identifying

---

Intertextuality," 35-45; see 43 for bibliographic references. By these notions, Eco describes how texts should be understood at even higher levels of sophistication. He identifies three levels of interpretation: conscious cases of direct intertextuality, in which an author is aware of influence from another text; subconscious intertextuality, in which subsequent readers are forced to recognize the influence of another text on an author; and finally, cultural intertextuality, in which influence derives from the realm of culture context. For a good, laconic description of Eco's goals in departing from facile descriptions of authorial intent, see the excellent book by the cognitive scientist Raymond W. Gibbs Jr., *Intentions in the Experience of Meaning* (Cambridge: Cambridge University Press, 1999), 264-66.

[81]See Phillips, "Biblical Studies and Intertextuality," 42.

[82]For the term *tri-lectic* I am indebted to Koog P. Hong, "Synchrony and Diachrony in Contemporary Biblical Interpretation," *CBQ* 75 (2013): 530.

[83]This is similar to the goal presented in Porter and Stovell, *Biblical Hermeneutics*, 24.

[84]I am indebted to Alkier, "Intertexutality," 8, here. He notes that he is depending on Umberto Eco's concept at this point.

[85]Chana Kronfeld, *On the Margins of Modernism: Decentering Literary Dynamics*, Contraversions: Critical Studies in Jewish Literature, Culture, and Society Series (Berkeley: University of California Press, 1996), 114-42.

allusions.[86] She thinks the reigning definition needs to be supplemented. Indeed, the literary history of the Bible depends on the national history of Israel. Furthermore, the sequence of events represented in the Bible depends on the known sequence of events in the social and cultural history of Israel.[87] Therefore, historical precedence is crucial, where it may be determined, when we are trying to determine that an allusion to another text is being invoked. Nevertheless, sometimes (especially in poetry) actual world referents of terms used by an author in a literary allusion sometimes diminish. Indeed, in Scripture there may sometimes only be an attenuated reference to a real-world term, person, or event in a poetic allusion since a poet may be inviting a reader to a putative, "imagined" world communicated in the text, one that could merely theoretically exist in the real world but does not.[88] Sometimes it is not a particular text that provides the source for an allusion, but rather echoed traditions. The archaeology of determining allusions is challenging.

Ben-Porat begins by clarifying terminological distinctions at the theoretical level. She regrets the neglect of vigorous analysis of allusion and attempts a clarification between literary allusions and other types of allusions. As for literary allusions she says,

> The literary allusion is a device for the simultaneous activation of two texts. The activation is achieved through the manipulation of a special signal; a sign (simple or complex) in a given text characterized by an additional larger "referent." This referent is always an independent text. The simultaneous activation of the two texts thus connected results in the formation of intertextual patterns whose nature cannot be predetermined.[89]

Ben-Porat's theory of allusion may be described as having several stages of recognition: "noticing the marker, identifying the source, bringing the

---

[86] Ziva Ben-Porat, "The Poetics of Literary Allusion," *PTL: A Journal for Descriptive Poetics and Theory of Literature* 1 (1976): 105-28, and Ben-Porat, "The Poetics of Allusion" (PhD diss., University of California, Berkley, 1967). For bibliography on other recent theoretical treatments on allusion, see Hebel, "Descriptive Poetics," 136.

[87] Lyle Eslinger, "Inner-biblical Exegesis and Inner-biblical Allusion: The Question of Category," *VT* 42, no. 1 (1992): 52-53.

[88] See Perri's nuanced discussion in "On Alluding," 292-98.

[89] Ben-Porat, "Poetics of Allusion," 108-9.

marked sign to bear on the interpretation of the sign which includes the marker, and also noting additional aspects of the source text which affect the reading of the alluding text generally."[90]

Ben-Porat takes pains to understand the nature of literary allusions in a way that goes beyond traditional dictionary definitions. According to her, the traditional views allow almost everything to come under the cover of allusion, making all literature "a massive tissue of allusion."[91] First, she asserts that the language of literature is opaque, "drawing attention to itself as well as its referents."[92] Second, she states that every reader is aware of certain conventions; every allusion is made within the bounds of a certain set of conventions constituting a genre. This point opens the way for the third point: the role of the reader. The nature of literature, according to Ben-Porat, is that "everything represented in a literature text is always presented only partially and with varying degrees of distortion."[93] It is, then, the reader's responsibility to provide the links to infer a pattern. Indeed, Ben-Porat is especially interested in bringing the role of the reader into the process of understanding allusions, something that has been strangely absent from traditional approaches to biblical literature.[94] Without neglecting the important philological and historical emphasis in biblical exegesis, by turning from merely the traditional text-oriented approach of biblical studies toward context-, author-, and audience-directed approaches to biblical allusions, we may further elucidate the meaning of a text.[95]

In this process of actualization, according to Ben-Porat, a reader goes through several stages. The reader takes an active, not passive, role in the interpretation of an allusion. In fact, the reader creates the complex patterns that form the makers in an allusion. "Recognizing, remembering, realizing, connecting"—all are important for a successfully performed

---

[90]Sommer summarizing Ben-Porat, in *Prophet Reads Scripture*, 15.
[91]Ben-Porat, "Poetics of Allusion," 24.
[92]Ibid.
[93]Ibid., 25.
[94]Ibid., 29.
[95]See, e.g., Perri, "On Alluding," 299–303.

allusion in literature.⁹⁶ This may sound dangerous especially to champions of the objective text common in many literary theories. Even so, Ben-Porat's point is that the reader plays a crucial and complex role in the development of a pattern whereby all elements of an allusion coalesce into the actualization of a meaningful allusion.

What must the reader do in these creative circumstances? "The reader must distinguish between a so-called 'allusion' to a word, which is actually a form of punning, and a literary allusion introduced by means of a word, which is a true allusion in the sense in which the term is used in this study," says Ben-Porat.⁹⁷ In a true allusion, in contrast to borrowing (i.e., citation), a reader implicitly agrees to invoke contextual meanings from the original context, incorporating something of the evoked text.⁹⁸

Ben-Porat's work on allusion is a good starting point; however, other scholars have developed certain criteria for determining the presence of an allusion as well. For example, Dennis R. MacDonald has set forth six helpful criteria for determining a conscious or deliberate allusion: accessibility, analogy, density, order, distinctive traits, and interpretability.⁹⁹ Order refers to sequential parallels between texts. "Distinctive traits" needs a little further explanation: since ancient authors use unusual details to alert a reader to the influence of one text on another, these clues can create deliberate allusion. The authorial intent behind particular allusions is MacDonald's interpretability. In other words, it involves the skill of grouping allusive functions. Richard Hays develops more criteria or tests for hearing echoes: availability, volume, recurrence, thematic coherence, historical plausibility, history of interpretation, and satisfaction.¹⁰⁰

---

⁹⁶Ibid., 301.
⁹⁷Ben-Porat, "Poetics of Allusion," 40.
⁹⁸Ibid., 92-93. She comments, "In a borrowing the reader agrees to disregard recognition of other texts within the text and not to activate the original context. The *only* criterion for allusion is the validity of the activation of elements from the summoned text."
⁹⁹Dennis R. MacDonald, introduction to *Mimesis and Intertextuality in Antiquity and Christianity*, ed. Dennis R. MacDonald (Harrisburg, PA: Trinity Press International, 2001), 2. The first two criteria (accessibility and analogy) concern popularity of a document and its likely availability to an author. Analogy for MacDonald is the search for similar texts and narratives by authors. Density is the third criterion: here someone may assess the "volume of parallels between two texts."
¹⁰⁰See Richard B. Hays, *Echoes of Scripture in the Letters of Paul* (New Haven, CT: Yale University Press, 1989), 29-32.

This is primarily an audience-oriented approach.[101] Others attempting to offer precision in this area are more concerned with an author-centered approach that maintains authorial intent with regard to allusions.[102] In modern biblical studies, Hays is often cited as a starting point for establishing allusions and echoes, although his criteria have not escaped criticism.[103] Likewise, Dale Allison has also established six criteria for determining allusions in the Bible.[104] Some biblical scholars have developed upwards of eleven criteria![105] Other scholars have produced even more stringent and (perhaps overly?) precise categories.[106]

Throughout the book, I have sought to help the reader with allusion competence by setting forth four categories with precise definitions: direct quote, subtle citation, allusion, and echo/reminiscence (see chap. 1). One of the chief questions in regard to intertextuality for this book has been determining when an author has deliberately selected and referred to a prior text. Trying to determine when an author is making associational links between texts is a challenge, especially if the allusion does not seem to be specifically marked. I would suggest that a prudential attitude is warranted when it comes to allusion hunting, for too often

---

[101]As is Christopher D. Stanley's groundbreaking work *Paul and the Language of Scripture*; see Stanley E. Porter, "The Use of the Old Testament in the New Testament: A Brief Comment on Method and Terminology," in *Early Christian Interpretation of the Scriptures of Israel: Investigations and Proposals*, ed. Craig A. Evans and James A. Sanders, JSNTSup 148 (Sheffield: Sheffield Academic Press, 1997), 92-93.

[102]See, e.g., Charles Lee Irons, *The Righteousness of God*, WUNT 2.386 (Tübingen: Mohr Siebeck, 2015), 301-6. See also Stanley E. Porter, "Allusions and Echoes," in *As It Is Written: Studying Paul's Use of Scripture*, ed. Stanley E. Porter and Christopher D. Stanley, SBLSymS 50 (Atlanta: Society of Biblical Literature, 2008), 29-40. Without going into detail, the problem as I see it is that Porter, who wants to maintain "authorial intent" for allusions and protect the notion that we find meaning in the actual words of the author of the text, argues that an author must know the work to which he or she alludes to be capable of making an allusion; however, for one thing, this does not take into consideration that an author may not be aware of the source of his or her use of stock phrases or concepts but may be merely picking up on common cultural patterns of the day. See the discussion above, especially Vincent Skemp's insights, under "History of Intertextuality Studies."

[103]See, e.g., Porter, "Use of the Old Testament," 83-84, and Alec J. Lucas, "Assessing Stanley E. Porter's Objections to Richard B. Hays's Notion of Metalepsis," *CBQ* 76, no. 1 (January 2014): 93-111.

[104]See Dale C. Allison Jr., *The New Moses: A Matthean Typology* (Minneapolis: Fortress, 1993), 19-23.

[105]Thompson, *Clothed with Christ: The Example and Teaching of Jesus in Romans 12.1–15.13*, JSNTSup 59 (Sheffield: JSOT Press, 1991), esp. 28-36.

[106]Beetham, *Echoes of Scripture*, 28-40.

we assume "that quotation or allusion is a conscious, almost forensic act on the part of an author."[107]

Conclusion

In this appendix I have tried to introduce the reader to some of the significant hermeneutical issues to be faced in intertextuality. Since I am convinced that students of the Bible and biblical scholars need to be aware of recent trends in other disciplines and develop further awareness of current practices, this appendix has trod through the murky waters of recent developments in linguistics and literary criticism especially as they touch on the birth and development of intertextuality. I have attempted, in a limited manner, to breach an impasse that has occurred in biblical studies and to ameliorate some of the present difficulties in hermeneutics.

---

[107]Phillips, "Biblical Studies and Intertextuality," 44.

BIBLIOGRAPHY

Abusch, Tzvi, John Huehnergard, and Piotr Steinkeller, eds. *Lingering over Words: Studies in Ancient Near Eastern Literature in Honor of William L. Moran.* Winona Lake, IN: Eisenbrauns, 1990.

Ackroyd, Peter R. *Exile and Restoration: A Study of Hebrew Thought of the Sixth Century B.C.* OTL. Philadelphia: Westminster, 1968.

———. "The Temple Vessels: A Continuity Theme." In *Studies in the Religion of Ancient Israel*, 166-81. VTSup 23. Leiden: Brill, 1972.

Adam, A. K. M., ed. *Handbook of Postmodern Interpretation.* St. Louis, MO: Chalice Press, 2000.

Aichele, George, Peter Miscall, and Richard Walsh. "An Elephant in the Room: Historical-Critical and Postmodern Interpretations of the Bible." *JBL* 128, no. 2 (2009): 383-404.

Alexander, Desmond T. *From Paradise to the Promised Land: An Introduction to the Main Themes of the Pentateuch.* Grand Rapids: Baker, 1995.

Allen, Leslie. *Psalms 101–150.* WBC 21. Waco, TX: Word, 1983.

Allison, Dale C., Jr. *The New Moses: A Matthean Typology.* Minneapolis: Fortress, 1993.

Altmann, Alexander, ed. *Biblical Motifs: Origins and Transformations.* Cambridge, MA: Harvard University Press, 1966.

Anderson, Bernhard W., with Steven Bishop. *Out of the Depths: The Psalms Speak for Us Today.* 3rd ed. Louisville, KY: Westminster John Knox, 2000.

Anderson, Bernhard W., and Walter Harrelson, eds. *Israel's Prophetic Heritage: Essays in Honor of James Muilenburg.* New York: Harper and Brothers, 1962.

Bailey, Kenneth E. *The Good Shepherd: A Thousand-Year Journey from Psalm 23 to the New Testament.* Downers Grove, IL: IVP Academic, 2014.

Bakhtin, M. M. *The Dialogic Imagination: Four Essays.* Edited by Michael Holquist, translated by Caryl Emerson and Michael Holquist. Austin: University of Texas Press, 1981.

Balentine, George L. "The Concept of the New Exodus in the Gospels." ThD diss., Southern Baptist Theological Seminary, 1981.

Banks, Diane. *Writing the History of Israel.* New York: T&T Clark, 2006.

Barr, James. *The Concept of Biblical Theology: An Old Testament Perspective.* Minneapolis: Fortress, 1999.

Barré, Michael L., and John S. Kselman, SS. "New Exodus, Covenant, and Restoration in Psalm 23." In *The Word of the Lord Shall Go Forth: Essays in Honor of David Noel Freedman in Celebration of His Sixtieth Birthday,* edited by Carol L. Meyers and M. O'Connor, 97-127. Winona Lake, IN: Eisenbrauns, 1983.

Barrett, P. W. "The Jewish Sign Prophets—A.D. 40–70: Their Intentions and Origin." *NTS* 27 (1981): 679-97.

Barstad, H. M. *A Way in the Wilderness: The "Second Exodus" in the Message of Second Isaiah.* Journal of Semitic Studies Monograph 12. Manchester: University of Manchester Press, 1989.

Barthes, Roland. *Image, Music, Text.* Translated by Stephen Heath. New York: Hill and Wang, 1977.

Bartholomew, Craig, et al., eds. *Out of Egypt: Biblical Theology and Biblical Interpretation.* Scripture and Hermeneutics 5. Grand Rapids: Zondervan, 2004.

Bater, Basil Robert. "The Church in the Wilderness: A Study in Biblical Theology." PhD diss., Union Theological Seminary in the City of New York, 1962.

Batto, Bernard F. *Slaying the Dragon: Mythmaking in the Biblical Tradition.* Louisville, KY: Westminster John Knox, 1992.

Baugh, Steven M. *Ephesians.* Evangelical Exegetical Commentary. Bellingham, WA: Lexham Press, 2016.

Beale, G. K. *The Book of Revelation: A Commentary on the Greek Text.* Grand Rapids: Eerdmans, 1999.

———. "The Cognitive Peripheral Vision of Biblical Authors." *WTJ* 76 (2014): 263-92.

———. *The Erosion of Inerrancy in Evangelicalism: Responding to New Challenges to Biblical Authority.* Wheaton, IL: Crossway, 2008.

———. *Handbook on the New Testament Use of the Old Testament: Exegesis and Interpretation.* Grand Rapids: Baker Academic, 2012.

———. *John's Use of the Old Testament in Revelation.* JSNTSup 166. Sheffield: Sheffield Academic Press, 1998.

———. *A New Testament Biblical Theology: The Unfolding of the Old Testament in the New.* Grand Rapids: Baker Academic, 2011.

———. Review of *Acts and the Isaianic New Exodus*, by David W. Pao. *Trinity Journal* 25 (2004): 93-101.

———, ed. *The Right Doctrine from the Wrong Texts? Essays on the Use of the Old Testament in the New*. Grand Rapids: Baker, 1994.

———. *The Use of Daniel in Jewish Apocalyptic Literature and in the Revelations of St. John*. Lanham, MD: University Press of America, 1984.

———. "The Use of Hosea 11:1 in Matthew 2:15: One More Time." *JETS* 55, no. 4 (2012): 697-715.

Beck, A. B., A. H. Bartelt, P. R. Raabe, and C. A. Franke. *Fortunate the Eyes That See: Essays in Honor of David Noel Freedman in Celebration of His Seventieth Birthday*. Grand Rapids: Eerdmans, 1995.

Beetham, Christopher A. *Echoes of Scripture in the Letter of Paul to the Colossians*. Biblical Interpretation 96. Leiden: Brill, 2008.

Bellis, Alice Ogden, and Joel S. Kaminsky, eds. *Jews, Christians, and the Theology of the Hebrew Scriptures*. SBLSymS 8. Atlanta: Society of Biblical Literature, 2000.

Ben-Porat, Ziva. "The Poetics of Allusion." PhD diss., University of California, Berkeley, 1967.

———. "The Poetics of Literary Allusion." *PTL: A Journal for Descriptive Poetics and Theory Literature* 1 (1976): 114-42.

Benson, James D., and William S. Greaves, eds. *Systemic Workshop*. Advances in Discourse Processes 15. Norwood, NJ: Ablex, 1985.

Bentzen, Aage. *King and Messiah*. London: Lutterworth, 1955.

Berding, Kenneth, and Jonathan Lunde, eds. *Three Views on the New Testament Use of the Old Testament*. Grand Rapids: Zondervan, 2008.

Berkhof, Louis. *Systematic Theology*. 4th ed. Grand Rapids: Eerdmans, 1984.

Best, Ernest. "Spiritual Sacrifice: General Priesthood in the New Testament." *Int* 14, no. 3 (July 1960): 273-99.

Bloom, Harold. *The Anatomy of Influence: Literature as a Way of Life*. New Haven, CT: Yale University Press, 2011.

———. *The Anxiety of Influence: A Theory of Poetry*. New York: Oxford University Press, 1973.

Boadt, Lawrence, and Mark S. Smith, eds. *Imagery and Imagination in Biblical Literature: Essays in Honor of Aloysius Fitzgerald, F.S.C.* CBQMS 32. Washington, DC: Catholic Biblical Association, 2001.

Bove, Mastrangelo. "The Text as Dialogue in Bakhtin and Kristeva." *Revue de l'Université d'Ottawa* 53 (1983): 117-24.

Brettler, Marc Zvi. *God Is King: Understanding an Israelite Metaphor*. JSOTSup 76. Sheffield: JSOT Press, 1989.
Bright, John. *Kingdom of God: The Biblical Concept and Its Meaning for the Church*. Nashville: Abingdon, 1953.
Brodie, Thomas L., Dennis R. MacDonald, and Stanley E. Porter, eds. *The Intertextuality of the Epistles: Explorations of Theory and Practice*. Sheffield: Sheffield Phoenix Press, 2006.
Brown, Raymond E. *The Death of the Messiah: From Gethsemane to the Grave*. 2 vols. Anchor Bible Reference Library. New York: Doubleday, 1994.
———. *An Introduction to the New Testament*. New York: Doubleday, 1997.
Brueggemann, Walter. *The Land: Place as Gift, Promise, and Challenge in Biblical Faith*. Overtures to Biblical Theology. 2nd ed. Minneapolis: Fortress, 2002.
———. *Message of the Psalms: A Theological Commentary*. Minneapolis: Augsburg, 1984.
———. "A Shape for Old Testament Theology, I: Structure Legitimation." *CBQ* 47 (1985): 28-46.
———. *Theology of the Old Testament: Testimony, Dispute, Advocacy*. Minneapolis: Fortress, 1997.
Bruno, Christopher R. "Readers, Authors, and the Divine Author: An Evangelical Proposal for Identifying Paul's Old Testament Citations." *WTJ* 71 (2009): 311-21.
Brunson, Andrew. *Psalm 118 in the Gospel of John*. WUNT 2.158. Tübingen: Mohr Siebeck, 2003.
Burnside, Jonathan. *God, Justice, and Society: Aspects of Law and Legality in the Bible*. Oxford: Oxford University Press, 2011.
Calduch-Benages, Núria, and Jan Liesen. *Deuterocanonical and Cognate Literature: Yearbook 2006; History and Identity: How Israel's Later Authors Viewed Its Earlier History*. New York: De Gruyter, 2006.
Cameron, Michael. *Christ Meets Me Everywhere: Augustine's Early Figurative Exegesis*. Oxford Studies in Historical Theology. Oxford: Oxford University Press, 2012.
Campbell, Anthony F. "Psalm 78: A Contribution to the Theology of Tenth Century Israel." *CBQ* 41 (1979): 21-42.
Caputo, John D., and Linda Martin Alcoff, eds. *St. Paul Among the Philosophers*. Indiana Series in the Philosophy of Religion. Bloomington: University of Indiana Press, 2009.
Carson, D. A., and John D. Woodbridge. *Hermeneutics, Authority, and Canon*. Grand Rapids: Zondervan, 1986.

Casey, Jay Smith. "Exodus Typology in the Book of Revelation." PhD diss., Southern Baptist Theological Seminary, 1981.

Cefalu, Rita. "Royal Priestly Heirs to the Restoration Promise of Gen 3:15: A Biblical Theological Perspective on the Sons of God in Genesis 6." *WTJ* 76 (2014): 351-70.

Ceresko, Anthony R. "The Rhetorical Strategy of the Fourth Servant Song (Isaiah 52:13–53:12): Poetry and the Exodus-New Exodus." *CBQ* (1994): 42-55.

Charlesworth, James H., ed. *The Messiah: Developments in Earliest Judaism and Christianity*. Minneapolis: Fortress, 1992.

Cheung, Alex T. M. "The Priest as the Redeemed Man: A Biblical-Theological Study of the Priesthood." *JETS* (September 1986): 265-75.

Childs, Brevard S. "The Sensus Literalis: An Ancient and Modern Problem." In *Beiträge zur alttestamentlichen Theologie; Festschrift für Walther Zimmerli zum 70. Geburtstag*, 80-93. Göttingen: Vandenhoeck & Ruprecht, 1976.

Clark, Katerina, and Michael Holquist. *Mikhail Bakhtin*. Cambridge, MA: Harvard University Press, 1984.

Clayton, Jay, and Eric Rothstein, eds. *Influence and Intertextuality in Literary History*. Madison: University of Wisconsin Press, 1991.

Clifford, Richard J. *The Cosmic Mountain in Canaan and in the Old Testament*. HSM 4. Cambridge, MA: Harvard University Press, 1972.

———. *Fair Spoken and Persuading: An Interpretation of Second Isaiah*. New York: Paulist Press, 1984.

Clowney, Edmund P. *Preaching and Biblical Theology*. Phillipsburg, NJ: P&R, 1961.

Coffey, John. *Exodus and Liberation: Deliverance Politics from John Calvin to Martin Luther King Jr.* New York: Oxford University Press, 2014.

Collett, Don. "Reading Forward: The Old Testament and Retrospective Stance." *Pro Ecclesia* 24, no. 2 (2015): 178-96.

Collins, Adela Yarbro. "Apocalyptic Themes in Biblical Literature." *Int* 53, no. 2 (April 1999): 123-24.

Cooper, Alan, and Bernard R. Goldstein. "Exodus and *Maṣṣôt* in History and Tradition." *Maarav* 8 (1992): 15-37.

Conrad, Edgar W., and Edward G. Newing. *Perspectives on Language and Text: Essay and Poems in Honor of Francis I. Andersen's Sixtieth Birthday, July 28, 1985*. Winona Lake, IN: Eisenbrauns, 1987.

Corley, Jeremy, and Vincent Skemp, eds. *Intertextual Studies in Ben Sira and Tobit*. CBQMS 38. Washington, DC: Catholic Biblical Association, 2005.

Cross, Frank Moore, Jr. *Canaanite Myth and Hebrew Epic: Essays in the History of the Religion of Israel.* Cambridge, MA: Harvard University Press, 1973.

———. "The Council of Yahweh in Second Isaiah." *JNES* 12 (1953): 274-77.

———. *Studies in Ancient Yahwistic Poetry.* SBLDS. Missoula, MT: Scholars Press, 1975. Reprint, Grand Rapids: Eerdmans, 1995.

Cross, Frank Moore, Jr., and David Noel Freedman. "The Song of Miriam." *JNES* 14 (1955): 237-50.

Crowe, Brandon. *The Obedient Son: Deuteronomy and Christology in the Gospel of Matthew.* BZNW. Boston: De Gruyter, 2012.

Culler, Jonathan. *The Pursuit of Signs: Semiotics, Literature, Deconstruction.* Ithaca, NY: Cornell University Press, 1981.

Currid, John D. *Ancient Egypt and the Old Testament.* Grand Rapids: Baker, 1997.

Dahl, Nils Alstrup. *Jesus in the Memory of the Early Church.* Minneapolis: Augsburg, 1976.

Daniélou, Jean. *From Shadows to Reality: Studies in the Biblical Typology of the Fathers.* Westminster, MD: Newman Press, 1959.

Daube, David. *The Exodus Pattern in the Bible.* London: Faber and Faber, 1963.

Davies, W. D. *Paul and Rabbinic Judaism: Some Rabbinic Elements in Pauline Theology.* London: SPCK, 1962.

Davis, Carl Judson. *The Name and Way of the Lord: Old Testament Themes, New Testament Christology.* JSNTSup. Sheffield: Sheffield Academic Press, 1996.

Dempster, Stephen. "Exodus and Biblical Theology: On Moving into the Neighborhood with a New Name." *Southern Baptist Journal of Theology* 12, no. 3 (2008): 4-23.

Denaux, A. "Old Testament Models for the Lukan Travel Narrative." In *The Scriptures in the Gospels*, edited by C. M. Tuckett, 271-305. BETL 131. Leuven: Leuven University Press, 1997.

Deterding, Paul E. "Exodus Motifs in First Peter." *Concordia Journal* 7, no. 2 (March 1981): 58-64.

Dillon, Richard J. "Mark 1:1-5: A 'New Evangelization." *CBQ* 76, no. 1 (January 2014): 1-18.

Doole, J. Andrew. *What Was Mark for Matthew?* WUNT 2.344. Tübingen: Mohr Siebeck, 2013.

Dozeman, Thomas B. *Exodus.* Eerdmans Critical Commentary. Grand Rapids: Eerdmans, 2009.

———. *God at War: Power in the Exodus Tradition.* Oxford: Oxford University Press, 1996.

———. *God on the Mountain: A Study of Redaction, Theology and Canon in Exodus 19–24.* SBLMS 37. Atlanta: Scholars Press, 1989.

Draisma, S., ed. *Intertextuality in Biblical Writings: Essays in Honour of Bas Van Iersel*. Kampen: Kok, 1989.
Dubis, Mark. "Research on 1 Peter: A Survey of Scholarly Literature Since 1985." *CurBS* 4, no. 2 (2006): 199-239.
Ducrot, O., and T. Todorov. *Encyclopedic Dictionary of the Sciences of Language*. Translated by C. Porter. Baltimore: Johns Hopkins University Press, 1979.
Dunn, James D. G. Review of *Jesus and the Victory of God*, by N. T. Wright. *JTS* 49, no. 2 (October 1998): 727-33.
Durham, John I. "Isaiah 40–55: A New Creation, a New Exodus, a New Messiah." In *The Yahweh/Baal Confrontation and Other Studies in Biblical Literature and Archaeology: Essays in Honour of Emmet Willard Harnick*, 47-56. Studies in the Bible and Early Christianity 35. Lewiston, NY: Edwin Mellen, 1995.
Duton, Denis. "Why Intentionalism Won't Go Away." In *Literature and the Question of Philosophy*, edited by Anthony J. Cascardi, 194-209. Baltimore: Johns Hopkins University Press, 1987.
Eliade, Mircea. *The Sacred and the Profane: The Nature of Religion*. New York: Harcourt, Brace & World, 1959.
Elias, Jacob W. "The Furious Climax in Nazareth (Luke 4:28-30)." In *The New Way of Jesus: Essays Presented to Howard Charles*, edited by William Klassen, 87-90. Newton, KS: Faith and Life Press, 1980.
Elliott, J. H. *A Home for the Homeless: A Sociological Exegesis of 1 Peter, Its Situation and Strategy*. Philadelphia: Fortress, 1981.
Elliott, Mark W., Scott J. Hafemann, N. T. Wright, and John Frederick, eds. *Galatians and Christian Theology: Justification, the Gospel, and Ethics in Paul's Letter*. Grand Rapids: Baker Academic, 2014.
Elton, G. R. *The Practice of History*. New York: Thomas Y. Crowell, 1967.
Enns, Peter. *Inspiration and Incarnation: Evangelicals and the Problem of the Old Testament*. Grand Rapids: Baker Academic, 2005.
Eslinger, Lyle. "Inner-biblical Exegesis and Inner-biblical Allusion: The Question of Category." *VT* 42, no. 1 (1992): 47-58.
Estelle, Bryan. "The Art of Synecdoche: Exodus & Conquest in Scripture." *Modern Reformation* 22, no. 6 (November–December 2013): 28-33.
———. "The Covenant of Works in Moses and Paul." In *Covenant, Justification, and Pastoral Ministry: Essays by the Faculty of Westminster Seminary California*, edited by Scott Clark. Phillipsburg, NJ: P&R, 2006.
———. "Noah: A Righteous Man?" *Modern Reformation* 19, no. 5 (September/October 2010).

———. "The Use of Deferential Language in the Arsames Correspondence and Biblical Aramaic Compared." *Maarav* 13, no. 1 (2006): 43-76.

Estelle, Bryan, J. V. Fesko, and David VanDrunen, eds. *The Law Is Not of Faith: Essays on Grace and Works in the Mosaic Covenant*. Phillipsburg, NJ: P&R, 2009.

Evans, C. Stephen. *The Historical Christ and the Jesus of Faith: The Incarnational Narrative as History*. Oxford: Oxford University Press, 1996.

Evans, Craig A., and James A. Sanders, eds. *Early Christian Interpretation of the Scriptures of Israel: Investigations and Proposals*. JSNTSup 148. Sheffield: Sheffield Academic Press, 1997.

Evans, Craig A., and Shemaryahu Talmon, eds. *The Quest for Context and Meaning: Studies in Biblical Intertextuality in Honor of James A. Sanders*. Leiden: Brill, 1997.

Evans, John Frederick. "An Inner-biblical Interpretation and Intertextual Reading of Ezekiel's Recognition Formulae with the Book of Exodus." ThD diss., University of Stellenbosch, 2006.

Fesko, J. V. *Beyond Calvin: Union with Christ and Justification in Early Modern Reformed Theology (1517–1700)*. Reformed Historical Theology 20. Göttingen: Vandenhoeck & Ruprecht, 2012.

———. "Vos and Berkhof on Union with Christ and Justification." *Calvin Theological Journal* 47 (2012): 50-71.

Fishbane, Michael. *Biblical Interpretation in Ancient Israel*. Oxford: Clarendon, 1985.

———. *Text and Texture: Close Readings of Selected Biblical Texts*. New York: Schocken, 1979.

Fisher, Edward. *The Marrow of Modern Divinity*. Fearn, UK: Christian Focus, 2009.

Fitzgerald, Aloysius, FSC. *The Lord of the East Wind*. CBQMS 34. Washington, DC: Catholic Biblical Association, 2002.

Fitzmyer, Joseph A. *The Semitic Background of the New Testament*. Biblical Resources. Grand Rapids: Eerdmans, 1997.

Ford, Josephine Massyngbaerde. "Shalom in the Johannine Corpus." *Horizons in Biblical Theology* 6, no. 2 (1984): 67-89.

Fox, Michael R., ed. *Reverberations of the Exodus in Scripture*. Eugene, OR: Pickwick, 2014.

France, R. T. "First Century Bible Study: Old Testament Motifs in 1 Peter 2:4-10." *Journal of the European Pentecostal Theological Association* 18 (1998): 26-48.

———. *The Gospel of Mark: A Commentary on the Greek Text*. NIGTC. Grand Rapids: Eerdmans, 2002.

Freedman, David Noel. "The Structure of Isaiah 40:1-11." In *Perspectives on Language Text: Essays and Poems in Honor of Francis I. Andersen's Sixtieth Birthday, July 28, 1985*, edited by Edgar W. Conrad and Edward G. Newing, 167-93. Winona Lake, IN: Eisenbrauns, 1987.

Frei, Hans W. *The Eclipse of Biblical Narrative: A Study in Eighteenth and Nineteenth Century Hermeneutics*. New Haven, CT: Yale University Press, 1974.

Funk, Robert W. "The Wilderness." *JBL* 78 (1959): 205-14.

Gage, Warren Austin. *The Gospel of Genesis: Studies in Protology and Eschatology*. Winona Lake, IN: Carpenter Books, 1984.

Galvin, Garrett. *Egypt as a Place of Refuge*. FAT 2.51. Tübingen: Mohr Siebeck, 2011.

Garr, Randall W. *In His Own Image and Likeness: Humanity, Divinity, and Monotheism*. Culture and History of Ancient Near East 15. Leiden: Brill, 2003.

Garrett, Susan R. "Exodus from Bondage: Luke 9:31 and Acts 12:1-24." *CBQ* 52, no. 4 (October 1990): 656-80.

———. "The Meaning of Jesus' Death in Luke." *Word and World* 12 (1992): 11-16.

Gibbs, Raymond W. *Intentions in the Experience of Meaning*. Cambridge: Cambridge University Press, 1999.

Gignilliat, Mark. "Paul, Allegory, and the Plain Sense of Scripture: Galatians 4:21-31." *JTI* 2, no. 1 (2008): 135-46.

Gillingham, Susan E. "The Exodus Tradition and Israelite Psalmody." *Scottish Journal of Theology* 52, no. 1 (1999): 19-46.

———. *The Poems and Psalms of the Hebrew Bible*. Oxford: Oxford University Press, 1994.

Glasson, T. Francis. *Moses in the Fourth Gospel*. Studies in Biblical Theology. London: SCM Press, 1963.

Goppelt, Leonhard. *A Commentary on 1 Peter*. Edited by Ferdinand Hahn. Translated and augmented by John E. Alsup. Grand Rapids: Eerdmans, 1993.

———. *Typos: The Typological Interpretation of the Old Testament in the New*. Translated by Donald H. Madvig. 1982. Reprint, Eugene, OR: Wipf and Stock, 2002.

Green, Joel B. "Identity and Engagement in a Diverse World: Pluralism and Holiness in 1 Peter." *Ashland Theological Journal* 55, no. 2 (Fall 2000): 85-92.

———. "Narrating the Gospel in 1 and 2 Peter." *Int* 60 (July 2006): 262-77.

Greenstein, Edward L. "Mixing Memory and Design: Reading Psalm 78." *Prooftexts* 10 (1990): 197-218.

Guthrie, Donald. *New Testament Introduction*. Rev. ed. Downers Grove, IL: InterVarsity Press, 1990.

Hafemann, Scott J., ed. *Biblical Theology: Retrospect and Prospect*. Downers Grove, IL: InterVarsity Press, 2002.

Halpern, Baruch, Jon D. Levenson, and Frank Moore Cross. *Traditions in Transformation: Turning Points in Biblical Faith.* Winona Lake, IN: Eisenbrauns, 1981.

Harmon, Matthew S., and Jay E. Smith, eds. *Studies in the Pauline Epistles: Essays in Honor of Douglas J. Moo.* Grand Rapids: Zondervan, 2014.

Haskell, Thomas L. *Objectivity Is Not Neutrality: Explanatory Themes in History.* Baltimore: Johns Hopkins University Press, 1998.

Hatina, Thomas R., ed. *Biblical Interpretation in Early Christian Gospels.* Vol. 3, *The Gospel of Luke.* JSNTSup 376. New York: T&T Clark, 2010.

———. *In Search of a Context: The Function of Scripture in Mark's Narrative.* JSNTSup 232. Studies in Scripture in Early Judaism and Christianity 8. London: Sheffield Academic Press, 2002.

Hays, Richard B. *The Conversion of the Imagination: Paul as Interpreter of Israel's Scripture.* Grand Rapids: Eerdmans, 2005.

———. *Echoes of Scripture in the Gospels.* Waco, TX: Baylor University Press, 2016.

———. *Echoes of Scripture in the Letters of Paul.* New Haven, CT: Yale University Press, 1989.

———. *Reading Backwards: Figural Christology and the Fourfold Gospel Witness.* Waco, TX: Baylor University Press, 2014.

Hays, Richard B., Stefan Alkier, and Leroy A. Huizenga, eds. *Reading the Bible Intertextually.* Waco, TX: Baylor University Press, 2009.

Heilig, Christoph, J. Thomas Hewitt, and Michael F. Bird, eds. *God and the Faithfulness of Paul: A Critical Examination of the Pauline Theology of N. T. Wright.* WUNT 2.413. Tübingen: Mohr Siebeck, 2016.

Higton, Mike. *Christ, Providence and History: Hans W. Frei's Public Theology.* London: T&T Clark, 2004.

Hill, David. "'To Offer Spiritual Sacrifices . . .' (1 Peter 2:5): Liturgical Formulations and Christian Paranesis in 1 Peter." *JSNT* 16 (1982): 45-63.

Hillers, Delbert R. *Treaty-Curses and the Old Testament Prophets.* Biblica et Orientalia 16. Rome: Pontifical Biblical Institute, 1964.

Hodge, Charles. *A Commentary on the Epistle to the Ephesians.* Grand Rapids: Eerdmans, 1950.

———. *A Commentary on the Epistle to the Romans.* Grand Rapids: Eerdmans, 1950.

Hoffmeier, James K., and Dennis Magary, eds. *Do Historical Matters Matter to Faith? A Critical Appraisal of Modern and Postmodern Approaches to Scripture.* Wheaton, IL: Crossway, 2012.

Hoffmeier, James K., Alan R. Millard, and Gary A. Rendsburg. *"Did I Not Bring*

Israel out of Egypt?" *Biblical, Archaeological, and Egyptological Perspectives on the Exodus Narratives*. Bulletin for Biblical Research Supplements 13. Winona Lake, IN: Eisenbrauns, 2016.

Holland, Tom. *Contours of Pauline Theology: A Radical New Survey of the Influences on Paul's Biblical Writings*. Fearn, UK: Mentor, 2004.

———. *Romans: The Divine Marriage*. Eugene, OR: Pickwick, 2011.

Hong, Koog P. "Synchrony and Diachrony in Contemporary Biblical Interpretation." *CBQ* 75 (2013): 521-39.

Horton, Michael S. *The Christian Faith: A Systematic Theology for Pilgrims on the Way*. Grand Rapids: Zondervan, 2011.

———. *Covenant and Eschatology: The Divine Drama*. Louisville, KY: Westminster John Knox, 2002.

———. *Lord and Servant: A Covenant Christology*. Louisville, KY: Westminster John Knox, 2005.

———. *People and Place: A Covenant Ecclesiology*. Louisville, KY: Westminster John Knox, 2008.

Howe, Bonnie. *Because You Bear This Name: Conceptual Metaphor and the Moral Meaning of 1 Peter*. Leiden: Brill, 2006.

Hunsinger, George, and William C. Placher, eds. *Theology and Narrative: Selected Essays*. New York: Oxford University Press, 1993.

Husbands, Mark, and Jeffrey P. Greenman, eds. *Ancient Faith for the Church's Future*. Downers Grove, IL: IVP Academic, 2008.

Hutton, Jeremy. "Isaiah 51:9-11 and the Rhetorical Appropriation and Subversion of Hostile Theologies." *JBL* 126 (2007): 271-303.

Idestrom, Rebecca. "Echoes of the Book of Exodus in Ezekiel." *JSOT* 33, no. 4 (2009): 489-510.

Irons, Charles Lee. *The Righteousness of God: A Lexical Examination of the Covenant-Faithfulness*. WUNT 2.386. Tübingen: Mohr Siebeck, 2015.

Isbell, Charles David. *The Function of Exodus Motifs in Biblical Narratives: Theological Didactic Drama*. Lewiston, NY: Edwin Mellen, 2002.

Itorgan, M. P., and P. J. Kobelski, eds. *To Touch the Text: Biblical and Related Studies in Honor of Joseph A. Fitzmyer*. New York: Crossroad, 1989.

Jefferson, Ann, and David Robey, eds. *Modern Literary Theory: A Comparative Approach*. 2nd ed. London: B. T. Batsford, 1986.

Jeremias, Joachim. *The Eucharistic Words of Jesus*. New York: Charles Scribner's Sons, 1966.

Jindo, Job Y. *Biblical Metaphor Reconsidered: A Cognitive Approach to Poetic*

Prophecy in Jeremiah 1–34. HSM 64. Winona Lake, IN: Eisenbrauns, 2010.
Jobes, Karen H. *1 Peter*. Baker Exegetical Commentary on the New Testament. Grand Rapids: Baker Academic, 2005.
Jobes, Karen H., and Moisés Silva. *Invitation to the Septuagint*. Grand Rapids: Baker Academic, 2000.
Johnson, Dennis. *The Message of Acts in the History of Redemption*. Phillipsburg, NJ: P&R, 1997.
———. *Triumph of the Lamb: A Commentary on Revelation*. Phillipsburg, NJ: P&R, 2001.
Kawashima, Robert S. "Comparative Literature and Biblical Studies: The Case of Allusion." *Prooftexts* 27 (2007): 324-44.
Keck, Leander E. "The Introduction to Mark's Gospel." *NTS* 12 (1966): 352-70.
Keel, Othmar. *The Symbolism of the Biblical World: Ancient Near Eastern Iconography and the Book of Psalms*. Translated by Timothy J. Hallett. Winona Lake, IN: Eisenbrauns, 1977.
Keesmaat, Sylvia C. "Exodus and Romans 8:14-30." *JSNT* 54 (1994): 29-49.
———. *Paul and His Story: (Re)Interpreting the Exodus Tradition*. JSNTSup 181. Sheffield: Sheffield Academic Press, 1996.
Kennedy, Joel. *The Recapitulation of Israel: Use of Israel's History in Matthew 1:1–4:11*. WUNT 2.257. Tübingen: Mohr Siebeck, 2008.
Kessler, Martin. *Battle of the Gods: The God of Israel Versus Marduk of Babylon; A Literary/Theological Interpretation of Jeremiah 50–51*. Assen, Netherlands: Van Gorcum, 2003.
Kiefer, Jörn. *Exil und Diaspora: Begrifflichkeit und Deutungen im antiken Judentum und in der Hebräischen Bibel*. Leipzig: Evangelische Verlagsstalt, 2005.
Kitchen, Kenneth A. *The Bible in Its World: The Bible and Archaeology Today*. Downers Grove, IL: InterVarsity Press, 1977.
Klassen, William, ed. *The New Way of Jesus: Essays Presented to Howard Charles*. Newton, KS: Faith and Life Press, 1980.
Kline, Jonathan G. *Allusive Soundplay in the Hebrew Bible*. Ancient Israel and Its Literature 28. Atlanta: SBL Press, 2016.
Kline, Meredith G. *By Oath Consigned: A Reinterpretation of the Covenant Signs of Circumcision and Baptism*. Grand Rapids: Eerdmans, 1968.
———. "The Feast of Cover-Over." *JETS* 37, no. 4 (1994): 497-510.
———. *Genesis: A New Commentary*. Edited by Jonathan G. Kline. Peabody, MA: Hendrickson, 2016.
———. *Glory in Our Midst: A Biblical-Theological Reading of Zechariah's Night Visions*. Overland Park, KS: Two Age Press, 2001.

———. *God, Heaven, and Har Magedon: A Covenantal Tale of Cosmos and Telos.* Eugene, OR: Wipf and Stock, 2006.
———. *Images of the Spirit.* Grand Rapids: Baker, 1980.
———. *Kingdom Prologue: Genesis Foundations for a Covenantal Worldview.* Overland Park, KS: Two Age Press, 2000.
———. "The Old Testament Origins of the Gospel Genre." *WTJ* 38, no. 1 (1975): 172-203.
———. *Structure of Biblical Authority.* Grand Rapids: Eerdmans, 1972.
Koch, K. "Ezra and the Origins of Judaism." *Journal of Semitic Studies* 19 (1974): 173-86.
Kraus, Hans-Joachim. *Psalms 60–150: A Commentary.* Translated by Hilton C. Oswald. Continental Commentaries. Minneapolis: Fortress, 1989.
Kristeva, Julia. *Desire in Language: A Semiotic Approach to Literature and Art.* Edited by Leon S. Roudiez. Translated by Thomas Gora, Alice Jardine, and Leon S. Roudiez. New York: Columbia University Press, 1980.
———. Σημειωτικη *[Sēmeiōtikē]: Recherches pour une sémanalyse.* Paris: Editions du Seuil, 1969.
Kronfeld, Chana. *On the Margins of Modernism: Decentering Literary Dynamics.* Contraversions: Critical Studies in Jewish Literature, Culture and Society Series. Berkeley: University of California Press, 1996.
Kselman, J. S. "Psalm 77 and the Book of Exodus." *Journal of the Ancient Near Eastern Society of Columbia University* 15 (1983): 51-58.
Kuhrt, Amélie. *The Ancient Near East, c. 3000–300 B.C.* 2 vols. New York: Routledge, 1995.
Kynes, Will. *My Psalm Has Turned into Weeping: Job's Dialogue with the Psalms.* BZAW 437. Boston: De Gruyter, 2012.
Laato, Antti. "The Composition of Isaiah 40–55." *JBL* 109, no. 2 (1990): 207-28.
———. *History and Ideology in the Old Testament Literature: A Semiotic Approach to the Reconstruction of the Proclamation of the Historical Prophets.* Coniectanea Biblica: Old Testament Series 14. Stockholm: Almquist & Wiskell International, 1996.
Lane, William L. *The Gospel According to Mark.* NICNT. Grand Rapids: Eerdmans, 1974.
Laniak, Timothy S. *Shepherds After My Own Heart: Pastoral Traditions and Leadership in the Bible.* New Studies in Biblical Theology 20. Downers Grove, IL: InterVarsity Press, 2006.
Laurent, Jenny. "The Strategy of Form." In *French Literary Theory Today*, edited by T. Todorov, 34-63. Cambridge: Cambridge University Press, 1982.

Leaney, A. R. C. "1 Peter and the Passover: An Interpretation." *NTS* 10, no. 2 (January 1964): 238-51.
Legaspi, Michael C. *The Death of Scripture and the Rise of Biblical Studies.* Oxford Studies in Historical Theology. Oxford: Oxford University Press, 2010.
Leithart, Peter J. *Deep Exegesis: The Mystery of Reading Scripture.* Waco, TX: Baylor University Press, 2009.
―――. "I Don't Get It: Humour and Hermeneutics." *Scottish Journal of Theology* 6, no. 4 (2007): 412-25.
Léon-Dufour, Xavier. *Dictionary of Biblical Theology.* 2nd ed. Translated by P. Joseph Cahill, with revisions and new articles translated by E. M. Stewart. Boston: St. Paul, 1967. Originally published under the title *Vocabulaire de theologie biblique.* Paris: Les Editions due Cerf, 1962.
Levenson, Jon D. *Sinai and Zion: An Entry into the Jewish Bible.* San Francisco: Harper & Row, 1985.
Lewis, C. S. *Reflections on the Psalms.* New York: Harcourt, Brace, 1958.
Lierman, John. *The New Testament Moses: Christian Perceptions of Moses and Israel in the Setting of Jewish Religion.* WUNT 173. Tübingen: Mohr Siebeck, 2004.
Lim, Bo. *The "Way of the Lord" in the Book of Isaiah.* Library of Hebrew Bible/Old Testament Studies 522. New York: T&T Clark, 2010.
Litwak, Kenneth. *Echoes of Scripture in Luke–Acts: Telling the History of God's People Intertextually.* JSNTSup 282. New York: T&T Clark, 2005.
Lodge, David, ed. *Modern Criticism and Theory: A Reader.* London: Longman, 1988.
Loewenstamm, S. E. "The Number of Plagues in Psalm 105." *Bib* 50 (1969): 491-96.
Long, V. Phillips. *Foundations of Contemporary Interpretation.* Vol. 5, *The Art of Biblical History.* Edited by Moisés Silva. Grand Rapids: Zondervan, 1994.
Longenecker, Bruce W., ed. *Narrative Dynamics in Paul: A Critical Assessment.* Louisville, KY: Westminster John Knox, 2002.
Longman, Tremper, III. *How to Read Exodus.* Downers Grove, IL: IVP Academic, 2009.
Longman, Tremper, III, and Daniel G. Reid. *God Is a Warrior.* Studies in Old Testament Biblical Theology. Grand Rapids: Zondervan, 1995.
Lucas, Alec J. "Assessing Stanley E. Porter's Objections to Richard B. Hays's Notion of Metalepsis." *CBQ* 76, no. 1 (January 2014): 93-111.
Lund, Øystein. *Way Metaphors and Way Topics in Isaiah 40–55.* FAT 28. Tübingen: Mohr Siebeck, 2007.

MacDonald, Dennis R., ed. *Mimesis and Intertextuality in Antiquity and Christianity*. Harrisburg, PA: Trinity Press International, 2001.
MacDonald, Nathan. "Israel and the Old Testament Story in Irenaeus's Presentation of the Rule of Faith." *JTI* 3, no. 2 (2009): 281-98.
Machen, J. Gresham. *The Christian Faith in the Modern World*. Grand Rapids: Eerdmans, 1947.
———. *The Christian View of Man*. London: Banner of Truth, 1937.
———. *Christianity and Liberalism*. Grand Rapids: Eerdmans, 1923.
———. *God Transcendent and Other Selected Sermons*. Grand Rapids: Eerdmans, 1949.
Macintosh, A. A. "Christian Exodus: An Analysis of Psalm 114." *Theology* 72, no. 589 (1969): 317-19.
Mallen, Peter. *The Reading and Transformation of Isaiah in Luke–Acts*. Library of New Testament Studies 367. New York: T&T Clark, 2008.
Mánek, Jindrich. "The New Exodus in the Book of Luke." *Novum Testamentum* (January 1957): 8-23.
Marcus, Joel. *The Way of the Lord: Christological Exegesis of the Old Testament in the Gospel of Mark*. Louisville, KY: Westminster John Knox, 1992.
Marshall, I. Howard. *The Gospel of Luke: A Commentary on the Greek Text*. NIGTC. Grand Rapids: Eerdmans, 1978.
Martens, Peter W. "Revisiting the Allegory/Typology Distinction: The Case of Origen." *Journal of Early Christian Studies* 16, no. 3 (Fall 2008): 283-317.
Martínez, F. García, ed. *Echoes from the Caves: Qumran and the New Testament*. Studies on the Texts of the Desert of Judah 85. Boston: Brill, 2009.
Mathewson, David. "New Exodus as a Background for 'The Sea Was No More' in Revelation 21:1c." *Trinity Journal* 24 (2003): 243-58.
———. *A New Heaven and a New Earth: The Meaning and Function of the Old Testament in Revelation 21.1–22.5*. JSNTSup 238. Sheffield: Sheffield Academic Press, 2003.
Mauser, Ulrich W. *Christ in the Wilderness: The Wilderness Theme in the Second Gospel and Its Basis in the Biblical Tradition*. London: SCM Press, 1963.
Mawhinney, Allen. "Baptism, Servanthood, and Sonship." *WTJ* 49 (1987): 35-64.
McCartney, Dan, and Peter Enns. "Matthew and Hosea: A Response to John Sailhamer." *WTJ* 63 (2001): 97-105.
McCasland, Vernon. "The Way." *JBL* (1958): 222-30.
McConville, J. G. "Ezra-Nehemiah and the Fulfilment of Prophecy." *Vetus Testamentum* 36, no. 2 (1986): 205-24.

McKim, Donald K. *A Guide to Contemporary Hermeneutics: Major Trends in Biblical Interpretation.* Grand Rapids: Eerdmans, 1986.

Mettinger, Tryggve N. D. *The Eden Narrative: A Literary and Religio-historical Study of Genesis 2–3.* Winona Lake, IN: Eisenbrauns, 2007.

Miller, Geoffrey D. "Intertextuality in Old Testament Research." *CurBR* 9, no. 3 (2011): 283-309.

Miller, Patrick D., Jr., Paul D. Hanson, and S. Dean McBride. *Ancient Israelite Religion: Essays in Honor of Frank Moore Cross.* Philadelphia: Fortress, 1987.

Moessner, David P. *The Lord of the Banquet: The Literary and Theological Significance of the Lukan Travel Narrative.* Minneapolis: Fortress, 1989.

Moi, Toril. *The Kristeva Reader.* New York: Columbia University Press, 1986.

Morales, L. Michael. *Cult and Cosmos: Tilting Toward a Temple-Centered Theology.* Biblical Tools and Studies 18. Leuven: Peeters, 2014.

———. *The Tabernacle Pre-figured: Cosmic Mountain Ideology in Genesis and Exodus.* Biblical Tools and Studies 15. Leuven: Peeters, 2012.

Morales, Rodrigo J. *The Spirit and the Restoration of Israel: New Exodus and New Creation Motifs in Galatians.* WUNT 2.282. Tübingen: Mohr Siebeck, 2010.

Morgan, Richard Lyon. "Fulfillment in the Fourth Gospel: An Inquiry into the Relationship of the Old Testament to the Fourth Gospel." ThM thesis, Union Theological Seminary in Virginia, 1956.

Morgan, Thaïs E. "Is There an Intertext in This Text? Literary and Interdisciplinary Approaches to Intertextuality." *American Journal of Semiotics* 3, no. 4 (1985): 1-40.

Moule, C. F. D. "The Nature and Purpose of 1 Peter." *NTS* 3, no. 1 (1956): 1-11.

Newman, Carey C., ed. *Jesus and the Restoration of Israel: A Critical Assessment of N. T. Wright's "Jesus and the Victory of God."* Downers Grove, IL: InterVarsity Press, 1999.

Niehaus, Jeffrey J. *Biblical Theology.* Vol. 1, *The Common Grace Covenants.* Wooster, OH: Weaver Books, 2014.

Nielsen, Kirsten. *Yahweh as Prosecutor and Judge: An Investigation of the Prophetic Lawsuit (Rib-Pattern).* JSOTSup 9. Sheffield: JSOT Press, 1978.

Nineham, D. E., ed. *Studies in the Gospels: Essays in Memory of R. H. Lightfoot.* Oxford: Basil Blackwell, 1967.

Ninow, Friedbert. *Indicators of Typology Within the Old Testament: The Exodus Motif.* Frankfurt: Peter Lang, 2001.

Nixon, R. E. *The Exodus in the New Testament.* London: Tyndale, 1963.

O'Connor, Michael P. *Hebrew Verse Structure.* Winona Lake, IN: Eisenbrauns, 1997.

O'Day, Gail R. "Jeremiah 9:22-23 and 1 Corinthians 1:26-31: A Study in Intertextuality." *JBL* 109, no. 2 (1990): 259-67.
Oropeza, B. J., and Steve Moyise, eds. *Exploring Intertextuality: Diverse Strategies for New Testament Interpretation of Texts*. Eugene, OR: Cascade, 2016.
Osborne, Grant R. *The Hermeneutical Spiral: A Comprehensive Introduction to Biblical Interpretation*. 2nd ed. Downers Grove, IL: IVP Academic, 2006.
Pak, Sujin. "Calvin on the 'Shared Design' of the Old and the New Testament Authors: The Case of the Minor Prophets." *WTJ* 73 (2010): 255-71.
———. *The Judaizing Calvin: Sixteenth-Century Debates over the Messianic Psalms*. Oxford Studies in Historical Theology. New York: Oxford University Press, 2010.
Pao, David W. *Acts and the Isaianic New Exodus*. Grand Rapids: Baker Academic, 2000.
Paul, Shalom M. *Isaiah 40–66: Translation and Commentary*. Eerdmans Critical Commentary. Grand Rapids: Eerdmans, 2012.
Perri, Carmela. "On Alluding." *Poetics* 7 (1978): 289-307.
Piper, Otto A. "The Origin of the Gospel Pattern." *JBL* 78 (1959): 115-24.
Pitre, Brant. *Jesus, the Tribulation, and the End of Exile: Restoration Eschatology and the Origin of the Atonement*. Tübingen: Mohr Siebeck, 2005.
———. "The 'Ransom for Many,' the New Exodus, and the End of the Exile: Redemption as the Restoration of All Israel (Mark 10:35-45)." *Letter & Spirit* 1 (2005): 41-68.
Plett, Heinrich F., ed. *Intertextuality*. New York: De Gruyter, 1991.
———. "Rhetoric and Intertextuality." *Rhetorica* 17, no. 3 (Summer 1999): 313-29.
Porter, Stanley E., and Beth M. Stovell, eds. *Biblical Hermeneutics: Five Views*. Downers Grove, IL: IVP Academic, 2012.
Poythress, Vern. *The Shadow of Christ in the Law of Moses*. Brentwood, TN: Wolgemuth & Hyatt, 1991.
Prosic, Tamara. *The Development and Symbolism of Passover Until 70 CE*. JSOTSup 414. London: T&T Clark, 2004.
Provan, Iain. *Seriously Dangerous Religion: What the Old Testament Really Says and Why It Matters*. Waco, TX: Baylor University Press, 2014.
Pryor, John W. "First Peter and the New Covenant (1)." *RTR* 45 (January/April 1986): 1-4.
———. "First Peter and the New Covenant (II)." *RTR* 45 (January/April 1986): 44-49.
Puckett, David L. *John Calvin's Exegesis of the Old Testament*. Columbia Series in Reformed Theology. Louisville, KY: Westminster John Knox, 1995.

Reid, Daniel. "The Christus Victor Motif in Paul's Theology." PhD diss., Fuller Theological Seminary, 1982.

Reiterer, Friedrich V., et al., eds. *Deuterocanonical and Cognate Literature: Yearbook 2006*. New York: De Gruyter, 2006.

Rendtorff, Rolf. *Canon and Theology: Overtures to an Old Testament Theology*. Translated and edited by Margaret Kohl. Minneapolis: Fortress, 1993.

———. "'Covenant' as a Structuring Concept in Genesis and Exodus." *JBL* 108, no. 3 (1989): 385-93.

Renfrew, Alastair, and Galin Tihanov, eds. *Critical Theory in Russia and the West*. Routledge Series on Russian and East European Studies 60. New York: Routledge, 2010.

Richardson, Alan. *An Introduction to the Theology of the New Testament*. New York: Harper & Row, 1958.

Robertson, David A. *Linguistic Evidence in Dating Early Hebrew Poetry*. SBLDS 3. Missoula: Scholars Press, 1972.

Robertson, O. Palmer. *The Flow of the Psalms: Discovering Their Structure and Theology*. Phillipsburg, NJ: P&R, 2015.

Rowe, C. Kavin. *Early Narrative Christology: The Lord in the Gospel of Luke*. Grand Rapids: Baker Academic, 2006.

Russell, Brian D. *The Song of the Sea: The Date of Composition and Influence of Exodus 15:1-21*. Studies in Biblical Literature 101. New York: Peter Lang, 2007.

Ryken, Phil. *Words of Delight: A Literary Introduction to the Bible*. Grand Rapids: Baker, 1987.

Sailhamer, John H. "Hosea 11:1 and Matthew 2:15." *WTJ* 63 (2001): 87-96.

Sarna, Nahum M. *Exploring Exodus: The Origins of Biblical Israel*. New York: Schocken, 1986.

———. *Genesis*. JPS Torah Commentary. Philadelphia: Jewish Publication Society, 1989.

Saussure, Ferdinand de. *Course in General Linguistics*. Edited by Charles Bally and Albert Sechehaye. Translated and annotated by Roy Harris. Chicago: Open Court, 1983.

Schilder, Klaas. *Christ in His Suffering*. Translated by Henry Zylstra. Grand Rapids: Eerdmans, 1938.

Schmid, H. H. "Creation, Righteousness, and Salvation: 'Creation Theology' as the Broad Horizon of Biblical Theology (1973)." In *Creation in the Old Testament*, edited by Bernhard W. Anderson, 102-17. Issues in Religion and Theology 6. Philadelphia: Fortress, 1984.

Schökel, Luis Alonso. *A Manual of Hebrew Poetics*. Subsidia Biblica. Rome: Pontifical Biblical Institute, 1988.

Schutter, William L. *Hermeneutic and Composition in 1 Peter*. WUNT 2.30. Tübingen: Mohr Siebeck, 1989.

Scott, James M. *Adoption as Sons of God*. WUNT 2.48. Tübingen: Mohr Siebeck, 1992.

Seifrid, Mark A. *Christ Our Righteousness: Paul's Theology of Justification*. Downers Grove, IL: InterVarsity Press, 2000.

Seitz, Christopher R. *The Character of Christian Scripture: The Significance of a Two-Testament Bible*. Studies in Theological Interpretation. Grand Rapids: Baker Academic, 2011.

———. "The Divine Council: Temporal Transition and New Prophecy in the Book of Isaiah." *JBL* 109, no. 2 (1990): 229-47.

———. *Figured Out: Typology and Providence in Christian Scripture*. Louisville, KY: Westminster John Knox, 2001.

———. *The Goodly Fellowship of the Prophets: The Achievement of Association in Canon Formation*. Grand Rapids: Baker Academic, 2009.

———. "Isaiah 40–66: Introduction, Commentary, and Reflections." In *The New Interpreter's Bible*, ed. Leander Keck, 6:307-552. Nashville: Abingdon, 1994.

———. *Prophecy and Hermeneutics: Toward a New Introduction to the Prophets*. Studies in Theological Interpretation. Grand Rapids: Baker Academic, 2007.

———. "The Prophet Moses and the Canonical Shape of Jeremiah." *Zeitschrift für die Alttestamentliche Wissenschaft* 101, no. 1 (1989): 3-27.

Selwyn, Edward Gordon. *The First Epistle of St. Peter: The Greek Text with Introduction, Notes and Essays*. London: Macmillan, 1946.

Seufert, Matthew. "Isaiah's Herald." *WTJ* 77 (2015): 219-35.

Seufert, Michael J. "A Walk They Remembered: Covenant Relationship as Journey in the Deuteronomistic History." *BibInt* 25 (2017): 149-71.

Simian-Yofre, Horacio. "Exodo in Deuteroisaías" [ET: Exodus in Deutero-Isaiah]. *Bib* 61 (1980): 530-53.

Smick, Elmer B. "The Mythological Elements in the Book of Job." *WTJ* 40 (1977–1978): 213-28.

———. "Mythopoeic Language in the Psalms." *WTJ* 44 (1982): 88-98.

Smith, Daniel Lynwood. "The Uses of 'New Exodus' in New Testament Scholarship: Preparing a Way Through the Wilderness." *CurBS* 14, no. 2 (2016): 207-43.

Smith, James K. A. *Who's Afraid of Postmodernism? Taking Derrida, Lyotard, and Foucault to Church*. Grand Rapids: Baker Academic, 2006.

Smith, Mark S. "Setting and Rhetoric in Psalm 23." *JSOT* 41 (1988): 61-66.

———. *Poetic Heroes: Literary Commemorations of Warriors and Warrior Culture in the Early Biblical World*. Grand Rapids: Eerdmans, 2014.

Smith, Mark S., with contributions by Elizabeth M. Bloch-Smith. *The Pilgrimage Pattern in Exodus*. JSOTSup 239. Sheffield: Sheffield Academic Press, 1997.

Snodgrass, Klyne. "1 Peter 2:1-10: Its Formation and Literary Affinities." *NTS* 24, no. 1 (1977): 97-106.

Soderlund, Sven K., and N. T. Wright, eds. *Romans and the People of God: Essays in Honor of Gordon D. Fee on the Occasion of His 65th Birthday*. Grand Rapids: Eerdmans, 1999.

Sommer, Benjamin D. *A Prophet Reads Scripture: Allusion in Isaiah 40–66*. Stanford, CA: Stanford University Press, 1998.

Spadaro, Martin C. *Reading Matthew as the Climactic Fulfillment of the Hebrew Story*. Eugene, OR: Wipf & Stock, 2015.

Stackhouse, John G., Jr., ed. *What Does It Mean to Be Saved? Broadening Evangelical Horizons of Salvation*. Grand Rapids: Baker Academic, 2002.

Stanley, Christopher D. *Paul and the Language of Scripture*. SNTSMS 69. Cambridge: Cambridge University Press, 1992.

Steinmetz, David C., ed. *The Bible in the Sixteenth Century*. Duke Monographs in Medieval and Renaissance Studies 11. Durham, NC: Duke University Press, 1990.

Stevenson, Gregory. "Communal Imagery and the Individual Lament: Exodus Typology in Psalm 77." *Restoration Quarterly* 39, no. 4 (1997): 215-29.

Stock, Augustine. *The Way in the Wilderness: Exodus, Wilderness, and Moses Themes in Old Testament and New*. Collegeville, MN: Liturgical Press, 1969.

Stordalen, Terje. *Echoes of Eden: Genesis 2–3 and Symbolism of the Eden Garden in Biblical Hebrew Literature*. Biblical Exegesis and Theology 25. Leuven: Peeters, 2000.

Strauss, Mark L. *The Davidic Messiah in Luke–Acts: The Promise and Its Fulfillment in Lukan Christology*. JSNTSup 110. Sheffield: Sheffield Academic Press, 1995.

Stuhlmueller, Carroll. *Creative Redemption in Deutero-Isaiah*. Analecta Biblica 43. Rome: Biblical Institute, 1970.

Sutanto, Nathaniel Gray. "On the Theological Interpretation of Scripture: The Indirect Identity Thesis, Reformed Orthodoxy, and Trinitarian Considerations." *WTJ* 77 (2015): 337-53.

Swartley, Willard Myers. *Mark: The Way for All Nations*. Scottdale, PA: Herald Press, 1979.

———. "The Structural Function of the Term 'Way' (*Hodos*) in Mark's Gospel." In *The New Way of Jesus: Essays Presented to Howard Charles*, edited by William Klassen, 73-86. Newton, KS: Faith and Life Press, 1980.

———. "A Study in Markan Structure: The Influence of Israel's Holy History upon the Structure of the Gospel of Mark." PhD diss., Princeton Theological Seminary, 1973.

Talbert, Charles H., and Jason A. Whitlark, eds. *Getting "Saved": The Whole Story of Salvation in the New Testament*. Grand Rapids: Eerdmans, 2011.

Talmon, Shemaryahu. *Literary Motifs and Patterns in the Hebrew Bible: Collected Studies*. Winona Lake, IN: Eisenbrauns, 2013.

———. *Literary Studies in the Hebrew Bible: Form and Content*. Jerusalem: Magnes Press, 1993.

Terrein, Samuel. *The Psalms: Strophic Structure and Theological Commentary*. Eerdmans Critical Commentary. Grand Rapids: Eerdmans, 2003.

Thielman, Frank. *From Plight to Solution: A Jewish Framework for Understanding Paul's View of the Law in Galatians and Romans*. Leiden: Brill, 1989.

Thompson, G. H. P. "Called-Proved-Obedient: A Study in the Baptism and Temptation Narratives of Matthew and Luke." *JTS* 11 (1960): 1-12.

Thompson, M. *Clothed with Christ: The Example and Teaching of Jesus in Romans 12.1–15.13*. JSNTSup 59. Sheffield: JSOT Press, 1991.

Timmer, Daniel C. *Creation, Tabernacle, and Sabbath: The Sabbath Frame of Exodus 31:12-17; 35:1-3 in Exegetical and Theological Perspective*. Forschungen zur Religion und Literatur des Alten und Neuen Testaments 227. Göttingen: Vandenhoeck & Ruprecht, 2009.

Todorov, Tzvetan. *French Literary Theory Today*. Cambridge: Cambridge University Press, 1982.

———. *Literature and Its Theorists: A Personal View of Twentieth-Century Criticism*. Translated by Catherine Porter. Ithaca, NY. Cornell University Press, 1987.

———. *Theories of the Symbol*. Translated by Catherine Porter. Ithaca, NY: Cornell University Press, 1982.

Tuckett, C. M., ed. *The Scriptures in the Gospels*. BETL 131. Leuven: Leuven University Press, 1997.

Tull, P. K. "Intertextuality and the Hebrew Scriptures." *CurBR* 8 (2000): 59-80.

Turner, Max. *Power from on High: The Spirit in Israel's Restoration and Witness in Luke–Acts*. Sheffield: Sheffield Academic Press, 1996.

Tuttle, Gary A., ed. *Biblical and Near Eastern Studies: Essays in Honor of William Sanford LaSor*. Grand Rapids: Eerdmans, 1978.

Udoh, Fabian E. *Redefining First-Century Jewish and Christian Identities: Essays in Honor of Ed Parish Sanders*. Christianity and Judaism in Antiquity Series 16. Notre Dame, IN: University of Notre Dame Press, 2008.

van Iersel, Bas, and Anton Weiler, eds. *Exodus, a Lasting Paradigm*. Edinburgh: T&T Clark, 1987.

VanDrunen, David. *Divine Covenants and Moral Order: A Biblical Theology of Natural Law*. Emory University Studies in Law and Religion. Grand Rapids: Eerdmans, 2014.

———. "The Importance of the Penultimate: Reformed Social Thought and the Contemporary Critiques of the Liberal Society." *Journal of Markets and Morality* 9, no. 2 (Fall 2006): 219-49.

———. "The Kingship of Christ Is Twofold: Natural Law and the Two Kingdoms in the Thought of Herman Bavinck." *Calvin Theological Journal* 45 (April 2010): 147-64.

———. "Legal Polycentrism: A Christian Theological and Jurisprudential Evaluation." *Journal of Law and Religion*. Forthcoming.

———. *Living in God's Two Kingdoms: A Biblical Vision for Christianity and Culture*. Wheaton, IL: Crossway, 2010.

———. *Natural Law and the Two Kingdoms: A Study in the Development of Reformed Social Thought*. Emory University Studies in Law and Religion. Grand Rapids: Eerdmans, 2010.

Vanhoozer, Kevin J. *The Drama of Doctrine: A Canonical Linguistic Approach to Christian Theology*. Louisville, KY: Westminster John Knox, 2005.

———. *First Theology: God, Scripture and Hermeneutics*. Downers Grove, IL: InterVarsity Press, 2002.

———. "Imprisoned or Free? Text, Status, and Theological Interpretation in Master/Slave Discourse of Philemon." In *Reading Scripture with the Church*, edited by A. K. M. Adam, Stephen E. Fowl, Kevin J. Vanhoozer, and Francis Watson, 51-94. Grand Rapids: Baker Academic, 2006.

———. *Is There a Meaning in This Text? The Bible, the Reader, and the Morality of Literary Knowledge*. Grand Rapids: Zondervan, 1998.

———. *Remythologizing Theology: Divine Action, Passion, and Authorship*. Cambridge: Cambridge University Press, 2010.

Vos, Geerhardus. *Biblical Theology: Old and New Testaments*. Grand Rapids: Eerdmans, 1948.

———. *The Pauline Eschatology*. Phillipsburg, NJ: P&R, 1986.
———. *The Teaching of the Epistle to the Hebrews*. Phillipsburg, NJ: P&R, 1956.
Wakeman, Mary K. *God's Battle with the Monster: A Study in Biblical Imagery*. Leiden: Brill, 1973.
Walsh, Carey, and Mark Elliott. *Biblical Theology: Past, Present, and Future*. Eugene, OR: Cascade, 2016.
Waltke, Bruce, with Cathi J. Fredricks. *Genesis: A Commentary*. Grand Rapids: Zondervan, 2001.
Waltke, Bruce, and James M. Houston, with Erika Moore. *The Psalms as Christian Worship: A Historical Commentary*. Grand Rapids: Eerdmans, 2010.
Walzer, Michael. *Exodus and Revolution*. New York: Basic Books, 1985.
Waters, Guy Prentiss. "Covenant Theology and Recent Interpretation of Paul: Some Reflections." *Confessional Presbyterian* 6 (2010): 167-79.
Waters, Guy Prentiss, and Ligon Duncan, eds. *Children and the Lord's Supper*. Fearn, UK: Christian Focus Publications/Mentor, 2011.
Watson, Duane F., ed. *The Intertexture of Apocalyptic Discourse in the New Testament*. SBLSymS 14. Atlanta: Society of Biblical Literature, 2002.
Watson, Francis. *Text and Truth: Redefining Biblical Theology*. Grand Rapids: Eerdmans, 1997.
Watts, Rikki E. *Isaiah's New Exodus in Mark*. Grand Rapids: Baker Academic, 1997.
Webb, William J. *Returning Home: New Covenant and Second Exodus as the Context for 2 Corinthians 6.14–7.1*. JSNTSup 85. Sheffield: JSOT Press, 1993.
Westerholm, Stephen. *Perspectives Old and New on Paul: The "Lutheran" Paul and His Critics*. Grand Rapids: Eerdmans, 2004.
Westermann, Claus. *Isaiah 40–66: A Commentary*. OTL. Philadelphia: Westminster, 1969.
———. *Praise and Lament in the Psalms*. Translated by Keith R. Crim and Richard N. Soulen. Atlanta: John Knox Press, 1981.
Wilder, William. *Echoes of the Exodus Narrative in the Context and Background of Galatians 5:18*. Studies in Biblical Literature 23. New York: Peter Lang, 2001.
Wimsatt, W. K., Jr., and M. C. Beardsley. "The Intentional Fallacy." *Sewanee Review* 54 (1946): 468-88.
Wjingaards, J. "A Twofold Approach to Exodus." *VT* 15 (1965): 91-102.
Wright, John. "Spirit and Wilderness: The Interplay of Two Motifs Within the Hebrew Bible as Background to Mark 1:2-13." In *Perspectives on Language and Text: Essays and Poems in Honor of Francis I. Andersen's Sixtieth Birthday, July 28, 1985*, edited by Edgar W. Conrad and Edward G. Newing, 269-98. Winona Lake, IN: Eisenbrauns, 1987.

Wright, N. T. *The Climax of the Covenant: Christ and the Law in Pauline Theology.* Minneapolis: Fortress, 1993.

———. *The Day the Revolution Began: Reconsidering the Meaning of Jesus's Crucifixion.* San Francisco: HarperOne, 2016.

———. *Jesus and the Victory of God.* Christian Origins and the Question of God 2. Minneapolis: Fortress, 1996.

———. *The New Testament and the People of God.* Christian Origins and the Question of God 1. Minneapolis: Fortress, 1992.

———. *Paul and His Recent Interpreters: Some Contemporary Debates.* Minneapolis: Fortress, 2015.

———. *Paul and the Faithfulness of God.* Christian Origins and the Question of God 4. Minneapolis: Fortress, 2013.

———. *The Paul Debate: Critical Questions for Understanding the Apostle.* Waco, TX: Baylor University Press, 2015.

———. *The Resurrection of the Son of God.* Christian Origins and the Question of God 3. Minneapolis: Fortress, 2003.

———. *Surprised by Hope: Rethinking Heaven, the Resurrection, and the Mission of the Church.* New York: HarperOne, 2008.

Young, Frances M. *Biblical Exegesis and the Formation of Christian Culture.* Cambridge: Cambridge University Press, 1997.

Zakovitch, Yair. *"And You Shall Tell Your Son . . .": The Concept of the Exodus in the Bible.* Jerusalem: Magnes Press, 1991.

Zevit, Ziony. "The Priestly Redaction and Interpretation of the Plague Narrative in Exodus." *Jewish Quarterly Review* 66 (1976): 193-211.

Ziesler, J. A. "The Transfiguration Story and the Markan Soteriology." *Expository Times* 81 (1970): 263-68.

Zimmerli, Walther. "Promise and Fulfillment." *Int* (1961): 310-38.

AUTHOR INDEX

Achtemeier, Paul, 287
Ackroyd, Peter, 207
Alexander, T. Desmond, 88
Allen, Leslie, 145, 146
Allison, Dale C., 126, 232, 233, 307, 350
Altick, Richard, 334n34
Anderson, Bernard, 142, 153
Augustine, 37-38, 53, 77
Bakhtin, Mikhail, 21-22, 47-48, 327-30, 335, 338, 346
Balentine, George L., 239
Barclay, William, 274n53
Barr, James, 12
Barré, Michael L., 129-31
Barstad, H., 152n16, 163
Barthes, Roland, 27-28, 318, 328n6
Batto, Bernard F., 117-18, 179n136
Baugh, Stephen M., 29
Bavinck, Herman, 87
Beale, G. K., 52, 224n91, 231, 232, 267, 299-301, 302, 305, 306, 307
Beardsley, M. C., 28n38, 335n37
Beetham, Christopher A., 33n69, 34, 36n85, 268, 334n34
Beker, J. C., 266
Bellis, A. O., 189-90
Ben-Porat, Ziva, 32, 346-49
Bentzen, Aage, 208n2
Best, Ernest, 294n43
Blenkinsopp, Joseph, 206
Bloom, Harold, 30-31
Boadt, Lawrence, 182
Bright, John, 149
Brown, Raymond, 288

Brueggemann, Walter, 2, 97, 131, 286
Brunson, Andrews, 128n25
Bucer, Martin, 54
Bullinger, Heinrich, 54
Burnside, Jonathan, 101n53
Calvin, John, 25n25, 77, 159, 319-20
   on allegory, 53-54, 59
   exegesis of, 50, 58-59
Campbell, Anthony F., 132, 134
Casey, Jay Smith, 234-35
Ceresko, Anthony, 50
Chandler, James K., 32
Charles, R. H., 301
Charlesworth, James H., 24, 157-58, 331
Chesterton, G. K., 263
Childs, Brevard, 54
Clifford, Richard, 114
Collett, Don, 58, 171
Collins, Adela Yarbro, 115
Conzelmann, Hans, 252
Craigie, Peter, 130n31
Cross, Frank Moore, 95, 111, 114, 139, 155n33
Crowe, Brandon, 219, 229
Culler, Jonathan, 332
Currid, John, 113-14
Dabney, R. L., 90
Dahl, Nils A., 247
Daube, David, 106, 280n86, 291n28, 323
Davies, W. D., 187, 264, 271-73
Davis, Carl Judson, 236n2
Derrida, Jacques, 328n6
Deterding, Paul E., 17, 292n33, 297

Dostoyevsky, Fyodor, 22, 329, 330n13
Dozeman, Thomas B., 97, 105n76
Duggan, Michael W., 199n70, 203
Dunn, James D. G., 243n37, 274n53
Dupont, Jacques, 253
Durham, John I., 179n134
Eco, Umberto, 333n25, 345-46
Elliott, J. H., 287
Ellis, Earle, 180-81
Ellul, Jacques, 212
Enns, 231
Erasmus, 54
Erderma, Erik A., 139n67
Evans, J. F., 197-98
Faulkner, William, 121
Fishbane, Michael, 22-23, 47-50, 140, 197
Fitzgerald, 190n29
Foucault, Michel, 328n6, 339n54
France, R. T., 212n23
Freedman, David Noel, 95, 111, 129-30
Frei, Hans, 41, 51, 53
Freud, Sigmund, 329
Gadamer, Hans-Georg, 20
Gaffin, Richard B., Jr., 37n94, 55n160, 230n119
Garr, Randall, 65, 66
Garrett, Susan R., 247-48, 249-50, 255
Gibbs, Raymond W., Jr., 1, 28n38
Gignilliat, Mark, 52
Gillingham, Susan, 133, 135
Goppelt, Leonhard, 291

Gorman, Michael J., 7n24
Green, Joel B., 255, 290n25
Grotius, Hugo, 60
Gunkel, Hermann, 153
Hanson, Paul D., 205, 224n91
Hatina, Thomas R., 213n29
Hays, Christopher, 339
Hays, Richard B., 5n15, 23, 26n31, 34-36, 38, 57n168, 209, 213, 230, 237, 246, 252, 264, 349-50
Heidegger, Martin, 19
Higton, Mike, 221
Hoglund, Kenneth G., 198-99
Hollander, John, 34
Holliday, W. L., 131n37
Horton, Michael S., 37, 87, 88, 104
Howe, Bonnie, 288, 289-90, 296
Idestrom, Rebecca, 192
Irenaeus, 54, 213
Jefferson, Ann, 28n41, 339n53
Jindo, Job Y., 226
Jobes, Karen, 291-92
John of Damascus, 92
Johnson, Dennis E., 257-58
Johnson, Mark, 101n49, 152n17
Keesmaat, Sylvia C., 264, 265, 280n85, 281-82, 334n31
Kelber, Werner H., 222
Kessler, Martin, 191
Kitchen, Kenneth, 112
Klein, David Jeffrey, 56
Kline, Jonathan, 49
Kline, Meredith G., 174, 178, 221n74, 283n106
    on creation and covenant, 87-88
    on Gospel genre, 225
    on Noachian covenant, 82, 84
    on Sethites, 75-76
Koch, K., 200, 205
Kraus, Hans-Joachim, 126-27, 142, 143n87, 146
Kristeva, Julia, 21-22, 27, 318, 327-32, 333n25, 334, 335, 339, 343, 346
Kronfeld, Chana, 19

Kselman, John S., 129-31
Kynes, Will, 26n29, 33
La Potterie, Ignacio de, 282n96
Lacan, Jacques, 329
Lakoff, George P., 101n49, 152n17
Leithart, Peter, 51-52
Levenson, Jon D., 98-99
Lewis, Bernard, 89
Lewis, C. S., 121
Lim, Bo, 167n84, 169, 170, 176n126, 205, 211n14, 224, 236n2
Litwak, Kenneth, 240, 244-45
Longman, Tremper, III, 113, 220
Lund, Øystein, 152, 165n69
Luther, Martin, 77
Lyotard, Jean-François, 4
MacDonald, Dennis R., 349
Machen, J. Gresham, 236
Mann, Thomas W., 121
Marcus, Joel, 211n14, 218, 223-24
Martin, Michael W., 225
Martyn, J. Louis, 266
Mathewson, David, 310, 311
Matthews, Kenneth, 72n46
Mauser, Ulrich W., 211
McCartney, Dan, 231
McCasland, S. Vernon, 211n18
McConville, J. G., 157, 205
Melanchthon, 54
Mendenhall, George, 73
Merrill, Eugene, 64
Mettinger, Tryggve N. D., 68n33
Michaels, Johann D., 40
Miller, Geoffrey D., 343n68
Miller, Patrick D., 79-80
Moberly, R. W. L., 61
Moessner, David P., 251-52
Moo, Douglas, 264
Morales, L. Michael, 78, 106, 277, 278n79, 297
Morris, Charles, 333n25
Motyer, J. A., 171
Moule, C. F. D., 287
Moyise, Steve, 299, 303n24
Muller, Richard A., 58

Ninow, Friedbert, 39, 42, 161n55, 171-72
Nixon, R. E., 159
Noth, Martin, 3, 96, 97, 98n27
Oden, Robert, 115
Origen, 51, 53-54, 213
Orosz, Magdolna, 11
Osborne, Grant R., 286, 340, 343n69
Pak, Sujin, 25n25
Pao, David, 224, 237, 238n12, 245, 253, 256-57, 258, 259-60, 261
Paul, Shalom, 150, 176n127
Peck, Thomas, 90
Pell, D., 151n17
Phillips, Peter, 334n30
Pierce, Charles Sanders, 328n6, 333n25
Pitre, Brant, 241n28, 326
Plett, Heinrich, 336, 338
Porter, Stanley E., 26n31, 31, 32-33, 36n85, 38, 350n102
Provan, Iain, 72
Quintilian, 59
Rad, Gerhard von, 63, 114
Reid, Daniel, 113, 220, 234n153, 323n12
Rendtorff, 62, 79
Ricoeur, Paul, 212
Robertson, David A., 110n92
Rowe, C. Kavin, 219-20, 239, 244
Russell, Brian D., 98, 101, 110, 132n40
Ryken, Leland, 8, 24
Sahlin, Harald, 264
Sailhammer, 231
Sanders, E. P., 6-7, 264-65
Sarna, Nahum, 71
Saussure, Ferdinand de, 327, 328n6, 332-33, 344
Schilder, Klaas, 12
Schmid, H. H., 62
Schneider, Michael, 327
Schökel, Louis Alonso, 119
Schutter, William, 286
Schweitzer, Albert, 6
Scott, James M., 273-74, 277-78, 279
Seitz, Christopher, 41, 55, 56
Semler, Johann S., 40

Seow, C. L., 116
Seufert, Michael J., 101n49
Shakespeare, 182
Shklovsky, Viktor, 32
Simian-Yofre, Horacio, 151-52n16, 163
Skemp, Vincent, 334
Sloan, Robert B., 243
Smith, Casey, 298-99
Smith, Daniel, 250
Smith, Mark S., 42, 95n15, 110-11, 131n33
Snaith, N. H., 152n20
Sommer, Benjamin D., 10, 20, 27, 341
Spadaro, Martin C., 226
Stanley, Christopher, 26n31
Stead, M. R., 342-43
Steck, O. H., 252
Steinmetz, David, 58
Stevenson, Gregory M., 136, 140, 141
Stock, Augustine, 208, 221, 298
Stuhlmueller, Carroll, 152
Swartley, Willard Myers, 223n83

Talmon, Shemaryahu, 8-9, 99, 102
Telfer, Charles K., 59n180
Thompson, G. H. P., 233
Thompson, John, 53
Tipton, Lane G., 57
Todorov, Tzvetan, 330n13
Tolkien, J. R. R., 314
Turner, Max, 245
Van Dixhoorn, Chad, 86n98
Van Wolde, Ellen, 339
VanDrunen, David, 72n44, 87-88, 89n113, 105, 275n57, 324
Vanhoozer, Kevin J., 22n11, 122
Vanhoye, Albert, 300
Vitringa, Campegius, 59-60
Vos, Geerhardus, 4, 44-45, 69n37, 300, 304n29
Wall, Robert, 47, 55n160
Waltke, Bruce K., 20-21
Walzer, Michael, 208, 314
Waters, Guy, 264
Watson, Francis, 62, 90-91, 270

Watts, Rikk E., 141, 154, 212-13, 214-15, 220
Weinrich, H., 151n17
Wellhausen, Julius, 108
Weren, W. J. C., 24
Westerholm, Stephen, 264
Westermann, Claus, 142, 149, 177, 263
Wilder, William, 272, 279-80
Williamson, H. G. M., 205-6
Wilson, Tim, 33n69
Wimsatt, 28n38, 335n37
Witte, Markus, 135
Woiwode, Larry, 270n35
Wolverton, W. I., 146
Wright, John, 9, 40, 102, 110n91, 173n108, 193-94n50, 216, 219, 232, 233n142
Wright, N. T., 15, 142n79, 205, 226, 241-42, 243n37, 263-64, 265-67, 270n34, 280-81, 317, 326
Young, Frances M., 53
Zehnder, Markus P., 150n9
Zimmerli, Walther, 157, 195, 224n91, 242

SUBJECT INDEX

Abrahamic covenant, 85-87, 131, 240, 243n37, 251
accessibility (allusions), 349n99
Achaemenid imperial history, 199
Acts. *See* Luke-Acts
Adam
   cultural activities of, 324
   curse of death on, 248
   probation of, 319-20
   as proto-typical priest, 67
   in Romans, 280
adoption, 273-74, 285, 312
Aeschylus, 263
Akkad, 117
Alexandrian theology, 50
alienation, 13, 315
all fallacy, 331
allegory, 39-40, 50-54
allusion, 10, 13, 19-20, 23, 25, 32-33, 268-70, 300, 315, 327, 346-51
allusion competence, 24, 332, 350
allusive sound play, 49
already/not yet principle, 242
analogical uses of Old Testament, 300
analogy, 52, 349n99
angel of the covenant, 215
Antiochene school, 53
Anzu, 115
Apocalypse. *See* Revelation
apocalyptic eschatology, 223
"Apocalyptic Paul," 266
apostasy, 133
archetype (Vos), 44
ark, 83n87
ark of the covenant, 176, 305

atonement, 290
audience, 38, 39, 269, 350
   See also reader
author, 39, 269, 340, 344-46
author-oriented intertextuality, 22, 25-28, 341-43
authorial intent, 27-28, 33, 36, 270, 335, 341, 349, 350n102
Avaris, 134
avian (bird) imagery, 13, 315
Baal, 124, 139
Babylon
   judgment on, 190
   return from, 167-68, 174-75, 185, 200-202, 206
Babylonian mythology, 172
baptism, 326
Barak, 109
Bible
   demythologizes ancient cosmologies, 116
   divine and human authors of, 25, 36-38
   inspiration of, 41
   meganarrative of, 5-6, 43, 94, 95, 122, 153, 269
   organic unity of, 38, 46
   spiritual vs. literal reading of, 58
biblical interpretation, as "tri-lectic," 346
biblical theology, 5, 12, 16
Bildfeld, 151n17
blood of Jesus Christ, 289
Book of Consolation (Isaiah), 150, 154, 176, 179n135
Book of Consolation (Jeremiah), 186

Cain, 71-74
calling on the name of the Lord, 75
Canaan, 94-95, 104, 316, 319-20
Canaanite mythological traditions, 136
canon, 56
categorical approach, 333n25
chaos, 119
child/childhood language, 277-78
Christian dispensation, as new exodus, 271-73
Christian liberty, 276
Christian life, 324
Christians, as new people of God, 294-96
christotelism, 57, 58n171
church
   as new Israel, 296
   as redefinition of people of God, 257
city of man, 70-76
clear allusion, 299
combat motif, 114-17, 139, 148, 172
combined allusions, 300
common curse, 69, 85
common grace, 70-76, 80, 118
community memory, 140
comparative method, 327n2
complexus, 59, 98n30, 180
conquest of the land, 97
consummation of the ages, 16, 312, 321
continuing exile, 205, 241-43, 265-67
corporate election, 267n20

Subject Index

cosmic mountain ideology, 64-65, 67, 94, 103, 122, 197, 315
cosmology, 61
covenant, 13-14
   of common grace, 82-83
   curses as national, 265n10
   in early chapters of Genesis, 62
   of Genesis 6:18, 80-82
   of grace, 69n36, 82-83
   lawsuit, 178-79, 189
   nomism, 264-65
   redemptive and nonredemptive, 84-85
   renewal, 195
covenant theology, promise and fulfillment in, 261-62
creation, 61-67
   and background of exodus motif, 82, 87, 119, 315
   and covenant, 13-14, 87-90
Creator/creature distinction, 139
cultural activities, 324
Cyrus, 158-59, 168-70, 174, 175, 201-2, 204
Davidic covenant, 131
Davidic king, 184-85
"de-authoring" of texts, 27
de-creation
   flood as, 160
   in Isaiah, 179
   plagues of Egypt as, 119
Dead Sea Scrolls, 151n10
Deborah, 109
Decalogue, 164
deformation, 132
deliverance politics, 70
desert, 99-100, 103, 221
   as conquered enemy, 167
   See also wilderness
Deutero-Isaiah, 150
diachronic intertextuality, 22, 25, 96, 329-30, 333, 338-39, 341-43
dialogism, 342
direct quote, 350
discipleship, 224
distinctive traits (allusions), 349

divine author, 46, 346,
   and authorial intent, 270
divine passives, 73
divine presence, 94
divine warrior, 16, 98, 113-16, 125, 139, 173, 277, 305, 316, 317-18
domain of darkness, 284
Dragon, 116
dry land, 119
dry-shod motif, 141, 148
dwelling with God, 312
east wind, 190
echoes, 33n69, 34-39, 349-50
   in Paul, 268-70
   within cultural intertexture, 334
Eden, 88
   as cosmic mountain, 67
   loss of divine presence, 94
   as sanctuary, 66, 67
effective history, 20
Egyptian Hallel, 126, 147
election, as corporate, 267n20
Elijah, 2, 215, 239, 246, 249, 250, 252, 254
Elisha, 246
end of exile, 241n28, 242, 243n37, 262, 265
ends of the earth, 162, 171-72, 257-59
Enlightenment, 40-41, 315, 340
entitlement to the world-to-come, 306, 319-21, 325
Enuma Elish, 115
eschatological moral standard, 276
eschatological rest, 66
   as final goal of exodus, 105
eschatology, 2, 321
evocation, 10, 30-31
exile, return from, 95, 152n20, 158, 200, 204-6, 241
exodus
   as means to an end, 104
   as mere liberation, 45, 67, 84, 100, 105, 125, 322
   as new creation, 93, 109, 119, 125
   as synecdoche for

salvation, 104, 120, 129, 224-25, 322
exodus motif, 2-8, 13
   adumbrated in early chapters of Genesis, 87
   eschatologized, 15, 148, 150, 161, 232, 317
   as paradigm, 14, 315, 318
   in Song of the Sea, 95
   in Synoptic Gospels, 262
Exodus-wilderness-Jericho pattern, 305-6
Ezekiel, 316
   new covenant in, 191-98
   new exodus in, 207
Ezra, exodus motif in, 199-203, 316
faithful shepherds, 185-86
Festival of Booths, 103
figural reading, 21, 25n25, 52
   See also typology
firstborn, 302
flood, 76
   as de-creation, 160
   as exodus from old creation to new, 82
forensic, in salvation, 93, 106, 323-24
fourfold sense, 50-51
framing discourse, 240
free-range allegory, 40, 53
Garden of Eden, 184, 318
gate liturgy, 126-27, 167
Gentiles
   and exodus tradition, 288
   inclusion of, 253, 259-61, 295
goal, of exodus motif, 316
God
   conquers enemies, 124
   enthronement over creation, 66
   faithfulness of, 144, 281, 313
   as father, 282
   graciousness of, 134-35
   as only king, 113
   presence with Israel, 97
   as sole agent of salvation, 109-10
   sovereign rule of, 142, 179-80, 293, 305, 312

Subject Index | 383

as warrior (*see* divine warrior)
Gospel genre, origins in exodus motif, 225
grand story. *See* Bible, meganarrative of
Hallel psalms, 126, 128
Ham, sin of, 83n87
heaven, 3n4, 266
  See also world-to-come
heavenly reality, 44-45
Hebrews (book), typology in, 44-45
hermeneutical horizon, 341-43
hermeneutical responsibility, 340
hermeneutics, three foci of, 344-46
historical criticism, 41, 339
historical prologue (treaty relationships), 200
history, as common grace, 118
Hittite suzerainty treaties, 164, 200
holiness, 78, 192, 288-89, 292
holy mountain, 100
Holy Spirit
  in Acts, 257-58
  guidance of, 285
  illumination of, 123
  inspiration of, 123
  presence and protection of, 176
hope, 289, 290
Hosea
  echoed in Galatians, 277
  echoed in Matthew, 227-32, 262
house of God, 287
human author, 36-38, 231
ideology, 212
idolatry, 193, 197, 266
image and shadow, 44
image of God, 65, 87
inauguration/consummation principle of eschatology, 205, 242, 243n37
indirect fulfillment, 301
influence, 30-31
inheritance, 104, 283, 284, 298, 309, 312

innerbiblical exegesis, 25-26, 29, 318
"intentionalist fallacy," 27n38, 335n37
interpretability (allusions), 349
intersubjectivity, 122, 335
intertextual coherence, 336
intertextuality, 10-11, 12, 19-25, 58, 314-15, 318, 327-51
intratexual coherence, 336
inverted use of allusions, 301
irony, 197
Isaianic new exodus, 14, 15, 43, 149, 152-80, 215, 316
Islam, 7
Israel
  apostasy of, 184
  as landlubbers, 125, 137
  as new creation, 125-26, 164
  rebellion of, 148
  as sacred space, 66
  as "turfed" people, 97, 104
  as typological son, 209n4, 218-19, 233
  as under the law, 274-80
J (Yahwist source), 109
Jabin of Hazor, 109
Jeremiah, 183-91, 206, 316
Jerusalem, 297
Jesus Christ
  as agent of new exodus, 208, 236, 241, 262
  as the antitypical prophet figure, 240
  as ascender, 101
  baptism of, 217, 219
  bound to his church, 260
  exodus of, 249, 251
  as faithful witness, 302
  as firstborn, 302
  journey to Jerusalem, 251, 255, 262
  as obedient Son, 221, 234
  as ruler of the kings of the earth, 302
  as second Adam, 68, 221, 234, 337, 248
  second advent of, 224
  synagogue reading of Isaiah, 244-48, 262

temptation of, 220, 232-34, 244, 254, 262
  as true son of Israel, 209n4, 216-22, 233
John the Baptizer, 216, 238, 243
Joshua, 48-49
Jubilee, 245
Judah, fall of, 183
Judahites, 145
judgment, 69, 241, 298
justification, 8
  by co-crucifixion, 7n24
  as entitlement to world-to-come, 319-20
  and sanctification, 325
kingdom of God
  and civil kingdom, 89-90
  inauguration of, 216, 317
kingdom of light, 284-85
kingdom of priests, 281, 295, 302-5, 317
kings, 304-5
Lamb that was slain, 303-4, 317-18
Lamech, 74-75
lament, 140-41, 146, 148
land, as inheritance, 104
language, and ideology, 212
law vs. Spirit, 279-80
led by the Spirit, 280
Leviathan, 115
lexemes, 332
liberation, exodus as, 45, 67, 84, 100, 105, 125, 322
liberation theologians, 70
light vs. darkness, 284, 285
linguistics, 344
literal and figurative language, 163
literary allusions, 347-48
literary prototypes, 300
literary typology, 46-50
literary-critical theories, 27
living stones, 294
Lord's Prayer, 282, 326
Lord's Supper, 264
Lothan, 139
love, in new-exodus community, 292-93
Lugal-e, 115
Luke-Acts, exodus motif in,

220, 236-62
Marduk, 124, 126-27, 139
Mark, exodus motif in, 209-16, 262
Mary, Magnificat of, 240
Matthew
  exodus motif in, 226-35, 262
  use of Old Testament, 226
  meaning in the text, 328-30
merism, 164
Messiah, 172, 179
Messiah-King, 147, 317
messianic secret, 218
metalepsis, 23
metanarrative, 4
metaphor, 163
mimesis, 109
Mosaic covenant, 70, 86, 131, 186
  conditional elements in, 177
  contingency in, 94
  as part of the covenant of grace, 105n72
Mosaic economy, 86n98, 94n9
Mosaic law, protological character of, 275-76
Moses
  and Ezekiel, 192
  as new Adam, 101
  prefigures Christ, 101
motifs, 8-10
Mount Sinai, 3, 98-99, 100, 101, 120, 122, 297
  as midway between Egypt and Canaan, 104-5
  represented presence of God, 103
Mount Zion, 98-99, 100, 101, 122, 167, 210, 297
mountain of God, 64, 88, 99-100, 122
  See also cosmic mountain ideology
myth, 117-18, 120
  in biblical literature, 10
  and history, 139
  as untrue, 125
mythohistory, 118

mythological themes of cosmology, 315
mythopoetic language, 116-17, 139, 147, 148
natural law, 186n13
Nebuchadnezzar, 183, 192
Nehemiah, 203-4, 316
new covenant, 43, 129, 148, 177, 185, 191
new creation, 93, 109, 179, 283, 309-13
new exodus, 3n5, 14, 15, 129-30, 163, 179, 307
  announcement from Jesus, 246
  eschatological quality of, 178
  fulfilled in Christ, 148
  and new covenant, 43, 93, 109, 191
  as new creation, 15, 161, 165
  as return from exile, 95, 152n20, 158, 200, 204-6, 241
new exodus community, 294-96
new heavens and new earth, 162, 304, 309
new Jerusalem, 311, 313
new perspectives on Paul, 6-7
new song, 162, 303, 304
Nicene Creed, 3n4
Noachian covenant, 72, 79-80
  as nonredemptive, 80-81
  and regulation of common world, 83-84, 118
Noah, 76, 78-79
Old Testament
  analogical uses of, 300
  christological sense of, 56-57
  indirect fulfillment of, 301
  as literary prototypes, 300
  thematic uses of, 300
  use in New Testament, 10
ontology, 55
oracles against the nations, 193, 206
oracles of judgment, 198
oracles of salvation, 194

originality in literature, 31, 129
P (Priestly source), 109
parable of the vineyard, 178
paraphrase, 31
paronomasia, 161
participatory, 93, 323-24
passive verbs, in Semitic languages, 73
Passover, 128, 264, 290
Passover lamb, 289, 290-91, 303-4
past, instills hope, 141
Paul
  Damascus road experience, 250, 255
  exodus motif in, 15-16, 264, 317
  writes from stance of fulfillment, 337
Persian Empire, 199
personification, 125
Peter, ecclesial reading of exodus motif, 16, 287-97, 317
Pharaoh, 120, 191
  defeat of, 148
  power and sovereignty of, 114
Phineas, 147
piety, 325-26
pilgrimage theme, 89
pillar of cloud and fire, 176, 280
plagues in Revelation, 306, 307
plagues of Egypt, 119, 142, 307
playfulness, 20
polycentrism (law), 72n44
polyphonic novel, 329
possible allusion, 300
postexilic period, exodus motif in, 14-15, 316
poststructuralism, 318, 333n25, 345
prayer, 325-26
priesthood of all believers, 294n43
probable allusion, 299-300
progress of redemption, 262
progressive revelation, 47

projective typology, 49
promise, 315
promise and fulfillment, 42-43, 261-62
Promised Land, 3, 103, 123, 131, 144-45, 148, 204, 222, 306, 309, 316, 320
prophecy fulfillment, 254
prophetic hope, 201, 202, 206, 316
prophetic indictment, 192, 316
protevangelium, 69
protological moral standard, 276
psalmody, 112
Psalms, exodus motif, 14, 121-48, 316
quadriga, 50-51, 53
Qumran, 157-58, 210-11, 257, 292n38, 296
quotations, 31, 327, 338
Rahab, 173-74
rainbow, 84
Rameses, 134
Ramesses III, pharaoh, 111
rationalism, 40
re-creation theme, 172
reader, 35, 39, 344-46, 348-49
reader-oriented intertextuality, 22, 25-28, 335n36, 336-40, 343
recognition formula, 192-93, 197, 198
redeemer, 189
redemption, 4-6, 69, 284, 290
 exodus typology in, 298, 301-2
Reformation, and allegory, 54
remembering, 135, 204
reminiscence. *See* echoes
repentance, 198
repetition, 108-9
rest, 66-67
restoration, 148, 283
 as new exodus, 229
 as typological and pre-eschatological fulfillment, 205-6, 207
resurrection, 283, 313
retrojective typology, 47-49, 140, 141

Revelation
 allusions in, 299-301
 exodus motif in, 16, 298-313, 317
reward, 295
rhetoric, 59
royal priesthood, 75, 281, 317
rule of faith, 54-57, 180-81
Rule of the Community (Qumran), 157
ruled reading, 56
Russian formalism, 329
Sabbath rest, 66-67, 106
salvation
 cloaked in exodus garb, 159
 corporate and individual categories of, 265-68
 forensic and participation metaphors for, 6-8, 93, 323-24
"salvation of God," 260
sanctification, 325
Satan, bondage to, 246, 248, 249, 250, 255, 262
Scripture. *See* Bible
sea
 conquering of, 123-25, 174
 disappearance of, 310-11, 174
 as enemy, 148
 myth of, 115-16
 as object of God's wrath, 136-39
 as symbol of chaos and evil, 311
sea of glass, 308
Sea of Reeds, 173-74
second exodus. *See* new exodus
Second Temple Judaism, 142, 211, 240, 242, 267
semiotics, 332, 344-45
sensus historicus, 59
sensus literalis, 59
sensus plenior, 38n97, 58, 171
Septuagint, 104, 188, 214, 218, 229, 243, 245, 247, 259, 269, 284, 295, 302, 337
servant of Yahweh, 170-71, 246
Sethites, 75-76, 77

shadows, 12, 42-46
sharing content (intertexuality), 29
sharing form (intertextuality), 29-30
sharing language (intexuality), 28-29
Shem, 76
Sinai. *See* Mount Sinai
Sinai covenant. *See* Mosaic covenant
slavery, 274, 284
slaves of God, 291
Son of God, 218
Song of Miriam, 95nn15-16
Song of Moses, 98, 305, 307, 308
Song of the Lamb, 303-4, 306, 308
Song of the Sea, 95-96, 98, 99, 101-2, 105, 120, 128, 133, 140, 161, 228, 282, 306, 308, 311, 315, 322
 dating of, 110-12
 as fulcrum of exodus story, 100
 as "new song," 304
 purpose of, 112-17
 and salvation, 106-10
 as triumph hymn, 111-12
sons of God (Genesis 6), 77
sonship, 218-19, 274
speech act, 343
Spirit vs. law, 279-80
Stephen, 247, 250, 262
structuralism, 328n6, 333n25, 339
subsequent readers, 269
subtle citation, 31, 350
suffering, 282-83
Sumer, 116
supercessionism, 5n15
symbols, 40
synchronic intertextuality, 22, 25, 96, 333, 336-40, 342-43
systematic theology, 322-23
tabernacle, 64-65, 94
Tanis, 134
temple, 65, 120
testing tree in Eden, 68
text, 39, 269, 344-46

meaning in, 328
as mosaic of quotations, 328-29
situated in cultural framework, 346
as transfinite, 330
as verbal sign complex, 345
text theory, 12-13
texts, dating of, 341
thematic uses of Old Testament, 300
theocracy, 68, 76
third heavens, 3n4
Tiamat, 124, 139
Tower of Babel, 86, 119
traditio, 23, 147n103
traditum, 23, 147n103
transfiguration, 239, 249-50, 254
transformation, 161
transposition, 343n68
transsemiotic universe, 330
transumption, 23
tree of life, 68
trial by ordeal
  exodus as, 93
  flood as, 79
triumph hymns, 111-12
trumpets, 305-6
two kingdoms, 89
type and antitype, 42, 43, 45
typology, 11-12, 13, 19-20, 29, 39-42, 50-54, 315
Ugarit, 117
Ugaritic mythology, 172
union with Christ, 7-8, 312, 323-25
universalism of new exodus, 180, 237
universalization theme (Revelation), 300-301
"universe of discourse" perspective, 346
Urbekenntnis, 3
Valley of Achor, 228
vaticinium ex eventu (prophecy after the fact), 183
vessels of the Lord, 175
vineyard song, 177-78
vineyard theme, 177-79
Vorbild-Nachbild (type-antitype), 42
water
  as act of de-creation, 160
  as chaos, 316
  as vivification, 160
"way" terminology
  in Isaiah, 150-52, 157, 163, 165, 172
  in Luke-Acts, 236, 246, 254-57
  in Mark, 209, 211, 214, 222-25, 262
"went forth," 123, 126

Westminster Confession of Faith and Catechisms
  on covenant of grace, 86
  on justification and union, 325
  on law, 94n9
wilderness, 88-89, 219, 280, 315
  in Isaiah, 161-62, 172
  in Luke, 239
  in Mark, 209, 210-12, 216-17
  transformation of, 174
  as transitory state, 102-3
wilderness wanderings, 96-98, 102, 122, 144-45, 159, 204, 233, 254, 279, 306
wind, 190
Wirkungsgeschichte, 20
wisdom, 133-34
witnesses, 258
world-to-come, 3, 9, 225, 309, 316, 318-20
  continuity with former world, 283
  Promised Land as, 125, 131
worship, 67, 311
wrath of God, 146-47
Yam (sea god), 124, 139
Zion. *See* Mount Zion
Zoan, 134

SCRIPTURE INDEX

OLD TESTAMENT

Genesis
1, *62, 63, 64, 65, 70, 72, 77, 78, 87, 97, 105, 164, 315*
1:1, *63*
1:2, *66, 119, 179, 221*
1:22, *184*
1:26, *65, 218*
1:28, *119, 184*
1:31, *66, 78*
2, *65, 68, 88*
2:2-3, *66*
2:4, *67*
2:15, *68*
2:16-17, *321*
3, *70, 74, 85*
3:11, *226*
3:14-21, *82*
3:15, *77*
3:15-21, *69, 85*
4, *70, 71, 72, 74, 75, 76, 78, 83, 280*
4:12, *71*
4:13-14, *71*
4:15, *71, 73, 74, 85*
4:17-26, *74*
4:18, *74*
4:19, *74*
4:23, *74*
4:24, *75*
4:25-26, *75*
5, *75, 76*
5:3, *218*
6, *76, 77, 82, 83*
6:1-4, *76, 78*
6:4, *78*
6:9, *78*
6:12, *78*
6:13, *80*
6:13-16, *81*
6:13-21, *80*
6:14, *77, 81*
6:17, *80*
6:18, *80, 81, 85*
7:1, *78*
7:11, *160*
8, *82*
8:1, *81*
8:20, *80, 84, 118*
8:20-22, *84*
8:22, *81, 82, 84*
9, *70, 72, 80, 82, 83, 84, 85*
9:1, *84*
9:1-7, *84*
9:8-17, *84*
9:20-29, *79*
9:22, *83*
9:25, *83*
9:25-26, *87*
11, *76, 86, 119*
12, *85, 86*
13:14-17, *95*
14:14, *247*
15, *86, 87*
15:6, *331*
15:13-14, *87*
15:14, *247*
17, *80*
22, *218*
31:40, *190*
41:52, *160*
46:26-27, *119*

Exodus
1, *94, 96, 105, 114*
1:7, *119*
1:10-11, *119*
1:11, *134*
2:3, *119*
3:5, *49*
3:7, *160*
3:12, *247, 297*
3:14, *302, 305*
3:17, *160*
3:19-20, *297*
4:22, *230*
4:22-23, *218, 323*
4:31, *160*
5:1, *67, 106*
5:5, *67*
6, *81, 196*
6:6-8, *103, 196, 269, 284*
7:8, *105*
7:16, *67, 106*
8:1, *67, 106*
8:20, *67, 106*
9:1, *67, 106*
9:13, *67, 106*
10:3, *67, 106*
11:1, *94*
11:8, *168*
12, *175, 290*
12:11, *175, 291*
12:11-12, *175*
12:33, *220*
12:39, *220*
12:41, *168*
13:3, *297*
13:3-4, *168*
13:9, *297*
13:14, *297*
13:16, *297*
13:21, *119, 176*
14, *106, 107, 109, 111, 120, 133, 140*
14:9, *176*
14:16, *190*
14:19-20, *134*
14:20, *176*
14:21, *119, 134, 190*
14:22, *190*
14:29, *119, 190*
14:31, *308*
15, *95, 97, 98, 111, 112, 114, 115, 120, 133, 135, 139, 140, 282, 307, 308, 315*
15:1, *110*
15:1-18, *95, 111*
15:1-21, *95, 98, 100, 101, 106, 132*
15:2, *128*
15:3, *112, 128*
15:6, *128*
15:8, *48, 109, 133, 134*
15:11, *308*
15:13, *98, 99, 305*
15:13-18, *305*
15:14, *305*
15:14-16, *111*
15:17, *98, 99, 227, 255, 306*
15:17-18, *113*
15:18, *105, 306*
15:19, *190*
15:19-21, *95*
15:22, *94, 101*
15:25, *220*
16:1, *168*
16:4, *220*
17:1-7, *168*
17:3, *200*
17:7, *159*
19, *42, 98, 101, 122, 185, 295*

19:1, *94, 98*
19:5, *94*
19:5-6, *295, 317*
19:6, *292, 302, 303, 305*
20:1, *185*
20:2-3, *193*
23, *215*
23:20, *176, 213, 214, 215, 223*
23:23, *176*
24, *228*
31:16-17, *66*
32, *187*
32:34, *176*
33:1, *200*
33:3, *155*
33:12, *200*
33:12-14, *155*
33:14, *67*
33:15-16, *159*
34:6, *136*

Leviticus
11:44, *288, 292*
18:5, *188, 203, 319, 337*
19:2, *288, 292*
19:3, *292*
20:7-8, *292*
20:26, *292*
22:17-25, *291*
23:5-8, *290*
25:10, *245*
26:14, *227*
26:27-33, *227*
26:41-42, *81*

Numbers
5, *79*
9:4-6, *290*
10:10, *94, 98*
10:11, *94*
10:33-34, *176*
13:22, *134*
14:14, *176*
14:34, *245*
20:1-13, *168*
24:5-7, *227*
26:51, *200*
28:16-25, *290*

Deuteronomy
1:31, *233*
1:33, *176*
4:34, *297*
5:15, *297*
6:16, *233*
6:21, *297*
7:8, *297*
7:19, *297*
8, *244*
9:26, *297*
11:2, *297*
16:3, *160*
18:15, *239*
18:18, *240*
26:6-7, *160*
26:8, *297*
27, *265*
27:26, *268*
28, *131, 162*
28:15, *227*
28:64-68, *227*
30, *337, 338*
30:1-14, *188, 319, 337*
30:11-14, *337*
31:14-22, *95*
31:16-17, *147*
31:16-18, *276*
32, *95, 282, 307*
32:4, *308*
32:5, *219*
32:10-11, *66, 119, 178, 179*
32:11, *66*
32:20, *219*
32:20-21, *147*
34:1-4, *233*

Joshua
1, *94*
3, *98*
3:7-8, *48*
3:13, *48*
5:15, *49*
6, *94*

Judges
4, *109, 112*
5, *112*
6:37, *190*
6:39, *190*
6:40, *190*

1 Samuel
2:1-10, *333*
18:7, *112*

2 Samuel
7:10, *227*
7:14, *282*
7:14-17, *273*

1 Kings
2, *135*
6:1, *120*
8:16, *135*
17:1-16, *246*
20:23-28, *100*

2 Kings
5:1-14, *246*
17:7-18, *133*
24, *192*

1 Chronicles
9, *175*
16, *142*
16:35-36, *145*

2 Chronicles
30:1-9, *290*
36:15-17, *187*

Ezra
1, *198*
1:1-11, *202*
7, *206*
7:12-16, *201*
7:12-26, *201*
9:8-9, *201*

Nehemiah
7:72, *199*
9, *203, 205, 206, 207*
9:12, *176*

Job
9:8, *64*
26:10, *64*
26:12-13, *173*
38:8-11, *64*

Psalms
1, *129, 130*
2, *218*
2:2, *230*
2:6-7, *230*
2:7, *218, 282*
2:12, *230*
3:5, *100*
8, *65*
14, *124*
15, *69, 126*
22, *282*
23, *129, 130, 131, 148, 185*
23:6, *130, 131*
24, *69, 126*
24:2, *64*
29:3, *64*
29:10, *64*
33:3, *162, 304*
33:6-7, *64*
34:13-14, *173*
40:3, *304*
40:6-8, *46*
43:3, *100*
48:2, *100*
51, *134*
60, *126, 142, 143, 144, 145*
68, *29, 45, 98, 99*
68:18, *26, 29*
68:33-35, *29*
74:11, *158*
74:12-17, *64*
74:15, *160, 161*
77, *47, 118, 135, 136, 137, 140, 141, 148, 282*
77:13-20, *140*
77:19, *141*
78, *98, 129, 132, 133, 134, 135, 136, 140, 148, 204*
78:12, *134*
78:12-39, *133*
78:13, *133*
78:14, *134, 176*
78:15-20, *168*
78:26, *100*
78:32, *135*
78:43, *134*
78:52, *155*
78:54, *100*
78:67, *135*
79:10, *158*

Scripture Index | 389

80:9, *227*
80:13, *158*
80:15, *230*
80:17, *230*
81, *147*
82:1-7, *78*
86, *308*
86:9-10, *308*
87:4, *173*
88, *302*
89:8-10, *64*
89:26-27, *230, 282*
89:27, *302*
89:37, *302*
90:12, *233*
95, *147*
96, *304*
96:1, *162*
96:1-4, *304*
98, *113*
98:1, *162, 309*
98:2, *308*
101, *128, 142, 145, 146*
103:6, *189*
104:5-7, *64*
105, *141, 142, 143, 145, 146, 148*
105:23-38, *144*
105:39-45, *144*
106, *141, 142, 145, 146, 148, 311*
106:7-12, *145*
106:28-31, *147*
106:45, *145*
106:47-48, *145*
113, *333*
114, *49, 123, 124, 125, 147, 311*
114:3, *125, 174*
118, *69, 126, 127, 128, 129, 147, 149, 294*
118:5-21, *128*
118:14, *128*
118:16, *128*
118:19-27, *127*
119:1-6, *276*
119:101, *276*
119:104, *276*
119:128, *276*
130, *129*
135:8-14, *140*

143, *130, 279, 331*
144:9, *162*
149:1, *162*

Proverbs
8:29, *64*
22, *344*
30:4, *64*

Isaiah
1, *178*
1:3, *178*
2, *178*
5, *30, 177, 178, 179*
5:1, *178*
6, *261*
6:9-10, *260*
8:14-15, *294*
8:18, *99*
11:1-10, *100*
11:9, *100*
19:11, *134*
19:13, *134*
19:20, *80*
24:1, *283*
26:2, *127*
27, *177*
27:13, *100*
28:16, *294*
30:4, *134*
32:15, *257*
36, *155*
40, *14, 20, 50, 115, 149, 150, 151, 152, 153, 154, 155, 159, 161, 162, 164, 169, 170, 171, 173, 175, 176, 177, 179, 180, 204, 210, 212, 217, 224, 238, 239, 240, 256, 261, 293, 316, 340*
40:1, *172*
40:1-11, *2, 153, 154, 155, 157, 261*
40:3, *24, 151, 157, 210, 213, 214, 215, 216, 224, 239, 240, 243, 331*
40:3-5, *153, 237, 240, 244, 254, 256, 262*
40:4-5, *239*

40:5, *154, 260*
40:6-8, *293*
40:9-10, *210*
40:12, *64*
40:21, *166*
40:27, *150, 158*
40:28, *66*
41:1-7, *158*
41:2, *206*
41:4, *166*
41:8-13, *158*
41:14-16, *158*
41:15-16, *158*
41:16-20, *49, 57*
41:17-20, *153, 158, 160*
41:18, *160*
41:20, *161*
41:22-29, *166*
41:25, *206*
42, *161, 163*
42:1, *218*
42:6-7, *162, 171*
42:8-9, *166*
42:9-10, *304*
42:10, *162*
42:13, *112, 161*
42:14-16, *153*
42:14-17, *161, 162, 163*
42:15, *161*
42:18-25, *164*
43, *164, 237, 295, 310*
43:1-3, *153*
43:1-7, *164, 165*
43:1-21, *167*
43:3, *164*
43:8-13, *166*
43:10, *257*
43:10-13, *302*
43:12, *257*
43:14-21, *153, 162, 165, 310*
43:16-21, *166*
43:18-19, *166, 310*
43:20-21, *295*
44:8, *257*
44:28, *206*
45:1, *206*
45:14, *301*
45:22, *258*
47:5, *170*
48, *168, 169, 175, 191*

48:15-21, *167, 168*
48:20-21, *153*
49, *168, 169, 170, 172, 191*
49:6, *171, 180, 258, 259, 261*
49:6-13, *169, 171*
49:8-12, *153*
49:23, *301*
50:2, *64*
51:3, *172*
51:9, *64, 138, 311*
51:9-10, *153*
51:9-11, *172, 173*
51:10, *138*
51:10-11, *174*
51:13-15, *174*
52, *191*
52:7-10, *176*
52:11-12, *153, 174, 175*
52:13, *50, 153, 172*
53, *303*
53:11-12, *172*
54:9, *64*
55, *179*
55:5-9, *177*
55:6-13, *176*
55:12-13, *153, 176, 177, 178*
56, *150, 179, 224*
58, *246*
58:6, *245*
58:8, *246*
61:1-2, *245*
61:6, *305*
63, *218*
63:8-9, *176*
63:9-13, *179*
63:11, *326*
63:11-14, *176*
63:19, *217*
65, *310*
65:17, *161*
65:17-20, *310*
66:20, *100*

Jeremiah
1, *184, 226*
1:1, *183*
2, *7, 187*
2:2, *219, 232*
2:2-3, *184*

2:3, *227*
2:5-6, *184*
2:6, *130*
2:8, *184*
3:11, *187*
4:19, *183*
5:22, *64*
7:28, *227*
9:1, *183*
10, *308*
10:7, *308*
10:19-20, *183*
11:1-8, *191*
11:18-23, *183*
12:1-4, *183*
15:10-21, *183*
16:1-4, *183*
17:12-18, *183*
17:14-26, *100*
18:18-23, *183*
20:7-18, *183*
22:1-4, *100*
23, *184, 206*
23:4-8, *185*
23:9, *183*
23:31, *184*
25:3-8, *191*
25:11-14, *206*
25:13, *188*
29:10-14, *206*
31, *191, 206*
31:23, *100*
31:31-34, *186, 191*
31:33-34, *186*
32:39, *195*
36:30, *190*
46, *188*
50, *184, 188, 189, 206, 333*
50–51, *191*
50:1, *189*
50:33-38, *188, 189, 190*
50:39-40, *190*
51:4, *191*
51:36, *190*

Ezekiel
1, *192, 195*
1:11, *200*
4:6, *245*
6:14, *192*
7:4, *193*
7:27, *192*
9, *206*
9:9, *192*
10, *192*
11:14-21, *193*
11:17-20, *194*
11:19, *194*
11:22-23, *192*
12:15, *192*
16, *278*
20, *193, 196, 316*
20:1-44, *195*
20:5, *197*
20:25, *197*
20:30-44, *196*
20:32, *197*
20:39, *198*
28, *67*
29:6, *193*
29:9, *193*
29:16, *193*
30:8, *193*
30:14, *134*
30:19, *193*
30:25, *193*
30:26, *193*
32:15, *193*
34:12, *155*
36:22, *176*
36:26, *194*

Daniel
2, *300*
2:28-29, *301*
7, *115*
9, *245*
9:16, *100*
9:20, *100*

Hosea
1, *187*
2, *278*
2:14-16, *227*
2:14-23, *219*
2:16-17, *232*
2:17, *277, 278*
2:17-18, *278*
2:21-22, *278*
2:23, *294, 296*
3:5, *100*
9:10, *227*

11, *164, 187, 278*
11:1, *219, 228, 229, 231, 232, 277*
11:3, *229*
11:10-11, *229*
11:11, *219, 232*
11:12, *278*
13:4, *227*

Joel
2:1, *100*
2:13, *145*
4:17, *100*

Amos
5:8, *64*
9:6, *64*
9:7, *80*
9:11-15, *100*

Micah
4:2, *100*
5:1-2, *100*
6:8, *276*

Nahum
1:4, *64*

Habakkuk
2:4, *331*
3:3, *100*
3:15, *64*

Zechariah
8:3, *100*
9, *115*

Malachi
3:1, *213, 214*

NEW TESTAMENT

Matthew
1, *230, 235*
1:1, *226*
2, *233, 235*
2:7-15, *229*
2:15, *228, 231*
3:3, *216*
3:15, *233*
4, *233*
4:1-11, *232*

4:5, *233*
4:8, *233*
5:18, *172*
8:26-27, *64*
22:30, *77*
23, *30*
25:31-46, *243*

Mark
1, *210*
1:1, *216*
1:1-3, *210, 213, 293*
1:1-13, *211*
1:1-15, *211*
1:2-13, *9, 40, 102, 173, 193, 210*
1:3, *216*
1:4, *216*
1:8, *221*
1:9, *221*
1:9-11, *218*
1:9-13, *217*
1:10-11, *217*
1:11, *218*
1:12, *221*
1:12-13, *220*
1:15, *211, 216*
3:7-12, *210*
6:3, *246*
8:27, *214, 222, 223, 224*
10:35-45, *241*
12:25, *77*

Luke
1, *240*
1:16-17, *243*
1:17, *239*
1:76, *239, 243*
3, *261*
3:1-6, *238*
3:2-6, *238, 239, 254*
3:4, *216, 243*
3:4-6, *237, 252*
4, *244, 246, 247, 248, 250, 253, 254, 261, 262*
4:6, *233, 248, 250*
4:9, *233*
4:16-20, *248, 254*
4:16-30, *245, 254*
4:18, *246, 253*

Scripture Index | 391

4:18-19, *244*
9, *249, 251, 254, 262*
9:1-50, *251*
9:30-35, *239*
9:31, *248, 249, 250, 254*
9:51, *251, 255, 262*
9:51-62, *252*
22:3, *248*
22:53, *248*
24, *259*
24:27, *253*
24:36-53, *253*
24:44, *253, 254*
24:44-49, *253, 254*
24:46, *253, 254*
24:46-47, *253*
24:47, *253, 254*

John
1:23, *216*
1:29, *222*
12:12-19, *128*
19:10, *90*
19:11, *90*

Acts
1:1, *238*
1:8, *257, 258, 259*
2:24, *248*
2:27, *248*
2:31-32, *248*
3:13, *172*
3:17-26, *239*
7, *247, 250, 255, 262*
7:6-7, *247*
7:7, *247*
7:9-23, *247*
7:41, *247*
7:44, *247*
9:1-2, *255*
9:2, *246*
12:1-24, *248*
13, *259*
13:37-39, *248*
13:46, *259*
13:46-47, *259, 260*
13:47, *259*
15, *238*
15:10-11, *277*
19, *256*
19:8-9, *255*
19:20, *237*

19:23, *256*
19:33-34, *256*
20:32, *248, 250*
22:3-5, *255*
24:10-23, *256*
24:14, *256*
26:18, *248, 250*
28, *261*
28:25-28, *260*
28:25-31, *172*

Romans
1:18, *267*
1:18-28, *147*
1:18-32, *267*
2:1, *268*
2:5-6, *243*
2:14-15, *186*
3, *280, 285, 317*
4, *86*
4:6-8, *276*
4:16-17, *86*
4:23-24, *86*
5, *267, 268*
6:2-4, *272*
6:2-11, *272*
6:14-15, *277*
6:17-18, *279*
7, *280*
8, *265, 281*
8:14-17, *281, 285*
8:14-23, *280*
8:14-30, *281*
8:18, *283*
9, *283*
9:22-23, *243*
10, *337, 338*
10:6-8, *337, 338*
12, *350*
13:1-7, *89*

1 Corinthians
5:7, *272*
9:25-27, *234*
10, *57, 180, 285, 328*
10:1-4, *326*
10:1-10, *16, 271*
10:2-4, *272*
10:3-4, *276*
10:10-11, *147*
10:12-13, *234*
12:13, *272*

2 Corinthians
3:1-18, *272*
5, *324*
5:1-5, *272*
8:7, *272*

Galatians
3, *86*
3:2, *280*
3:8, *29, 46*
3:9, *276*
3:10, *268, 277*
3:10-14, *265*
3:12, *277*
3:13, *274, 277*
3:16, *46*
3:19, *46*
3:23, *46*
3:23-29, *275*
4, *33, 273, 279*
4:1-7, *274, 285*
4:1-9, *274, 277, 279*
4:3, *274, 275, 276*
4:4, *274, 277*
4:4-7, *279*
4:5, *274, 277*
4:8, *275*
4:9, *275, 276, 278*
4:21, *277*
4:21-31, *52*
4:23-31, *33*
5, *279, 285*
5:1, *272, 277*
5:3-4, *277*
5:16-17, *279*
5:18, *272, 274, 279*
5:25, *272*

Ephesians
4, *99*
4:7-10, *26*
4:7-16, *29*
4:8, *29, 45*
4:11, *29*
5:14, *29*

Colossians
1:12, *284*
1:12-14, *16, 269, 284, 285*
1:13, *248*
2:8-23, *276*

3:1, *272*
3:1-4, *276*

1 Thessalonians
2:10-11, *272*
4:7, *272*
4:8, *272*
5:5-11, *272*

2 Thessalonians
1:7-10, *243*

Hebrews
2:14-15, *248*
3:1-11, *67*
3:7, *147*
4, *5, 321*
7:27, *294*
9, *46*
9:14, *291*
9:24, *45*
10:1, *44*
10:4-5, *45*
10:5, *29*
10:10, *45, 294*
11:1-40, *276*
11:4, *71*
12, *122*
12:18, *101*
12:22, *101*

James
1:27, *291*
4:6, *29*

1 Peter
1, *16, 296, 317*
1:1, *16*
1:2, *292*
1:3, *288, 293*
1:13-21, *288, 289, 292*
1:16, *292*
1:17, *287*
1:22-25, *292*
2:1-10, *294*
2:4-10, *294*
2:5, *287, 294*
2:9, *288, 296, 302*
2:9-10, *294*
2:11, *287*
2:13-16, *291*
2:18, *287*

2:22-25, *172*
3:7, *287*
3:19-20, *77*
3:20, *79*
4:7, *291*
4:10, *287*
4:17, *287*
5:6, *297*
5:8, *291*

2 Peter
1:15, *249*
2:4, *77*
3:13, *104*

Jude
6, *77*

Revelation
1, *300*
1:1, *301*
1:4, *300*
1:4-6, *301*
1:5, *300*
1:5-6, *303, 304*
1:13, *300*
2:17, *304*
3:9, *301*
3:12, *304*
4:6, *310*
5, *308*
5:2, *303*
5:4, *303*
5:5-6, *303*
5:6, *303*
5:9-10, *298, 303*
5:9-11, *306*
5:10, *302, 304*
5:13, *311*
7:1-3, *311*
8:6-12, *301*
8:8-9, *311*
10:2, *311*
10:5-6, *311*
10:8, *311*
11:14-19, *305*
11:15, *105, 306*
11:15-18, *308*
11:16-17, *305*
11:17, *305*
11:19, *298*
12, *115*
12:1, *306*
12:9, *300*
12:18, *310, 311*
13:1, *310*
14:7, *311*
14:7-8, *250*
14:20, *306*
15, *309*
15:1, *307*
15:1-4, *306*
15:2, *310*
15:2-4, *308*
15:3, *298*
15:4, *308*
16, *311*
16:1-14, *301*
16:5, *305*
17:14, *304*
18:10-20, *311*
19, *308*
19:11-16, *305*
20, *309*
20:1-7, *174*
21, *93, 95, 105, 299*
21:1, *64, 304, 310, 311*
21:1-5, *161, 310*
21:1-8, *67, 309, 313*
21:2, *304, 313*
21:2-3, *311*
21:3, *3, 312*
21:5, *304, 310, 312*
21:6, *171, 312*
21:7, *312*
21:8, *312*
21:9-10, *106, 313*
22:1-3, *67, 106*

Finding the Textbook You Need

The IVP Academic Textbook Selector
is an online tool for instantly finding the IVP books
suitable for over 250 courses across 24 disciplines.

ivpacademic.com